BARGAIN HUNTING

IN THE BAY AREA

BARGAIN HUNTING
IN THE BAY AREA

BY SALLY SOCOLICH

CHRONICLE BOOKS

SAN FRANCISCO

Library of Congress Cataloging-in-Publication
Data available.

Designed by Tim Clark
Printed in the United States of America.

ISBN 0-8118-1776-8

Distributed in Canada by Raincoast Books,
8680 Cambie Street, Vancouver, B.C. V6P 6M9

10 9 8 7 6 5 4 3 2 1

Chronicle Books
85 Second Street
San Francisco, CA 94105

Web Site: www.chronbooks.com

Contents

How to Be a Bargain Hunter

Twenty years ago, I used to climb three flights of stairs, undress between pipe racks, pay cash, and be made to feel like the owner was doing me a favor by letting me buy at a discount. Today I can drive to a regional outlet center and enjoy all the amenities of most full service retail stores. Every strip center seems to be anchored by a big box discounter. Are there any challenges or mysteries remaining for bargain hunters? Yes! Now more than ever, this book is relevant. You need to know which retailers are doing what; are the bargains bogus or for real? You'll get the lowdown on who has the best deals and prices—and the best selection. This book will save you time because I've done the footwork and made the calls. As the evolution and revolution in off-price and outlet retailing continues on a very visible level, I've discovered and profiled new outlets that tend to keep an almost subterranean existence below the radar of most shoppers. They represent the best of what this book is all about.

The Bay Area has had its share of store openings, closings, expansions, contractions, and moves, all of which are reflected in this new edition. My standards haven't changed. Outlets and off-price stores must still measure up in price and integrity. Each store must offer greater savings than its competitors in the overall Bay Area retail marketplace. I'm not bothered by the lack of retail amenities found in many outlets or warehouse-style businesses, but I do try to warn you when this is the case so that you'll approach the business with the right expectations. It's not my intention to tell you what to buy (I leave that to product-buying guides like Consumer Reports and other publications). Rather, my mission is to direct you to those sources where, whatever you buy, you'll be getting the best value for the money you spend. Many of these stores and outlets are well known to consumers by now; others benefit from the high-profile brands they stock. I've limited or eliminated my comments regarding many of the well-known bargain sources, giving more space to those that are more obscure.

Remember that bargains are relative. Your income level, value system, and exposure to merchandise in all price ranges and qualities will provide you with your uniquely personal perception of a "bargain." Bargain hunting appeals to shoppers at all income levels, but you must often think in terms of trade-offs. To capture savings you may have to drive forty to ninety miles north or south to one of the outlet centers or to a community on another side of the Bay: is it worth it? At some stores and outlets, the hours may be inconvenient, the inventory unpredictable, the service indifferent, the parking nonexistent, or the neighborhood plagued by SWAT-team-like meter maids. Only you can decide how much inconvenience equals the trade-off—saving money. Don't confuse "cheap" with "value." A $10,000 dining room suite purchased for $6,700 is as good a "value" as a $1,500 dining room suite purchased for $900. Likewise, a $300 cashmere sweater purchased for $150 is as good a "value" as a $40 cotton sweater purchased for $20. It's the savings that count, more than just the final price. And remember: nothing is a bargain if you don't need it. One of the biggest problems at outlets and discount stores is the compulsion to buy simply because everything seems so cheap. To truly save money, quit while you're ahead.

While I hope that this book will save you some time when it comes to comparison shopping, it can still be worth your while. It always helps to know your market. Timing, overhead, special promotions, stock liquidations, and other factors can be reflected in the prices offered by particular outlets. Please refer to the Glossary of Bargain-Hunting Terms on page 342 for a full explanation. It's time to admit that there's a lot of outlet merchandise being sold at phantom values—labels that once denoted quality are now trading on long-lost reputations. It appears that some manufacturers have a two-tiered distribution system: one quality for major full-price retailers, a knock-off and lesser quality for outlet stores. Those swayed by "labels" should know that by now labels do not necessarily indicate quality or value. Likewise, don't be fooled by "suggested retail prices"; some appear to have been arbitrarily chosen to create the illusion of a greater discount. Caveat emptor should be a part of all your buying decisions.

Fortunately, there are still many "only-in-the-Bay-Area" outlets that showcase the talents and diversity of local manufacturers and businesses. May they thrive forever! In addition, major companies (outside the Bay Area) have instituted "outlet divisions," which has led to the "factory stores" that show up in regional outlet centers across the country. They may not always meet the expectations of consumers who first cut their bargain-hunting teeth shopping at the original and unique factory outlets (many have vanished from the scene) that were profiled in earlier editions of this book. Yet, factory stores located far from the company's factory or distribution sites provide an opportunity to buy quality goods at modest to maximum discounts that were unavailable to Bay Area consumers before these companies went into the outlet business.

This edition of Bargain Hunting in the Bay Area includes more than 700 stores offering solid values. With few exceptions, I expect a store or outlet to offer at least 20% off the retail price, though most entries offer far greater reductions. When possible, I have quoted prices to indicate the kinds of bargains available at the various stores. These prices are based on research conducted in the late spring of 1997. This book is intended as a guide, not an endorsement of the stores listed. I have no affiliation with the stores reviewed; no one paid to be in this book; no "printing charges" were assessed (a practice sometimes utilized by other guidebooks); nor were my comments subject to store approval.

A Word of Warning Before You Set Out

Since store hours—and even locations—are subject to change, I recommend that you call those shops you intend to visit before driving miles across town. Addresses and phone numbers were correct at the time of publication, but these may change. Subsequent printings will include corrections, and readers are encouraged to notify me in care of the publisher of any such changes. Also, don't hesitate to let me know when a store doesn't measure up to my description. I want to know whether you were satisfied with the experience. Be fair—I need your name in case I have to contact you to establish that your letter is not an envious competitor's sour grapes. Be assured I will keep your name in confidence if I believe it's important to pass along your criticisms to the store involved. Your "happy reports" are appreciated, as well—I love them! And I would be delighted to hear from other bargain hunters regarding new listings for future editions or other suggestions you may have. Please send any and all comments to my publisher:

Chronicle Books
85 Second Street, Sixth Floor
San Francisco, CA 94105

Happy hunting!
Sally Socolich

How to Use This Book

Bargain Hunting in the Bay Area is arranged by general merchandise category. Under each subject heading, store names are listed in alphabetical order. Some subjects, such as Apparel/Fashion, House and Home, and others, have been divided into subcategories. For each store, I give the address, phone number, hours, parking availability, and means of payment accepted (cash only, cash or check, and/or credit cards). If a store takes credit cards, it will also take checks unless otherwise noted. Credit card codes: MC—MasterCard, AE—American Express, DIS—Discovery, DC—Diners Club, CB—Carte Blanche, and VISA. Following this information, sometimes I'll list other outlet centers or other stores, that is, where branch stores or similar services are offered.

Because many stores sell a wide variety of merchandise, I have made a limited number of cross-references that I thought would be helpful to a bargain hunter. These appear at the end of each section. And please consult the indexes at the end of the book: Store listings on 347, arranged alphabetically; Geographical listings on page 357, arranged by city; and Subject listings on page 373, arranged by product or service supplied.

An important note about phone numbers! In late 1997 or in 1998, area codes 415, 510, 408, and 916 are subject to change in some communities. Where possible, I have used information provided by Pacific Bell to list phone numbers using the new area codes in affected communities. If an area code has changed and your call won't go through, call information for the new number.

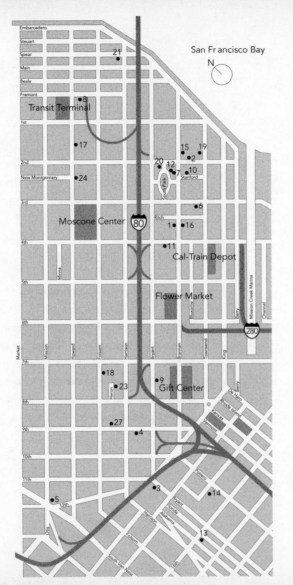

SAN FRANCISCO BARGAIN-HUNTING MAP

1   Allen, Allen USA
2   Bridal Veil/Traditional White
2   Bridal Warehouse
3   Byer
4   Christine Foley
5   Color Exchange
6   Cut Loose
7   Discount Bridal
6   Dress Market
8   Fritzi
9   Georgiou
10   Gunne Sax/Jessica McClintock
11   Harper Greer
12   Isda & Co.
13   Josef Robe
14   Leather To Go
15   Lilli Ann
16   Lisa Violetto Accessories
17   Marguerite Rubel Raincoats/Jackets
18   Martha Egan Company
19   N. E. Wear
20   New West
21   Rock Express
22   San Francisco City Lights
23   Siri
24   Spaccio
4   Urban Athletic

Women's Apparel/Fashion

Rather than follow an alphabetical arrangement for all apparel, I've listed all categories in women's apparel first, followed by men's, then family, which includes children's. Next come fashion-related sections (cosmetics, jewelry, shoes, etc.).

I've divided the women's apparel listings into several sections so that you can locate the resources that best meet your shopping needs. The first is devoted to all the outlet and off-price stores in the South of Market and surrounding areas of San Francisco. It's a focal point for bargain hunters, so you can plan shopping days in the City by quickly perusing the listings. For special sizes, manufacturers' outlets elsewhere, and off-price, chain, and specialty stores, please refer to the sections that follow.

San Francisco's Factory Outlets and Off-Price Stores

Covering South of Market (SOMA), parts of the Mission and Potrero districts, and surrounding areas

The glory days of SOMA shopping may have passed, but, fortunately, there are still some important outlets, and new outlets have opened. The biggest problem confronting SOMA shoppers on weekdays is the dearth of parking that's contributed to the closing of so many former outlets. Your best bet is to shop on Saturdays or be prepared to vigilantly feed the meters (metermaids will cut you no slack) or pay the high rates at parking lots.

Factory outlets: Many of the stores listed here and throughout the Apparel/Fashion chapter are factory stores or factory outlets, typically owned and operated by clothing manufacturers or importers, and often located on or near the manufacturers' plants. Some offer little in the way of

retail store amenities; others have gone high-tech. Some may not take credit cards, have unconventional hours, or have difficult parking resulting in very limited hours of operation. Be sure to call ahead to verify hours and addresses. I've noted in parentheses which stores are factory outlets.

ALLEN, ALLEN USA OUTLET (FACTORY OUTLET)
426 Brannan Street, San Francisco. (415) 543-3882. M–Sat 10–5. MC, VISA. Parking: street or pay lots.
Just when I'm convinced nothing new or of interest will happen again in SOMA, a new outlet comes on the scene. Allen, Allen, USA is a major catalog company of contemporary women's and young women's apparel. The catalog's past-season merchandise, seconds, and current overruns are sold

for 33–60% discounts. Although the overall orientation is contemporary, it's not so far out that you can't find some pretty mainstream fashions. There are dozens of sweater styles in each catalog (some little bitty things, some oversize and long; some slinky, some bulky). Recent catalogs have shown modern shapes in long tunic dresses, empire dresses, short A-line and swing dresses, pants and palazzos (many with drawstring waists and pockets), denim overalls, and lots of coordinates in absolutely fabulous fabrics (burlap or gauzy linens, flax, washable crushed velvets, corduroys, cotton knits, twills, rayon or polyester jacquards, thermals, cotton cashmere). If you want a glimpse of what's coming into the outlet down the line, check the current catalog chained to the front counter. A very good outlet for young women of *Friends* orientation and their up-to-date empty nester moms. Mostly weekend casual and casual dressy clothing, but some styles can go to "work." A caveat: dealing with "leftovers" means that sometimes it's hard to match up all the coordinates to complete an outfit. Sizes: S–XL.

BILL'S SWEATER OUTLET (FACTORY OUTLET)
2101 Bryant Street, San Francisco. (415) 285-9999. M–F 8:30–5:30, Sat 10–4. Cash/Check. Parking: street.

I suspect that not too many go out of their way to check out this outlet, and that's too bad. This outlet is somewhat primitive and small (shelves mounted around its small lobby are overflowing), but it's stocked with choice goods. You'll find mostly women's sweaters and a limited number of very special men's sweaters. The sweaters are fully fashioned, knit to shape and size before the sides and sleeves are stitched together—the way all quality sweaters should be made. Most of the sweaters are made under private labels for designers, fashion houses, department stores, or catalog companies, which accounts for the fashion styling and the wonderful textures and yarns (cashmere, mohair, cotton, and silk). A special "Penelope" label has been created for the company's own line that sells in boutiques around the country. Prices hover around wholesale, with greater discounts on prototype samples. Give a holler if no one's around, and presto, someone will appear to give you the lowdown on prices and willingly take your money. Prices range from $35–$85.

BYER FACTORY OUTLET (FACTORY OUTLET)

1300 Bryant Street, San Francisco. (415) 626-1228. W–Sat 10–5. MC, VISA. Parking: lot.
(Other outlets: BFO/Byer Factory Outlet, Mervyn's Plaza, Santa Clara; Great Mall, Milpitas.)
Byer California manages to satisfy legions of budget shoppers, many of whom consider regular pilgrimages to its factory stores a must—most prices at $8–$49 are too hard for teens and their moms to resist! At the outlet, discounts are usually 40–60% off original retail. These aren't seconds but first quality. Younger working gals stretch dollars on blouses, pants, and sophisticated coordinates or dresses; they can save on a New Year's Eve knockout prior to the holidays. Byer offers modestly priced lines of Junior, Misses, and Petite dresses and related sets, jackets, and sportswear (sizes 3–18); Large fashions (1X–3X); Girls sportswear and dresses (4–6X and 7–14). Some of the labels you'll recognize: Byer Too, Pacquette Too, Ms. Choice, Amy Byer, and Amy Too. The Santa Clara and Milpitas outlets are posh compared to the San Francisco store and have a nicer selection and more current fashions. No returns or exchanges are allowed in San Francisco; 15-day exchange in Santa Clara and Milpitas.

CHRISTINE FOLEY (FACTORY OUTLET)

430 Ninth Street, San Francisco. (415) 621-5212. M–Sat 10–4. MC, VISA. Parking: street.
Christine Foley's hand-loomed 100% cotton sweaters are very special, offering whimsical designs, bold colors, and real originality. Most styles can be worn by girls or boys, women or men. They're not cheap, and you're likely to find them in elegant department stores or boutiques. This colorful little outlet disposes of discontinued styles, color imperfections, and seconds. Prepare for the prices. Wholesale prices on children's sweaters (sizes 2–12) range from $60 to $88; adult sweaters (S, M, L) range from $138 to $166. Retail prices are at least double. Seconds are reduced the most, up to 70% off retail; stickers reveal the defects.

COLOR EXCHANGE OUTLET (FACTORY OUTLET)

1565 Mission Street (off South Van Ness), San Francisco. (415) 522-5243. W–F and 1st Sat of the month 11–2:30. MC, VISA. Parking: street.
I like this outlet, but many may find it difficult to get to the store during its rather limited hours. 90% of the inventory jammed on the racks by color group is first-quality past-season merchandise.

Color Exchange makes a line of garment-dyed related separates. Basic styles return each season in new colors augmented by new designs to keep the line going forward. The cardigan-style tops, pants, vests, big shirt tops, and skirts are transitional for year-round wear in the Bay Area, and useful for resort or cruise vacations anytime. The look is casual and comfortable, in large part because of the fabrics—100% cotton knits, corduroy, French terrys, etc. Savings are 50% off retail. Expect to pay $10–$30 on most past-season goods. The line is sold to department stores and catalog companies like Sundance and Horchows. Sizes: S–L (fits 4–14).

**CUT LOOSE FACTORY OUTLET
(FACTORY OUTLET)**

690 Third Street, San Francisco. (415) 495-4581. M–Sat 10–5:30. MC, VISA. Parking: street. (Factory warehouse sales first weekend each month: 1780 Armstrong Avenue, San Francisco.)
You can have it two ways here: shop at the main outlet for 50% savings and more on past- and current-season overruns, or wait for the factory warehouse sales, when seconds are sold at truly skinflint

prices. Cut Loose offers upscale designs for weekday and weekend wear, garment-dyed separates in distinctive fabrics—textured cottons, crinkled rayons, washed linens, corduroys—and a wonderful variety of solid colors. Prices range from $3 to $65 on separates: pleated pants, leggings, tights, assorted blouse and top styles, skirts (straight, full, short, long), and dramatic oversized jackets. The cut is generous on most styles—perfect for less-than-perfect bodies. Keep it simple and basic, or show your fashion savvy by choosing from sophisticated separates. Sizes: S–XL; Plus sizes 1X–3X. If you're on the mailing list, you won't miss out on any sale opportunity at either site. *Note: Cash only at factory sales.*

DRESS MARKET

688 Third Street, San Francisco. (415) 495-6768. M–Sat 10–5:30. MC, VISA. Parking: private lot.
There's enough variety in this outlet's selection to satisfy women with diverse fashion tastes—in fact, it has a split personality of sorts. One half could easily be called the cruise, resort, or vacation outlet, since it presents soft, comfortable ethnic fashions: wonderful loose-flowing separates and dresses in

gauze, chiffon, and natural fibers with exotic prints, often made in Indonesia or India. You'll also find a small mainstream collection of daytime and social occasion dresses, and samples in sizes 8–12 from Wild Rose (dresses, sets, and jumpsuits), Dani Max, R. J. Stevens, Dawn Joy, Breaking Loose, and Casper at 50% off retail. Count on some weekend wear: shorts, fancy T-shirts, Renee Hauer sweaters and leisure sets—all first-quality overruns, samples, and, sometimes, past-season goods. Prices are nicely discounted all the time. Sizes: 4–16. Exchanges within 14 days.

ESPRIT FACTORY OUTLET (FACTORY STORE)
499 Illinois (at 16th Street), San Francisco. (415) 957-2550. M–F 10–8, Sat 10–7, Sun 11–5. Hours subject to change during special sales and holiday season. MC, VISA, AE, DIS. Parking: free lot. (Other outlets: Gilroy, Napa centers.)
The Esprit Outlet is more than an outlet, it's a major tourist attraction. Whatever your age, Esprit can cover you from head to toe. The outlet sells seasonal overruns, returns, and samples. Its shoe department is very popular. If you find the outlet prices still too steep, your best strategy is to wait for the fabulous sales, when prices may be reduced an additional 30–40% off the lowest marked price. Otherwise, check the bargain bins in the back. You'll find everything Esprit, including the Dr. Seuss collection for children and adults. Sizes range from Infant 12mos to Toddler 36mos (boys, too) up to Junior 13/14 and Women's. Exchanges with receipt, within 14 days of purchase, for merchandise credit good for one year. Call for special sales and directions.

FRITZI FACTORY OUTLET (FACTORY OUTLET)
218 Fremont Street (bet. Howard and Folsom), San Francisco. (415) 979-1394; recording for directions (415) 979-1399. M–Th 9–5, F–Sat 8–5. MC, VISA, DIS. Parking: street.
The fun at Fritzi is buying the latest look for a price that causes you no remorse if you don't want to wear the garment next year. Savvy shoppers line up for special sales every Friday morning from 8 to 10, when selected items are marked down an additional 20–75%. You'll have to fight traffic to get there, but it's worth the hassle! Fritzi is a reliable source for those who have to consider price first and foremost: dresses for $28; sets (coordinating tops and skirts) for $22; tops, blouses, pants, and

skirts for $6–$15. Even better, women will find larger sizes; styles that appeal to grownup taste; dresses and sportswear for girls and preteens; even maternity fashions. Fritzi labels: Fritzi California, FR Sport, Jaclyn T (more sophisticated styling and fabrics), Fritzi Petite, Fritzi Woman, You Babes and My Michelle (Juniors), You Babes (girls, teens, and kids—created for price-conscious customers). Sizes: Large tops and bottoms 1X–3X (fits 16–24); Girls S, M, L (7–14); Toddlers 2–4T, Kids 4X–6X; and Junior and Misses 3/4–13/14; Missy and Petite tops and bottoms S–L (fits 6–14). The outlet is crowded on Saturdays, so if you can shop during the week, you'll only have to worry about a parking place. All sales final.

GEORGIOU FACTORY OUTLET (FACTORY OUTLET)

925 Bryant Street (bet. Seventh and Eighth streets), San Francisco. (415) 554-0150. M–Sat 10–5. MC, VISA, AE, DIS. Parking: private rear lot, enter on Langston (alley next to store).
(Other outlets: 579 Bridgeway, Sausalito; Milpitas, Vacaville centers.)
If you're dazzled by Georgiou's fashions, you'll be thrilled with its outlet's past-season overruns, over-stocks, and missed shipments, and you'll probably get a buzz buying the "old stuff" on $1–$9 racks. All Georgiou's fashions are made of natural fibers: wool, cashmere blends, silk, linen, rayon, and cotton, with each new color and print designed to coordinate with existing colors in its line. You can build a wardrobe of career separates piece by piece. Most styles qualify as contemporary classics—they'll remain au courant for seasons to come. Younger women especially love the detailing, buttons, and figure-flattering fit on many of the career suits. Holiday suits, ensembles, and dresses have real pizzazz. The colorful and fun cruise, leisure, and resort lines made from 100% cotton will survive many fashion seasons. Misses sizes 4–16. Prices are 50–80% off retail. Georgiou accessories at discount prices are just what you need to pull your outfit together. The outlet has a high-tech look, wonderful lighting, and an accommodating staff. Ask for a Club Georgiou card (for extra discounts) and don't miss Georgiou's special sales—one of my best buys in 1997 was a $280 wool crepe suit marked down to $65. Wow!

GUNNE SAX/JESSICA McCLINTOCK OUTLETS (FACTORY OUTLET)

35 Stanford (bet. Second and Third streets, enter from Brannan or Townsend), San Francisco. (415) 495-3326. M–Sat 9:30–5, Sun 11–5. MC, VISA, AE. Parking: very limited street.
(Other outlet: 494 Forbes, South San Francisco, (415) 737-2525.)

The Gunne Sax outlets are supermarket-sized! They are two of the Bay Area's few resources for prom and party dresses, which is wonderful if you're enchanted with the feminine, romantic Jessica McClintock look or excited by the more contemporary Scott McClintock line. Suits, skirts, dresses, and blouses come in a wide variety of fabrics for daytime or evening occasions. Many brides and bridesmaids have found beautiful dresses here that would have been off-limits at full retail prices. There are also infant christening gowns and First Communion dresses. Except for a few samples and irregulars, most of the inventory is past-season. Discounts are 50–80% off retail. The prices are tempting, but take care to scrutinize for flaws, which are easily acquired on delicate fabrics. Sizes: Junior 3–13; Women's 4–16, Plus 14W–24W (Scott McClintock only); Girls dresses in 2–4T (very limited), 4–6X, 7–14; Preteen 6–14. All sales are final. *Warning: Don't park in the alley in front of the SOMA outlet! This is prime meter maid territory. Shopping is much easier at the South San Francisco location: more focused merchandising and ample parking.*

ISDA & CO. OUTLET (FACTORY OUTLET)

29 South Park (bet. Bryant and Brannan, Second and Third streets), San Francisco. (415) 512-1610. M–Sat 10–5:30. MC, VISA. Parking: street.

Isda & Co. offers something that is often difficult to find when shopping South of Market: better quality and sophisticated styles for upscale shoppers. It has earned a Golden Shears Award and many articles in the fashion press with its clean, chic, well-tailored designs for women who have grown up and want high-quality clothes at affordable prices. If you admire the Donna Karan line, you'll surely love Isda's designs. You can create your own ensemble from related separates: Combine a skirt (short or long), walking shorts, or pants with vest tops or hip-length, slimming jackets. You'll find elegant mercerized cotton knit T-shirts and fine-gauge mercerized sweater knits and vests. These tops are soft and lustrous and look very expensive. The fabrics are the best: quality rayon suitings, tropical weight wool, 100% cotton (in sophisticated white blouses), and rayon/linen blends. At the outlet, past-season groups are at least 50% off retail. That translates to about $146 for a jacket, about $70 for pants, or about $56 for a skirt, with even greater markdowns on way-past-season styles. It may become more difficult to create ensembles as the season progresses and styles sell out. Sizes: 2–14 or S, M, L.

MARGUERITE RUBEL RAINCOATS/JACKETS (FACTORY OUTLET)

543 Howard Street, 2nd Floor, San Francisco. (415) 362-2626. M–F 8–3, Sat 8–11:30. MC, VISA. Parking: street.
Marguerite Rubel can be unnerving for first-time shoppers; she is refreshingly honest, painfully direct at times, and altogether something of a character. Once you get past her gruff demeanor, you'll end up firm friends. Her World Map jackets made for George Bush and Bill Clinton have garnered exceptional publicity. She enjoys a good reputation for the classic and innovative styling of her raincoats, blazers, jackets, coats, and sportswear. Velvets have always been a part of her line, and she keeps up-to-date by including poplins, silklike polyesters, and other fabrics. Recently, her best-selling styles have included updated quilted baseball or weekend jackets, some with appliqués or patchwork utilizing 200 squares in each jacket. Some of the inventory appears to have been around since the beginning of time, but retro-fashion buyers love it. You'll find many one-of-a-kind jackets, coats, and overruns from her sportswear. It's a grab bag of fashions with some real treasures; if you've ever wanted a dramatic velvet cape or wrap, this is your place. You can expect 40–50% savings, but not Nordstrom's service, and you're in for a scold if you don't handle the fashions with care. *Quilters note: Velvet scraps are sold in dozens of colors at $3/pound, with a 25-pound minimum.*

MARTHA EGAN COMPANY (FACTORY OUTLET)

1127 Folsom Street (bet. 7th and 8th streets), San Francisco. (415) 252-1072. M, T, Sat 10–4; W–Fri 10–6. Cash/check. Parking: street.
The line is vintage-inspired with a retro orientation, capturing the look of the '40s. Dresses (in short or

long versions) may be oversized—some semi-fitted. Some overalls, vests, and pajama pants, too. Soft European rayon crepes and failles are fabrics of choice for fall and winter collections (georgettes and sheers for spring), while unusual buttons provide special accents. Check the end-of-season racks for 30–50% discounts, or $10–$20 racks for last-chance super buys. Prices at retail range from $75 to $150. Sizes: S, M, and L (fits 8–14). This is a small studio outlet offering a very personal shopping experience for the right customer.

NEW WEST

2 South Park, San Francisco. (415) 882-4929.
M–Sat 10–5, Sun Noon–5. MC, VISA, AE.
Parking: street.
(Other store: 2967 College Avenue, Berkeley.)
New West buys popular lines of women's and men's contemporary sportswear from status stores in New York. The labels will leave you agog! Some of these fashions are slightly irregular, some have been repaired (broken zippers, popped seams, missing buttons), but no one seems to mind. The men's department serves guys who want good deals on casual weekend separates, great ties, Saturday night out-to-dinner clothes, and trendier sportcoats and suits. The women's lines appeal to ladies who frequent contemporary sportswear departments of major stores or specialty shops. There's usually a collection or two that's just right for the partying crowd. Prices are generally 40–60% off original retail and often more (I spotted one status designer men's suit marked down from $1,800 to $425). Women's sizes 4–14. The College Avenue location is classier yet, to fit in with the Elmwood shopping district. Finally, New West allows exchanges for store credit.

ROCK EXPRESS (FACTORY OUTLET)

350 Spear Street (bet. Folsom and Harrison), San Francisco. (415) 597-9799. W–F Noon–6, Sat 10–4. MC, VISA, AE, DIS. Parking: street (limited).
Rock Express grew out of concert merchandising for Bill Graham's Winterland Productions, which produces the licensed merchandise of more than seventy-five entertainers, sells rock-and-roll commodities to retail outlets, and prints T-shirts for major corporations and fundraising events. Rock Express sells "leftovers" from all of its various enterprises, leading to some very nice surprises at the outlet.

T-shirts get the most rack space; you'll also find jackets and sweatshirts in a variety of sizes, styles, and colors. Collectors may discover memorabilia that ends up in the outlet from time to time. Sizes for the whole family, but little in the popular XL or XXL.

SIRI (FACTORY OUTLET)

7 Heron Street (alley off 8th Street bet. Harrison and Folsom streets), San Francisco. (415) 431-8873. M–F 10–6, Sat 10–5. MC, VISA. Parking: street.

An out-of-the-way location for an out-of-the-ordinary collection of feminine fashions. Siri's fashion studio is a combination retail boutique and outlet. Her elegant collection of daytime and special occasion dresses and sportswear is sold to status stores and boutiques. Prices on dresses range from $150 to $500; on sportswear from $90 to $250. The styles are timeless and classic, yet offer originality for those who don't want to look like department store clones. Women in their twenties, thirties, and forties are prime targets for this sophisticated line. Beautiful fabrics (many designed in-house), interesting textures, and distinctive colors are hallmarks of each collection. Expect savings of 50–75% off retail on past season styles (many one-of-a-kind beauties). Sizes: 2–12.

SUSAN LAWRENCE

119 Sacramento Street, San Francisco. (415) 399-0222. M–F 10–6, Sat 11–5. MC, VISA, AE. Parking: pay lots.

Executive women from the Financial District, their assistants, and recent college grads come here for the suits, dresses, and blouses that their jobs require, finding premium lines that are sold concurrently in status downtown stores. The more traditional labels include Jones New York, Saville, Christian Dior, Evan Picone, Tahari, and Donna Ricco, starting at $169. Contemporary suits and dresses with European styling (fitted jackets and shorter yet businesslike skirts) from Expressions, Sunny Names, and Rina Rossi are priced from $149 to $199. Pantsuits are back in the workplace in both contemporary and missy styles starting at $149. Susan Lawrence offers discounts ranging from a modest 20% up to 35% (average about 25%). Sizes: 4–14. Alterations can be provided in-store. This shop offers a winning combination: good prices and professional and personal service.

WESTON WEAR INC. (FACTORY OUTLET)

*900 Alabama Street (corner 21st Street, one block
from Harrison), San Francisco. (415) 550-8869.
One weekend each month. Fri 2–6, Sat 11–3. MC,
VISA. Parking: street.*

Weston Wear is innovative and sometimes strikingly
avant-garde, but also practical and mainstream.
Some dresses are high on the sex appeal quotient,
perfect for women with a let's-have-fun attitude.
Moms and daughters can enjoy exploring the racks
at the monthly factory sales; younger women will
find festive Saturday night clothes (lots of slinky
short dresses); mainstream moms can spruce up
with contemporary separates or dresses. Many
styles are body-hugging, figure-flattering designs—
if you've got the figure. The fabrics are key to the
line and fit—stretch knits with spandex or lycra,
also slinky stretch velvets and laces, even sheer
nylon mesh (with lining). The company's contemporary styling has made the cut and shows up at
chic boutiques like Fred Segal in Santa Monica,
and is worn by celebs on TV's *Melrose Place*,
Beverly Hills 90210, and *General Hospital*. The
company sells many of its styles under the private
labels of department and specialty chain stores.

Prices, at wholesale or below on overruns, discontinued styles, seconds, and samples, range from
$5 to $50. Sizes: 1, 2, & 3 (fit 4–12). To be notified
about the factory sales, call and have your name
added to the outlet's mailing list. Postcards sent
quarterly announce sale dates for three months at
a time.

Also See

Under Men's Sportswear:
N. E. WEAR

Under Men's Suits:
SPACCIO

Under Active Sportswear:
**SAN FRANCISCO CITY LIGHTS; URBAN
ATHLETIC**

Under Lingerie:
JOSEF ROBES

Under Late Additions:
LILLI ANN OUTLET

Famous Labels/Factory Stores

Factory stores: This is a designation I've given to stores owned by companies that have created a thriving and profitable side business by operating not just one, but dozens of factory-owned stores throughout the country. Major brands like Liz Claiborne, Jones New York, OshKosh B'Gosh, and Van Heusen go this route. This strategy makes sense in today's retail environment: in this way, clothesmakers are not entirely dependent on department stores, or subject to market forces over which they have little control. Factory stores usually offer more of a manufacturer's products or lines than any one retail or department store, and the prices and discounts can range from very modest (and disappointing) to quite impressive. To keep stores well stocked, many companies manufacture or buy merchandise specifically for their outlet divisions. I feel that often this "special" merchandise does not offer the same quality or value as the company's regular merchandise manufactured for full-price retailers. Modest discounts (25–30%) most often apply to current, first-quality merchandise.

Factory stores owned by major manufacturers are usually found in the outlet centers on the perimeter of the Bay Area. At times it seems like everyone in these areas is participating in an ongoing game of musical chairs as they hopscotch from one space to another, or move from one outlet center to another when leases come up for renewal.

In the following listings, very well known designers or brand names are afforded minimal space. I'm assuming the name will define the merchandise. However, the locations of the outlets and range of discounts are important in determining whether a trip is worthwhile. Many outlets offer extra-special promotions and discounts during national holidays—e.g., Martin Luther King's Birthday,

Presidents' Weekend, Labor Day, etc. These holidays are an especially good time to plan a visit to an outlet center.

For daily hours, see the Appendix.

ADOLFO II/AILEEN

Outlets at Gilroy, Gilroy. (408) 847-3534. Daily. MC, VISA, DIS. Parking: lot.
Adolfo Sport, Adolfo II, Aileen, and Rafael emphasize leisure and lifestyle clothing for women who want to add a little pizzazz to their wardrobes. Shoppers here can find any number of styles when looking for leisure sets; fancy, dress-up, T-shirt tops; and coordinated sets. Aileen's prices and its all-encompassing size selection make it a favorite with mature women who also appreciate its understated and trend-proof image. Every season, related separates in 100% cotton are reintroduced in new colors and prints, with modest style innovations. You can buy separates from any section. Prices on in-season styles are reduced about 35% off retail, but watch for racks with additional markdowns. Sizes: Misses 8–20; Petite 8–18; Plus 18W–28W. Exchanges allowed with receipt and hang tags.

ANN TAYLOR LOFT

1221 Marina Boulevard, Marina Square, San Leandro. (510) 351-8348. Daily. MC, VISA, AE. Parking: lot.
(Other stores: Gilroy, Napa, Petaluma centers.)
These stores are real crowd pleasers though I'm not sure about the bargain angle. Apparel sold in this Ann Taylor division is made specifically for Loft stores to address the budget needs of women who find its regular stores too pricey. The company chooses proven style winners from its retail division and manufactures knock-offs for the Loft stores. Jackets from coordinate groups ranged in price from $98 to $137 in early 1997; you can capture a professional look with a nice cotton or silk blouse—many styles are priced at $39–$59, on average. The selection is always up-to-date. Count on an extensive sportswear category with lots of denims, knit tops, etc., a respectable shoe department, and, best of all, an extensive petite department. About half the space at the Petaluma store is devoted to clearance inventory from Ann Taylor's specialty store division. Some great past-season markdowns to 70% off retail. Sizes: Petite 2–12; Misses 2–14. Returns and refunds.

ANNE KLEIN

Outlets at Gilroy, Gilroy. (408) 842-7660. Daily.
MC, VISA. Parking: lot.
(Other outlets: Pacific Grove, Tracy centers.)
Anne Klein is one of the best outlets for upscale fashions and really delivers on price, quality, and selection. Some style groups are from previous seasons, while the rest are current. Anne Klein II collections are the big attraction. Prices at the outlet are guaranteed to satisfy the savviest shopper. Solid 40% discounts are the norm on most groups, but look for extra specials. You'll also find modestly discounted Anne Klein accessories, including handbags, scarves, hats, fashion jewelry, and watches. Sizes: Petite 2–14; Misses 4–16. Exchanges accepted within seven days for store credit only.

BCBG

Napa Factory Stores, Napa. (707) 254-7984. Daily.
MC, VISA, AE, DIS. Parking: Lot.
This line is a great favorite with the twenty-something crowd. The body-conscious fashions and contemporary styling add up to a collection of trendy career and party clothes. There's an element of retro in some of the styles, and the slinky little dresses are perfect for Saturday night "club cruising." Skirts are slim and long or very, very short. Lots of tunic sets, little jackets, and career suits, but not much in the way of casual weekend sportswear. Prices range from $25 to $100 at an average 50% discount. New arrivals are marked down 30% and end up at 70% off on final sale racks. The shoe racks carry the same fashion-forward styling—a perfect complement to the apparel collections. Sizes: 2–14.

CAROLE LITTLE OUTLET

Outlets at Gilroy, Gilroy. (408) 847-4411. Daily.
MC, VISA, AE. Parking: lot.
(Other outlets: Napa, Pacific Grove centers.)
Carole Little is noted for "easy" clothing: mainstream yet chic, with contemporary and classic career and weekend apparel. The related separates are dramatic and make a statement, and on their own they have a distinct character. Dresses and sweaters are staples. Collections are priced from 40% to 75% off original retail. Each season's line of color-themed styles offers tremendous versatility for building an outfit. Sizes: 2–24. Plus gals love the attention from the company's Carole Little II Collection. Store exchanges within five days only.

CHAUS FACTORY OUTLET

Outlets at Gilroy, Gilroy. (408) 847-1396. Daily. MC, VISA, AE, DIS. Parking: lot.
Chaus is strictly for ladies who appreciate its styles in easy-care synthetics, washable rayons, and blends; comfort design (many elastic waists and over-blouses to hide the tummy); and avoidance of trendiness in its related separates and dresses. However, that doesn't mean the line is dull—anything but! It's ideally suited to retirement and traveling, while popular with working women as well. The outlets are well stocked and the selection of sizes is guaranteed to please: Petite 4–14; Misses 6–16; Chaus Women 16–24 and 1X–3X. Markdowns 30–60% off retail, with frequent promotions and special sale racks. Sign up! Its mailing list sends word of special sales.

CHICO'S FACTORY STORE

Factory Stores at Vacaville, Vacaville. (707) 453-1336. Daily. MC, VISA, AE. Parking: lot.
I love leftovers! Especially Chico's distinctive color-coordinated in-house-designed casual clothing in 100% cotton, silk, and rayon. Loose fitting and designed for easy care, these creative designs feature attractive, bold colors in casual contemporary motifs with just a hint of ethnic. Combine pieces from the related separates for a knockout ensemble! Save 25–50% off every day; look for 50%-off promotions on discontinued color groups. Sizes: 1, 2, 3 for women 7/8–14/16. And you can't possibly leave without adding a piece of dramatic fashion jewelry.

DONNA KARAN COMPANY STORE

St. Helena Factory Outlets, St. Helena. (707) 963-8755. Daily. MC, VISA, AE. Parking: lot.
(Other outlets: Milpitas center.)
Donna Karan's elegant, upscale St. Helena outlet is equal to her reputation. Noted for her remarkable sense of style and signature collections, her company store is merchandised with recent overruns as well as past-season inventory. The 35–50% discounts off retail on most everything make the trip worthwhile for a Donna Karan or DKNY customer, but the apparel is still somewhat pricey. Retail prices on many Donna Karan collection pieces are often over $1,000. DKNY and sportswear collections approach affordability for most women. Lots of denim, classy and elegant career silk blouses (many body-suit

styles), related separates, coats, handbags, belts, sunglasses, fashion jewelry, scarves, and more. A small men's boutique on the first floor has sport-shirts, suits, sweaters, etc. The company offers a 14-day period for exchanges or merchandise credits. The Milpitas store is smaller, with less emphasis on the higher-priced collections. Full range of sizes (some 2s–14), including Petites; Men's S–XXL.

ELLEN TRACY OUTLET

Napa Factory Stores, Napa. (707) 226-2994. Daily. MC, VISA, AE. Parking: lot.
From day one, this outlet has been drawing hordes of women from all over the Bay Area. Do yourself a favor and shop during the week to avoid the long lines for dressing rooms on weekends. This is a four-star outlet offering Ellen Tracy's sophisticated apparel from career, sportswear, and after-five collections. From the company's perspective, the collections sold in its outlet are well past season, beyond the point when local stores may still be selling the merchandise. Yet, since manufacturers and stores work so far ahead of a season, almost everything in the outlet is timely from a shopper's point of view. Initially, new merchandise hits the

outlet with prices reduced 40% off original retail. February and August are set aside for major end-of-season sales. Sizes: Petite 0–12; Misses; 2–16; Plus sizes 14–24. Refunds or exchanges within 14 days.

EVAN PICONE

Petaluma Village Factory Outlets, Petaluma. (707) 769-1803. Daily. MC, VISA, AE. Parking: lot.
The scenario: You have a job interview and need a stylish but classic suit with a knee-length skirt or longer. An easy-to-maintain fabric that won't look haggard at the end of the day, plus a coordinating blouse in washable silk or polyester would be nice, too. You'll find it all and more at the Evan Picone outlet that showcases collections of career coordinates, suits, casual sportswear, dresses, coats, and fashion accessories. The current, first-quality fashions are introduced at 30% discounts; progressive markdowns follow. Add your name to the mailing list so that you won't miss any special sales. Beautiful store with accommodating size range! Sizes: Petite 2–14; Misses 4–16; Women's 14W–24W.

EXECUTIVE SUITE—JONES NEW YORK
Outlets at Gilroy, Gilroy. (408) 842-2555. Daily.
MC, VISA, AE. Parking: lot.
Both women and men can walk in the door and
walk out with a new suit. Women's suits start at
$219 (retail about $370). Women can also pick up
an ensemble (dress and jacket). There are always a
few rounds of classy career dresses. The men's
side has suits at $239 or two for $450, more contemporary suits for $259, and blazers at $160. The
quality, selection, and values make these suits a
solid blue-chip investment. Sizes: Women's 4–16,
Petite 2–14; Men's 36S–48L.

GUESS? OUTLET
Outlets at Gilroy, Gilroy. (408) 847-3400. Daily.
MC, VISA. Parking: lot.
A little of everything Guess? for teens and adults:
discontinued, seconds, and irregulars, resulting in
30–70% discounts. You'll find great buys on Guess?
shoes designed to complement its apparel: Western
boots, clogs, and clunky street shoes for women
and men. Large store, lots of energy: Guess? heaven
for the faithful.

J. CREW
Outlets at Gilroy, Gilroy. (408) 848-1633. Daily.
MC, VISA, AE. Parking: lot.
(Other outlet: Napa center.)
A mixed bag of bargains, with some discounts so
chintzy you'll wonder if the company realizes that
consumers expect savings—other pricing and
markdowns so good that they prompt a grab-it-
and-go response. All the merchandise at these
outlets is from J. Crew's catalog division, lagging
behind by about two catalog cycles. Discounts
20–70% off original catalog retails. The women's
and men's selections are equally balanced, with a
little of everything originally offered in the catalog.
Attentive staff and beautiful merchandising makes
shopping a pleasure. You've got 10 days for
exchanges or cash refunds.

JONES NEW YORK COUNTRY
Napa Factory Stores, Napa. (707) 226-7567. Daily.
MC, VISA. Parking: lot.
(Other outlets: Gilroy, Folsom centers.)
The orientation is dressier casual clothing and
ensembles and separates for business casual. The
image is classic, but not dull. Nice wool blazers,

more refined sweaters and vests, and traditional slacks in winter and fall collections; linens, silks, khaki, and dressy denims for spring and summer collections. The quality is excellent both in fabric and construction. Good values for the price—although not greatly discounted. Sizes: 4–14.

JONES NEW YORK FACTORY STORE

Outlets at Gilroy, Gilroy. (408) 848-1411. Daily. MC, VISA. Parking: lot.
(Other outlets: Napa, Tracy; Jones N.Y. Factory Finale, Folsom, Petaluma, Monterey centers.)
Career women need no introduction to Jones New York: beautifully made, simply designed career apparel, a staple in department stores. Discounts at its factory store are 25–35% off retail, not much better than a good department store sale, but the styles are all current, first quality, and top of the line. For best buys catch the end-of-season sales. Lovely stores! Sizes: Petite 2–14, Misses 4–16. Factory Finale stores liquidate fashions from other factory stores around the country. Discounts here are an additional 40% on past-season merchandise—some way past-season. Even so, the fashions fly out the door, many selected to complete

ensembles started the year before. All sales final at Finale stores.

JONES NEW YORK SPORT

Napa Factory Stores, Napa. (707) 224-7151. Daily. MC, VISA. Parking: Lot.
(Other Outlet: Gilroy center.)
Just the ticket for your weekend unwind—a collection of casual clothing that takes active lifestyles into consideration. More laid back than the country collection (listed above). Lots of denim and knits. Sizes: 4–14 or S, M, L.

KASPER A.S.L.

Napa Factory Stores, Napa. (707) 252-9253. Daily. MC, VISA. Parking: lot.
(Other outlet: Gilroy center.)
These are wonderful stores with collections of feminine suits for women wearing Petite or Misses sizes (some styles to 18). Prices on very current inventory are 25–35% off major store retails, and as the season progresses, markdowns reach 50%. Kasper's suits and pantsuits have wonderful detailing and there's styling for all "suit" occasions. Pick an understated, traditional suit for executive situa-

tions, or choose to emphasize your femininity with suit jackets that nip in at the waist, that may have dressier buttons, bolder colors, trim on the lapels—items that allow one to feel dressed up for weddings or other social and civic occasions. Accessorize your suits with some elegant blouses and dressy lightweight sweaters. *Note: Plus sizes may be hitting the outlets before the end of the year.*

KORET OF CALIFORNIA FACTORY STORE

Outlets at Gilroy, Gilroy. (408) 842-3900. Daily. MC, VISA, DIS. Parking: lot.
The Koret faithful will find 30–40% savings on current-season overruns, resulting in a $30–$50 price range. You can put together a nice ensemble from the collections of related separates in mainstream styles. Many fabrics are washable, even the wool jackets/blazers. Collections are geared for the office and weekend, but some are fancy enough for dressy occasions. At the other end of the spectrum, Koret offers some very appealing and more contemporary sportswear groups. The size range is most accommodating: Petite 4–16; Women's 16–26/28; and Misses 6–18. Exchanges only within 30 days.

LAURA ASHLEY

Outlets at Gilroy, Gilroy. (408) 848-5470. Daily. MC, VISA. Parking: lot.
The Laura Ashley outlet is sure to please the fans of this company. It's everything you would expect—lots of apparel for women and children (dresses, hats, shoes, some wedding fashions, etc.). These are past-season closeouts, some fairly recent, and discontinued inventory from its home furnishings and accessories division. It's a lovely store with discounts ranging from 20–60% off retail. I particularly appreciate the fabric, wallpaper, and trim selection priced at 50% off retail. Buy all you need at one time, since whatever you buy may not be there the next time you visit.

LIZ CLAIBORNE OUTLET

Outlet at Gilroy, Gilroy. (408) 847-3883. Daily. MC, VISA, AE. Parking: lot.
(Other outlets: Napa, Tracy centers)
Everything Liz and more. A few other labels are taking up space: Russ Togs, Russ Sport, Crazy Horse, and Villager. About 60% of the inventory sold in the outlet is marked down 30% off retail, the rest 40–50% off. It's at least one season behind

department stores and has already gone through one markdown cycle. In-season merchandise is usually excess from the year before; however, the stores are large and well stocked with Liz fashions for women and men. The handbag, hosiery, shoe, fragrance, and fashion jewelry departments are reasons to stop in if the apparel is not your preferred line. Petites are bound to be very pleased with their choices! I think the discounts are a little chintzy considering the status of the merchandise. Sizes: Petite 2–14; Women's 4–14; Large 14–22 (Elizabeth by Liz Claiborne).

LUCIA

Outlets at Gilroy, Gilroy (408) 848-3877. Daily. MC, VISA. Parking: lot.
(Other outlet: Vacaville center.)
This line resembles Villager, Country Suburban, Pendleton, and other somewhat conservative lines; it's sold through major stores under a private label and to specialty stores under the Lucia, That's Me, and TM Sport labels. Lots of nice suits, blazers, sweaters, pretty blouses, skirts, pants, etc., all very feminine in lovely colors combined with nice prints. These are mostly career clothes, along with festive

and fancy sets for dressier needs and nice collections of sportswear for the weekend. Posted signs note each week's discount, usually 40–50% off the tagged price. Prices range from $20 to $50. Sizes: Petite 4–16; Misses 4–16; Junior 3/4–15/16.

MAX STUDIO OUTLET

Pacific West Outlet Center, Gilroy. (408) 842-3636. Daily. MC, VISA, AE. Parking: lot.
(Other outlet: Napa center.)
The Max Studio Outlet is for those who don't conform or play it safe and want to stand out from the boring and blah. You'll find contemporary sportswear, sometimes avant-garde and updated groups of career, casual, and day-to-evening fashions. The fabrics make the difference: Lycra blends in body-hugging groups with short, short skirts or shorts, pants, and sassy jackets or tops; soft crepes or double knits resulting in figure-flattering styles. The career groups stand out. Some groups have flowing pants or longer skirts, but each group usually features a short skirt for the woman with great legs. Special Editions of its most popular styles are made for the outlet. Prices are reduced about half on all past-season styles, but look around for extra

specials and additional 30% discounts. Sizes: XS–XL (fits 2–14). Exchanges within 10 days on non-sale merchandise for store credit only.

MONDI

Great Mall of the Bay Area, Milpitas. (408) 935-9203. Daily. MC, VISA, AE, DIS. Parking: lot.
Mondi is a company with headquarters in Germany and an international reputation. It has boutiques in all the capitals of the world and shows up on the pages of *Vogue, Elle,* et al. If you've shopped its pricey boutiques on Rodeo Drive in Beverly Hills, or in Century City, or Carmel, then you'll be prepared for the pricing and sophisticated styling. Past-season collections (at least a year old) of women's apparel for all activities from beachcombing to elegant galas are banished to this outlet and reduced in price from 33–50% off original retails. The styles are original, creative, and designed for women trying to avoid the generic collections of department stores. Even at discount, the prices on fall collection jackets may range from $150 to $250; pants average $100 ($200–$200 at retail); blouses may be $50 to $150. Accessories and shoes complete the picture. Sizes: 4–14.

MYCRA PAC DESIGNER OUTLET

525 Center Street, Rheem Shopping Center, Moraga. (510) 631-6878. M, W, & F 11–5. MC, VISA. Parking: lot.
This old Bank of America building is an unlikely place to find a fast-growing company of stylish all-weather apparel. You can buy Mycra Pac coats and jackets at Harrods in London and in status stores around the country. The fashion-forward designs are hot sellers in many upscale catalogs. They're made from high performance fabrics that are treated with Dupont Teflon to be water- and wrinkle-resistant, and they're low maintenance too. About 90% of the coats are designed to be reversible—there may be a subtle and sophisticated animal print on one side, a rich solid color on the other. Many styles have a daytime to evening option—like black velvet reversing to a bronzed high-tech fabric. Most coats have collars that pull up into rain hoods. Even better, each coat or jacket comes in its own carrying case, usually a cleverly designed compact handbag-styled pouch that gives no clue to the coat contained inside. Needless to say, they're simply great coats for women on the go and fashion-conscious world travelers. The coats and jackets

(really two coats or jackets in one) are priced from $200 to $350 at retail. At the company's elegant little outlet, prices are reduced about 50% (sometimes more) on discontinued styles, production samples, and occasional seconds. At any one time there'll be about six or seven racks of Mycra Pac fashions; enough to make a trip worthwhile. Lucky Lamorinda ladies are close at hand for frequent sorties to the outlet to get the first crack when "new" discontinued styles are put out on the racks. This outlet bears watching; the company continues to push the envelope with new fabrics, designs, and fabrications, and inevitably these will end up in the outlet. Whatever you buy, you're likely to consider it a wardrobe treasure, good for many seasons to come. Sizes: 0, 1 & 2 (fits petite through medium/large). The building stands alone in the middle of the shopping center parking lot near T.J. Maxx.

ROBERT SCOTT & DAVID BROOKS

Napa Factory Stores, Napa. (707) 253-7993. Daily. MC, VISA. Parking: lot.
(Other outlet: Gilroy center.)

This company sells many groups under private label to national catalog companies and upscale specialty stores around the country, including Talbots. Most of the clothing is current season, sold at 30% discount (end-of-season closeouts usually 60% off on final markdowns). The look is classic, tasteful, and updated. The quality of fabrics and manufacture is first rate, accounting for the slightly higher prices than at many other factory stores. Spring blazers may be about $114, shorts about $42, and blouses $36. I love the career groups, casual coordinates, and extensive sweater collection. Other cottons in very appealing cardigan and pullover styles have designs and contrasting trims to coordinate with sportswear groups. Limited dress selection. Sizes: 2–18 or S–XL (few Petites). This store rates high for its beautiful, timely fashions and immaculate merchandising.

ST. JOHN

Great Mall of the Bay Area, Milpitas. (408) 942-0440. Daily. MC, VISA. Parking: lot.
This maker's enduring styles in wrinkleproof knits travel beautifully—one reason why so many women consider them to be wardrobe treasures. Discriminating shoppers don't flinch at the prices. Even at an average 50% off original retail on past-season collections, those unfamiliar with the line may be stunned. Don't expect to find St. John's basic styles—they're never discontinued. Seasonal collections (including some dazzling holiday), cotton sport, accessories (jewelry, scarves, belts, handbags), and some shoes to match color collections get the spotlight. Sizes: 2–16 Misses. Located near the Great Auto courts entrance.

TSE CASHMERE

Napa Factory Outlets, Napa. (707) 259-9444. Daily. MC, VISA, AE. Parking: lot.
Expect to find TSE's ultraluxurious classic and fashion-oriented cashmere sweaters and sportswear for women and men at 33% discounts everyday, or wait for end-of-season markdowns at 75% off. Holiday weekends are always celebrated with extra special sales and markdowns. Anything that might show up in the company's collections may show up in the outlet. Some cashmere silk and linen blends, plus very delicate, superfine knits distinguish the summer collections. Fall collections include cashmere knits, wovens, and meltons, wool crepe, and superfine wool. Some Infants, Childrens sizes; even blankets, throws, etc. from the home collections show up from time to time. *Note: TSE is pronounced "say."*

Also See

Under San Francisco's Factory Outlets and Off-Price Stores:
BYER FACTORY OUTLET; ESPRIT; GEORGIOU FACTORY OUTLET

Under Men's Sportswear:
MOST LISTINGS

Under Family, Men's & Women's, General Clothing
DOCKERS; EDDIE BAUER; LEVI'S; GAP; GUESS?

Under Shoes:
BASS; TIMBERLAND

Bay Area Manufacturers' Factory Outlets

The following outlets are owned and operated by Bay Area manufacturers or importers. We're lucky to have them; most are treasures, and they reflect both the originality and diversity of the local apparel industry. They're true to the original concept of "factory outlet"—what outlets were before major companies highjacked the terminology and applied it to their "outlet divisions." As time allows, try to visit as many as you can to identify which outlets are going to come through with bargains in your personal "style." In addition to each outlet's ongoing business, most have very special sales during the year for mailing list customers. To reach the backstreet locations of some outlets, you may need a map of the area. The hours may be limited (and often change), so do call ahead before venturing miles out of your way. In addition to these, you'll find other factory outlets listed throughout the apparel chapters.

ANNE MARIE DESIGNS

509 "B" Street, Antioch. (510) 757-7066. By appointment (groups invited) and M–Sat 9–4 during seasonal sales. MC, VISA. Parking: street.
The lines: 100% cotton, garment-dyed, preshrunk, and handpainted or embroidered active sportswear sold primarily to resort-oriented specialty stores. It's a little pricey, with shorts, pants, and tops, oversize tops, jumpsuits, and cardigan-style long jackets selling for 50–75% off retail (past-season styles). Prices start at $15 for each piece and may be as much as $48. The line is wonderful! Whimsical handpainting or embroidery that's not overdone creates perfect, casual party, resort, or dining-out clothes. Ladies in search of an understated look can grab the "naked" and unadorned styles. The outlet's downside? You may not find matching coordinates in all color groups, especially on way-past-season merchandise. Sizes: XS–XL (fits 6/8–14/16); one-size-fits-all jackets; some Plus

size collections 0–2X. Call to have your name added to the mailing list for seasonal sales.

BEBE OUTLET
Great Mall of the Bay Area, Milpitas. (408) 263-BEBE. Daily. MC, VISA. Parking: lot.
Bebe's retail stores are popular with younger career women. The collections of chic and updated career suits and separates in distinct fabrics, with elegant European tailoring and subtle shaping, are stylish enough to go straight from the office to a dinner date. Retail may not accommodate the just-getting-started career woman; at the outlet at 30–70% off, past-season fashions are within reach. (At retail most fall jackets range from $169 to $189; at the outlet they sell from $80 to $132. Most pants retail from $78 to $124; they sell from $62 to $87 at the outlet.) Women who don't have the legs for the 17-inch skirts may opt for pants to coordinate with the jackets. Love the weekend collections, too! Sizes: 2–12.

C. P. SHADES OUTLET
206 G Street, Petaluma. (707) 773-3290. M–Sat 10–6, Sun Noon–5. MC, VISA, AE. Parking: street.
If you're a C.P. Shades loyalist, then you won't mind the drive to Petaluma to buy seconds, past-season merchandise, and samples at its attractive but spartan outlet. Women embrace this line for its casual sophistication and unusual fabric interpretations. If you ever have to spend the night sleeping in your clothing, you won't be distressed or uncomfortable if you're wearing this line. Though fabrics are laundered (think wrinkles), they still retain a certain elegance. Combined with the overall unstructured fit (think baggy and loose) the result is one of maximum ease of care and comfort. Linens, velvets, cottons, rayon jacquards, etc. are used in creating collections of related separates. Long skirts, many styles of loose pants with elastic waists, tops in styles for maximum layering are sold at 25–60% discounts at the outlet. Some current merchandise is not discounted at all. Frustration is guaranteed when you find a wonderful jacket/top or bottom and then realize the coordinating elements are no longer available. Maximum discounts can be retrieved from the

boxes of damaged garments. Ten-day exchange for store credit only.

EMERYVILLE OUTLET

1467 Park Avenue, Emeryville. (510) 655-9578. M, T, F 10–4. Cash/Check. Parking: street.
You can call these fashions shifts, floats, dresses, sundresses, caftans, patiowear, cruisewear, or casualwear—anything but muumuus! The comfortable, loose garments combine fabrics, ribbon, and corded trims, use of patchwork, insets, bands, and borders in 100% cotton and better cotton blends. Some are dressy enough for entertaining, some casual and chic enough for sunning on the deck of a cruise ship, while others are perfect for around the house. Sizes: Petite through X-Large (4–20). Prices at $14–$49 reflect an average of 50% or more off retail. Sew-it-yourselfers will love the selection of leftover fabrics in prints, stripes, and solids, in 45- and 60-inch widths, priced at $2–$5/yard.
Directions: Take the Powell Street Exit east from I-80, turn right at Hollis Street. Follow Hollis to Park Avenue, turn right.

JACQUELINE WEST OUTLET

805 Gilman Street, Berkeley. (510) 528-8698. M–Sat 10–5:30, Sun Noon–5. MC, VISA. Parking: street.
If you're known by the company you keep, then Jacqueline West is riding high. Barbra Streisand relaxes in her French smock dress, and Julia Roberts and other celebs have focused attention on her Henry-Ts (named after Henry Miller). This T-shirt, made from the softest knit imaginable, is fitted and flattering—it's a best-seller in stores around the country (Barney's N.Y. and other status stores). Other styles in her line of casual, contemporary weekend wear are made from natural fibers, i.e., washed linens, cottons, raw silks, and merino wools. Everything is made for comfort. Most separates and dresses are loose and shapeless (many designs influenced by military or Chinese apparel) to fit lots of body types. Colors, for the most part, are earthy. Prices at the outlet are 30–50% off retail on past-season overruns and slightly imperfect fashions. Check the bargain boxes filled with assorted leftovers priced at $5, $10, and $15. This easy wear is European-sized: 1, 2, and 3 (fits 6–14). All sales final.

KAREN ALEXANDER OUTLET

4083 Emery Street (between Park and 40th streets), Emeryville. (510) 653-8121. M–Sat 10–4. MC, VISA. Parking: street.

One of the smallest outlets, but also one of the best. Karen Alexander makes a line of very special dresses that are always feminine whether they're reflecting a 1920s Gatsby-era look, a retro 1930–40s look, or bridging eras up to a sophisticated '90s look. Many styles are romantic, figure flattering, with flowing skirts that tend to run long—just above the ankle on average-height women. (Tall women in particular love this line.) There's versatility in the collection with dresses that offer split skirts, sarong skirts, drop-waist styles, jumper styles, long sheaths, fluttering skirts, and always the signature design details that set this line apart. Cottons, denim, linens, and rayons; velvets, organzas, crepes, and jacquards for after-five and holiday collections are used in the fabrications. Wonderful prints and textures too. Choose a style for going out to brunch, a wedding, out to dinner, the office— some styles will even feel just right on the sidelines of the kids' soccer games (jumpsuits). Prices on end-of-season closeouts range from $79 to $120 at 50% off retail. Don't miss occasional warehouse sales where dresses are priced at $25 for samples and from $49 to $99 for other styles. Sizes: 4–14.

LAFA KNIT CORPORATION OUTLET

291 Utah Avenue (at Littlefield Avenue), South San Francisco. (650) 875-1989. M–Sat 10–5. MC, VISA. Parking: street/lot.

You can't be expected to recognize this name because the company is primarily a private label sweater manufacturer for many stores and designer collections. Its outlet is where surplus inventory and samples are sold without any fanfare or obvious effort to showcase the sweaters. Removed from a retail store's careful merchandising, closer scrutiny is required to appreciate and liberate the many better-quality sweaters. There's not a lot of any one style or group—which lends a somewhat hodgepodge aspect to the selection. There are lots of fine-gauge flat knits, merino wool knits, chenille knits, rib knits, cotton, and cotton/lycra blends. You'll find tricot knits in the body hugging sweater tops, as well as cropped styles, vests, and some more mainstream styling in the cardigans and jackets (sometimes with coordinating skirts and pants), assorted pullover styles, and sweater dresses. A smaller selection of men's sweaters is also sold. Prices are reduced at minimum of 50% off store retails—during end-of-season sales the prices are reduced to an almost ridiculous level (the best time to replenish your sweater wardrobe). If you're cruising through this industrial area, give yourself an extra few minutes to case the outlet. Sizes: S–L.

LAS MANOS

427 Allan Court, Healdsburg. (707) 433-9348. Fri 10–3 (call for expanded summer hours). Cash/check. Parking: lot.

Some drawbacks: a long drive to Healdsburg, and limited hours. However, if you're a fan of contemporary, casual clothing with a somewhat ethnic orientation, you'll hit paydirt at the Las Manos outlet. The company has ten local specialty boutiques and ships its line to specialty stores in Sun Belt states and resorts everywhere. The clothes are made in Bali or in Guatemala from distinctive fabrics. Lots of batiks, ikats, and wrinkle-resisting crinkle fabrics in cottons and rayons. At the outlet, prices are reduced 30–70% off store retails on the dresses and related separates. Other retail store clearance inventory shows up—some great fashion jewelry, hats, and shoes add to the selection of seconds and past-season merchandise. Sizes: Petite to XL. All sales final. Located just a few blocks from the downtown square.

M.A.C. SPORT OUTLET

7049 Redwood Boulevard #104, Novato. (415) 898-1622. M–F 10–6, Sat 10–5, Sun Noon–5. MC, VISA, DIS, AE. Parking: lot.

M.A.C. Sport's line consists of preshrunk custom-dyed apparel, most in 100% cotton knits and wovens. Past-season styles are reduced about 50% below normal retail, with added discounts on seconds. These are California casual, related components designed for women seeking weekend or updated business wear. Collections appearing throughout the year include long slim or tie back dresses and jumpers, more structured weekend outdoor clothes in corduroys and twills, soft coordinates in cotton or rayon knits, classic contemporary styles in washed linen, and more. You have options whether your look is loose and drapey, or whether you like something with a little cinching to flatter the figure. Many styles are designed and made just for the outlet; others are seconds and overruns. At any one time, you'll have about eight different exciting colors to work with. You can mix and match from its one-size-fits-all in most tops, or S, M, L in other styles. You may not find every element of a complete ensemble. Fashions are priced $5–$55. *Directions: From 101 North, take the Rowland Avenue exit, go west across overpass, turn right at first set of stoplights onto Redwood Road. Turn left at Lamont (look for Redwood Chevrolet) and left again onto the frontage road. Drive to the end of cul-de-sac.*

MELIOR COMPANY STORE
1001 Camelia Street (one block south of Gilman), Berkeley. (510) 559-7070. T–Sat 11–5. MC, VISA, AE. Parking: street.
Career women are beating a path to Melior's elegant, boutiquelike outlet. The designs, manufactured locally, are interpretations of current and classic trends, the look is easy and toned down, with a soft structure and clean line. Women in Melior suitings and separates convey simplicity and subtle sophistication—bridging the gap from daytime to evening when required. The imported European fabrics are distinctive for their unique texture, tactile appeal, and rich, muted tones. You'll pay far less than for similar high-end designer goods, especially shopping here where prices are reduced 50% off retail on overruns and end-of-season closeouts. Skirts, pants, jackets (and occasional tops and dresses) range from $50 to $150. Sizes: 0–3 (fits 4–14).

MISHI
801 Delaware Street, Berkeley. (510) 525-1075. M–Sat 10–6, Sun 11–5. MC, VISA, DIS. Parking: lot. (Other outlet: 201 Western, Petaluma.)
Mishi is known for its contemporary, natural-fiber, garment-dyed sportswear line: "lifestyle" clothing that escapes being trendy without being dull. It's popular with sophisticated women who appreciate styles that camouflage midlife figure imperfections. The colors in the line change every season, providing the faithful with an excuse to buy something up-to-date. Mishi's stores devote half their space to showcasing current and recent styles at full retail prices, while the outlet half offers past-season closeouts and samples. Some very tempting fash-

ions are sold from other popular ethnic and lifestyle casual clothing manufacturers—unfortunately at full price (although on sale from time to time). Outlet inventory at 50% off is priced at $15 to $45. The moderately priced fashion accessories sold here are not discounted but are carefully selected to go with the apparel. Sizes: S, M, L (4–14), and some XL (16).

OUTBACK

2517 Sacramento Street, Berkeley. (510) 548-4183. M–F 11–6, Sat 11–6, Sun Noon–5. MC, VISA, DIS, AE. Parking: lot.

Outback manufactures fashion-forward, contemporary clothing whose most loyal customers are inventive women typically 30 to 50, although younger women are just as inclined to embrace the look, which is achieved with original prints, unusual fabrics (many knits), and design details. If you're interested in an up-to-date, new image, explore the Outback! You'll find seasonal overruns, discontinued styles, and samples at 20–50% off original retail. (Some current fashions are not discounted.) You'll also find funky costume jewelry as well as children's clothing at good discounts.

Check the racks of attire from small manufacturers with the same fashion-forward outlook, selling at modest discounts. Sizes: S–XL (fits 4–14); some Large 1X–3X.

PAPY BOEZ OUTLET

1041 Murray Street, Berkeley. (510) 849-2856. M–Sat 10–5. MC, VISA. Parking: street.

Papy Boez and Harvest are two very popular labels that show up in national catalogs and boutiques around the country. Designed locally and made in India from cottons or rayons colored with vegetable dyes, this charming and timeless line is more mainstream than many imported lines that convey an ethnic or avant-garde image. I can picture Martha Stewart and Cal coeds appearing equally at ease wearing these dresses, jumpers, blouses, and separates. The line is set apart by its detailing (tucks, appliqués, pattern mixing, embroidery, etc.), and original hand-painted or hand-blocked printed fabrics. New collections reflect updated and contemporary styling in linens (coordinates with jackets, vests, skirts, and shirts), and some wonderful and sophisticated sweaters. During quarterly sales usually held in April, July, August (back-to-school), and for the holidays (Thanksgiving to Christmas), past-season styles and slightly imperfect fashions are priced 60–75% off retail. Prices range from $7.99 for blouses to $60 for linen collections. Sizes: Small/Medium or Medium/Large. *Directions: Murray is a small side street that angles off from the intersection of 7th Street and Ashby. Outlet is midblock between 7th and San Pablo Avenue.*

SWAN & SWAN FACTORY SALES

409 First Street, Petaluma. (707) 778-1133.
Occasional F and Sat sales 10–4. Cash/Check.
Parking: street.
This Petaluma company manufactures women's T-shirts to be worn as a fashion top rather than something to knock around in. They are hand-embroidered in Mexico with clever, whimsical, or just-plain-pretty patterns. Some designs are romantic, others have themes—resorts, animals, flowers, Western, etc. Prices at retail are fairly steep ($40–$60), considering that these are T-shirts, after all. At warehouse sales that occur three to four times a year, all the T-shirts sold are seconds—most with minute flaws that will not deter those bent on buying gifts. Prices typically range from $12 to $24 for short- or long-sleeved styles. The seconds available in Swan's new collection of dresses are priced from $15 to $38. Sizes: S, M, L. Call or write to have your name added to the mailing list.

TOM TOM FACTORY OUTLET

1716-B Fourth Street, Berkeley. (510) 559-7033.
M–Sat 10–6, Sun 11–6. MC, VISA, DIS.
Parking: street.
Tom Tom makes a line of garment-dyed clothes that are easy to wear and easy to care for. The company has been around for years, but it has left its funky image behind and grown up with its customers. These are typically women in the workforce who want contemporary clothing that's unstructured and comfortable—they're not dressing as accountants or courtroom lawyers with stiff, conservative, and usually predictable suitings. The Tom Tom look works well on the job, around town, and for Saturday night occasions—such as when you want something with a little pizzazz for restaurant dining or socializing with friends. Styles are accommodating: take your pick from form-fitting styles or those designed to flow around the body and cover up all one's imperfections. At the outlet,

you save 50% off retail prices on the company's first-quality overruns or past-season fashions. Natural fibers like linen, rayon, flax, cotton, and blends are fabricated in a new palette of colors each season. An extra dimension is achieved with the textures and weaves of many fabrics. Prices generally range from $20 to $70 on the jackets, big coats, jumpers, dresses, skirts, pants, etc. Everything is washable and all shrinkage has been eliminated in the dyeing process. Sizes are simple—Small, Medium, and Large—and they easily accommodate women in sizes 6–14. Tom Tom shares this building with the popular Sweet Potatoes Outlet for children.

V. C. TORIAS THE OUTLET

783 Rio del Mar Boulevard #47, Aptos. (408) 687-0744. Sun–M 10–4, T–F 10–6, Sat 9–5. MC, VISA. Parking: lot.

Aptos is a bit of a drive, but worth the trek if you want bold, bright, casualwear that qualifies as wearable art. The owner/artist/designer has created this eye-catching line for women who don't want to conform to the standard fashion-page image. These women may not have perfect bodies; they may, in fact, go up and down in size with frustrating regularity. Working in high-quality rayon, linen, cotton knit, and washable velvet, the basic silhouettes—dresses, pants, shorts, shirts, and jackets—are transformed with hand-painting and appliqué. These distinctive fashions have been worn by Rue McClanahan on *Golden Girl,* and by the cast of *Sisters.* No two pieces are exactly alike. Other benefits—garments need no ironing, and they wash and travel well. One-size labels can accommodate women from sizes 2 to 22 (certain styles are more flattering to particular sizes). Sold at retail to better boutiques and resorts, at the outlet, overruns, design samples, and outdated styles are discounted 25–50% off original retails. Tops and bottoms range from $25 to $100 ($98 to $175 retail); dresses from $75 to $200 ($150 to $300 retail). *Directions: Take Hwy. 1 south to Aptos. Take the Rio del Mar exit and head west. Located on the second floor of the Deer Park Marketplace.*

WE BE BOP

*1380 Tenth Street, Berkeley. (510) 528-0761. M–F
10–5, Sat 10–6, Sun Noon–5. MC, VISA.*
Parking: street.

We Be Bop fashions have pizzazz! They're made
from natural fibers, usually cotton or rayon. The
batik fabrics are distinctive, an interplay of prints and
patterns combined in most garments using unique
colors. The owners develop the designs in collabo-
ration with Balinese craftspeople. Some garments
are straightforward, others so clever you almost need
a manual to figure out how to tie or wrap them. In
any case, women with an individualistic sense of style
embrace the look. Large-sized women are not over-
looked and can wear the styles with great panache.
Prices are discounted 30–50% off retail (ranging
from $20 to $80), sometimes more on way-past-
season closeouts. As offbeat as this line may sound,
it shows up in some pretty mainstream stores. Sizes:
S, M, L; one-size-fits-all; Large sizes to 4X.

Bay Area Off-Price/Chain Discount Stores

Many of the chain off-price stores have been around so long and are so familiar that Bay Area shoppers hardly need any introduction to them. They consistently offer a good product mix for consumers who appreciate shopping close to home. Before seeking out a specialty discount boutique, call first to make sure it's still in business at the same address with the same hours (they are an endangered retail species).

CASUAL CORNER OUTLETS

Great Mall of the Bay Area, Milpitas. (408) 956-9640. Daily. MC, VISA, AE, DIS. Parking: lot.
(Other outlets: Petaluma, Tracy, Vacaville centers.)
The "outlets" (forty-three around the country) carry the same categories of merchandise that one might find at its full-priced mall stores, but there is a difference. The outlet division has its own buyers committed to finding merchandise that conveys the "Casual Corner" image, but at a more affordable price. You

won't find anything originally sold through its regular stores. Even so, women seem to appreciate the prices on all the casual weekend apparel groups, career and soft dresses, related separates, suits, blouses, outerwear, and some very special fashion sweaters. Everything is first quality and in-season. In spring '97, linen blazers at $59 and linen-rayon blend pants at $39 were great buys. Sizes: 4–16.

DRESS BARN

1670 S. Bascom Avenue, Hamilton Plaza, Campbell. (408) 377-7544. M–F 10–9, Sat 10–6, Sun Noon–5. MC, VISA. Parking: lot.
(Other stores: fourteen in greater Bay Area—refer to Geographical Index for location nearest you.)
The selection here is dedicated to a clearly defined target customer (career women aged 18–45). Besides career apparel, you'll find a very nice dress line, suits, separates, activewear, coats, and accessories. Sizes: 4–14. Most Dress Barn

locations have a Petite department. Most discounts are approximately 25–35% off department store prices; clearances and special promotions up to 60% off.

GROUP USA

Great Mall of the Bay Area, Milpitas. (408) 935-8787. Daily. MC, VISA, AE, DIS. Parking: lot.
This outfit refined its concept operating eighteen East Coast outlets before launching this first West Coast store. Practice makes perfect. This store is a boon to career women with its offerings of current collections of apparel from brand-name companies usually associated with major department stores. Kenar, Expressions, Rena Rossi, Saville, Jones New York, Michael, Bicci, Dani Max, Albert Nipon, David Bijoux, and Larry Levine were some of the labels on spring '97 fashions. The career selection (primarily suits) is evenly balanced between contemporary styling for a more fashion-forward customer and updated classic (more mainstream) styling for traditionalists. Discounts start at 30% off regular retail and are often much greater. The social dressing and after-five department is one of the best around with some real dazzlers for cruises, proms, and elegant black-tie affairs. The handbag and shoe departments offer the "look" of more expensive lines. Faux leathers keep prices for handbags under $40. A nice blouse selection, coat department, some dresses and coordinated sets, a decent Petite department, scarves, and fashion jewelry complete the picture. Sizes: Missy/Petite 2–14.

HIT OR MISS

4130 Mowry Avenue, Fremont Hub, Fremont. (510) 794-5607. M–F 10–9, Sat 10–6, Sun 11–5. MC, VISA, AE, DIS. Parking: pay garage. (Other stores: twenty-one in greater Bay Area— refer to Geographical Index for location nearest you or call (800) 94-STYLE.)
Hit or Miss sells stylish work and weekend apparel at value prices. You'll find an in-depth selection of dresses, weekend sportswear, related separates, all-weather and wool coats, suits, dresses, blouses, jackets, and fashion accessories. Savings usually 20–50% off retail; sizes 3/4–13/14 (rarely 16s). Good service, good savings, tasteful merchandising, and convenience—a winning combination. Refunds and exchanges.

INGA'S/CASUAL ELEGANCE

504 Sycamore Valley Road West, Danville Livery Mercantile, Danville. (510) 837-1123. M–Sat 10–5:30. MC, VISA, AE. Parking: lot.

Inga, a former model who knows the fashion biz inside and out, buys all her fashions in New York—from showrooms, manufacturers, and reps. Dealing with smaller designers and companies with names you may or may not know, she chooses styles that are up-to-date without being trendy, styles that appeal to sophisticated women with multifaceted lifestyles and that address the relaxed side of glamour. This is a great place to shop for a sophisticated cruise wardrobe. Quality combined with value are Inga's goals. There's a little of everything: after-five (some mother-of-the-bride dresses), elegant daytime, some weekend and casual sportswear, star-status sweaters, and a few career suits. Buying right allows her to pass on savings that average 40% off retail on current-season merchandise. Most suits or two- or three-piece ensembles range from $159 to $279. I coveted the silk blazers marked down to $245 from $395. Inga's can't be all things to all people, but the woman who resists being a department store clone will love this place.

Inga's service—akin to that of a personal shopper—is thrown in for free. Sizes: 4–14 (some 16s).

LOEHMANN'S

75 Westlake Mall, Daly City. (415) 755-2424. M–F 10–9, Sat 10–7, Sun Noon–6. MC, VISA. Parking: lot.
(Other stores: Sacramento; San Francisco; San Ramon; Sunnyvale.)

Loehmann's is the original off-price fashion store, with a solid reputation for designer and couture lines at discount prices, covering all the basics and then some: cocktail, dressy, fine furs, in-between, career apparel, coats, lingerie, hosiery, fragrances, swimsuits, activewear, sportswear, shoes, and accessories. If you can spot designer clothes without a label, you'll recognize fashions from many status designers. Prices are guaranteed at least 33% off retail, and there is a reliable quantity always priced at 50% off. The San Francisco store excels in its selection of career apparel. Exchanges for store credit within seven days. Sizes: 4–16 with a few racks of Plus sizes and a fair selection of Petites.

RAFFIA

2175 N. California Boulevard #205-A, Tishman Center, Walnut Creek. (510) 937-0232. M–F 8–5. MC, VISA, AE, DIS. Parking: lot (validated).
Raffia is located on the mezzanine of an office building in Walnut Creek's "golden triangle" next to BART. It's convenient for all the office workers in the area and is a source of discount prices on well-known sportswear lines. You'll find women's sportswear and sweaters, men's active and casual sportswear, plus a small selection of fashion and sport shoes, handbags, watches, even some tennis equipment. It's "roulette" shopping at its best!

RAGSMATAZZ

2021 Broadway, Oakland. (510) 763-3735. M–F 10–6, Sat 11–5. MC, VISA. Parking: street. (Other stores: South Shore Center, Alameda; 622 Clement Street, San Francisco.)
Ragsmatazz provides a fun, colorful, fairly current selection of junior-oriented and contemporary fashions (including some surprising labels). Fashion shoes, purses, wallets, and backpacks from a leading manufacturer are very popular with shoppers. Discounts are 40–60% off retail. If you love trendy junior styles, you'll want to check out the new shipments frequently. Moms and sisters can buy clever and cute sportswear from Spumoni for younger girls (sizes 12mos to Girls 14—best selection at Clement Street store). Sizes: Junior 1–13; Women's 4–16. Exchanges are allowed up to seven days after purchase with receipt.

SANDY'S—THE UNIQUE BOUTIQUE

3569 Mt. Diablo Boulevard, Lafayette. (510) 284-2653. M–F 10–6, Sat 10–5:30. MC, VISA. Parking: lot.
Sandy's gets a high rating. Sandy has the magic touch at selecting upscale, intriguing women's apparel for discriminating customers. This has been a secret source for many local women. The store is so beautiful, you'll feel that you're shopping in a very special boutique and, once initiated, you'll return again and again. Although Sandy's caters to the up-to-date mature woman, younger women will find fancier dresses for parties, proms, and weddings. Regulars grab the Max Studio, Carole Little, Tadashi, Arthur Max, Wild Rose, MZM, Laundry, Componix, CPX, Jonathan Martin, Nina Picalino, Bonnie Marx, and other lines of dresses,

related separates, sportswear, and jumpsuits. Sandy buys lots of wonderful fashion jewelry, hats, handbags, and watches. You'll see discounts of 30–50% off retail, and everything is current. Sizes: 2–18 (a few 20s). If you're willing to go a little out of your way to seek out Sandy's (next to the chic Tourelle Restaurant), you won't be disappointed.

WESTPORT LTD.

Factory Stores of America, Vacaville. (707) 449-0833. Daily. MC, VISA, AE, DIS. Parking: lot. (Other outlets: Anderson/Shasta, Folsom, Lathrop, Milpitas, Pacific Grove centers.)
Westport Ltd. offers a well-rounded, always-current selection: Ascending in quality and price, you'll find career suits, lovely daytime go-to-lunch-or-meeting dresses, sophisticated career dresses, and separates. Discounts are 20–50% off, maybe more on frequent in-store unadvertised specials. Sizes: 4–16. Returns, exchanges, and refunds.

Women's Accessories

CHARISMA (MAIL ORDER)
14550 Apache Avenue, Largo, FL, 33774. (800)
TRY-HOSE. MC, VISA, DIS, C.O.D.
If you're fed up with spending too much money replacing pantyhose, call Charisma, the U.S. distributor of a Canadian line. Though the difference between the U.S. 15-denier standard and Charisma's 20-denier hose may seem negligible, it makes a world of difference in terms of wear. Washing: Just throw the hosiery in a mesh bag and run it through your washing machine and dryer. Charisma's prices are an extra incentive. You must buy its one-size Regular (90–155 pounds) sandal foot by the dozen—select any combination of twenty colors. Price: $33/dozen. Other sizes available by the dozen and individually: Tall (140–190 pounds); control-top Regular or Tall; Princess (180–210 pounds); and Queen (225+ pounds). More expensive special groups of opaque and maxi-support hosiery can be ordered individually, knee-highs by the dozen. Your pantyhose by the dozen will arrive in a plain plastic bag to keep prices down. Charisma also has a network of sales representatives around the country who buy at lower-than-mail-order prices and make a few bucks on each pair sold. Get details or place orders using Charisma's 800 number.

LISA VIOLETTO ACCESSORIES
425 Brannan Street, San Francisco. (415) 543-
6261. M–Sat 11–5. MC, VISA. Parking: street.
If you love fashion accessories and wonderfully unique jewelry, you'll want to sashay in here and spend some time. Lisa Violetto is a local designer and manufacturer of fashion jewelry and accessories. Her line of necklaces, earrings, and jacket clips is sold to boutiques and major stores. The line is constantly evolving, but in early 1997 the emphasis was on Austrian crystal beads and vintage-inspired designs made with antique gold or silver plating.

The popular Y-necks were hot sellers. Prices at the outlet are reduced 40–50% off original retails on the leftovers—surplus inventory, samples, discontinued styles, etc. In addition, Lisa makes some wonderful hats, scarves, and—using beautiful fabrics—velvet throws for home or body, Victorian evening bags, and decorative pillows. To balance out the selection, other fashion jewelry and home accessory designers are sending in discontinued pieces and samples: Ellen Blakeley (mirrors), Arianne Millinery (hats), New York's Reesa Roberts (intricate relinked chain jewelry), Ferrara (belts and necklaces), Sunday Bazaar (sterling silver and semiprecious stone jewelry), Namast in Los Angeles (delicate necklaces). Others will be joining the scene in the months ahead. Many of the small designers sell "under the glass" and to posh stores. This is a charming outlet, organized like a classy upscale boutique yet offering downscale pricing.

1928 DESIGNER BRANDS/ACCESSORIES

Factory Stores at Vacaville, Vacaville. (707) 449-8106. Daily. MC, VISA. Parking: lot.
(Other outlets: Folsom, Gilroy, Pacific Grove centers.)
Stop in for the "extras" to fill the spaces in your jewelry chest and dresser drawers. You'll save a minimum of 40–50% every day on costume jewelry from the 1928 Jewelry Co. (including the Aurora collection), Napier, Swarosky, Kenneth Jay Lane, Catherine Stein, Jody Coyote, and Robert and Roman. Look for famous-maker handbags and small leather goods; 1928, Pulsar, Citizen, Gucci, Bulova, and Seiko watches to 50% off; sunglasses; Buxton wallets; men's jewelry; scarves; hair accessories; jewelry boxes; picture frames; and more. Solid discounts on gold chain, Italian sterling silver, and Langstrom's Black Hills gold.

SOCKS GALORE & MORE

Factory Stores of America, Vacaville. (707) 448-2420. Daily. MC, VISA, DIS. Parking: lot.
(Other outlets: Gilroy, Folsom centers.)
You want socks, you got socks! You'll find socks for everyone in the family. Over 60,000 pairs of designer brand socks (with and without labels) are sold for

20–80% off retail. Whatever your size or needs, you've got options. Money back guarantee.

SUCCESSORIES
152 Reina Del Mar (on Highway 1), Pacifica. (650) 359-0260. Daily 11–6. Cash/Check. Parking: street.
This eclectic selection of fashion jewelry, belts, hats, handbags, hair accessories, clothing, scarves, and other fancies showcased by Bay Area designer sales rep Pamela Winston-Charbonneau for is worth the trip. Most jewelry pieces are contemporary, collectible, and qualify as artwork. The prices are surprisingly affordable ($6–$150), especially at the 30–60% discount offered here. The artists/designers include Famous Melissa (jewelry made from computer chips and components), Broken Bottles (jewelry and housewares made from recycled glass), Cute As a Button (rings made from antique buttons set in silver), Spinoso (scarves), and several others. It's artistic and unusual. Look for the little red caboose that houses this gem on Hwy. 1.

SUNGLASS CITY
623 San Anselmo Avenue, San Anselmo. (415) 456-7297. M–Sat 10–5:30, Sun 10–5. MC, VISA, AE. Parking: street.
If you're serious about sunglasses, Sunglass City is the place to go. The folks here are specialists who can give you all the technical information you need to make an intelligent choice. You'll find top brands like Ray-Ban, Vuarnet, Revo, Serengeti, Armani, Persol, Hobie, Ski Optiks, and Suncloud at 15–40% off retail. Ray-Bans are always 30% off list. Vuarnets are discounted 15–20%. If you're like me and only buy glasses you can afford to lose, check the inexpensive lines, $3.95–$20.

TOTES FACTORY STORE
Factory Stores at Vacaville, Vacaville. (707) 449-8707. Daily. MC, VISA. Parking: lot.
(Other outlets: Anderson/Shasta, Pacific Grove centers.)
Women and men can poke around here and come up with treasures so inventive, clever, and practical that it's hard to leave without a tote of some kind. Check the selection of rainwear for women, children, and men, ranging from lightweight to heavyweight.

Plus there are umbrellas in all configurations, duffel bags, lightweight luggage, sunglasses, portfolios, notebooks, and more goodies to solve many gift-giving dilemmas. A universally popular store!

Also See

Under Women's Apparel/Fashion:
ALL SECTIONS

Under Cosmetics and Fragrances:
ALL LISTINGS

Under Handbags and Luggage:
ALL LISTINGS

Under Shoes:
ALL LISTINGS

Under Family, Men's & Women's, General Clothing:
THE BIG FOUR; STEIN MART

Large Sizes

ALL THE MORE TO LOVE (CONSIGNMENT)
1355 Park Street, Alameda. (510) 521-6206. M–Sat 10–6, Th until 7, Sun 11–4. MC, VISA. Parking: street.
A consignment shop where some better-quality like-new dresses or ensembles show up. Otherwise, it's a mixed bag of apparel for large-size women in all categories. Good prospects for women in transition up or down the scale. Shoes, accessories, and jewelry too.

CASUAL CORNER WOMAN
Great Mall of the Bay Area, Milpitas. (408) 934-9788. Daily. MC, VISA, AE, DIS. Parking: lot.
Just like the Petites who shop Casual Corner's Petite Sophisticate Outlets or the Misses-size women who shop Casual Corner Outlets, women sized 14–24 can find well-priced collections of casual sportswear and career apparel at Casual Corner Woman. The company does a very nice job of selecting stylish, mainstream fashions that are appropriately in season. Ensembles, related separates, sweaters, some dresses, and small groups of extra-fancy special-occasion fashions are ready for the taking.

DRESS BARN WOMAN/WESTPORT WOMAN
1660 S. Bascom Avenue, Hamilton Plaza, Campbell. (408) 371-7730. M–F 10–9, Sat 10–8, Sun 11–6. MC, VISA, AE, DIS. Parking: lot. (Other Westport Woman outlets: Folsom, Gilroy, Milpitas, Vacaville centers.)
Dress Barn Woman and Westport Woman (same ownership) are worthwhile destinations for all large-size ladies. Their selection of large-size fashions at 20–50% off retail is impressive. In December, you'll find dazzling holiday dresses; in summer, vacationwear. Everything—coats, jackets, swimwear, sweaters,

casual weekend garb, activewear, and accessories—appears very current. Sizes: 14–24 (a few 26s), or 1X–3X. Exchanges and cash refunds are available within 14 days. How nice!

FULL SIZE FASHIONS

Factory Stores of America, Vacaville. (707) 447-9505. Daily. MC, VISA, DIS. Parking: lot. (Other outlet: Anderson/Redding center.)
Since Full Size Fashions is dedicated to addressing the "whole woman," you'll find lingerie (panties, bras, girdles), sleepwear, bathing suits, coordinated groups of sportswear and career fashions, dresses, separates (jeans, sweaters, tops, etc.), and cover-ups, all discounted 30–50% off original retail. This isn't a resource for expensive designer label apparel at discount; its lines are moderately priced at retail. Young women, career women, and even silver-haired senior ladies can find fashions for their lifestyles. Sizes: dresses (full and half sizes) 16–32; tops 36–60; bottoms 30–54. Exchanges only within two weeks.

HARPER GREER

580 Fourth Street, San Francisco. (415) 543-4066. M–Sat 10–6, Sun Noon–5. MC, VISA, AE, DIS. Parking: street.
Large-size career women will find better quality and good design at Harper Greer. Since 1989 it has sold all its designs exclusively through its company store; it delivers sophisticated clothing in silk, wool, cotton, and better synthetics in chic and updated styles. Career coordinates, dresses, and a tempting selection of separates for workdays and weekends will keep you going in and out of the dressing rooms. Dresses range in price from $69 to $249 (executive boardroom dress); jackets in several lengths and career blazers range from $96 to $229. Obviously, the higher prices are for fine-quality wool, silk, or linen. Sizes: 14–26 (depending on style or cut many fit larger sizes). Tailor on premises for quick alterations.

MAKING IT BIG SPECIALTY STORE AND OUTLET

135 South West Boulevard, Rohnert Park. (707) 795-6861. M–Sat 10–6, Sun Noon–5. MC, VISA, AE, DIS. Parking: lot. Catalog requests to: 501 Aaron Street, Cotati, CA, 94931 or call (707) 795-1995.

This company fills a special niche in the large-size marketplace. It manufactures garment-dyed cottons (both wovens and knits), washable rayons, and ethnic prints. Cotton dresses and sportswear are made in sizes 32–72. Catalog prices usually range from $30 to $60 on its sportswear separates. It's a crossover line, going from work to weekend wear. Its new and expanded store is equally divided into a retail boutique showcasing the full-price current-season merchandise, and an outlet for all its catalog over-runs, past-season merchandise, seconds, and sale markdowns. Outlet discounts range 20–70% off retail. Get on the mailing list for its semiannual blowout sales.

SEAMS TO FIT

6527 Telegraph Avenue (between Alcatraz and Ashby), Oakland. (510) 428-9463. M–F 11–6, Sat 10–6, Sun Noon–4. MC, VISA, DIS. Parking: street.

Seams to Fit is in part the clearance center for Says Who, a large-size specialty store. It also connects with manufacturers to buy seconds and overruns, which it sells for discount prices alongside consigned merchandise. If you're planning a career change but can't afford a new wardrobe, if your body size has changed, or if you just want to buy clothing at affordable prices, you'll want to pick through the racks. The consigned clothing may have a bit of history, but it's still pretty fresh, or it would not have been accepted for resale. You'll find seconds and overruns in new fashions from Chez, Red's Threads, Vicki Vi, Liz & Jane, Fennini, August Silk, We Be Bop, and Says Who private label fashions, plus any and all major brands on consignment.

SIZES UNLIMITED

*1809 Willow Pass Road (Park and Shop Center),
Concord. (510) 825-2022. M–F 10–9, Sat 10–7,
Sun Noon–5. MC, VISA, AE. Parking: lot.
(More than twenty Northern California stores.)*
Sizes Unlimited has updated and improved all its
full-size fashions. Women of all ages find attractive
sportswear, career apparel, lingerie, sleepwear,
and outerwear at pleasing prices. Weekly promotions keep bargain hunters happy and "card holders" get special discount coupons. Sizes: 14–32.
Returns and refunds allowed.

Also See

Under San Francisco's Factory Outlets and Off-
Price Stores:
**BYER FACTORY OUTLET; CUT LOOSE; FRITZI;
GUNNE SAX**

Under Famous Labels/Factory Stores:
**AILEEN; CAROLE LITTLE; CHAUS; ELLEN TRACY;
EVAN PICONE; KASPER ASL; KORET; LIZ
CLAIBORNE; LUCIA**

Under Bay Area Manufacturers' Factory Outlets:
EMERYVILLE OUTLET; WE BE BOP

Under Family, Men's & Women's, General Clothing:
**BURLINGTON COAT FACTORY; MARSHALL'S;
ROSS DRESS FOR LESS; STEIN MART; T.J.
MAXX**

Under Clearance Centers:
NORDSTROM RACK; TALBOTS

Under Gitwares and Home Decor:
**RED ROSE COLLECTION CATALOG
OUTLET STORE**

Lingerie, Sleepwear, and Robes

BARBIZON FACTORY OUTLET

Factory Stores at Vacaville. (707) 447-0482. Daily. MC, VISA, DIS. Parking: lot.

For sheer savings, embark on what will be the first of many pilgrimages to one of these beautiful stores. You'll find truly sweet discounts on this fresh and lovely selection of current, first-quality sleepwear and lingerie: batiste gowns, matching peignoirs, featherweight flannels, and cuddleskin nightgowns and pajamas. The supporting cast includes bras, panties, teddies, camisoles, terry robes, tap pants, and slips. Discounts are 50% off original retail, even greater on special promotions and end-of-season clearances. Every spring, Jantzen bathing suits and Vanity Fair robes grace the racks before the holidays. Sizes range from Small to XL, although the biggest selection is in S, M, L. Bras range from 32 to 42DDD. Occasionally, you'll find Lady Barbizon in sizes 1X–3X. Vacaville receives clearance inventory from other outlet stores, resulting in some extra-thrifty buys. Exchanges or refunds anytime.

FARR*WEST FACTORY OUTLET

294 Anna Street, Watsonville. (408) 728-0880, (800) 848-7891. M–F 10–4. MC, VISA. Parking: lot.

It may be a drive, but once there you'll find 66–75% reductions on tap pants, petti pants, half slips, full slips, camisoles, wraps, panties, garter belts, and chemises. These are samples, discontinued styles, and irregulars priced $3–$23 at 60–90% off retail. Farr*West produces fine lingerie collections in woven goods: polyester "taffecrepe," stretch charmeuse, crepe georgette, cotton batiste, and a very high quality noncling woven polyester charmeuse. Sizes: P–XL, slips 32–40, and 1X–4X. *Directions: Take the Airport exit from Highway 1. The first street is Westgate, turn right, then left on Anna.*

JOSEF ROBE OUTLET

2525 16th Street (2nd floor), San Francisco. (415) 252-5522. M–Sat 9–5, Sat 10–4. MC, VISA. Parking: street.

This is for those who have no qualms about spending a little more for quality. Josef Robes makes luxury robes for hotels and for the general public. Retail robes are sized by height and circumference to insure a proper fit for all body types. There are numerous styles, including both wrap robes and pullover robes in 100% cotton in basic white or fashion colors. These are expensive for velour or terry cloth robes, often selling at retail for $100 and up. First-quality robes are sold for a 20% discount, but pick up a second and you'll save at least 50%—that means as little as $40 on a short white kimono-style terry robe, or about $55 on a logo robe from the Post Resort or the Inn at Spanish Bay. Many seconds priced $40–$80. More discounts will be found in corners of the outlet that showcase Early Gilbert's boutique line of form-fitting lingerie in stretch laces and fabrics; Parks for Recreation's line of men's body-conscious underwear and workout wear; and Barbara Hume's samples from her fine line of handwoven (and expensive at retail) classic apparel (jackets and vests) and coordinating sportswear separates.

L'EGGS, HANES & BALI

Petaluma Village Factory Outlets, Petaluma. (707) 778-1056. Daily. MC, VISA. Parking: lot.
(Other outlets: Folsom, Gilroy, Milpitas, Pacific Grove, Vacaville centers.)

From the name you can assume that you'll find pantyhose, knee highs, lingerie, men's underwear, Isotoner gloves, thermal underwear, socks, and children's underwear and socks. These are close-outs or slightly imperfect goods (usually nonconforming colors). Sizes to 50DD bras for women and undershirts in XXL and Tall for men. The variety in Bali lingerie is gratifying. Larger gals will be particularly pleased with the panty selection that goes to size 13. Savings 20–60% off original pricing. Returns and refunds.

MAIDENFORM OUTLET

Factory Stores of America, Vacaville. (707) 451-1211. Daily. MC, VISA, AE. Parking: lot.
(Other outlets: Gilroy, Pacific Grove, Tracy centers.)
At Maidenform you'll find bras (32A–42DDD, also full-figure), camisoles, tap pants, full slips, bustiers, half slips, garter belts, sleepwear, and lounge wear in Regular and Queen sizes. The lingerie ranges from basic to elegant in fashion colors and dependable neutrals; also sleepwear and robes designed for good-looking comfort. Discounts are 25–60% off.

NAP OUTLET

Petaluma Village Factory Outlets, Petaluma. (707) 766-8081. Daily. MC, VISA, AE. Parking: lot.
This is truly a manufacturer's outlet—you'll love it, I promise. Lovely fabrics, interesting textures, great prints and colors, and wonderful styling all add up to a collection of sleepwear, robes, and lingerie that's exceptional in every way. This is a great place to choose your next "reward." The line, which is sold in upscale stores (sometimes under private label), is quite versatile. Women approve of the contemporary, comfortable, and cozy look and feel in most sleepwear groups. (You may never quite make it out of some of the thermal knit groups and into your daywear if you're having a day at home.) Loved the terry velour robes, pajama and robe sets, sleepshirts, and gowns—in fact, everything designed for slumber. There's a smattering of sensuous and fancy satin peignoir sets and body suits, plus some lacy bras and panties made for a famous lingerie company—the name must remain a secret. The men's section is equally impressive, with silk or polyester boxers, flannel or cotton kimonos in great paisleys or masculine prints and colors. Almost everything is 100% cotton except for specialty collections. Prices are nicely discounted (about 30–60% off) to take the sting out of this pricier line. Additional discounts on occasional irregulars and featured specials. Sizes: S–L, 1X–3X.

OLGA/WARNER'S OUTLETS

Outlets at Gilroy, Gilroy. (408) 842-3799. Daily. MC, VISA, AE, DIS. Parking: lot.
(Other outlets: Folsom, Gilroy, Petaluma centers.)
The selection of Olga and Warner's styles in sleepwear, controlwear, panties (sizes 4–10), bras (sizes 32AA–42DDD), slips, camisoles, bodysuits, and

swimwear (seasonal) is very impressive. The discounts on the overruns, discontinued, and irregular styles range from very modest to sensational. The staff is always ready to assist with measurements and fitting if requested.

Also see

Under Bay Area Off-Price/Chain Discount Stores
LOEHMANN'S; STEIN MART

Under Clearance Centers:
ALL LISTINGS

Under Fabrics:
THAI SILKS

Under Family, Men's & Women's, General Clothing:
BURLINGTON COAT FACTORY; JOCKEY; MARSHALL'S; ROSS; T.J. MAXX; VF FACTORY OUTLET

Maternity

DAX & COE MATERNITY FACTORY OUTLET

935 El Camino Real, Menlo Park. (650) 327-4371.
M–F 10–6, Sat–Sun Noon–5. MC, VISA.
Parking: street.
This line was worn by the Duchess of York and
Melanie Griffith. Its success is easy to understand,
since it's fabricated in 100% cotton knits and
includes a wonderful sweater group that will still
be wearable after the baby comes. The outlet is
wonderful, with samples, prior-season merchandise,
and seconds in groups of coordinates, some career
and casual dresses ($15–$50), tops ($10–$50),
shorts, pants, and skirts ($10–$35). Prices are
40–75% off original retail. Sizes: 4–14 or S, M, L.

FASHION AFTER PASSION (CONSIGNMENT)

1211 Park Street, Alameda. (510) 769-MOMS. M–F
10:30–6:30, Sat 10:30–6, Sun 11–3. MC, VISA, DIS.
Parking: street.
To add a few pieces to your temporary maternity
wardrobe, Fashion After Passion offers good buys;
it's packed with sportswear and separates, nursing
clothing, and season maternity apparel. Better
dresses and career apparel are in short supply and
don't stay in the store long. All sizes in lines that
were originally moderately priced. The full line of
undergarments and bras to 46H are in good supply
but not discounted. A consignment children's
department allows moms to get a head start on
baby's wardrobe.

MATERNITY WORKS

Outlets at Gilroy, Gilroy. (408) 847-7560. Daily.
MC, VISA, AE. Parking: lot.
(Other outlets: Napa, Petaluma centers.)
If you're set on maintaining a professional image and putting on the ritz through the ninth month, or if you just want to look your best when your waist grows to 44 inches, then make the trek to Maternity Works. Owned by the Mothers Work (a company that's brought the Mimi specialty retail chain, the Pea in the Pod and Motherhood stores, and Maternité catalog into its fold), this is the best maternity outlet I've found yet, with satisfying discounts and markdowns (30–75% off), a stylish selection of apparel for all occasions, and quality that should meet the requirements of the most discriminating shopper. About 50% of the merchandise is past-season closeout inventory from its regular stores, and the remaining selection is a collection designed for its outlet division offered at special value pricing. The private label outlet merchandise measures up in every way to the regular lines. The company designs and manufacturers almost everything in the United States, but a few outside lines are carried (bras, panties, panty-hose, etc.). This is a great resource for professional women! I loved the inventory of past-season holiday fashions, the many styles of jumpsuits, dresses, the one-piece slip skirt (top with any jacket), the denim collection, knit tops and pants, and many nursing style fashions. Overall, a nice mix of traditional and contemporary fashions (under the Mimi label).
Sizes: Petite to XL.

MOM (MATERNITY CENTER OF MARIN)

874 Fourth Street, San Rafael. (415) 457-4955.
M–Sat 10:30–5. MC, VISA, DIS.
Parking: street/city lots.
You'll want to hit the racks here for consignment clothing that encompasses all categories of maternity apparel. Don't miss the new apparel (past-season overruns) at nicely discounted prices. Good selection of necessities for the nursing mom. Consignments accepted anytime!

MOTHERHOOD MATERNITY OUTLET

Factory Stores of America, Vacaville. (707) 446-4792. Daily. MC, VISA, AE. Parking: lot.
(Other outlet: Shasta/Anderson center.)
Motherhood Maternity's leftover and surplus inventory from its 200 stores is very current and beautifully displayed. The modest 20% discounts on very current fashions are better than none at all, but you'll have to watch for end-of-season markdowns to get gratifying 50% discounts. The selection reflects the complete "cover" Motherhood offers for expectant moms: lingerie, sleepwear, swimsuits, sweaters, sportswear, dresses (career and dressy), jumpsuits, pantyhose, etc. Sizes: S, M, L (occasionally some XS and XL).

NATURAL RESOURCES

4081 24th Street, San Francisco. (415) 550-2611. M–F 10:30–6, Sat 11–5. MC, VISA. Parking: street.
As a resource center for pregnant women and new families, Natural Resources offers classes, a reference library, health-care products, breastfeeding supplies, and more. You'll also find closeouts and overruns of new maternity fashions and consignment maternity apparel. Nice discounts on the new merchandise; consignment prices for shoestring budgets.

TODAY'S MATERNITY

Great Mall of the Bay Area, Milpitas. (408) 941-9492. MC, VISA, DIS. Parking: lot.
Those "anticipating" will be pleased to see the markdowns on current season fashions. Count on a minimum of 20% off retail, sometimes more (up to 40% off retail) when the store buyer scores a particularly good purchase from the many established manufacturers that supply the inventory. Better collections of casual and career clothing are accorded about equal space, but there are usually some dressier fashions for special occasions, plus lingerie, some whimsical specialty T-shirts, and just about anything else that is needed for cover while waiting for baby. Sizes: Petite through X-Large.

Also See

Under Family Apparel:
ALL SECTIONS

Petites

Many stores in all clothing categories may have a small selection of Petite sizes; you can find them at Loehmann's, Marshall's, Dress Barn, Aileen, Anne Klein, Donna Karan, Koret Factory Stores, Lucia, Liz Claiborne, Chaus, Jones New York (all divisions), Westport Ltd., Carole Little, Robert Scott & David Brooks, Ross Dress for Less, T.J. Maxx, Burlington Coat Outlet, Nordstrom Rack, Off Fifth, Talbots, Group USA, Mondi, Ellen Tracy, Evan Picone, Kasper ASL, and St. John. The selections range from two to three racks to whole sections of a store or outlet specifically devoted to Petite customers. Check the Store Index for the page numbers of these stores.

PETITE SOPHISTICATE OUTLET
Petaluma Village Factory Outlets, Petaluma. (707) 763-8097. Daily. MC, VISA, AE, DIS. Parking: lot. (Other outlets: Milpitas and Vacaville centers.) There's a slew of terrific fashions to cover all a Petite needs. Career suits, activewear (or spectator) casual weekend collections, dresses, related separates, sweaters, and accessories. A division of Casual Corner, these specialty stores have won a loyal following of diminutive women. While the merchandise in the outlets does not come from its full-price retail division, the same image is conveyed. Discounts are 20–50% off retail on comparable merchandise, averaging about 40%. Fashions are in season and first quality. Make a splash with less cash if you're 5'4" or under and wear sizes 2–16. Refunds and exchanges.

Wedding and Formal Wear

BRIDAL VEIL OUTLET/TRADITIONAL WHITE
625 Second Street, San Francisco. (415) 777-9531. M–Sat 10–5:30. Cash/Check. Parking: pay lots.
Here you'll save at least 20–50% off retail on samples and discontinued headpieces and veils for brides and bridesmaids. Prices range from $45 to $145, while retail prices would be more like from $150 to $300. You'll find veils in informal to cathedral lengths, and headpieces in tiara, crown, bandeau, juliet, wreath, pillbox, and other styles. Many have exquisite beading and appliqués on fabrics that include silk shantung and satin. You'll find accessories like ring bearer pillows, gloves, guest books, shoes etc. Special orders and custom designs are available, but at strictly "custom" prices. A new aspect of the outlet concerns bridal gowns available in both vintage (used) and new (from American manufacturers). New gowns are sold off the rack at a very modest savings, with prices generally ranging from $275 to $1,000. Gowns can be special-ordered, custom-designed, and made to order. The vintage gowns (some on consignment) can be very good values for brides striving for something a little different.

BRIDAL WAREHOUSE
625 Second Street #218 (bet. Brannan and Townsend), San Francisco. (415) 882-4696 or (800) 567-4696. M–Sun 10–5, Closed Wed. MC, VISA. Parking: street.
The Bridal Warehouse is a new type of bridal store, stocking gowns in a complete size range for purchase off the rack. Some gowns are made overseas and imported by companies advertising in bridal magazines. In spring 1997, many gowns were in synthetic fabrics, heavily beaded, and very ornate

in both full and sheath styles. Prices ranged from $300 to $600 on average (some lower, some higher priced). Two racks held higher-quality samples of special-order gowns (prices reduced about 15–20% off retail). Before shopping at a "warehouse" store, visit a few bridal shops first to get a feel for quality and price. Sizes: 2–20 in stock. Bridesmaid dresses are 15% off when at least three are ordered. Check the racks for prom dresses and good values on beaded mother-of-the-bride dresses.

CHERYL T'S BRIDAL & TUXEDO

3229 Stevens Creek Boulevard, San Jose. (408) 244-5158. M–Th Noon–8, Fri Noon–6, Sat 10–5, Sun Noon–4. MC, VISA. Parking: lot.
At Cheryl T's sample sizes range from 8 to 12, and when these gowns are discontinued they are sold for 50% off the original price. Closeout racks have really low prices on discontinued sample brides-maid and mother-of-the-bride dresses. Most of these dresses are a little tired! New bridal gowns can be special ordered from samples—tagged with manufacturer's name, retail price, discount price of 10% if ordered with a 50% deposit, and 20% dis-count price if ordered and paid for in full five months

in advance. These gowns, currently advertised in bridal magazines, include Demetrios, Ilissa, Alfred Angelo, Bill Levkoff, Watters & Watters, Jordan, Princess, Jasmine, Bianchi, Joelle, and Jim Hjelm. You may not find all these brands' styles, but you can special order. Samples of bridesmaid dresses offer the same applied discount rate. And bring the fellas along for new tuxedos sold or rented at discount prices.

DISCOUNT BRIDAL OUTLET

300 Brannan Street (bet. Second and Third streets), San Francisco. (415) 495-7922. M–Sat 10–5, Sun 11–5. MC, VISA. Parking: street.
You won't find the elegant salon feeling of most bridal shops here; its no-frills, no-glamour, close-to-tacky decor keeps prices down. But if you covet gowns in the $250–$1,000 range at retail, you're a good candidate for the selection. Of course, dresses at more modest prices are available, too. Discounts are about 20% off retail, but may be more since many salons take a higher markup. You can buy right off the rack for a wedding on Saturday. Other dresses may be ordered for delivery in a week or two, or at most two to four months. Discontinued

styles may be discounted as much as 50% off retail, while fluffy petticoats are 20–30% less than salon prices. I spotted a few dogs, but in order to get the best styles, the owner sometimes has to take a loser. The same discounts apply to gowns for bridesmaids and flower girls, or a dress for a prom or a *quincinera*. Large selection of gowns in sizes 4–42 (off the rack or special order).

HE-RO OUTLET

Great Mall of the Bay Area, Milpitas. (408) 934-9582. Daily. MC, VISA, AE. Parking: lot.
The main attraction here is the glittering selection of scene-stealing after-five fashions from Black Tie, Oleg Cassini, Niteline, and Roufogali. Elegant beaded and sequined dresses, evening suits with beaded trim, party pants, full-length and street-length heavily beaded gowns, and little strapless dresses with jackets are always on hand. Mothers of the bride or groom may even find a knockout dress or suit. New style trends are reflected in the dresses without embellishments or at the most very lightly embellished on after-five dresses. Prices are discounted 30–70% off retail (averaging about 40%). At that, a dazzling full-length heavily

beaded dress may range from $300 to $650, a shorter version from $225 to $400. If you find a dress you love, but it's not available in your size, it can be special ordered for delivery in five to seven days. Note: Protect your investment. Don't leave without obtaining a referral to a nationwide cleaning service that specializes in beaded formal wear and wedding gowns. The service is easy to use with an 800 number and UPS shipping.

Another facet of this store is the section (about 20%) devoted to classy sportswear and sophisticated daytime wear: Kenar, Regina Porter, Terry Jon (suits), Halsey (vests, sweaters, and blouses), and Carryback (linen blouses). European-inspired dresses and suits set you apart from the conventional Talbots customer while Schraeder Sport offers traditional dresses for the more conservative woman. Sizes: 4–18.

NEW THINGS WEST

350 South Winchester Boulevard (off Stevens Creek), second floor, San Jose. (408) 241-8136. M–F 11–8, Sat 10–6, Sun 1–5. MC, VISA, DIS, AE. Parking: lot.

New Things West has multiple personalities. First, retired samples of bridal, bridesmaid, formal wear, and some MOBs from its first floor main store (Bay Area Bridals) are sold at modest to maximum discounts. Bridesmaid dresses start at $19.99, bridal gowns from $99, and prom dresses generally range from $19 to $79. Clearance racks of formal wear (some mother-of-the-bride and cocktail dresses) are always reduced a minimum of 60%, many 80%. Naturally, you'll find some forlorn fashions on the racks, but also some real beauties. The "new" bridal department at New Things West covers the spectrum, with gowns priced for every budget. The owner utilizes his connections to buy special closeouts and factory overstocks. These are discounted a minimum of 20% off regular retail and some styles can be special ordered. There are gowns available off the rack in sizes 4–44. Any sample is available as a special order. Also, nice clearance dressy shoe department with outstand-ing values. *Note: If you strike out in the clearance department, don't leave without checking out the full-service salon.*

Rental and Previously Worn

CHERISHED

1150 Civic Drive, Walnut Creek. (510) 280-0128. T–Th 11–7, Fri–Sat 10–5. MC, VISA, AE. Parking: street.

Consignment shopping for wedding gowns makes sense when you're trying to trim wedding costs. The owner brings her special understanding and expertise to the business—for many years she owned an upscale bridal salon. Whether you're hoping to spend a modest $200 or ready to pay more than $1,000 for a gown that may have been worn at an elegant country club reception, chances are you'll find many to consider within your budget. The gowns are in excellent condition, a requirement for consignment. Prices are approximately half off the original price. The styles reflect anything that may have been shown in bridal magazines from the past few years. Some gowns are new—retired try-on samples or canceled orders from the inventory of other bridal salons. These are also reduced in price from 40% to 60% off original retail. Sizes generally range from 4–38. Bridal veils and some mother-of-the-bride gowns available too. If you're retiring a gown, bring it in—you'll split the selling price 50/50 with the owner.

FORMAL RENDEZVOUS

118 South Boulevard (south end of B Street), San Mateo. (650) 345-4302. By appt. T–F Noon–6:30, Sat 10–5. MC, VISA, AE. Parking: street.

At this boutique-style salon crammed with beautiful fashions, those needing a wedding, cocktail party, formal, or semiformal dress have a good chance of finding a real dazzler. It may be a showstopping beaded and sequined formal, tea-length cocktail dress, even a basic black cocktail dress. The selection provides options for women of varying ages and style orientations, in sizes 4–20. Most designer dresses and bridal gowns come with status labels like Bob Mackie, Sho Max, Oleg Cassini, Demetrios, and Victor Costa. To allow the staff time to give you the personal service and attention you may require, appointments are preferred.

ONCE WORN GOWNS

901-A Irwin Street (corner of Third Street), San Rafael. (415) 485-5550. M–Sat 10–6, Wed until 8 (limited hours Oct–Dec; call first). MC, VISA, layaways. Parking: private lot off Third Street.

If you have a hard time justifying the cost of a new bridal gown or the money just isn't there to buy one, then consider the alternative offered by Once Worn Gowns. This upstairs boutique specializes in selling once-worn gowns placed on consignment by women in the area. In the selection of approximately 200 wedding gowns, there are many styles and no single look. You may find a gown you've admired in a bridal magazine, a custom-made gown, or a gown originally sold off the rack. The goal is to satisfy the needs of a diverse clientele. The largest selection is found in the $200–$500 range, which represents a savings of at least half off retail. The more expensive designer gowns, originally priced $1,000–$3,000 at retail (many in beautiful silk fabrics), come in frequently but usually sell quickly. Another plus—there's no guesswork involved. What you see is what you get. When selecting a gown from a bridal salon, often the sample you try on is much too big or too small, requiring you to "guess" that it will be perfection when delivered in the right size. I particularly liked the selection of bridal veils and headpieces priced $45–$150. Also, shoes, petticoats, bras, a good selection of bridesmaid dresses (occasionally even four or five matching gowns), some mother-of-the-bride dresses, junior bridesmaid dresses, and flower girl dresses. Sizes: 2–30. Alterations can be handled by a resident seamstress and bridal designer. This woman is also available to make custom wedding gowns of your own design. The other side of this business may appeal to any recent bride (or member of the wedding) who may want to turn their dress into cash. Consignees receive 50% of the selling price. *Note: A move is being contemplated to larger quarters in late 1997. Call for new location.*

Also See

Under San Francisco's Factory Outlets and Off-Price Stores:
GUNNE SAX; GEORGIOU

Under Famous Labels/Factory Stores:
ELLEN TRACY; MONDI; ST. JOHN

Under Bay Area Manufacturers' Factory Outlets:
KAREN ALEXANDER

Under Bay Area Off-Price/Chain Discount Stores:
GROUP USA; LOEHMANN'S

Under Family, Men's & Women's, General Clothing:
BURLINGTON COAT FACTORY

Under Clearance Centers:
ALL LISTINGS

Men's Sportswear

CALIFORNIA BIG & TALL

822 Mission Street (bet. Fourth and Fifth streets), San Francisco. (415) 495-4484. M–Sat 10–6, Th until 7, Sun Noon–5. MC, VISA. Parking: Fifth and Mission Garage (pay).

Everything sent to California Big & Tall from the 17 Rochester Big & Tall stores is initially marked down at least 20–40% off retail; some racks add up to 60% and more. The bargains are usually past-season styles and include suits, sportcoats, sportshirts, sweaters, wool and poly/wool slacks for workday and weekend clothing. Some basics like underwear and belts are not discounted. Sizes: suits 46–60 Reg, Long, and Extra Long; shirts to 20-inch neck, 38-inch sleeve. A small shoe selection to 16 Medium, 15 Wide. As at most clearance centers, not everything is wonderful, but there are many good-quality buys. Alterations extra; all sales final.

CHAMPS SPORTS

Great Mall of the Bay Area, Milpitas. (408) 956-0771. MC, VISA. Parking: lot.

Whether you're a fan of the NBA, NFL, or NHL, or you want to sport your favorite university or college logo, you have a good chance of finding something to broadcast your loyalty at Champs Sports. However, 49er and Raider logos are seldom found. Save 50% on past-season styles of apparel (tanks, tops, sweats, outerwear, wind or jog suits, shorts, etc.) and about 20–50% off on discontinued styles of athletic shoes. Current merchandise is regular retail price, although there are always promotional racks and specials posted around the store.

GANT

Petaluma Village Factory Outlets, Petaluma.
(707) 778-9285. Daily. MC, VISA. Parking: lot.
(Other outlets: Gilroy, Vacaville centers.)
Mainstream sportswear for the average guy is what
Gant is all about. You'll find a handsome collection
of shirts, pants, sweaters, and more with traditional
styling priced at 30– 50% off retail. Sizes: S–XXL in
tops; 30–44 pants.

G.HQ. OUTLET

Great Mall of the Bay Area, Milpitas. (408) 263-
8571. Daily. MC, VISA, AE. Parking: lot.
Part showcase for its current collections and part
clearance center for its eight Southern California
stores, G.Hq. is popular with twenty-somethings
and men who are not afraid to be on the forefront
of fashion trends. Most of the selection is geared
toward "dress casual"—shirts, sweaters, slacks, sportcoats, and suits that fit right in the Saturday night
club scene, have a little extra pizzazz for dates and
restaurant dining, or are more relaxed for Friday
casual days at the office. The clearance inventory
in the back half of the store is marked down 25–50%
off original retail, since this merchandise is slightly
past-season. Sizes in European-styled sportcoats
are S–XL; pants from waist sizes 29–38.

GUESS? CLASSICS

Outlets at Gilroy, Gilroy. (408) 848-8875. Daily.
MC, VISA, AE. Parking: lot.
There should be a sign on the window that reads:
"For Men Only." This factory store is stocked with
dress casual sportswear, weekend sportswear, golf
collections, and a smaller selection of Guess? Boys
in sizes 8–20. Strike just the right note on Fridays
with a loose-fitting wool blazer marked down to $98
from $142 (further reduced to $65 during special
sale periods). Match it up with pants for $30 (retail
$45). Savings generally range from 25% to 50%.

HAGGAR CLOTHING CO.

Outlets at Gilroy, Gilroy. (408) 842-4983. Daily.
MC, VISA, AE, DIS. Parking: lot.
Taking the coordinate concept used in selling
women's clothing, Haggar sells suit jackets and
suit pants separately. The pants are sold in finished
lengths in waist sizes 30–44; jackets sizes 26–48 in
Short, Medium, and Long. Some suit fabrics are
labeled "washable." This is a moderately priced

line sold in many major national chain stores. Prices are reduced 25–50% off major store retails. There's also a nice selection of casual sportswear and pants (waist sizes 29–50) in a variety of styles and fabrics that he can wear while he's doing whatever!

IZOD FACTORY STORE

Outlets at Gilroy, Gilroy. (408) 847-1448. Daily. MC, VISA, AE, DIS. Parking: lot.
(Other outlets: Pacific Grove, Truckee, Vacaville centers.)
It's been years since the Izod logo set you apart, but the line is still appealing and much desired. Golfers in particular love the Izod Factory Store, where I spotted the classic "links" cardigan and many styles of pullovers, twill and cotton/linen slacks, shorts, shirts for any weather or season, and accessories, all at 20–50% discounts. Izod's smaller sportswear collection for women particularly appeals to a more mature and mainstream customer. Sizes: S–XXL, some Big and Tall sizes. Refunds and exchanges within 60 days.

JOHN HENRY & FRIENDS

Pacific West Outlet Center, Gilroy. (408) 848-1777. MC, VISA, DIS. Parking: lot.
(Other outlet: Milpitas, Monterey centers.)
Naturally you'll find John Henry shirts (a popular department store label), but also Thomson slacks, and a colorful and more sophisticated selection of sportswear and ties from Perry Ellis. Men can break out of the executive mode with a whimsical "theme tie." This is another excellent resource for men, with merchandise nicely presented and prices nicely discounted. Sizes: shirts 14 1/2–18, sleeves to 34/35; pants to 42. Exchanges and cash refunds.

N. E. WEAR

96 Townsend Street (off Second Street), San Francisco. (415) 357-1002. M–F Noon–5:30, Sat 10–5:30. MC, VISA, AE. Parking: street.
You'll find clothing here that you can enjoy wearing anytime, anyplace, N. E. Wear! It's a line with a European attitude, an outdoor feel, and an American appeal. The fabrics are the stand-out factor in this line: sherpa fleece with great textural interest; soft, cotton, flat-back rib knits; double-

sided polar fleeces; sanded twills and interlock knits; and wide-wale corduroys. One cruise through the racks and women will start thinking gifts—gifts their fellas will actually wear. Along with the wonderful fabrics, the quality is evident in the construction, which is why the line is sold at better department and specialty stores and at classy resorts like La Costa, Pebble Beach, and the Sonoma Mission Inn. You can pick up a cozy and comfortable top in several styles—a simple crew neck pullover, a five-button pullover, a shirt jacket, or a mock turtle just for starters. A range or stadium coat in sherpa fleece may set you back about $60—a real bargain, everything considered. Action pants, sportshirts, lightweight jackets, shorts, fleece caps, polo-style shirts, and hooded tops are some of your other style options. Long or short skirts, vests, camp-style shirts, and assorted tops, jackets, and dresses coordinate the women's selection. Prices on these past-season styles, over-runs, samples, and occasional irregulars are 40–70% off original retail. Sizes: Men's S–XL; Women's XS–L. All sales final.

NAUTICA OUTLET

Napa Factory Stores, Napa. (707) 252-3992. Daily. MC, VISA, AE, DIS. Parking: lot.

This is the consummate headquarters for the sailing crowd. It's true that some men may find Nautica's prices steep at retail, but that's directly related to the quality of its well-made line and the quality of its fabrics. You'll get some price relief with discounts that average about 35% off retail. A $76 sweatshirt that looks as good a year later as the day you bought it will set you back about $48; a casual $300 jacket (perfect for cold days out on the Bay) may be reduced to $200 or $149 on special end-of-season racks. The store is done up with taste and style, the better to showcase the classic, clean lines of Nautica's first-quality pants, shorts, shirts, sweaters, jackets, sweats, and all the other bits and pieces. Sizes: S–XXL (with accommodating athletic cut).

ROBERT TALBOTT FACTORY OUTLET

The Village Center, Carmel Valley. (408) 659-4540. M–Sat 10–5, Sun Noon–5. MC, VISA, AE. Parking: lot.

The next time you're visiting Carmel, take a ride out to the Robert Talbott Factory Outlet. You'll

save at least 50% on fine ties that typically retail for $42–$80. Many have minute to major flaws like slubs in the fabric, wrinkles, and pulled threads. Prices are discounted accordingly. Frequent in-store specials feature ties as low as $5. Also, fabulous buys on elegant discontinued fabrics such as silks (all types), wool challis, and fine cottons. The shirt selection has been expanded. Both the shirts and shirt fabrics are in demand because of the superior quality of the cotton fabric and the high thread count. Don't overlook the good deals on bow ties, cummerbunds, and pocket squares either.
Directions: From Highway 1, take Carmel Valley Road 13 miles to the Village Center; turn right at the Texaco station.

TOMMY HILFIGER OUTLET STORE

Napa Factory Stores, Napa. (707) 224-4299. Daily. MC, VISA, AE. Parking: lot.
Mailing customers get cards three to four times a year offering additional discounts during extra special sales. Altogether, the savings reach sublime levels ($65 sportshirts reduced to $24.99). At any other time, the savings are modest—25–35% off retail on average. Even so, business is brisk, as fans of this line relish the opportunity to buy current and past-season overruns. Tourists can load up and have the sportswear shipped home via UPS.

VAN HEUSEN FACTORY STORES

601 Mission Street, San Francisco. (415) 243-0750. M–Sat 9–6, Sun 11–5. MC, VISA, DIS.
Parking: street.
(Other outlets: Folsom, Gilroy, Milpitas, Petaluma, Vacaville centers.)
The Van Heusen Factory Group comprises over 400 off-price stores selling Van Heusen and other labels directly to the consumer. You can always find dress shirts in dozens of fabrications in regular and European (slim) fits, sizes 15–18½. You'll also want to browse through racks of casual sportswear for both men and women, geared for traditional tastes.

Also See

Under San Francisco's Factory Outlets and Off-Price Stores:
BILL'S SWEATER OUTLET; CRISTINE FOLEY; NEW WEST DESIGN

Under Famous Labels/Factory Stores:
**EXECUTIVE SUITE; DONNA KARAN; J. CREW;
LIZ CLAIBORNE; TSE CASHMERE**

Under Bay Area Off-Price/Chain Discount Stores:
RAFFIA

Under Family Clothing:
ALL LISTINGS

Under Active Sportswear:
**COLUMBIA SPORTSWEAR COMPANY; FILA
FACTORY OUTLET; SIDE OUT; URBAN ATHLETE;
OSHMAN'S CLEARANCE CENTER**

Under Children's Clothing:
BUGLE BOY

Under Shoes:
TIMBERLAND

Under Sporting Goods:
ALL LISTINGS

Men's Suits

AFTERWARDS

1137 El Camino Real (at Santa Cruz), Menlo Park. (650) 324-2377. M–Sat 10–6, Th until 8. MC, VISA. Parking: street.

Afterwards is a consignment store offering an intriguing selection of new and used men's suits from upscale stores: you'll always find some Polo by Ralph Lauren and occasionally status labels like Brioni, Mani, or Armani. Since the owners have good industry connections, men will find new "samples" from Robert Talbott and Ferrell Reed (ties), Alexander Julian, Trafalgar (belts), J. Abboud (sweaters), and others. Afterwards also takes new excess inventory on consignment. New merchandise is marked at about 50% off retail; consignment inventory is about 75% off original retail. Prices are $100–$400 plus. The women's half of the store is equally impressive, with better labels. These folks obviously refuse more than they accept for consignment.

BROOKS BROTHERS FACTORY STORES

Outlets at Gilroy, Gilroy. (408) 847-3440. Daily. MC, VISA, AE. Parking: lot.
(Other outlets: Petaluma, St. Helena centers.)
Brooks Brothers career clothing appeals equally to men and women, with dependable basics and fine quality. Prices are discounted about 30% on average, with extra point-of-purchase markdowns to 50% off on selected groups every day. The company has expanded its sportswear: casual slacks, shirts, and sweaters. Pick up some essentials—ties, pajamas, socks, belts, and more. Sizes for men: 36 Short to 48 Long and Extra Long; dress shirts from 14 (32-inch sleeve) to 17½ (36-inch sleeve). I loved the women's career clothing—suits, separates, and silk sets and dresses. Returns within 30 days with receipt. No alterations.

CLOTHING BROKER

5327 Jacuzzi Street, Richmond. (510) 528-2196.
MC, VISA. F 10–7, Sat 10–6, Sun 11–5.
Parking: lot.
(Other stores: 3280 Victor Street, Santa Clara,
(408) 748-7637.)

The Clothing Broker stores are located in industrial parks, are open only three days a week, and use minimal advertising: a successful formula for very low pricing. Each store is well stocked with suits and sportcoats in sizes 36S to 60 Regular. In spring 1997 navy blue blazers were $109; most suits ranged from $99 to $179 (international collections from Begair, Lebus, and others to $269). All-wool tuxedos were $169. The company buys directly from manufacturers or manufacturers' reps and occasionally buys closeouts. There is an extensive selection in Big and Tall from 40 Portly to 60 Long to a 22-inch neck in shirts. Dress shirts were priced from $12.99 to $24.99. Ties from $7.99 to $14.99. A separate vendor maintains a very nice shoe department with styles from Johnston & Murphy, Florsheim, Stuart James, Bally, and others for $54–$119. Most slacks were priced $39–$44. This is a pipe-rack operation but nicely presented; all in all, I think Clothing Broker does a very good job, satisfying all but the most elite shoppers. Alterations done on site for a fee. Returns, exchanges, and refunds. Call for directions.

GOOD BYES

3464 Sacramento, San Francisco. (415) 346-6388.
M–Sat 10–6, Th until 8, Sun 11–5. MC, VISA.
Parking: street.

Good Byes offers cut-above consignment men's apparel. In labels, you'll find everything from Gap to Gucci. You'll find prices starting at $50, averaging about $125, and topping out at about $300. Sizes usually 36–46. Good selection of slacks, dress shirts, ties (many new), belts, and shoes. The owner has a pipeline to an upscale line of men's sportswear, resulting in new merchandise (mostly samples) in all categories of men's apparel. Go to the women's side for tempting buys.

MODA FASHION APPAREL OUTLET

Great Mall of the Bay Area, Milpitas. (408) 935-8060. Daily. MC, VISA, AE, DIS. Parking: lot. (Other outlet: Petaluma center.)

How about some name dropping? Valentino, Giorgio Armani, Emmanuel Ungaro, Calvin Klein, Joseph Abboud, and others. Impressed? You will be when you see the men's suits, sportcoats, slacks, overcoats, casualwear, and supporting cast of accessories (ties, belts, etc.). The smaller women's collection (apparel mostly from Emmanuel and Armani) is equally impressive. The company makes apparel under about 60 different labels for famous designers and brands. The "leftovers" are sold here for about 40% off retail prices. Note: The Petaluma store sells men's apparel only. Sizes: Men's suits 36S to 50L.

PRESIDENT TUXEDO OUTLET

1933 Davis #190, Westgate Shopping Center, San Leandro. (510) 562-9551. M–W 10–6, Th 10–8, F 10–7, Sun 11–4. MC, VISA. Parking: lot.

If you've added up the cost of renting a tuxedo and accessories, you'll find that buying used equals about two rental charges, maybe less, and the tux will be in the closet for future use. Most used wool-blend jackets at the President Tuxedo Outlet are priced at about $110; pants range from $40 to $50. You can buy used or new shirts and accessories. The retired rental inventory in the clearance section reflects the selection found at its twenty-six regular stores. You'll find new tuxedos (all wool or wool blend) that are priced reasonably. Alterations are extra. Sizes for everyone, including a few boys' sizes.

SPACCIO

645 Howard Street (at New Montgomery), San Francisco. (415) 777-9797. M–Sat 9–6, Sun Noon–5. MC, VISA, AE, DIS. Parking: free garage on side of building.

This major Italian manufacturer sells direct at consumer-friendly prices. Bottom line: savings of 30–40% off other store retails. Spaccio makes Italian suits in four different cuts, including one that comes close to the American traditional fit. Italian suits use very fine fabrics like lighter-weight merino wool or wool gabardine (rather than the worsted wool used by most American manufacturers). You'll find somber and dignified fabric suitings along with standout bold colors appealing to a younger fashion-liberated customer. Sizes 36S to 52XL. Prices range from $299–$699 everyday; during special sales prices dive for drop-dead deals. Alterations can be done on the premises for a modest fee. Completing the selection: sportcoats, full-length topcoats, light-weight contemporary fashion sweaters, well-made and elegant slacks, Italian ties, and dress shirts of fine 100% cotton.

Also See

Under Men's Sportswear:
POLO/RALPH LAUREN

Under Famous Labels/Factory Stores:
DONNA KARAN; EXECUTIVE SUITE; JONES NEW YORK; EVAN PICONE

Under Family, Men's & Women's, General Clothing:
BURLINGTON COAT FACTORY; STEIN MART

Under Clearance Centers:
NORDSTROM; OFF FIFTH

Family, Men's & Women's, General Clothing

The Big Four:
ROSS, MARSHALL'S, T.J. MAXX, BURLINGTON COAT FACTORY

Think of these stores as your "four best friends": Ross, Marshall's, T.J. Maxx, and Burlington Coat Factory do an admirable job of providing solid discounts and a head-to-toe selection of apparel, accessories, and shoes for each family member. Each store has its own personality and slight differences in merchandising. In my comparison surveys, I've often found that prices on many brand names at these four stores are significantly lower than those found at the factory stores or outlets.

Highlights: Burlington Coat Factory has the best selection of coats and outerwear (some skiwear) in all sizes and styles for adults and children of any Bay Area store. Its men's and young men's departments are the best of the four—Big and Tall sizes,

too! Also great home and kitchen accessories, shoes, linens, and, at some stores, baby furniture. T.J. Maxx comes up with surprising status labels in women's apparel and has a discriminating selection of giftware, a satisfying shoe department, linens, and good Petite- and Plus-size selections. Ross offers moderately priced fashions (selected stores receive upscale labels), plus shoes, fragrances, picture frames, handbags, and body and bath products. Marshall's captures occasional groups of better women's apparel. Check in for fragrances, jewelry, giftware, and linens.

Women's Petite and Plus fashions get respectable rack space at all four stores, and men's and children's selections are generally excellent. Each company's stores are stocked according to the customer base of their area. If you feel your store doesn't have enough "good stuff," try another location. These stores are consumer-friendly, allowing returns, exchanges, and refunds. For the Marshall's nearest you, call (800) MARSHALL (627-7425); for Ross (800) 945-ROSS (945-7677); T.J. Maxx (800) 2TJ-MAXX; Burlington Coat Factory (415) 495-7234.

Other Stores

ASHWORTH

Factory Stores of America, Vacaville. (707) 447-0237. Daily. MC, VISA, AE, DIS. Parking: lot.
Ashworth sportswear, designed as a golf collection, goes just about anywhere. At pro shops, prices are a lot higher; here they're just about right. PGA tour star Freddy Couples endorses Ashworth. Men shop on one side of the store, women on the other. Sweaters, slacks, shorts, tops, and jackets from about $15 to $39.

BIG DOG SPORTSWEAR

1299 Marina Boulevard, Marina Square, San Leandro. (510) 895-1510. Daily. MC, VISA, DIS, AE. Parking: lot.
(Other outlets: Folsom, Gilroy, Milpitas, Napa, Pacific Grove, Petaluma, Tracy, Vacaville centers.)
Reflecting the Southern California lifestyle and a sense of whimsy with its St. Bernard logos, Big Dog sportswear for men, women, and kids is great fun. Savings are about 25–40% off on sweats, T-shirts, graphic ties, shorts, pants, shirts, jackets, and beach towels. Sizes from 6mos to 5X (real big and real tall!). Great for lighthearted gifts. For a "warm and fuzzy" gift, pick up an adorable stuffed "big dog" with ageless appeal.

CALVIN KLEIN OUTLET STORE

Outlets at Gilroy, Gilroy. (408) 847-7889. Daily. MC, VISA, AE, DIS. Parking: lot.
(Other outlet: Napa center.)
Don't let money come between you and your Calvins! Shop at the outlet and you'll save 30% to 50% on average on a great selection of first-quality sportswear for men, women, and children. Denim fashions are always in evidence—you'll save about $20 on basic jeans that retail for about $54. There are smaller sections with 40% discounts on average devoted to Calvin's bridge collections—some career separates and casual clothing for women; men's linen blazers, dressier slacks, and shirts for dress-down Fridays. T-shirts go with every fashion category in the store, and you'll also find belts, socks, underwear, caps, etc. One of the better designer

outlets. Sizes: Kids 8–20; Girls 7–16; Men's S–XL, waists 28–40, length 30–34; Women's misses and petite 2–14. Exchange and refunds within 14 days.

CRAZY SHIRTS FACTORY STORE

Great Mall of the Bay Area, Milpitas. (408) 934-9425. MC, VISA. Parking: lot.

Visit many tourist locations around the country, or go down to Fisherman's Wharf, and you're likely to cruise through one of Crazy Shirts' twenty-seven stores selling specialty active wear. The company is proud that all its apparel is made in America of 100% cotton. At the outlet you'll find that most tops sport a colorful tourist logo, although there are occasional blank tops. These are usually first-quality, discontinued colors or designs or past-season overruns. The tourist logos are very well done, the colors crisp, and the quality superior to most tourist-oriented merchandise. Almost everything is reduced 50%. Good source for T-shirts and fleece or sweat tops. Sizes: S–XL (a few XXLs).

DOCKERS OUTLET

Napa Factory Stores, Napa. (707) 252–7526. Daily. MC, VISA, AE, DIS. Parking: lot.

A prominent sign in the store reads "Quality control experts never miss a thing. If there's a blemish in the fabric, a shade off color, or a variance in size, the merchandise is labeled as irregular." Even so, you'll be challenged trying to identify the imperfections on merchandise that accounts for about half the inventory in the outlet. It's well stocked with fashions from the entire Dockers collection of casual clothing for men, women, and children. Men can pick up pants from the Slate collection, golf shirts, sweaters, ties, and just about anything else in the men's Dockers' line. Prices are reduced 25–35% on average, up to 50% on some displays.

EDDIE BAUER OUTLET STORE

1295 Marina Boulevard, Marina Square, San Leandro. (510) 895-1484. M–F 10–9, Sat 10–6, Sun Noon–5. MC, VISA, AE, DIS. Parking: lot. (Other stores/outlets: Sunrise Shopping Center, Citrus Heights; Hilltop Mall, Richmond; Gilroy center.)

Eddie Bauer's outlets emphasize its casual apparel and outerwear for men and women: pants, shirts, dresses, sweaters, and jackets. You'll also find some shoes, socks, backpacks, luggage, watches, sunglasses, and small accessory items. Catalog overstocks, discontinued products, surplus from its retail store division, and some apparel made specifically for its outlet stores make up the selection. Prices are reduced 40–70% off original. Exchanges or cash refunds with receipt.

GAP OUTLET

Great Mall of the Bay Area, Milpitas. (408) 946-1760. Daily. MC, VISA, AE, DIS. Parking: lot. (Other outlet: Gilroy center, Vacaville)

Gap heaven for the faithful. The outlets are just as tempting as the regular stores. The difference? Large quantities of slightly irregular merchandise at about 50% off retail pricing, plus first-quality past-season merchandise at 25–40% reductions. Shop the outlet as a family—men, women, teens, and tots can load up. Some Banana Republic and Old Navy labels show up on the racks.

GEOFFREY BEENE

Factory Stores of America, Vacaville. (707) 452-0603. Daily. MC, VISA. Parking: lot. (Other outlets: Folsom, Gilroy, Pacific Grove centers.)

Geoffrey Beene factory stores are stocked with an impressive array of men's fashions. Everything is very current and stylish, and priced an average 25–50% off. A versatile array of sportshirts, occasional sportcoats, slacks, lots of denim pants and shirts, activewear, robes, gorgeous ties, and a posh stock of dress shirts make it possible for a fella to build a wardrobe that everyone will admire. Most stores have a split personality, devoting about half the space to a well-designed collection of women's sportswear. Refunds and exchanges allowed.

GUESS? OUTLET

Outlets at Gilroy, Gilroy. (408) 847-3400. Daily. MC, VISA. Parking: lot.

A little of everything Guess? for teens and adults: discontinued, seconds, and irregulars, resulting in 30–70% discounts. You'll find great buys on Guess? shoes designed to complement its apparel: Western boots, clogs, and clunky street shoes for women and men. Large store, lots of energy: Guess? heaven for the faithful.

JOCKEY

Factory Stores of America, Vacaville. (707) 451-8119. Daily. MC, VISA, AE, DIS. Parking: lot. (Other outlets: Folsom, Gilroy centers.)

There's a lot more to Jockey than men's briefs: you'll find underwear for women and children, casual shirts, pantyhose, tank tops, etc. Sizes for all dimensions. All first-quality goods at average 30% off retail.

LEVI'S OUTLET

Napa Factory Stores, Napa. (707) 252-6926. Daily. MC, VISA, AE, DIS. Parking: lot.

This outlet is the real thing. Owned by Levi Strauss, it is accordingly well stocked with jeans of every description for men, women, and children. All your favorite styles are priced 30% off retail, on average. Also, shirts, jackets, and other Levi's sportswear to make sure you're covered head to toe before leaving.

LEVI'S OUTLET BY MOST

Factory Stores of America, Vacaville. (707) 451-0155. Daily. MC, VISA, DIS, AE. Parking: lot. (Other outlets: Anderson/Redding, Folsom, Gilroy, Milpitas, Petaluma, Tracy centers.)

This company sells Levi's irregulars and closeouts. In some instances the flaws were obvious, like small spots from sewing machine oil or unequal fading on stonewashed jeans, but most of the time I was at a loss to find anything wrong with the apparel. You'll find all the Levi's labels: Dockers for women and men (men's pants usually at $19.99–$29.99); popular pants styles from the 501, 540, 550, and 560 collections; many styles for students, girls, and boys (all sizes covered), all at about 50% discounts! Plus shirts in an endless selection, casual tops, belts, socks, and a little bit of everything Levi's. Children's wear discounts are modest—about 25% off original retail. Great store, great selection, great bargains!

LONDON FOG FACTORY STORES

Factory Stores of America, Vacaville. (707) 447-1196. Daily. MC, VISA, AE, DIS. Parking: lot. (Other outlets: Anderson/Redding, Gilroy, Pacific Grove, St. Helena, South Lake Tahoe centers.)
This is London Fog's headquarters for outerwear and rainwear for men and women. It's all quite nice, and nicely discounted. The factory stores primarily showcase men's and women's raincoats, all-weather coats (many with zip-out linings), jackets, and heavyweight down jackets (for the slopes), all with water-repellent fabrics, at 50% discounts. Sizes: Petite 2–20; Misses 2–26 1/2; Men's 36–52 in Short, Regular, and Long. Some children's outerwear, too! If you think you might need to exchange an item, don't cut off the tags.

MILLER STOCKMAN WESTERN WEAR OUTLET

Vintage Oaks Shopping Center, Novato. (415) 898-4154. M–F 10–9, Sat 10–9, Sun 11–6. MC, VISA, AE, DIS. Parking: lot. (Other outlet: Milpitas center.)
Urban cowboys or cowgirls and those who really ride the range will want to check out the bargains here. The store's inventory, from the Rocky Mountain Clothing Company, Miller Stockman retail stores, and Miller Stockman's catalog division, offers Western fashions and accessories head to toe. There's a variety of brand names: irregulars in pants from Wrangler and Rocky Mountain; also Nocona, Larry Mahan, Tony Lama and Justin boots. The boot selection takes up one wall, with over 3,000 pairs for women and men. Shoe sizes: Men's sizes 6½–13 (all widths); women's 5–10. Most boot prices reduced about 25–40% off retail. Rocky Mountain pant sizes: Men's 28–40 (cowboy and slim fit); women's 00 (tiny) to 20. *Note: Hats are not discounted.*

PANGEA OUTLET

110 Howard Street, Petaluma. (707) 778-0110. Sat only 9–4 (May–Dec), 10–2 (Jan–Apr). Cash/Check. Parking: street.

Pangea screenprints and embroiders messages on T-shirts, jackets, sweatshirts, and other garments customers may want their message or logo on. Flawed merchandise and test prints are tossed into the reject box, where you can hunt for T-shirts, all for $2. About 70% of the merchandise is first-quality, the remaining irregulars have minor flaws. Seconds in T-shirts are priced $3–$4, firsts $6–$9; seconds in sweatshirts $5–$12, firsts $8–$12. Sizes for the whole family.

POLO/RALPH LAUREN FACTORY STORE

3300 Broadway Road, Bayshore Mall, Eureka. (707) 444-3075. M–Sat 10–9, Sun 11–6. MC, VISA, AE, DC. (Other stores: Anderson/Shasta, Atascadero, Barstow, Mammoth Lakes centers.)

The Polo/Ralph Lauren Factory Stores are in remote sites for a very good reason—they're safely removed from important retail accounts. Discounts are 30–50% off original retail; 30% on current-season overruns, while greater discounts apply to mer-chandise that may be one or two years old or irregular. About 95% of the merchandise is first-quality; the remaining irregulars have minor flaws. If you time your visit right, you'll catch additional markdowns on the already well-priced merchandise (get on the mailing list!). Polo's "designer collec-tions" aren't stocked, but you'll find just about everything else in its extensive line, including men's and women's apparel from the classic collection, boy's clothing, and homewares (towels, duvets, comforters, sheets, bed skirts, and rugs). Refunds (usually a MC, VISA, or AE credit) on merchandise returned within seven days in person or by mail. Exchanges for credit are accepted up to 30 days after purchase.

REEL STUDIO STORE

Outlets at Gilroy, Gilroy. (408) 842-9393. Daily. MC, VISA. Parking: lot.

A captivating store for cartoon and movie buffs. Most merchandise is related to major studios (Walt Disney, Looney Tunes/Warner Bros., etc.) or cultural icons like Barbie, Betty Boop, Hello Kitty, and Sanrio. The manufacturer makes clothing under licensing agreements for sale to mass merchandisers and sells its leftovers through the outlet. Sweaters, sweatshirts, T-shirts, overalls, underwear, and more are available for men, women, tots. and teens. Much of the merchandise is unisex—just zero in on a favorite character represented with a whimsical image. There's a small selection of accessories, too (caps, tote bags, stuffed animals). Prices reduced 20–40% off original retail.

ROYAL ROBBINS FACTORY OUTLET

841-A Gilman, Berkeley. (510) 527-1961. M–F 10–6, Sat 10–5, Sun 11–5 (extended summer hours). MC, VISA, DIS. Parking: lot.
(Other store: 1508 Tenth Street, Modesto.)
Royal Robbins classic clothing for outdoor—and indoor—living is sold nationally through well-known mail-order companies and stores specializing in men's and women's outdoor wear. At the outlets you'll find seconds (very small flaws) on current collections and overruns from preceding seasons. The clothing is transitional for year-round use and is designed to wash and dry easily—a boon for adventure travelers. Many collections are made from 100% cotton or other natural fibers in distinctive patterns and weaves; other fabrications are in

Italian fleece—microfibers with moisture transport systems that make wear and care a snap. Many styles are unisex. Prices at the outlets are 35–70% off retail. The line includes sweaters, belts, hats, skirts, pants, shorts, dresses, shirts, and tops. The outlets are nicely stocked and a pleasure to shop. Exchanges and credits are allowed, but no cash refunds.

STEIN MART

Great Mall of the Bay Area, Milpitas. (408) 934-1550. MC, VISA, AE, DIS. Parking: lot.
It may look like a better department store with its tastefully merchandised displays—until you check the price tags and find 25–60% discounts off traditional retailer prices. Stein Mart is a welcome addition to the Bay Area shopping scene. With more than 123 stores in the Midwest and Southeast, this is its first store in California. It brings refreshing new choices and a more refined approach to discount shopping. The family's apparel needs are covered with men's, women's, and children's departments. I particularly liked the more upscale women's "boutique" department, which offers a bridge to designer fashions and the wonderful and versatile

selection of stylish dresses for all occasions. This store has the most extensive and best accessory department of all the major chain discounters—wonderful fashion jewelry, handbags, belts, scarves, etc. The gift, linen, gourmet, kitchen, and home accessories department is also very impressive. Keep your eyes peeled for famous names that show up from time to time: Baccarat, Lalique, Wilton Armetale, Orrefors, Lipper, and more. The accessories are displayed with real cachet—it's easy to visualize a new birdcage, Chinese porcelain planter, elegant frame, sculpture, bookends, patio dinnerware set, copper kitchenware, vases, decorative pillows, or other pièce de résistance filling a spot in your home. On top of everything, Stein Mart offers a high level of customer service.

THE SWEATSHIRT COMPANY

Factory Stores of America, Vacaville. (707) 451-0307. Daily. MC, VISA. Parking: lot.
(Other outlets: Folsom, Gilroy centers.)
The Sweatshirt Company sells crew neck sweatshirts, track pants, and hooded sweatshirt jackets in sizes ranging from Infant to Adult XXXL and some Talls. All its first-quality goods are sold for 30% off full retail. Also, sweatshirts with college logos or unique pocket treatments and printed T-shirts. Prices range from $6.99 to $25.

VF FACTORY OUTLET

Factory Stores of America, Vacaville. (707) 451-1990. Daily. MC, VISA. Parking: lot.
(Other outlet: Gilroy center.)
The VF Factory Outlet offers a wealth of merchandise and good values for the whole family. You'll find fashions sporting labels from Healthtex (newborn to teenagers), Jantzen and JanSport (sportswear and swimsuits), Vanity Fair (intimate, daywear, and sleepwear), Wrangler and Lee (men's, women's, and youth fashions—jeans, shirts, shorts, and jackets). These are first-quality fashions, plus irregulars and way-past-season merchandise marked down substantially. Overall discounts are 50% off every day. Sizes for everyone: women's fashions from Junior size 1 to Women's 26; Men's pants to waist sizes 44, lengths to 36. If you need Boys Husky sizes they can be ordered, along with just about anything else in these brands. Returns and refunds okay.

WOOLRICH

American Tin Cannery, Pacific Grove. (408) 644-9218. Daily. MC, VISA, DIS. Parking: lot.

One glance at the apparel at Woolrich and you'll think of weekends in the country. The store showcases far more of its sportswear and outerwear collections for men and women than you'll ever see in any one store. Rugged, warm, and weatherproof outerwear (jackets, coats, windbreakers, parkas), fishing vests with dozens of pockets, warm bulky sweaters, plus pants, skirts, shirts, hats, caps, packs, and slippers, prove there's lots more to the line than you might have imagined. There are the enduring, classic Woolrich styles and some groups designed with more fashion. The women's groups offer some surprises—charming prints, novelty fabrics, and chic jackets and coats. Woolrich blankets (often tagged as seconds) are good buys, too. Expect to save 20–60% off retail on past-season overruns and seconds. A very nice store for traditionalists.

Also See

Under Clearance Centers:
ALL LISTINGS

Under San Francisco's Factory Outlets and Off-Price Stores:
ROCK EXPRESS

Under Active Sportswear:
ALL LISTINGS

Under Appliances, Electronics, and Home Entertainment:
WHOLE EARTH ACCESS

Under General Merchandise:
PRICE/COSTCO; WAL-MART

Active Sportswear

Aerobics, Camping, Dance, Exercise, Golf, Skiing, Tennis, etc.

BODY BODY
224 Greenfield Avenue, San Anselmo. (415) 459-2336. M–F 9–8, Sat 9–6. MC, VISA. Parking: street.
Body Body offers a collection of bodywear at modest discounts: past-season apparel 20–40% off and some current styles at minimal 10% discounts. Racks are jammed with brand-name apparel devoted to the workout crowd, plus a nice collection of active sportswear. Sizes 4–14, small selection of XL to fit up to size 18. Leotards and tights for kids at 20–33% off retail.

COLUMBIA SPORTSWEAR COMPANY FACTORY OUTLET
Outlets at Gilroy, Gilroy. (408) 848-3740. Daily. MC, VISA, AE, DIS. Parking: lot.
Columbia Sportswear is your destination for bargains in women's and men's skiwear and outerwear in high-tech fabrics, plus apparel for hunters and fishers (vests, parkas, caps, shirts, and pants), and sportswear for women, men, and children. Adults can buy shoes from a new line of casual and functional footwear while everyone in the family can suit up in snowboard apparel from Convert. Closeouts average 30% discount, seconds are usually 50% off original retail. The company does not warranty the outlet's goods for waterproofing or construction. Sizes: Women's S–XL (4–18); Men's: S–XXXL; Children's 2T–16.

DANSKIN
Factory Stores of America, Vacaville. (707) 448-9313. Daily. MC, VISA, DIS, AE. Parking: lot.
(Other outlets: Folsom, Gilroy, Pacific Grove centers.)
Whatever your size, Danskin has got you covered. Dancewear, aerobic wear, Dance France (Petite sizing), Danskin Plus (sizes 14–24), and Danskin Pro (for heavy use by serious athletes involved in daily training) are reduced 30–50%. Great colors, prints, and styles add up to a sizzling selection. Girls can

get ready for the gym or dance studio with Danskin's collection in sizes 2T–14.

FILA FACTORY STORE

Pacific West Outlet Center, Gilroy. (408) 848-3452. Daily. MC, VISA, AE. Parking: lot.
(Other outlet: Tracy center.)
If wearing expensive tennis clothes might improve your game, consider the togs at the Fila Factory Store. It sells past-season merchandise, samples, and overruns. Fila uses quality fabric, resulting in clothes that are made well to wear well. Prices are reduced approximately 40%, more affordable but still not inexpensive. Current merchandise is discounted a minimum of 40%. Although limited in style and size, the selection of tennis skirts, golf/warm-up suits, ski vests, sweaters, bathing suits, shorts, shoes, etc. changes frequently. Sizes: Women's 4–14, Women's shoes 5½–10; Men's 44½–56, Men's shoes 6½–13. Exchanges only within 30 days.

ONE STEP AHEAD

Great Mall of the Bay Area, Milpitas. (408) 956-1244. Daily. MC, VISA. Parking: lot.
This line in 100% cotton in sizes 5/6 to 16/18 will inspire you to work up a sweat at aerobic classes or on gym equipment. Top off your leotards, tights, bra tops, etc. with a stylish coverup, fleece, or French terry top from its line of supercomfy sportswear. Past-season fashions discounted 25–50% off retail.

OSHMAN'S CLEARANCE CENTER

Great Mall of the Bay Area, Milpitas. (408) 935-8775. Daily. MC, VISA, AE. DIS. Parking: lot.
Oshman's Clearance Center is where the company sends "leftovers" from all its stores. Anything that may have sold at its other stores can wind up here. Figure most merchandise is past-season, or end-of-season clearance, customer returns, or slightly damaged. Discounts start at about 40% off original retails and dive from there. The most consistent category of "leftovers" is apparel from all departments including aerobic/workout apparel and a seemingly endless supply of T-shirts. Free weights, work benches, and other fitness equipment are a

rarity. Pieces that do occasionally hit the floor have been demos or are customer returns.

SAN FRANCISCO CITY LIGHTS FACTORY OUTLET

333 Ninth Street (bet. Folsom and Harrison), San Francisco. (415) 861-6063. M–Sat 10–6. MC, VISA. Parking: street.

San Francisco City Lights is an innovative manufacturer of body- and aerobic wear. Aerobics buffs beat a path here for wholesale prices or better on discontinued styles, seconds (usually dye imperfections), and overruns. The basics: leggings in five different lengths, leotards, unitards, briefs, several styles of bra tops, body belts, crop tops, plus a selection of sweats in soft fleece. You'll find the hottest new colors in fabrics made from comfortable 90% cotton and 10% lycra. Many of the fashions (particularly the coordinating sportswear) are perfect for casual weekend activities. I loved the washed linens, nubby knits, and other innovative textured fabrics! The children's collection of playwear will win the heart of moms. Sizes: Children's 2T–14; Women's S, M, L fits 4–12 (to 14 in some styles). All sales final. Communal dressing room, so don your best underwear.

SIDEOUT SPORT

Outlets at Gilroy, Gilroy. (408) 848-8040. Daily. MC, VISA. Parking: lot.
(Other outlet: Folsom center.)

If you know the name Mike Whitmarsh (beach volleyball's first Olympic silver medalist at the 1996 summer games), you'll know what this outlet is all about. He's an all-time champion who wears and promotes this line. Sideout should be de rigueur for the volleyball crowd. An average 25% is discounted on Sideout's slightly past-season shorts, shirts, sweats, and tank tops. Expect greater discounts on occasional seconds and it's-got-to-go sale racks. Carry the image to the fullest extent with bags, sandals, watches, stickers, balls, and nets. The newer sportswear—Polo-style shirts and casual shirts (in handprinted fabrics from Bali)—are perfect for standing or sitting on the sidelines.

STARTER SPORTSWEAR

Outlets at Gilroy, Gilroy. (408) 847-1147. Daily. MC, VISA, DIS. Parking: lot.

Starter manufactures apparel for some names you may have heard of—NFL, AFL, NBA, NCAA—as well as colleges and universities around the country.

Not only sportswear, but the actual team uniforms! You can tell the world the name of your game or team with Starter's logo jackets, jerseys, warm-up suits, sweats, shorts, T-shirts, and outerwear. Discounts are 20–60% (average 40%) off retail on past-season merchandise and some seconds. Sizes: from small tots to XXXXL. A popular store with sports fans.

T.L. BRODERICK CO.

2605 Lafayette Street, Santa Clara. (408) 748-0880. M–F 10–8, Sat 10–6, Sun Noon–5; closed April 1–Sept 1. MC, VISA. Parking: lot.
If price rather than jet-set appearance is your criterion in family skiwear or snowboard apparel, stop off at T.L. Broderick Co. for discounts on brand-name apparel, goggles, gloves, socks, caps, sweaters, and snowboards. It sells its in-house lines of well-made, moderately priced down or polyester jackets and ski bibs for men, women, and children, and snowboard clothing and accessories. Discounted lines include Columbia, CB Sports, Fera, Helly Hansen, Pacific Trail, Airwalk, and Liquid. Prices are reduced 30–60% on the first-quality selection. Sizes: Children's 2–16;

Women's 6–16 or XS–XXL (some Petites and Talls in stretch pants); Men's 28–44 or XS–XXL (to XXXXL in ski bibs); some items in Tall sizes. The store is easy to miss; call for directions.

URBAN ATHLETIC

434 Ninth Street, San Francisco. (415) 255-8881. M–F 8–4, call for Sat hours. Cash/Check. Parking: street.
The Urban Athletic outlet is the place for activewear and comfortable weekend separates when comfort is key. Take your pick from leggings, crop tops, leotards, bike shorts, hooded tops, baggy shorts, and T-shirts in cotton/lycra blends or French terry, fleece, thermal knits, and sports rib fabrics. Organic fabrics are in classic neutrals—beige, gray, cream, and white. Thermal knits are prewashed and preshrunk. Prices range from $5 to $24 (wholesale prices on samples, discontinued patterns, and overruns). Sizes: S, M, L (fits 4–14). All sales are final.

Also See

Under Women's Apparel/Fashion:
ALL LISTINGS

Under Men's Apparel:
ALL LISTINGS

Under Family Clothing:
ALL LISTINGS

Under Clearance Centers:
ALL LISTINGS

Under Shoes:
ADIDAS; NIKE FACTORY STORE; REEBOK FACTORY STORE

Children's Clothing

BABY GUESS? GUESS KIDS?

Outlets at Gilroy, Gilroy. (408) 847-6333. Daily. MC, VISA. Parking: lot.

I always thought that parents who paid premium dollars for the Baby Guess? line had rocks in their heads, but I'm reconsidering after seeing the cute line at Baby Guess? and Guess Kids?. Best buys are captured on the irregulars with red tags, usually priced at 50% off original retail. Overstock and seasonal merchandise is always at least 35% less than full-price boutiques. Everything's more affordable, with shortalls at $17, denim jackets at $25. Sizes: Infant 3mos to 14.

BIOBOTTOMS RETAIL OUTLET

620 Petaluma Boulevard North, Petaluma. (707) 778-1948. M–F 10–6, Sat 10–5, Sun Noon–4. MC, VISA. AE, DIS. Parking: lot.

Biobottoms sends out a catalog with appealing fashions for infants through preteens, including coveralls, long johns, dresses, pants, tops, shorts, and bathing suits, all in 100% cotton. At its outlet/retail store you'll find overruns and discontinued goods from previous catalogs, samples, and a large selection of seconds at 30–70% off; additionally, some styles from the current catalog are often available at a 10% discount. Diapering with cloth is a specialty, and there's a complete supply of Biobottoms, diaper covers, and other diapering goods in the stores at full price. Write for a catalog: P.O. Box 6009, Petaluma, CA 94953.

BUGLE BOY OUTLET

Factory Stores of America, Vacaville. (707) 446-9297. Daily. MC, VISA, AE. Parking: lot.

(Other outlets: Anderson/Redding, Folsom, Milpitas centers.)

Boys, teens, and young men can have it any way they want at Bugle Boy. Racks are jammed with pants and shorts in all sizes. Generally, the discounts are 22–30% on current-season merchandise and get better during the frequent in-store promotions. Girls, teens, and women get a little rack space, too. Sizes: Girls 4 to Women's 16/18; Boys 4 to Men's 40; decent selection of Boys Huskies 8–16, Infants and Toddlers sizes. No cash or credit card refunds. Exchanges only within 30 days.

CARTER'S CHILDRENSWEAR

Great Mall of the Bay Area, Milpitas. (408) 942-9110. Daily. MC, VISA, DIS, AE. Parking: lot. (Other outlets: Folsom, Gilroy, Pacific Grove, Vacaville centers.)

Carter's is well stocked with everything Carter's makes. Great selection of playwear, sleepwear, and layettes. Everyday discounts are 30% off retail. There are lots of irregulars in the layette, sleepwear, and playwear selection, but they're clearly marked and in no way less desirable. Carter's also makes clothing exclusively for its own stores, and prices are quite pleasing. Sizes: Preemie to 6X for girls; to 7 for boys.

CHICKEN NOODLE OUTLET

605 Addison Street, Berkeley. (510) 848-8880. April–June, Oct–Dec M–F 10–5. MC, VISA. Parking: lot.

Chicken Noodle children's playwear is every bit as cute as the name would imply—wonderful prints and practicality along with clever and engaging design details. The 100% cotton fabrics in wovens or knits predominate. Deck out your boys from a small selection of Infant sizes to 7; your girls in Infant to 14. Prices are reduced 40–60% off retail on past-season overruns, ranging from $5 to $35 (special dresses); seconds (very small quantities) are marked way down. The accessories caught my eye: hair bows and hats, plus the few styles of mom's dresses, short sets, and jumpers to match with daughters. Bundled remnants of fabric are priced $3–$4/yard. *Directions: From 80 take the University Avenue exit east, turn right at Sixth Street. Go one block to Addison, turn right, and drive to end of street (toward Aquatic Park). Building and parking are on right. The outlet is sometimes closed during heavy shipping periods—call ahead.*

CHOICES/ANDY'S DAD'S PALCE

899 Howard Street, Yerba Buena Center, San Francisco. (415) 495-2628. M–F 11–6, Sat 10–6. MC, VISA, AE. Parking: street.
(Other stores: Andy's Dad's Place, 160 Bon Air Center, Greenbrae.)

Multiple Choices is aptly named! You've got choices whether you're shopping for school-age kids ages 6 to 18 (including the "surf" brands that boys have to have) or men's fun sportswear. Look for racks of girls' play clothes and sweat fashions. Expect 30–70% discounts on top-selling department store brands: Stussy, Mossimo, Quiksilver, OshKosh, Billa Bong, O'Neill, Rusty, Red Sand, Gotcha, and more. Parochial school uniforms are always on hand at discount prices. Exchanges any time!

CREME DE LA CREME

Outlets at Gilroy, Gilroy. (408) 842-2512. Daily. MC, VISA, AE, DIS. Parking: lot.
(Other outlet: Folsom center.)

The perfect place for baby and shower gifts. An adorable line of cuddly clothing fabricated in 100% cotton. Charming prints and the softest fabrics adorn the sets, jumpers, rompers, etc.

Often spotted on the racks of upscale stores. Sizes: Layette to 6X.

DAISY ADRIANA

2327-B Blanding Avenue, Alameda. (510) 522-2601. M–Sat 10–5. MC, VISA. Parking: street.

This outlet has such an out-of-the-way location that I worry that many mothers and grandmothers will miss the action. Daisy Adriana is a new line just starting to show up in upscale department stores. The precious dresses and rompers are made from beautiful 100% cotton prints and solids, many with wonderful detailing and trims. The look? Traditional and pretty! Toddler styles often have diaper covers to go along with the dresses—really cute! Sizes 9mos to 14. At retail, the 4–6X dresses and rompers range from $50 to $60 (an elegant holiday dress may be $70 to $100 plus). At the outlet everyday prices on overruns are about 40% off retail, but end-of-season progressive mark-downs go down to sublime levels. Best buys? Check the $10–$12 rack, the fabric remnant bin ($3–$4), and bins of excess trims. An extra bonus? The racks of Queen Anne's Lace sleepwear and Eileen West dresses.

Directions: From Fwy. 880, take 23rd Street bridge to Park Street, turn right at Blanding.

DONNA CAPOZZI, INC. OUTLET

1003 Camelia Street, Berkeley. (510) 558-1100. M–Sat 10–5. MC, VISA. Parking: Lot.
There's a new look in the Donna Capozzi line that many moms will embrace for their daughters. Its styling is more contemporary and the look is achieved in large part through the use of women's apparel fabrics. Rayons and rayon blends, georgettes, crepe satins, linens, and wonderful knits are used in the fabrications. It's perfect for girls who can't abide frills and poufy old-fashioned dresses. Stop in for 50% discounts on first-quality overruns, samples, and past-season merchandise. A small selection of fabrics and buttons are usually set out in sale bins. Sizes 12mos to Preteen. Don't drive away without taking a peek at the Melior Outlet for contemporary women's career clothing right next door. *Note: Located in the space formerly occupied by Mousefeathers.*

FLAPDOODLES

Outlets at Gilroy, Gilroy. (408) 842-3081. Daily. MC, VISA, AE, DIS. Parking: Lot.
Working mothers must love this line. No ironing required! The 100% garment-dyed (eliminates any shrinkage) cotton play clothes come in a spirited selection of colors. The style is relaxed and contemporary, which means everything runs a little big. Mix and match for creative outfitting and functional fun: tops, bottoms, socks, T-shirts, leggings, hair accessories, jumpers, rompers, swimwear, outerwear, and more. An added plus—the Marisa Christina sweaters for children. Save 25–50% off retail prices on sizes Layette through 14.

KIDS R US

220 Walnut Street, Mervyn's Plaza, Redwood City. (650) 367-6005. M–Sat 10–9, Sun 11–6. MC, VISA, AE, DIS. Parking: lot.
(Other stores: Colma, Newark, Sunnyvale.)
Kudos to Kids R Us for providing a one-stop resource for busy parents seeking solid values, name brands, good selection, and maximum convenience when shopping for their children (ages newborn to about 13). From no-nonsense basics to

accommodating a child with a penchant for trendy styles, you'll shop with success! And everyday discounts average about 30% off retail, even more on end-of-season specials or promotions.

OSHKOSH B'GOSH

Outlets at Gilroy, Gilroy. (408) 842-3280. Daily.
MC, VISA, AE, DIS. Parking: lot.
(Other outlets: Petaluma, Vacaville centers.)
For the best deals at these large and colorful factory stores, look for the yellow tags that say, "No one's perfect, though we try, so when we're not, it's your best buy." Otherwise, discounts are modest—averaging about 25% off retail. Sizes: Girls to 14; Boys to 16; plus a few rounds of adult-sized overalls for men.

PETALS FACTORY OUTLET

1120 Hilltop Mall, Richmond. (510) 222-9941.
M–Sat 10–9, Sun 11–7. MC, VISA, DIS.
Parking: lot.
Petals has accounts across the country and four retail stores in the Bay Area. It has set aside about half the space in this store to sell clearance inventory from past-season collections at 25–50% off retail. Intricate designs and detailing plus better-quality, unusual fabrics and prints make up the charming Petals line of dresses and jumpsuits for little girls (sizes 12mos to 16). Retail prices start at $10 and go as high as $170. Petals dresses are perfect for dressing up and looking pretty, and they can do double duty as school clothes. The new Rapscallions line of coordinated playwear in Lycra and knits displays whimsical styling, and little girls love the fancy activewear, dancewear (for tumbling and ice skating), and swimsuits designed with lots of frills and saucy skirts. I doubt anyone will be able to resist the adorable hats, headbands, hair bows, and purses designed to accessorize the dresses. All sales final.

REBECCA RAGS, INC. OUTLET

10200 Imperial Avenue, Cupertino. (408) 257-7884. M–F 9–4:30 (Some Sats, call first). MC, VISA.
Parking: lot.
Rebecca Rags makes a charming line of children's clothing! Many of its styles are made from lovely velours in vibrant colors, others in soft flannels or cotton knits. Rebecca Rags designs are appealing, with unique appliqués on the dresses, jumpers,

and warm-up suits in sizes 6mos to 14. The quality is excellent. Ruff! Raggs is a boys' line that moms will love. The outlet is jammed with end-of-season overruns, seconds, and production samples. Prices are 20% above wholesale, much less if the item is damaged or way past season. Exchanges only on first-quality goods, no exchanges on seconds.

ROSE CAGE

10 Cleveland Street (off Seventh Street), San Francisco. (415) 431-8562. M–Sat 10–5. Cash/Check. Parking: street.

This small outlet yields fetching girls' fashions in sizes Infant and 2T–14. Rose Cage has made a name for itself with clever and distinctive appliqués on its tops; its related separates are made from 100% cotton knits (some fleece in fall collections) in whimsical prints and solids, and sell in the outlet as overruns at 25–50% off original retail. Prices range from $5 for tank tops to $16 for dresses. The skirts, bike and regular shorts, skorts, T-shirts, peplum tops, etc. are priced $7–$12. You can also find items useful for craft projects: rosettes, bows, embellishments, printed appliqués, and lace. If the outlet is locked, someone will let you in to shop.

Parking is easier on Saturdays. *Note: Call for new location in 1998.*

SF BLUES OUTLET

Outlets at Gilroy, Gilroy. (408) 847-9111. Daily. MC, VISA. Parking: lot.

SF Blues stands out with its appealing use of bright colors and practical styles for its European-styled play clothes. The line includes precious playsuits, sportswear, and baby sacks made from fine-quality 100% cotton stretch terry, velour, cotton flannel, and denim in charming prints—all available at 50–70% discounts. Many unisex styles are offered; all items come in sizes Newborn to 10. Each season features innovative fabric choices for related separates, playsuits, fetching caps, reversible jackets, and darling sweaters (included in some fall groups). Most overruns, discontinued styles, and samples in playsuits are $5–$46. Get your name on the mailing list for special invitations to end-of-season blowouts held at its San Francisco warehouse!

SARA'S PRINTS (FACTORY OUTLET)

3018-A Alvarado Street, San Leandro. (510) 352-6060. Quarterly sales. MC, VISA. Parking: lot.
Sara's Prints are made in Israel from fine Egyptian or Israeli cotton, the softest fabric imaginable. The colorful and whimsical prints are highlighted against the fresh white background of all garments. The line consists of layettes, caps, and booties, rompers, diaper sets, coveralls, playsuits, polo-style shirts, dresses, turtlenecks, boys' undershirts and briefs, girls' panties and camisoles, long underwear sets, and playsets for boys and girls. The Mother and Daughter sleepwear collection ranges from oversized T-shirts to nightgowns. Retail prices are moderate depending on your budget. During quarterly one- to two-week factory sale events, past-season merchandise and seconds are sold for a minimum 50% off retail. A phone call will get your name added to Sara's mailing list.

STORYBOOK HEIRLOOMS

Outlets at Gilroy, Gilroy. (408) 842-3880. Daily. MC, VISA, AE, DIS. Parking: lot.
Storybook Heirlooms, an upscale catalog company of "timeless clothing for girls," sends its catalog surplus inventory here: a wonderful selection of girls' clothing and accessories in sizes Infant through 16. You'll find top-quality merchandise bearing the Storybook Heirloom label and fashions from other recognized manufacturers. Since the lines are moderately to very expensive at retail, prices may still seem high even at discount. Discounts start at 20% on recent merchandise and go to 30–60% on the older stuff. You can find special-occasion wear, dresses, casual sportswear, petticoats and slips, darling footwear, and mother-daughter coordinates. Join the mailing list for invitations to the occasional major blowout sales at its Hayward warehouse. Call (800) 825-6565 for a complimentary catalog.

SWEET POTATOES FACTORY OUTLET

1716 Fourth Street, Berkeley. (510) 527-7633. M–Sat 10–6, Sun 11–6. MC, VISA, DIS. Parking: lot.
Sweet Potatoes active sportswear features bright colors, prints, plaids, and fun details. Dresses, overalls, shirts, jog sets, jumpsuits, tights, leggings, socks, skirts, hats, suspenders, and turtlenecks add up to many options when outfitting the kids. You'll love the whimsical Yazoo line for girls in sizes 4–14; Spuds for boys in sizes 12mos–7; Sweet Potatoes

for Infants to 10; New Potato and Marimekko for Layette to Toddler; and the new Ruth Hornbein sweaters, Claude Vell with sophisticated French styling, and Big Fish swimwear collections. The seconds, overruns, samples, and past-season styles are discounted 30–60%, which doesn't make them cheap by any means since they are boutique-priced at retail. For your projects, you can often pick up leftover fabrics, trims, and patches (10¢ to $4). Some very petite women find the preteen sportswear just right for their tiny proportions. Note: The company's success may necessitate a move later in 1997, but it won't go far. Make sure you're on its mailing list.

TRUMPETTE OUTLET

108 Kentucky Street, Petaluma. (707) 769-1173. M–Sat 10–5, Sun Noon–5. MC, VISA. Parking: street.

Maybe you've seen the adorable infant and tod-dler suits with "Got Milk?" "Automatic Sprinkler" or "Tax Deduction" emblazoned across the front. If you've been captivated by these whimsical out-fits, this is the company you want to connect with. Those sayings may no longer be available, but you can be sure that equally clever and appealing quotes or phrases will have been created. Original and fun silk-screened graphics (critters, fruits, veggies, etc.) adorn the front of many other outfits all made from 100% garment-dyed cotton. Jumpers, potty pants, big pants, dresses, jackets, and henley T-shirts are staples of the line. You'll want to buy one or several of these outfits if there are any kids in your sphere or if gift-giving is on the horizon. You'll save about 40% off original retails on the first-quality overruns and past-season collections. A typical infant jumper goes for about $19.50 at the outlet. Sizes: 0 (infant) to 7.

WEE CLANCY FACTORY SALES

2682-J Middlefield Road, Redwood City. (650) 366-5597. Th–Sat 10–4, Sat 9–1. MC, VISA. Parking: lot.

Peninsula moms love to cruise through Wee Clancy's racks finding new booty for their girls, especially wonderful European-styled dresses and playwear often made from exceptional 100% cotton. Many dresses and fancy jumpsuits made in elegant fabri-cations with velvets, taffetas, silks, and glitter metallic are perfect for VIP and religious occasions. Wool coats and capes fulfill every little girl's fantasy. Clancy, a new label, is designed for the 7- to 16-

year-old girl with more contemporary inclinations. The detailing, fabrics, and intricate designs justify Wee Clancy's prices. Frequent specials where additional discounts are taken at the register make these dresses more affordable for everyone. These dresses are guaranteed to make any little girl feel very pretty and special. The outlet sells seasonal overruns, samples (size 4), and sometimes slightly imperfect merchandise. Average outlet price is $30 to $35. Sizes: Infant to 16. Get on the mailing list!

Also See

Under Family Clothing:
MOST LISTINGS

Under Clearance Centers:
ALL LISTINGS

Under San Francisco's Factory Outlets and Off-Price Stores:
CHRISTINE FOLEY

Under Baby and Juvenile Furniture/Equipment:
ALL LISTINGS

Under General Merchandise:
PRICE/COSTCO

Clearance Centers

For Major Department Stores and Retail Chains

CONTEMPO CASUALS OUTLET

Vintage Oaks Shopping Center, Novato. (415) 892-5706. M–Sat 10–9, Sun 11–6. MC, VISA, AE, DIS. Parking: lot.

Heads up! This is one for young women, and they're really gonna love it. At this clearance center for Contempo Casuals, the mall headquarters for teen trendsetters, everything is priced at least 50% off retail and, prices on many groups or categories of merchandise are marked down to 70–80% off retail: some jeans and pants go for $2, $4, or $9. You'll find every category of apparel that the company sells: coats, activewear, bathing suits, dresses, pants, sweaters, skirts, blouses and tops, even prom dresses. I spotted some "uglies" in the selection, but 14- to 17-year-old girls may think they're totally awesome! Sizes 1–13 in the Contempo line designed for the 17- to 25-year-old market. The prices and selection are so enticing that teens and younger women are in for a shopping bonanza!

NORDSTROM RACK

81 Colma Boulevard, 280 Metro Center, Colma. (650) 755-1444. M–Sat 10–9, Sun 11–7. Nordstrom Card, MC, VISA, AE. Parking: lot.
(Other store: Marina Square, San Leandro, (510) 614-1742.)

The Rack's inventory consists of clearance and out-of-season fashions from the main Nordstrom stores, as well as special purchases from regular Nordstrom manufacturers (easy to spot since some of this stuff would never be selected for the stores). Expect to save 30–70% off Nordstrom's original retail, and 30–50% on special purchases. I think some of the best buys and quality are found in the men's department. The emphasis at The Rack is on apparel and shoes for the entire family. Exchanges, refunds, and Nordstrom's unconditional guarantee.

OFF FIFTH (SAKS FIFTH AVENUE OUTLET)

Great Mall of the Bay Area, Milpitas. (408) 945-9650. Daily. MC, VISA. Parking: lot.
(Other outlet: Petaluma center.)

Saks has opened so many Off Fifth stores around the country that my worst fears have been realized—a decline in the overall quality of the inventory and more and more special-purchase fashions just for the Off Fifth division. Some very high profile designer names that were evident during the first year of operation are now harder to find. However, I still recommend scouring the racks for the real deals: merchandise that previously graced the racks of Saks Fifth Avenue stores or was destined for the Folio catalogs. Discriminating shoppers can cull through the career suits and coordinates (including Petite sizes) and casual sportswear, dresses, coats, footwear, and accessories and leave with satisfying bargains. I do like the men's department! Men's suits, sportcoats, sportswear, furnishings, outerwear, and footwear should prompt many couples to plan tandem shopping sprees. Prices range 40–75% below original Saks Fifth Avenue prices.

TALBOTS OUTLET

1235 Marina Boulevard, Marina Square, San Leandro. (510) 614-1090. M–F 10–9, Sat 10–7, Sun 11–6. MC, VISA, AE. Parking: lot.

I have friends that arrive at the Oakland Airport and insist on a ten-minute detour down the freeway to the Talbots Outlet before going anyplace else. That's because Talbots really comes through with quality goods and solid discounts (30–60% off). It's a great favorite—drawing women from all over Northern California. Year-round, you're likely to find "nice" dresses for special occasions, some with extra dazzle for the holidays. There's a small children's department with worth-the-trip bargains. Extras include career and casual shoes, lingerie and loungewear, bathing suits, and fashion accessories. I liked the career and dress departments best of all. Savvy shoppers, don't ignore the postcards announcing special sale events. Talbots rewards petite ladies with a very extensive selection of fashions and has a better-than-average inventory of clothing for that often-neglected 14- to 20-size woman. Kudos to the staff for their gracious service. Sizes: Petite 2–16; Misses 4–20. Refunds and exchanges.

TRAVELSMITH CATALOG OUTLET

811 University Avenue, Berkeley. (800) 950-1600 for hours. MC, VISA, AE, DIS. Parking: street/lot. The address was tentative at press time, but the new TravelSmith outlet is a must for folks who rely on the popular catalog for duds and accessories for their travels. Call the 800 number for the facts on its Bay Area site, set to open in the fall of 1997. Expect 20–70% off catalog retails on returned catalog merchandise (classified as seconds), samples, and catalog overstock inventory. Apparel will constitute 80–90% of the outlet's inventory, with the rest encompassing gadgets, accessories, and luggage oriented toward the needs of world travelers. TravelSmith has garnered a loyal following of catalog shoppers who appreciate apparel for men and women that addresses the special concerns of travelers trying to pack a carry-on case with enough clothing to see them through weeks of touring. You'll find apparel with a range of useful attributes, including light weight, wrinkle resistance, heat defiance, easy care, fast drying, convertible styling (like pants with legs that zip off to become shorts), and more. Many jacket, vest, and pant styles have security pockets or multiple compartments (like the photojournalist's vest). The overall catalog collection provides styles that work whether you're going on a backroad trek, visiting a museum, or daytripping from a cruise ship. Shoes are also a big catalog item, and you can see some of the best buys here on catalog returns.

Leather Apparel

LEATHER OUTLET/DOWN UNDER IMPORTS

950 Detroit Avenue #14, Concord. (510) 687-8883. F–Sun Noon–5. MC, VISA. Parking: lot.
The Leather Outlet sells leather fashions (lamb, calf, cowhide, wild boar) from better U.S. companies. The outlet is small but versatile. Men can opt for bomber styles, motorcycle jackets (with requisite zippers and snaps), blazers, flight jackets, and long fingertip jackets, some with zip-out inserts for warmth. Women will find racks of chic butter-soft jackets in vibrant colors and some Western-style fringed jackets. Prices are around wholesale. Most men's jackets are $59–$229 in sizes 36–64; women's $99–$269 in sizes XS–XXL (5/6–20).

LEATHER TO GO

200 Potrero, San Francisco. (415) 863-6171. M–F 9–4, Sat 10–2 (during December). MC, VISA. Parking: street.
Maybe you've seen President Clinton in his casual mode sporting his favorite brown cowhide jacket. The jacket came from this local company—a source of much pride and satisfaction. Buy this jacket and others at Leather to Go's factory showroom, where samples, imperfects, closeouts, and first-quality overruns are 40% off retail. If approximately $80–$300 sounds like a good price range for better-quality leather jackets in bomber, Western, and blazer styles, or suede and shearling outerwear, you'll be right at home here. The company sells through fine stores, specialty shops, and catalogs in the United States, Europe, and Asia. Jackets with some famous labels show up on the racks. These are often production samples made for private label collections sold by well-known designers or status brands. It also makes jackets for law enforcement agencies, athletic teams, etc. Sizes: Men's 36–46 or S–XXL; Women's 6–16.

LEATHERMODE OUTLETS

Great Mall of the Bay Area, Milpitas. (408) 956-1899. Daily. MC, VISA, AE, DIS. Parking: lot. (Other outlets: Gilroy, Tracy centers.)

Leathermode is well known in Southern California with its fifteen retail stores. Excess inventory, past-season styles, and closeouts on apparel, casual luggage, handbags, executive cases, and accessories keep this outlet well stocked. First-quality fashions with labels from Guess?, Kenneth Cole, Avirex, Michael Lawrence, Jones New York, Nine West, and more are reduced 20–60% off original retail. Couples can find cowhide or brushed-leather bombers, motorcycle jackets, men's full-length coats, or three-quarter-length lambskin ladies' jackets. Leather portfolios, attachés, and similar goods are all very nicely priced. Men's jackets range from $89 to $399; women's from $79 to $499. Sizes: Men's to XXL; women's to XL. A very good leather source!

WILSONS LEATHER OUTLET

Great Mall of the Bay Area, Milpitas. (408) 934-9095. Daily. MC, VISA, AE, DIS. Parking: street.

Whatever your leather fantasy, they've got it here. Of course the company has the right pipeline to the goods. Men and women can buy jackets, coats, pants, vests, hats, whatever! Basics, classics, and some real high-fashion contemporary styles are in the mix. Prices reduced 20–40%.

Also See

Under Famous Labels/Factory Stores:
ANNE KLEIN; ELLEN TRACY; DONNA KARAN; J. CREW; MONDI

Under San Francisco's Factory Outlets and Off-Price Stores:
GROUP USA; LOEHMANN'S

Under Family, Men's & Women's, General Clothing:
LONDON FOG; POLO/RALPH LAUREN; WOOLRICH

Under Men's Clothing:
CLOTHING BROKER; G.HQ OUTLET; MODA

Under Clearance Centers:
ALL LISTINGS

Under Handbags and Luggage:
LEATHER LOFT

Recycled Apparel

Consignment, Resale, and Thrift Shops

In today's politically correct environment there's a certain cachet to buying resale. Consumers from all income and education levels enjoy the pursuit and pleasure of finding great buys from resale, consignment, and thrift shops. A consignment shop is where one is likely to find the best quality. Usually their prices are higher than thrift shops. The affluent use these shops as a discreet way to recycle their clothing and recoup some of the original cost. Most resale shops operate on a consignment basis. Usually the potential seller brings in any items she wants to dispose of, and the store agrees to try to sell them for her for a certain percentage of the price. Other stores agree on the price the item will go for (the amount depending on the item's condition and age), and this is split fifty-fifty with the shop owner. Strictly resale shops buy outright. Either way, it's a winning proposition for everyone involved: The original owner makes a profit, the store owner makes a profit, and customers are able to buy clothes that might otherwise be out of reach. Expect to save 50–70% buying this way; when you pay $40 for a dress, it probably cost about $200 new.

At many shops, you'll find some very sophisticated clothes with designer labels. Often clothing may be as good as new—an indication that the original owner may never have worn the item. Even the best of us make mistakes with our purchases: we buy a garment that's a tad too tight and then never quite get our weight down to wearable size, or the color or style seems all wrong after consideration (and returning the merchandise to the store is no longer an option). Finding these shops is not difficult. Many advertise in community newspapers, while a quick perusal of the Yellow Pages of your phone book under "Clothing: Used" will provide a list of shops closest to you. Some shoppers "follow the money" by choosing shops in areas that are obviously supplied by an affluent clientele.

There are hundreds of resale shops around the Bay Area, and it may take time to find the one(s) that suits your fashion personality. Stores do vary, particularly in the standards applied to the merchandise they accept. The most discerning resale shops accept only recent fashions, in like-new condition, with recognized labels that denote quality. Some feature vintage or retro clothing, and prices may be based more on the collectible status of the goods. Always ask if there's more to see, since some shops keep the best merchandise in the back room for their regulars. As you begin your explorations, be prepared to see some stores that will leave you cold, with merchandise that's out-of-date, too tired, and presented in such a hodgepodge fashion that you can't generate any enthusiasm for shopping. If the store smells like old clothes and sweat, just leave and keep on trekking; there's a store somewhere that's perfect for you. Resale stores specializing in children's clothing are a boon to budget-pressed parents. Fortunately, there are several free publications that focus on the services, concerns, and interests of parents and their children. *Parents' Press, Bay Parent, Bay Area Baby, Valley Parent, Peninsula Parent,* and others are widely distributed at places where children and parents congregate: preschools, clinics, doctors' offices, supermarkets, and children's toy, apparel, and specialty stores. These publications are filled with advertising from children's resale and consignment stores. Many of these children's shops are also very good sources for used shoes, toys, baby equipment, books, and maternity clothing.

Cosmetics and Fragrances

In almost every shopping center around the Bay Area you'll find a beauty supply store that offers more merchandise than you'll find in most drugstores and supermarkets. Even though the selection of hair-care, nail, and, sometimes, skin-care and beauty aids is extensive, prices all around are pretty competitive. Often these stores offer incentives for return visits, such as a card to tote up cumulative totals in purchases leading to rebates or extra discounts. It pays to stick with one store if this is the case.

CALIFORNIA THEATRICAL SUPPLY

132 Ninth Street, Second Floor, San Francisco. (415) 863-9684. M–F 10–4. MC, VISA. Parking: street (until 4 p.m.).

This company deals mainly with local and national television personalities, theater and opera stars, and performing troupes. The shelves offer a rainbow collection of cosmetics that fill the requirements of stage and studio. Geared for the pros, the staff is not equipped to spend time giving makeup lessons or helping you make decisions. Kryolan, Dermacolor, Mehron, and Ben Nye are the professional lines offered, along with some generic products in lipsticks, eyeshadows, foundations, pancakes, powders, blushes, mascaras, pencils, and a baffling array of brushes. Professionals buy nose putty, eyelashes, moustaches, wigs, feathers, and other tricks of the theatrical trade. Plastic surgeons refer patients here for the store's line of camouflage makeup. Planning a face-painting party for kids or fund-raisers? This is where to buy the makeup/paints that are guaranteed to wash off. Prices, while not discounted, are substantially lower than on comparable lines in department stores. You'll also see many products no longer found in department store selections.

COLOURS & SCENTS

Outlets at Gilroy, Gilroy. (408) 842-3575. MC, VISA, AE, DIS. Parking: lot.
(Other outlets: Milpitas, Pacific Grove, Napa.)
If Elizabeth Arden is your preferred brand, you'll like what you see here. The discounts are modest at best: $5–$10 off on most products. You'll save a few dollars on Ceramide Time Capsules, or about 18% on Visible Difference. Borghese makeup, moisture treatments, and body creams are well stocked. Ultima II comes through with some of the best discounts—almost half off. A nice discount fragrance selection balances out the inventory of these elegant stores. Look around for extra specials—your best buys. Order by phone if you don't like to drive.

NEW YORK COSMETICS AND FRAGRANCES

318 Brannan Street, San Francisco. (415) 543-3880. M–F 10–6, Sat 10–5, Sun Noon–5. MC, VISA, DIS. Parking: limited street.
If you're trying to trim your budget, consider buying your makeup here. This company does some of its business on a wholesale basis with hair and beauty salons, selling cosmetics under its own salon label. At the outlet, you can buy the unbranded, naked product at a minimal markup. Lipsticks, foundations, nail polish, eyeshadow, blush, and mascara cover the basics. Whenever it can get a good buy on brand-name cosmetics like Calvin Klein, Estée Lauder, Clinique, or Lancôme, it passes on the discounts. Brand-name fragrances are 10–70% off retail. Request a catalog for easy ordering by phone or mail.

PERFUMANIA

359 Grant Avenue, San Francisco. (415) 956-1229. M–Sat 10–7, Sun 11–6. MC, VISA, DIS. Parking: pay lots.
(Other stores/outlets: Anderson/Redding, Concord, Daly City, Folsom, Gilroy, Milpitas, Petaluma, Pleasanton, Richmond, Tracy, Vacaville.)
The first thing to do when stopping in is to pick up the monthly flyer that highlights selected fragrance specials: great savings on promotional merchandise, unboxed products, miniatures, testers, and other brand-name products. Your best bet? Special boxed gift sets. Overall, 20–60% off on your favorite fragrances for women or men.

PRESTIGE FRAGRANCE AND COSMETICS

Factory Stores of America, Vacaville. (707) 449-8067. Daily. MC, VISA, DIS, AE. Parking: lot.
(Other stores/outlets: Gilroy, Lake Tahoe, Milpitas, Pacific Grove, Petaluma, Tracy.)

PFC stores are owned by one of the biggest cosmetic companies in the country. You can get nationally advertised lines formulated for specific skin types, or products to minimize aging. Waiting for you: cosmetics and skin-care lines at 30–70% off retail. Also, discontinued products and leftovers from special promotional campaigns that are super buys with the additional discount at PFC. The same conditions apply to the fragrances and fragrance-based products (body powders, lotions, and soaps). Suntan products, men's fragrances, nail-care needs, and other beauty-related items round out the selection. Check the "annex" for the best buys going.

Also See

Under Family, Men's & Women's, General Clothing:
ROSS

Handbags and Luggage

AMERICAN TOURISTER/SAMSONITE

Factory Stores of America, Vacaville. (707) 446-1595. Daily. MC, VISA, AE, DIS. Parking: lot. (Other outlets: Folsom, Gilroy, Tracy centers.)
American Tourister's factory store is well stocked with molded and soft-sided luggage, along with sport bags, backpacks, handbags, Buxton wallets, travel accessories, and business cases. These are closeouts and irregulars with minor cosmetic flaws. You'll also find a fair amount of first-quality merchandise. Discounts overall are 40–70% off retail.

BORSA FINE LEATHERS

Great Mall of the Bay Area, Milpitas. (408) 263-9867. Daily. MC, VISA, AE, DIS. Parking: lot.
Borsa was created by an Italian manufacturer as a store name since the manufacturer was reluctant to draw too much attention to the label on its leather goods, which are well known in Europe and Japan. In the United States much of what it makes is sold under private label by other well-known companies or designers. The label Castello may not be a household word, but that takes nothing away from the very fine quality of all of its leather handbags, wallets, and professional cases. Made to the company's specifications in China from Italian top-grain leathers, the line is very European in style and definitely classy. Prices on its handbags generally range from $100 to $200 at discount; small leather goods and wallets from $9 to $50; and document cases/totes from $200 to $300. Other better quality and fine handbag lines are also carried: Kenneth Cole, Liz Claiborne, Perlina, Valentino, Romeo (from Italy), and others are discounted at least 20% off—and usually more. Look for designated weekly specials of another 20% off. The clasps or fastenings on many handbags are gold-plated or solid brass. A lifetime maintenance policy on Borsa's handbags allows you to return items at any time for repairs or cleaning (they'll even refurbish edges that may get a little

worn with use). Returns and refunds up to five days, returns up to fourteen days. Close to Airplane Court entrance at the mall.

BRUCE ALAN BAGS, ETC.
Outlets at Gilroy, Gilroy. (408) 848-4104. Daily. MC, VISA. Parking: lot.
The handbags range from low-priced to quite pricey, but all are discounted 20–40% off retail. Career basics and many special fashion bags in leather, fabric, and novelty fabrications sport famous and less-known labels. Also: totes, executive cases, luggage, sport bags, duffels, travel accessories, security pouches, and other goodies. Nice selection overall.

CALIFORNIA LUGGAGE OUTLET
Outlets at Gilroy, Gilroy. (408) 847-4181. Daily. MC, VISA, AE, DIS. Parking: lot.
(Other outlets: Vacaville, Napa centers.)
You have to wonder if anyone buys luggage at retail anymore. This store is owned by El Portal Luggage & Leather Goods, usually found in shopping malls. It's capturing some business from bargain hunters by offering 20–50% discounts on major brands: Tumi, Samsonite, Delsey, Skyway,

Travelpro, and Lark. All types of luggage, plus backpacks, soft weekend bags, travel accessories, games, and more.

CHOICE LUGGAGE
1742 El Camino Real, Mountain View. (415) 968-3479. M–F 10–7:30, Sat 10–6. MC, VISA, AE. Parking: lot.
Choice offers bargain prices on an extensive inventory of brand-name garment bags, carry-on luggage, and tote bags from moderate to top-of-the-line companies. You'll find Lark, Skyway, Samsonite, Atlantic, Atlas of Boston, Halliburton, Andiamo, Travelpro, Delsey, Eagle Creek, and others. It also stocks small travel accessories, men's over-the-shoulder pouches, fine leather wallets, and attachés. Exchanges allowed only within 30 days of purchase.

THE COACH STORE
St. Helena Factory Outlets, St. Helena. (707) 963-7272. Daily. MC, VISA, AE. Parking: street.
(Other store: Carmel.)
At Coach Stores, everything is "value priced," 20–50% off retail. The leathers may have surface

flaws, but usually the merchandise is simply discontinued. Travelers might consider its leather duffels, carry-ons, and totes. Men should stop in for an executive case, belt, wallet, or travel kit, and examine its handsome line of ties. Ladies will naturally zero in on the handbags that constitute about 75% of the store's overall selection. Anything made by Coach might be available, including pocket diaries or organizers. Prices average 26% off original retail; 50% discounts can be found on the special sale tables. All merchandise bears a discreet mark inside noting that the item was purchased from a Coach value-priced store. This should not deter you from buying any item as a gift.

EDWARDS LUGGAGE OUTLET

Great Mall of the Bay Area, Milpitas. (408) 934-9559. Daily. MC, VISA, AE, DIS. Parking: lot.
Edwards puts on a new personality with this clearance outlet, a fun, high-energy store in keeping with the Great Mall's orientation. Customers love the mock airline cabin with seats and overhead bins. The focus is on travel everything: a variety of luggage, attachés, travel aids (security, passport

cases, personal accessories, etc.), games, maps, and books. Discontinued inventory from its posh full-price stores—agendas, business cases, computer bags, and women's small leather goods—are sold at 20–50% off original retail. Better brands of luggage such as Hartmann, Tumi, Lark, and Samsonite are 30–50% off retail on seconds, overruns, and discontinued colors.

GLASER DESIGNS

32 Otis Street (at S. Van Ness and Mission), San Francisco. (415) 552-3188. M–F 9:30–5:30, Sat Noon–5. MC, VISA. Parking: street/pay lot off Brady Alley.
The emphasis here is on high-end, long-lasting handmade travel gear that costs a lot, but less than comparable lines sold in status stores. Glaser's handsome travel and custom-finished leather/fabric garment and stadium bags cost $500–$700; packing cases are in the $400–$500 range. Customers have inspired innovations like the "insiders"— stretch-proof nylon mesh containers to organize travel goods. Business travelers also appreciate its Traveler's briefcases, which double as computer

bags ($700–$800). Garment bags are designed to "stand" when folded so that they won't collapse on your garments. You'll find a few seconds year-round, but most customers are willing to pay premium prices for the regular merchandise and feel the quality/price/value ratio is reasonable.

GRAFFEO LEATHER & HANDBAG OUTLET

1232 Burlingame Avenue, Burlingame. (650) 342-6276, (800) 472-3336. M–Sat 10–5, Sun 10–5 (Oct–Dec). MC, VISA, AE. Parking: street.

Graffeo sells under private label through a fascinating list of stores. All its handbags, leather goods, and luggage are very versatile, encompassing an attractive selection (generally in black, brown, or natural) of ladies' handbags, totes, backpacks, executive attachés, portfolios, specialty bags (camcorder, cellular phone, and laptop computer cases; shave kits; etc.), garment bags, carry-ons, and a luggage line. These pieces feature clever compartments, organizing aspects, pockets, and detachable straps. The handbags are soft and casual, while making the grade as an "executive" accessory. At the outlet these leather goods are sold at wholesale prices. Some guidelines: handbags $10–$39;

totes and backpacks $44–$69; carry-ons $79–$99; garment bags $199; executive cases $49–$99. Nylon sport bags, duffels, and carry-ons are well priced at $10–$20. Graffeo makes connections and opportunistic buys at various trade shows in the course of doing its business. That explains the displays of picture frames, leather jackets, other brands of luggage and handbags, fashion scarves, and unexpected treasures—all offered at solid discount prices.

GRIFFCO HANDBAG CO.

204 Martin Luther King Way (at Second Street), Oakland. (510) 444-3800. M–F 9–5, Sat 9–4:30. MC, VISA. Parking: side lot.

Griffco manufactures more than forty styles of soft, casual, genuine leather handbags in a wide array of colors. They aren't for elegant dressing, but rather for everyday use. Factory prices are $10–$36 on the handbags. Small backpacks, men's bags, and shaving bags are well priced, with soft-sided briefcases at $39–$65. Leather book bags are $55, while luggage carry-ons are an exceptional value at $76. If you need repairs later on your purchase, no problem. All bags guaranteed!

HANDBAG FACTORY OUTLET

2100 Fifth Street, Berkeley. (510) 843-6022. M–F 8:30–5, Sat 10–4:30. MC, VISA. Parking: lot.

You'll bag some great buys here, even though the prices are not cheap. This anonymous outfit manufactures a moderate- to high-priced line (retail $36–$200). The handbags have casual inclinations but they're classy enough for executive dressing. You'll find discontinued items, samples, and seconds with minor flaws for 30–60% off retail. All its bags are made from superior-grade leathers. You'll have your choice of style with compartments and pockets. Expect to spend about $80 for a midsized bag. The color range is very good, with all the basics and some fashion hues. Fanny packs, backpacks, and wallets are also popular here; the wallets and belts at discount are from other manufacturers.

HARBAND'S LUGGAGE

46 Kentucky Street, Petaluma. (707) 769-0610. M–F 10–6, Sat 10–3. MC, VISA, AE, DIS. Parking: street/lot.

Harband's portfolios and attaché cases are a very good gift resource. Fine leather is its specialty, although vinyls and hard cases are also available.

Samsonite, Briggs & Riley, Schlesinger, Korchmar, Leathermill, Remin, and Kart-a-Bags are some of its lines. The discounts are typically a modest 20% (sometimes more) off manufacturers' list prices; special sales take prices down to 50% off. Little leathers—wallets, passport cases, travel accessories—are also discounted.

LEATHER LOFT

Factory Stores of America, Vacaville. (707) 446-7262. Daily. MC, VISA, DIS, AE. Parking: lot. (Other outlets: Folsom, Gilroy, Milpitas, Petaluma, Pacific Grove centers.)

Leather Loft stocks its 150-plus factory stores with handbags, belts, wallets, briefcases, travel and desk accessories, gifts, designer accessories, and a small array of leather jackets. The selection includes timeless classic styles as well as the latest color or design. You'll find first-quality merchandise and closeouts. Discounts are 25–60% off retail. Handbags for every budget from $25 to $150. The leather jackets deserve a close look!

LUGGAGE CENTER

828 Mission Street (across from Fifth and Mission Garage), San Francisco. (415) 543-3771. M–F 8:30–6, Sat 10–5, Sun 11:30–5.
Parking: street/pay lots.
(Other stores: Berkeley; Burlingame; Cupertino; Dublin; Emeryville; Los Gatos; Mountain View; Pleasant Hill; Redwood City; Sacramento; San Jose; San Rafael; Vacaville; Walnut Creek. See Geographical Index.)

The Luggage Center offers solid discounts to first-class as well as economy-minded travelers. The luggage is first-line merchandise, open stock, and special purchases from companies like Skyway, Samsonite, Eagle Creek, Delsey, Travelpro, Halliburton, and others. There are no seconds. Savings are 20–50%. The inventory includes all types of luggage, and a wide variety of travel accessories, totes, attachés, and wallets. Exchanges and refunds within 30 days with receipt.

LUGGAGE TO GO

75 Bellam Boulevard, Marin Square, San Rafael. (415) 459-5167. M–Sat 10–6, Sun Noon–5. MC, VISA, AE. Parking: lot.

This store's discounts are 20–60% off retail on luggage (many current styles and fabrications), plus bonus pricing on special manufacturers' promotions, factory purchases, and leftovers from the owner's Beverly Hills store. Attachés, luggage, and almost anything required for carrying goodies on a trip are stocked. The selection is particularly choice for those wanting better lines not often found at discount. You'll like these labels: Samsonite, Lark, Delsey, Halliburton, Travelpro, Hartmann, the French Co., and more. The beautiful Italian leather collection is for the very chic. Monogramming is free—how nice!

MALM WAREHOUSE & REPAIR

1429 Burlingame Avenue, Burlingame. (650) 343-0990. M–F 9–6, Sat 10–6, Sun Noon–5. MC, VISA, AE, DIS. Parking: street.

Malm offers new suitcases, carry-ons, garment bags, and more from its inventory of discontinued and slightly irregular luggage. Hartmann, Tumi,

Lark, Delsey, and Samsonite are some of the brands you'll find at 25–50% markdowns. Take care of details with a discounted portfolio, attaché, toiletry kit, business case, agenda, or small leather good. Repairs, too—a complete service for luggage and attachés. Free monogramming.

MCM COMPANY STORE
Napa Factory Stores, Napa. (707) 254-0274. Daily. MC, VISA. Parking: lot.
(Other outlet: Pacific Grove center.)
One of the best outlets for upscale shoppers. MCM (a Germany-based company) has more than 250 boutiques in major cities around the world. MCM's leather goods—handbags and luggage—are sold here for 30% off retail (50% and more off on discontinued styles). The classic Signature Collection that made MCM famous features very functional coated linen-canvas with brass and leather details. It's a pricey line with many bags originally going for $400–$700 at retail and luggage pieces to $1,000. MCM's top-of-the-line Nature collection of fine leather goods is also gracing the shelves at the outlets along with the popular Corrida line. Take a peak at the sportswear—collections of bright, casual separates reflecting great design and quality. Make a statement with jeans, workout wear, and hot resort pieces. *Très chic!*

ROCKRIDGE LUGGAGE
5816 College Avenue, Oakland. (510) 428-2247. MC, VISA, AE. M–F 10–7, Sat 10–6. Parking: underground garage.
This company manages to cram an extensive selection of luggage from many recognized companies into its small space: Tumi, Boyt, Lark, Samsonite, Travelpro, Andiamo, Eagle Creek, Jansport, and others. Discounts everyday are 20–40% off retail. Students will have any number of choices when it comes to choosing a pack to tote heavy textbooks, while executives can find a leather attaché, portfolio, or briefcase in just the right configuration and size. Travel carts, small leather goods, gift items, and pens are the right price for gift givers.

SAMSONITE COMPANY STORE

Outlets at Gilroy, Gilroy. (408) 847-1879. MC, VISA, AE, DIS. Daily. Parking: lot.
(Other outlet: Milpitas center).
Samsonite now owns American Tourister and Lark, which makes these stores virtual clones of the American Tourister outlets. Same discounts apply on the Lark, Samsonite, U. S. Luggage, Jansport, LaSalle, and Jourdan collections of luggage, duffels, totes, and travel accessories.

SVEN DESIGN

2301 Fourth Street, Berkeley. (510) 848-7836. M–F 10–5, Sat 1–5. MC, VISA. Parking: street.
Sven's outlet showcases its line, which it sells primarily through craft shows and boutiques, although selected styles show up in status department stores. About 75% of the selection here is current season offered at 20% discount. Handbag prices are $22–$100; you'll find deeper discounts (40–50% off retail) only on closeouts and discontinued styles. Its drum-dyed leather requires skilled artisanry (which means higher prices). Fine-quality construction features suit the most exacting requirements. Handbags come in neutrals and fashion colors, plus a few

styles in exotic leathers or tapestry fabrics, serving traditional and contemporary tastes. You'll also find totes, book bags, fanny packs, and minibags/wallets with detachable straps. The handbags here are not inexpensive, but if quality is your concern and you feel that a little saving is better than none, you'll be very pleased.

THE WALLET WORKS

Pacific West Outlet Center, Gilroy. (408) 842-7488. Daily. MC, VISA, DIS. Parking: street/pay lots.
(Other outlets: Napa, Petaluma, Pacific Grove centers.)
The Wallet Works is perhaps known best for its wallets, available in department stores around the country. Think of a leather item in any configuration made to hold money, credit cards, or passports, and it'll be here, plus portfolios, soft luggage, fanny packs, daily organizers, tote bags, and portable coolers. The handbag selection is tempting, too. The few seconds are clearly marked, with extra discounts as the tradeoff. Discounts range from a modest 20% to 60% off retail.

Also See

Under Family, Men's & Women's, General Clothing:
ALL LISTINGS

Under Shoes:
ETIENNE AIGNER; TIMBERLAND

Under Women's Apparel/Fashion:
ALL LISTINGS

Under Famous Labels/Factory Stores:
ANN TAYLOR; ANNE KLEIN; LIZ CLAIBORNE

Under Women's Accessories:
DESIGNER BRANDS AND ACCESSORIES

Under Appliances, Electronics, and Home
Entertainment:
WHOLE EARTH ACCESS

Under General Merchandise—Discount Stores,
Warehouse Clubs:
ALL LISTINGS

Jewelry and Watches

Fine and Costume Jewelry, Diamonds, and Watches

Some ABCs on Buying Fine Jewelry
If you're buying fine jewelry for the first time, you're probably quite wary, because diamonds, gemstones, and gold don't come with labels and brands that make comparison shopping easy. You may feel ill-equipped to determine quality and value, to be sure that you're buying at a fair price, or know if you're paying more than you have to. If you are armed with some basics about buying jewelry—using common sense, taking time, asking questions, and, above all, comparison shopping—you need not hesitate to venture out of malls or high-profile jewelers to make your purchase.

A word about diamonds: Two diamonds that look alike at first may be very different, and two diamonds of equal size can have very unequal values. Since no two diamonds are alike, experts use four criteria to determine a diamond's value: the "Four Cs"—carat, color, clarity, and cut. The differ-ent combinations of all these characteristics determine the quality and value of a diamond.

AZEVEDO JEWELERS & GEMOLOGISTS, INC.
210 Post Street, Third Floor, Suite 321, San Francisco. (415) 781-0063. T–Sat 10–5. MC, VISA. Parking: pay lots.
Azevedo offers a beautiful selection of diamonds, colored stones, gold jewelry, and cultured pearls at substantial savings; its success is due to low overhead, careful buying, and referrals from satisfied customers. Appraisals are done by graduate gemologists. Its showroom is very classy, but most of the jewels are kept under wraps for obvious security reasons. Azevedo features jewelry designed by Oscar Heyman & Bros. at the lowest prices you'll find in the Bay Area. This is one of six American Gem Society stores in San Francisco.

BEAD BRAIN OUTLET

2700 18th Street (at York bet. Bryant and Potrero), San Francisco. (415) 621-8815. T–Sat Noon–6. MC, VISA, AE. Parking: street.

Bead Brain is an outlet for Jan Michaels, whose fashion jewelry always looks more expensive than it is. It is made from primary materials like brass chain and stampings, acrylic components, and glass stones and beads. Antique brass and antique silver plating characterize the basic finishes of both the contemporary women's and men's accessories. The finished jewelry selection ranges from the conventional to Baroque to contemporary styles—accents that really make an outfit. Also, necklaces, pins, hair accessories for women; cuff links, tie clips, money clips, and suspenders for men. Closeouts go for at least 50% off retail. Aspiring jewelry designers can find all the components (beads, findings, stones, stampings) to make one-of-a-kind jewelry pieces at el cheapo prices. Women have been known to lose all track of time when poking through the leftovers. Regular workshops are offered in jewelry making, metal work, mosaic and wirework household designs.

BEADCO/SMALL THINGS COMPANY

760 Market Street (Phelan Building), Suite 860, San Francisco. (415) 397-0110. M–F 10–4; other hours and Sat by appt. Cash/Check, VISA. Parking: pay lots.

This company's talent lies in finding maximum value for the best price, using connections developed over the years. If you're interested in a special gift—pearls, lapis, jade, diamonds, precious gemstones, gold, or silver—Beadco probably has it in stock, or can find it, usually at a price 30–60% lower than conventional retailers. Contact Beadco if you need pearls restrung, plating, jewelry repaired (including sterling silver and costume jewelry) or remodeled, a custom design, or an appraisal. Creating innovative wedding rings is the store's special pleasure. Unless you're coming in for repairs, it's essential to call for an appointment.

BRODER JEWELRY COMPANY

210 Post Street, Room 611, San Francisco. (415) 421-9313. M–F 9–3:30, Sat by appt. Cash/Check. Parking: pay lots.

Mr. Broder does custom design, appraisals, and repair work for many of San Francisco's finest jewelry stores and works closely with a private clientele, creating special pieces like rings, pendants, and bracelets. However, he does not sell watches or other items usually found in jewelry stores. His closet-sized office has no stock on hand, so this is definitely not a store for casual browsing. If you have a picture of a design, bring it in, or Mr. Broder can create one. His low overhead accounts for the low prices on diamonds and colored stones and on anything he can special-order from a large number of manufacturers and their catalogs. Naturally, if you need a ring sized, repaired, or reset, his talents are at your disposal. One of the few jewelers who works in platinum. A 50% deposit is required before custom orders are started.

CRESALIA JEWELERS DIAMOND EXPERTISE

111 Sutter Street (at Montgomery), San Francisco. (415) 781-7371 or (800) 781-7371. M–Sat 9:30–5:30. AE, MC, VISA, DIS. Parking: validated parking in garage next block.

Cresalia displays an extensive selection of diamond rings, fine jewels, and watches. It designs and manufactures its own rings and carries well-known brands as well. You'll recognize the compa-nies in its selection: Artcarved, Italiano gold, Kobe pearls, Krementz, Gorham, Reed & Barton, Lunt, Wallace, Ballou, Sheffield, Kirk, and Cross pens just for starters. Prices are guaranteed to be 25–50% below regular retail prices. Cresalia has a staff of graduate gemologists from the Gemological Institute of America to help you choose a diamond or gem, and to grade and appraise jewelry you own. If you're shopping for elegant gifts, you'll appreciate the extensive array of silverware, crystal, clocks, hollowware, china, and dinner accessories that can be wrapped and shipped UPS if requested.

EVANTON NIEDERHOLZER JEWELERS

503 Magnolia Avenue, Larkspur. (415) 924-7885. T–Sat 10–5. MC, VISA. Parking: street.

This is where "people in the know" go for quality jewelry at lower prices: gold and silver accessories, jewelry, diamond rings, wedding sets, and precious stones. There are substantial savings on prestige watches from companies like Omega; sterling silver flatware and hollowware from Gorham, Reed & Barton, Towle, Lunt, and others; Colle crystal and small gift items from Christian

Dior, Sasaki, Royal Worcester, and Spode. Custom jewelry design services provided.

THE FENTON COMPANY

210 Post Street, Suite 203, San Francisco. (415) 563-0258. By appt. Cash/Check. Parking: pay lots.
Joan Fenton serves as a personal jewelry shopper. In her twelve and a half years in business, Joan has helped many brides, professional women, and "awfully smart men." She keeps no inventory, and her low overhead lets her pass on good prices to her discriminating clientele. She knows how to get things done and brings a sense of style and charm along with her expertise to her business. Call for an appointment to assess your needs. When Joan knows what you want, she can present choices that meet the specifications of size and price that you've requested. Using her trade resources, she'll either find it for you or have it custom-designed at wholesale prices plus a slight markup, generally 10–20%.

FOSSIL

Outlet at Gilroy, Gilroy. (408) 848-2709. Daily. MC, VISA, AE, DIS. Parking: lot.
Fossil achieved fame with its fashion watches, popular with a younger and hipper crowd. It didn't take long before the company was expanding into sunglasses, belts, ties, sweatshirts, women's handbags, and fashion jewelry. All these things are sold at about 30% off original retail. There's usually a $19.99 watch or sunglasses special on selected styles. Look for other exceptional savings on closeouts and discontinued styles.

GUARDIAN INTERNATIONAL

150 Bellam Boulevard, Suite 250, San Rafael. (415) 258-0601. M–F 9–5, Sat by appt. MC, VISA. Parking: street.
Guardian International has solid credentials. When buying directly from this source, you'll save about 35% off the "major store price." If you need something fast, you'll be able to find something that's just right. Guardian provides extraordinary quality in original custom designs, and special orders are its forte. It keeps a good inventory of diamonds up to one carat, and can readily provide larger sizes

upon request. If you're in the market for a status watch (most priced over $1,000 at retail) such as Bertolucci, Omega, Cartier, Rolex, and many more, you can pick a style from a notebook full of catalogs, and on most lines you'll pay just 10% over Guardian's cost. Don't come in expecting to see several cases of fine jewelry. It's more of an office serving its private clientele (the public) on an appointment basis.

HOCHERMAN & SON JEWELERS

760 Market Street, Suites 346–348, San Francisco. (415) 986-4066. M–F 8:30–4:30 by appt. MC, VISA. Parking: pay garages.

"Bargain" is a relative term; if you haven't had to adjust your spending because of the recession, Hocherman may be the perfect resource when you're contemplating fine jewelry purchases. It's not set up for casual browsing, since most of its work is done on a custom design basis. Many couples come here seeking unusual settings (true works of art) for wedding rings and will spend $6,000–$8,000 for a ring that would cost $12,000–$14,000 at a Union Square jeweler. Of course, other customers spend much less, especially on wedding

bands, gemstone jewelry or pearls, or jewelry resetting. If you'd like estate jewelry reset or want to rework original wedding sets into something more up-to-date, consider this resource. The company keeps an extensive selection of loose diamonds and gemstones on hand, and works with you to develop a design for your jewelry piece. There are modest charges for designing the model and renderings, and work proceeds with a 50% deposit.

K-GOLD CO.

2229 Bunker Hill Drive (off Hwy. 280), San Mateo. (650) 349-2912. M–Sat by appt. Cash/Check. Parking: street.

If you have old jewelry tucked away and you'd like to have it updated, reset, or repaired, this company can do the job. For years K-Gold has worked with prominent jewelry stores creating custom designs and repairing gold, platinum, and precious stones. It has also created replacement jewelry for insurance claims. You can bring in stones for setting, or stones can be purchased for you if you know what you want. No inventory is kept on the premises. If you want a wedding set, ring, or piece designed, you can browse through wholesale catalogs, or you can bring in a picture. When updating jewelry, the gold or platinum in your jewelry can be reused. (No work is done with sterling silver jewelry.) Although this small studio is not a conventional retail setting, I think customers will feel very comfortable here. However, it's important to schedule an appointment, since K-Gold is not set up for walk-in business. I think you'll find the savings very worthwhile, and the work is done to the highest standards.

MOVADO COMPANY STORE
St. Helena Premium Outlets, St. Helena. (707) 967-0738. Daily. MC, VISA, AE. Parking: lot.
Upscale buyers are very impressed by the watches they see under lock and key at Movado. Most are seconds with small cosmetic surface imperfections. Others are discontinued styles. Whatever the "flaw," the movements inside are perfect and the watches are under full warranty. You don't have to be rich to shop here, since you can find many styles priced $100–$300. On the other hand, you can buy a handmade Piaget 18K solid-gold watch with sapphire crystal for $4,000 (retail originally $14,000). Movado's 14K solid-gold watches are priced at $375 and up, while its sportier Esquire line goes

for $30–$177. Overall discounts are 20–70% off original retail. Buy with care since there are no refunds; exchanges only within 10 days with receipt for an item of equal or higher value. This elegant store hardly seems to fit the term "bargain," but you will be surprised.

PETER JACOBS JEWELRY RESOURCES
369-C Third Street, Montecito Plaza Shopping Center, San Rafael. (415) 459-4300. M–Sat 10–6, MC, VISA, DIS. Parking: lot.
Peter Jacobs was a distributor of fine jewelry to department stores; he's kept the resources to buy direct and sell to consumers, who now pay him what department stores paid. He keeps a notebook filled with ads from local department stores and mall jewelers to compare their prices with his for the same items. The difference is impressive. You'll find gold jewelry (bracelets, chains, necklaces, earrings, charms, and pins), gemstones, diamonds, pearls, and sterling silver jewelry. I was very impressed with his selection of wedding sets and bands (most are tucked away in the safe). After receiving an education on diamond buying, you'll be able to select a diamond that suits the

ring and your budget. Better watches can be purchased on a special order basis with savings of about 30%. Whenever possible, Jacobs tries to accommodate special needs and requests.

A PIECE OF THE RAINBOW

1015 Camelia Street (one block south of Gilman), Berkeley. (510) 527-2431. M–F Noon–6, Sat 10–4. Cash/Check. Parking: street.

This company manufactures (to my mind) a somewhat esoteric line of funky, novelty, whimsical, and appealing rhinestone jewelry. Collectors buy some very special Dorothy Bauer pieces under the glass at better stores. Prices are half off wholesale. Most pins are $7.50–$30 (some can go as high as $100); earrings $10–$40. Some themes: sports, wildlife, domestic pets, Christmas, patriotic symbols, flowers, recreational activities, and words and expressions (like one the I should have: "I Love to Shop"). These are all discontinued, prototypes, samples, mistakes, and occasional seconds. A popular store for collectors of rhinestone jewelry.

TAYLOR & JACOBSON

1475 N. Broadway (Lincoln Broadway Building), Suite 490, Walnut Creek. (510) 937-9570. M–F 9–6 by appt. MC, VISA. Parking: garage across street.

The best values are often found in the least likely locations. This company does most of its business with stores that use its custom fabricating, diamond-setting, and repair service. Essentially a wholesaler, it also works directly with local consumers. It doesn't claim to sell at wholesale prices (how refreshing!), but it certainly offers substantial savings. It has a display case with many dazzling rings; however, most of its available settings are kept in trays or are represented in wax patterns that you can try on. Engagement rings and wedding sets are a specialty. Services include repair, remounts, sizing, repronging, reshanking, and polishing. You can choose from loose stones including diamonds, jade, lapis lazuli, pearls, and other precious and semiprecious beauties. Appointments are essential to get through the locked doors.

ZWILLINGER & CO.

760 Market Street (Phelan Building), Suite 800, San Francisco. (415) 392-4086. T–Sat 9:30–5. MC, VISA, AE, DIS. Parking: downtown pay garages. You'll feel more comfortable if you wear your Sunday best before entering the vaultlike security doors of this firm, which has been in the same location for the past forty-seven years. For those great occasions in life—engagements, anniversaries, and graduations—when you desire a very special memento, a piece of fine jewelry can be purchased here at considerable savings (20–50% off retail). Prices on 14K and 18K gold and platinum jewelry, watches, and diamond rings are very impressive. You can create your own wedding set by selecting a mounting with or without stone, and then pick a center diamond of the size and quality to fit your budget. The selection of loose diamonds is breathtaking! Discriminating women and men appreciate the large array of fashion jewelry from such noted designers as Charles Garnier, Winward, Judith Conway, Garaveli Aldo, Gemveto, and others usually seen advertised in *Architectural Digest, Connoisseur, Town & Country,* et al. If Zwillinger doesn't have a particular piece in stock, bring in a picture; chances are the piece can be ordered or custom-made for you. Watches from Omega, Movado, Seiko, and other status brands ($3,000-plus range) are available. Graduates from the Gemological Institute of America are on staff. Appraisals and full jewelry repairs are done. Zwillinger buys diamonds and replacement jewelry for several large insurance companies. First-time jewelry buyers will be in good hands.

Also See

Under Women's Accessories:
ALL LISTINGS

Under Giftware and Home Decor:
ALL LISTINGS

Under General Merchandise:
ALL LISTINGS

Shoes

ADIDAS

Outlets at Gilroy, Gilroy. (408) 842-1638. Daily. MC, VISA, AE, DIS. Parking: lot.

If the company's advertising campaigns are on target, Adidas needs no introduction. Count on shoes for active sports—basketball, soccer, running, and training. Discounts range from 30% to 50% on average, up to 75% off on the these-have-got-to-go special markdowns. Shoes may have small cosmetic blems or be discontinued styles. Sizes: Men's 6½–15; Women's 5–10; Youth 8½–6; Children 4–8. All sales final. An extra—Adidas nylon jogging sets priced at $59.

ATHLETE'S FOOT OUTLET

1237 Marina Boulevard, Marina Square (next to Talbots), San Leandro. (510) 895-9738. M–F 10–9, Sat 10–7, Sun 11–6. MC, VISA, AE, DIS. Parking: lot. (Other outlets: Milpitas, Novato centers.)

Most parents cringe at the prospect of outfitting their children with new shoes, especially the Nike, Reebok, and Adidas types. Athlete's Foot Outlets carry the major high-profile brands of shoes for crosstraining, tennis, soccer, football, basketball, aerobics, running, track, and all-around everyday wear. Prices at this self-service store are reduced 15–60% off retail, averaging about 30% off retail, plus occasional super markdowns. Sizes for the whole family start with Infant 0–8, children's 1½–6, Youth 10½–13, Women's 5½–11, Men's 6½–15. Also, T-shirts, shorts, sweats, and warm-ups. Refunds or exchanges within 30 days with receipt.

BANISTER SHOE STUDIO

Great Mall of the Bay Area, Milpitas. (408) 956-9928. Daily. MC, VISA, AE, DIS. Parking: lot.
(Other outlets: Folsom, Gilroy, Pacific Grove centers.)
These outlets are part of the Nine West Group and showcase all its labels. Women's fashion shoe collections from Calico, Bandolino, Easy Spirit, Evan-Picone, Amalfi, Pappagallo, and others are moderately discounted everyday. Prices are more enticing during special sale times. The shoes are nicely displayed in sizes 6–10 (a few 11s).

BASS SHOE OUTLET

Outlets at Gilroy, Gilroy.(408) 842-3632. Daily. MC, VISA, DIS. Parking: lot.
(Other outlets: Lake Tahoe, Pacific Grove, Petaluma, Truckee, Vacaville centers.)
Finding the perfect vacation walking shoe is difficult, especially if you're trying to find a style that won't get you arrested by the fashion police. Bass provides the comfort and style to take you through hours of museums and miles of city streets. You'll find the original Bass Weejuns, Sunjuns, and Saddles, as well as the latest fashion footwear to take you from the beach to the boardroom. Prices reflect 16–30% discounts on most styles and up to 50% discounts on some seconds. Also, belts, duffels, totes, wallets, shoelaces, mink oil, and more at discount prices. A few stores showcase Bass's weekend sportswear lines for men, women, and kids.

BIRKENSTOCK FOOTPRINT

Outlets at Gilroy, Gilroy. (408) 848-1602. Daily. MC, VISA, AE. Parking: lot.
Those funny-looking shoes are no longer considered funky. Mainstream America has embraced the comfort of the contoured footbed. It helps that Birkenstock now makes so many styles that there's one for every personality and situation. There are Birkenstocks to slip on, buckle up, or lace, with open or closed heels and toes. You'll find styles for beachcombing or for wearing into the office on dress-down Fridays, and you'll find "professionals"—shoes for those who stand on their feet or walk on the job. This is the only outlet in the country, and here prices are reduced 30–50% off original retail on discontinued styles or seconds. (The seconds have cosmetic imperfections.) All shoes in European sizing—refer to wall charts for translation. American

sizes: Men's 5–17½; Women's 4–13½; Kids 7–3. Options are expanded with the unisex styling of many shoes.

BOOT FACTORY

Factory Stores at Vacaville, Vacaville. (707) 449-6429. Daily. MC, VISA, DIS, AE. Parking: lot. (Other outlet: Gilroy center.)
Take the whole family up to the Boot Factory for rompin', stompin' Western-style boots, and serious work and outdoor boots. You'll find cosmetic irregulars or discontinued styles from a famous Texas-based maker of traditional boots and its Western-inspired, more contemporary label. Prices $40–$400; most average $75–$100. About half the shelf space is devoted to sturdy and heavy casual boots; insulated, waterproof, and leather hiking boots; and some steel-toe work boots for men. Catch these labels: Wolverine, Doc Martens, Caterpillar, Georgia Boots in steel or nonsteel toes. Take a hike in Hi-Tec, HH Brown, Khombu, and Timberland. Kids love the cowboy/cowgirl boots! Sizes: Women's 5–11; Men's 7–13, some wide widths for men and women. Most boots appear discounted about

35–40% off original retail (during special sales prices to 60% off).

BROWN BROS. SHOE WAREHOUSE

848 Lincoln Avenue (at Ninth Street), Alameda. (510) 865-3701. M–Sat 9:30–6. Cash/Check. Parking: street.
Brown Bros.' shoes are all first quality, in up-to-date styles from Florsheim, Stacy Adams, Dexter, Sperry Topsiders, and Rockport. It's strictly a men's shoe store with sizes 6–15 to EEE widths. It sells athletic shoes for solid discount prices and has some of the lowest-priced work boots that I've found, which is why so many hardworking fellas come here from miles around. You'll always find a good shoe at a reasonable price, usually 25–35% off retail. Exchanges and refunds allowed.

CAROLE'S SHOE WAREHOUSE

890 Ralston Avenue, Belmont. (650) 596-2924. M–Sat 10–6, Sun Noon–5. MC, VISA, DIS, AE. Parking: lot.
Carole's is a self-service operation displaying an intriguing selection of shoes warehouse-style. There are funky, fashion, conventional, and sporty

styles—occasionally including a few dogs. Buying liquidations, overruns, and clearance inventories yields an extensive variety of dress heels (including chic imports from Italy and Spain), boots, and casuals. Fellas can buy nice Italian dress and casual shoes (average price $40–$80). Savings 30–60% off retail (average discount 40–50% off). Sizes: Women's 5½–12; Men's, a few 5s to 13. The racks of women's apparel offer some unpredictable and surprisingly good buys—worth a peek.

COLE-HAAN

Napa Factory Stores, Napa. (707) 258-0898. Daily. MC, VISA, AE, DIS. Parking: lot.
If you love Cole-Haan shoes but hate the price tags, you'll find a measure of savings at its elegant factory store. Collections of shoes for women and men are about one season behind and priced 20–50% off retail. In addition to its signature shoe styles, Cole-Haan stocks nicely executed luggage, handbags, belts, and small leather goods. Those seeking shoes in narrow or wide widths, small or extra-large sizes, will want to splurge when they find these shoes available—an unpredictable occurrence. Those wearing medium or narrow

widths have the most options when shopping. Sizes: Women's 5–11 AAAA–W; Men's 7–15 B–D (a few Es).

CONVERSE

Factory Stores of America, Vacaville. (707) 447-7657. Daily. MC, VISA, DIS, AE. Parking: lot.
Converse needs no introduction to anyone who's shopped for athletic or sport shoes; men and women, even infants and toddlers, can find shoes for active lifestyles. Since Converse is sold throughout the Bay Area and the country, all shoes are marked as "irregulars" (wink wink) to avoid alienating full-price retailers. Savings 30–50% off retail. Sizes: Infant 1–13½; Girls and Boys 1–6; Women's 4–11; Men's 6–14 (some styles to 19). If you've got a hard-to-find size, talk with the staff to see if a special order is possible.

DSW SHOE WAREHOUSE

Great Mall of the Bay Area, Milpitas. (408) 941-0490. MC, VISA, AE, DIS. Parking: lot.
The best shoe discount operation to open in the Bay Area in 1997! With over 36,000 pairs of shoes on hand every day, priced at 20–50% off depart-

ment store retails, it's a virtual amusement park of shoes. Shoe fanatics will have a field day cruising up and down the aisles of self-service displays picking up fun, fanciful, practical, utilitarian, classy, and classic shoes. In fact, that selection is the key to DSW's success—which was well established with 31 stores in 18 states before opening its first California store here. Outrageous trendsetting styles take care of the fashion forward crowd, but executive career women, soccer moms, teenagers, and comfort-oriented senior citizens can also find a fit and style. Count on familiar name brands in moderate to better price ranges. However, no Ferragamos or other very exclusive and expensive women's shoes. Lots of sport shoes, but no Nike or Reebok brands. The men's selection takes up about 20% of the stock with equally good values and across-the-board selection of sport, casual, and dress shoes. You can bank on regular deposits of new styles to make each visit worthwhile. Sizes: Women's 5–12; Men's 7–13 (few 6s and 15s). The narrow and wide widths are easily identified by florescent stickers on the outside of shoe boxes.

EASY SPIRIT

1253 Marina Boulevard, Marina Square, San Leandro. (510) 352-8804. Daily. MC, VISA. Parking: lot.
(Other outlets: Gilroy, Vacaville.)
If you're standing on your feet all day, in uniform or out, then comfy shoes are essential. Easy Spirit shoes have gained great popularity for their comfort-enhancing features. At the outlet you'll find serious work, dress, and casual styles, flats and heels, reduced about 20–30% everyday with frequent promotions that bring prices down even more. I also spotted a few Selby labels in the selection. Men have a corner of the store where they can pick up oxfords, loafers, even wingtips. Sizes: Women's 4½–12, widths AA–EE; Men's 8–13, widths Medium–EE.

ENZO ANGIOLINI

Great Mall of the Bay Area, Milpitas. (408) 934-1349. Daily. MC, VISA, AE, DIS. Parking: lot.
This label is made by Nine West. It's a more expensive line for women, European-inspired, featuring Italian leathers in a more tailored collection of shoe styles. Retail prices range from $68 to

$150; at this outlet you'll save 20–40% every day. The shoe styles convey classic silhouettes with contemporary fluidity and they're destined to outlast the season. Casual boots, booties, flats and loafers, daytime heels (in beautiful leathers and nubuck), fabric shoes (for evening), and a few metallics define the collection. The store is pretty posh—complementing this quality selection nicely. Sizes: Women's Medium width 5–11, Narrow and Wide 7–10. Returns and refunds.

ETIENNE AIGNER
Factory Stores of America, Vacaville. (707) 452-1385. Daily. MC, VISA, AE. Parking: lot.
(Other outlet: Gilroy center)
This is a real winner for women's shoes, an elegant factory store beautifully merchandised with upscale-quality shoes, handbags, leather accessories, gloves, and leather jackets. Those familiar with this line will not be disappointed with the extensive selection of classic, tailored, and dress shoes. Sizes: Women's 5½–10 (a few 5s and 11s); widths: Narrow to Wide. Prices on handbags (all leather) vary from $39 to $110, with the average price nesting at $63. Discounts are 33% off retail across the board.

During special sale promotions many groups are posted with additional 20% markdowns. Add your name to the mailing list; it's your only pipeline to special promotions and discount coupons. Exchanges only allowed within 14 days with receipt.

FAMOUS FOOTWEAR/FACTORY BRAND SHOES
1600 Saratoga Avenue, Westgate Mall, San Jose. (408) 378-5064. M–F 10–9, Sat 10–7, Sun 11–6. MC, VISA. Parking: lot.
(Other stores: Anderson/Redding; Carmichael; Fremont; Gilroy; Milpitas; Roseville; Sacramento; San Jose; Stockton; Vacaville.)
Famous Footwear and Factory Brand Shoes offer a full selection of moderately priced brand-name shoes, discounted a minimum of 10% to a maximum of 40% off retail. Its strength lies in the selection of what I call family basics and "sensible" shoes for women. Expect a complete range of sizes and styles for the whole family.

FLORSHEIM FACTORY OUTLET

*Great Mall of the Bay Area, Milpitas. (408) 945-9428. Daily. MC, VISA, AE. DIS. Parking: lot.
(Other outlets: Anderson/Redding, Gilroy, Petaluma, Vacaville centers.)*
This well-known company now offers 20–50% discounts on overruns, closeouts, and slightly blemished (surfaces only) shoes. Men can revel in the selection of everything Florsheim: dress shoes and boots (including the top-of-the-line Royal Imperial group), casual street and outdoor shoes, Comfortech styles, tennis shoes, and slippers during the holidays. Sizes: Men's 6–15, A–EEE. Refunds or exchange on unworn shoes.

FOOTLOCKER OUTLET

*Great Mall of the Bay Area, Milpitas. (408) 946-0408. Daily. MC, VISA. Parking: lot.
(Other outlets: Gilroy center.)*
Selling both new shoes at full retail and discontinued styles from famous makers like Adidas, Nike, Vuarnet, and Reebok, the Footlocker outlets function as clearance centers for the company's retail stores. Clearance inventory yields savings of 25–60% off retail.

HUSH PUPPIES FACTORY OUTLET

Outlets at Gilroy, Gilroy. (408) 848-1180. Daily. MC, VISA, AE, DIS. Parking: lot.
Hush Puppies have taken on a whole new personality. The classic suede styles remain, but the company has added fashion colors, canvas, and new leathers in its new collections. Savings are 10–50% off retail on the outlet's first-quality selection. Styles for the whole family. Sizes: Women's 4–12 Narrow–XW; Men's 6–16 Narrow–XXW. Other brands from the company's family—Wolverine boots and shoes, Cat footwear.

JOAN & DAVID/A STEP FORWARD

*2010 Mountain Boulevard, Montclair Village, Oakland. (510) 339-0500. M–Sat 10–6, Sun 10–5. MC, VISA. Parking: lot.
(Other outlets: Gilroy, Pacific Grove, St. Helena centers.)*
Most Joan & David loyalists buy these shoes as an investment. The line's popularity is due in part to its classic styling, even though each season "the classics" reflect a new interpretation of fashion trends and colors. The prices are higher than other outlet stores that focus on American brands. You'll

usually save 40–50% off original retail. Expect to pay at least $79–$89, up to $169 (original retail $325). Boots are $129–$269 (original retail to $450). Sizes: Women's 5–10 (occasionally larger sizes, and some Narrows are available). Handbags and belts are an extra plus. At outlet center stores, discriminating shoppers appreciate the exquisitely made updated sportswear collection from Joan & David. Beautiful fabrics and quality construction justify the high prices on this line.

JOHNSTON & MURPHY FACTORY STORE

Factory Stores of America, Vacaville. (707) 446-4652. Daily. MC, VISA, AE, DIS. Parking: lot.
(Other outlet: Napa center.)
A 25% discount off a $10 item isn't much, but 25% off $200 is $50, an entirely different prospect. So I'm satisfied with the 20–40% discounts here. You'll find discontinued styles, past-season shoes, and occasional slight imperfects, plus markdowns on current-season men's shoes. Johnston & Murphy's quality is a given in its lines of classic dress, dress casuals, comfort dress, modern classic (more Italian), or athletic casuals. Expect classic wingtips retail priced at $195 to be about $129, or

golf shoes at $170 to be $139. Sizes: Men's 7–15 A–EEE. Sign up for mailing list specials. No-hassle refunds or exchanges.

KENNETH COLE

Outlets at Gilroy, Gilroy. (408) 848-2026. Daily. MC, VISA, AE. No checks. Parking: lot.
(Other outlet: Napa center.)
I love this line of footwear for men and women. Its best customers are 20- to 30-year-olds who seek comfort, plus some flash, glamour, and sexiness in their lives. Kenneth Cole's line is a forerunner of fashion and trends—the line is trendy without being extreme. The quality is great. Many women's shoes are menswear-influenced (oxfords, chukka boots, ghillie-laced shoes, and kiltie shoes), yet there are more feminine styles and some styles just perfect for brides. At retail the shoes are usually priced from $89 to $160. Good selection of men's shoes. I wish the company would be more aggressive with its discounts. Discounts of 18-30% are unlikely to increase the pulse rate of seasoned bargain hunters (look for mailings announcing annual sales when prices are 50% off outlet prices). Men's ties, hosiery, luggage, briefcases, small leather

goods, eyeglasses, and handbags add spice to the shoe collection. Sizes: Women's 5½–12; Men's 7–13 (some Wide).

NATURALIZER OUTLET

Factory Stores of America, Vacaville. (707) 452-1083. Daily. MC, VISA, DIS. Parking: lot.
If Naturalizer, Life Stride, Connie, or Natural Sport are your brands, then stop in for 30–50% discounts on a wide selection for women of all ages. Lots of no-nonsense comfort shoes! Very good choices of in-season styles; great markdowns on slightly past-season goods. Sizes: Women's 5–11 (some 4s and 12s); widths: Slim (AAA) to Wide (WW) in some styles.

NIKE FACTORY STORE

Pacific West Outlet Center, Gilroy. (408) 847-4300. Daily. MC, VISA, AE. Parking: lot.
(Other outlet: Folsom center.)
You won't find the latest, hippest, or hottest styles from Nike here. However, you may find fairly recent popular styles priced about 30% off retail as blems. The selection of blems, closeouts, and discontinued styles covers just about all of Nike's

sport shoes. Sizes: Infant 2–8; Preschool 8½–13; Girls 1–6; Boys 1–6; Women's 5–12; Men's 6–15. Discounts are 20–40% off retail. Half of the store is devoted to many styles of first-quality discontinued apparel for active sports or simple leisure for men, women, and children. Discounts average 30% off retail. Exchanges only; no cash refunds.

NINE WEST FACTORY STORE

1251 Marina Boulevard, Marina Square, San Leandro. (510) 614-0758. M–F 10–9, Sat 10–7, Sun 11–6. MC, VISA. Parking: lot.
(Other outlets: Folsom, Gilroy, Milpitas, Petaluma, Tracy, Vacaville centers.)
Nine West offers a mixed bag of bargains, from hardly worth noting to dazzling. You'll save just $5 on some current women's styles, but more like 30–60% on last season's regular prices. The selection covers a little of everything Nine West. Look for two-for-one price offers on absolutely going, going, gone past-season styles! Sizes: Women's 5½–10 (a few 5s and 11s). The outlets accept returns and give refunds within 21 days on unworn shoes with receipt.

REEBOK FACTORY STORE

Factory Stores of America, Vacaville. (707) 452-0235. Daily. MC, VISA, AE. Parking: lot.
(Other outlets: Gilroy, Pacific Grove, Petaluma, Tracy centers)

The Reebok stores are upbeat and energizing, but for me that doesn't make up for the fact that the discounts are often downright chintzy. However, you may find a shoe that addresses your needs on the more deeply discounted closeout tables. The stores also carry Reebok activewear for the whole family. Shoes in sizes for tiny tots, kids, teens, women, and up to great big lugs (Men's size 15–16).

ROCKPORT OUTLET

Outlets at Gilroy, Gilroy. (408) 848-8837. Daily. MC, VISA, AE. Parking: lot.
(Other outlets: Pacific Grove, Tracy, Vacaville centers.)

If this is your label, then this is the place to shop. You'll find a combination of discontinued styles, current overruns, and some blems (cosmetic only) sold at average 30% discounts. Not all sizes available in each style. *Note: Vacaville's Reebok Outlet*

has a respectable Rockport selection. Sizes: Women's 5–11; Men's 7–15.

SAS FACTORY SHOE STORE

Outlets at Gilroy, Gilroy. (408) 842-2185. Daily. MC, VISA, DIS. Parking: lot.

If you spend hours on your feet each day, the prospect of so many comfort-oriented shoes will be exciting. If you're a true bargain hunter, you'll be a little disappointed at the discounts that range from a teensy 10% to a maximum of 25% off retail. Most SAS shoppers find compensation in the depth of the first-quality selection and extensive size range. Sizes: Women's 4–12 Slim–WW; Men's 6–15 Slim–DD.

SHOE DEPOT

280 Metro Center, 43 Colma Boulevard, Colma. (650) 755-0556. M–F 9–9, Sat 9–7, Sun 10–6. MC, VISA. Parking: lot.

When a steel-toe boot or heavy work shoe is necessary for OSHA's safety requirements on the job, Shoe Depot is the place; it has more work shoes than I've seen anywhere, starting at hard-to-find small sizes (6) and going up to 14, in widths D–EEE.

The discounts are decent. You'll also find athletic-style, casual, dress comfort, and traditional dress shoes. Some famous brands: Nunn Bush, Stacy Adams, Florsheim, Rockport, Dexter, Gorilla, Wolverine, and Georgia.

SHOE LOFT

225 Front Street (off California), San Francisco. (415) 956-4648. M–F 10–6, Sat 11–5. MC, VISA, AE, DIS. Parking: pay lots.
A dedicated portion of the Financial District's lunchtime women shoppers comes to the Shoe Loft for its better brands and size selection. It buys "after sale" stock from posh retail shoe stores. Of course, the standard sizes and widths are prevalent (Women's 4–12), but the hard-to-fit may find odd sizes as well (a few triple and quad widths). Prices are generally $25–$70.

SHOE PAVILION

899 Howard Street, Yerba Buena Square (at Fifth Street), San Francisco. (415) 974-1821. Daily. MC, VISA, AE, DIS. Parking: street/pay lots. (Other stores/outlet centers: 16 Bay Area stores; see Geographical Index.)

Shoe Pavilion describes itself as the "leading off-price retailer of quality brand-name footwear on the West Coast," offering women's shoes with 30–70% discounts daily on major brands. Although I feel the rapid expansion of this company has led to a decrease in the selection of "better" shoe brands, for the most part, the styles are very current and service is very accommodating. Prices range from $10 to $89 for shoes. Most discounts on current styles are in the 35% range. Check the displays that highlight the latest arrivals in full size ranges. Even shoes on the self-serve racks are often backed by additional sizes in the stock room, so don't hesitate to ask for your size. Good selection of men's shoes, too!

STRIDE-RITE

Outlets at Gilroy, Gilroy. (408) 842-1011. Daily. MC, VISA. Parking: lot.
Closeouts, slight irregulars, and past-season styles from Stride-Rite's shoe divisions are offered at 30% off every day. Specials on the "dump" tables take discounts down to 50–60% off retail. Sperry Top-Siders, Keds, and Stride-Rite shoes come in all sizes for everyone in the family.

TIMBERLAND

Napa Factory Outlets, Napa. (707) 259-1191.
Daily. MC, VISA, AE. Parking: lot.
(Other outlets: Gilroy center.)

Timberland has been a rising star in the shoe industry. Its rugged outdoor shoes have become fashionable as everyday streetwear. With success comes excess, and that leads to outlet stores. Discontinued styles and factory blems (cosmetic flaws) are discounted 30–50% off retail. There's a little of everything made by Timberland in the selection and it's all guaranteed. Sizes: Women's 5–10; Men's 7–13. About half the space at Timberland's outlets is devoted to its apparel (sportswear and outerwear) and accessory divisions for men and women. Just like the shoes, many styles of its weathergear are waterproof. Handbags, backpacks, duffel bags, gloves, and caps provide customers with head-to-toe cover options.

VANS

Factory Stores of America, Vacaville. (707) 447-8368. Daily. MC, VISA. Parking: lot.
(Other outlets: Anderson/Redding, Folsom, Gilroy, Petaluma, Tracy centers.)

Vans updates the classic canvas boat shoe with bold colors and prints. Entire families can choose comfortable fun shoes at this outlet; irregulars and discontinued styles keep the racks well stocked. Both lace-up and slip-on styles are available, plus some in suede. Vans fills a special niche with its snowboard and skateboarding shoes. Since the styles are more or less unisex, you can purchase by fit, or stick to Toddler 5–10½; Boys 2½–6; Youth 11–2; Women's 4–10; Men's 6½–13. Discounts 30–65% off original retail.

VERY SAN FRANCISCO

123 Second Street (between Mission and Howard), San Francisco. (415) 777-3140. MC, VISA, AE. Parking: street/pay lots.

A somewhat funky off-price store catering to the working crowd around the SOMA Financial District. Women's shoes are definitely geared to a younger crowd with labels like Doc Martens, Paulina,

Timberland, and then some Rockport for the comfort-first customer. Fashion-forward heels and flats along with urban street chukka boots suit everybody from secretaries to bike messengers. Men can buy a cross section of boots, casuals, or dress shoes from Rockport, Dexter, and others. Discounts are minimal to modest, but better than paying full retail. Check the racks at the back of the store for the best deals. An eclectic selection of giftwares and accessories add a little something extra to the mix of bargains.

WALKING CO./MEPHISTO OUTLET

Great Mall of the Bay Area, Milpitas. (408) 262-5105. Daily. MC, VISA, AE, DIS. Parking: lot. Before going on vacation, stop by this outlet, which is owned by the reliable Walking Company specialty shoe chain (eighteen retail stores). The Mephisto brand is the headliner here, with discount prices (30–50% off) on men's and women's discontinued styles and surplus inventory. These shoes are noted for the durability, comfort, support, and breathability of the natural materials used in each handmade pair of shoes. Other popular brands of walking shoes are carried: Rockport, Teva, Easy Spirit, Clark's, Soft Spots, and Timberland at close-out prices. Sizes: Women's 5–11½; Men's 5½–13½.

Also See

Under Famous Labels/Factory Stores:
ANN TAYLOR LOFT; GUESS?; LIZ CLAIBORNE

Under Bay Area Off-Price/Chain Discount Stores:
GROUP USA; LOEHMANN'S; RAFFIA

Under Family, Men's & Women's, General Clothing:
BURLINGTON COAT FACTORY; MARSHALLS; T.J. MAXX; J. CREW; STEIN MART

Under Children's Clothing:
KIDS R US

Under Clearance Centers:
NORDSTROM RACK; OFF FIFTH; TALBOTS

Under Appliances, Electronics, and Home Entertainment:
WHOLE EARTH ACCESS

Under Baby & Juvenile Furniture/Equipment
LIL' THINGS; TOTALLY 4 KIDS

Appliances, Electronics, and Home Entertainment

The superchains dominate the Bay Area appliance and home electronics market. Their volume purchasing power gives them a price advantage, but if you read the want ads, you'll see that they pay their sales "counselors" hefty commissions. These stores are careful to avoid blatant bait-and-switch tactics, but you can be sure that a salesperson is motivated to trade you up to models or brands that offer a larger commission and/or greater profits. In my opinion, most chains offer a "price guarantee" that is almost worthless. Each store appears to carry many exclusive models (known as "derivatives"). Typically the only difference between models at competing stores are in exterior color, finish, or other minor cosmetic or technical features. Good luck comparison shopping on the basis of model numbers! Since the numbers differ, it's very hard to meet the requirements for the price guarantee. Instead, you must note the features in detail to get a feel for comparative pricing. And when the sales-person starts pushing an extended service warranty, remember that stores consider such a warranty the best way to increase profits in times of intense competition for market share, which otherwise keeps profit margins low. These stores have driven many smaller operations out of business, but independents survive who operate with small margins, no commissions, and without the high overhead of the superchains. Shop smart! Take careful measurements of the existing space or cavity in your home for a replacement appliance so you don't spin your wheels selecting something that doesn't fit. Standard sizes of twenty years ago are not the standard anymore.

ABC APPLIANCE SERVICE

*2050 Taraval Street (at 31st Avenue), San
Francisco. (415) 564-8166, (800) 942-1242. M–Sat
9–4, Sun 10–1. MC, VISA, DIS. Parking: street.*
ABC's modest store lacks razzle-dazzle merchandising glamour. Its secret for low prices on major
brands of kitchen and laundry appliances is volume
purchasing. Most built-in appliances on display are
connected to gas, water, or electricity, allowing for
working demonstrations. That's convenient! Check
out the new displays of imported kitchen sinks and
faucets. ABC can provide immediate delivery on
most of the lines it carries. Phone quotes are given
(sometimes grudgingly when busy). Delivery
charges vary with the size of your order and distance involved.

AIRPORT APPLIANCES

*20286 Hesperian Boulevard, Hayward. (510) 783-
3494. M–F 9–8, Sat–Sun 10–6. MC, VISA, DIS.
Parking: lot.*
To survive competition from superstores, Airport
Appliances offers an aggressive pricing policy. The
selection of major brands in laundry and kitchen
appliances includes high-tech lines like Creda,

Bosch, Asko, Best Hoods, Thermador, Dacor
Gaggenau Dynasty, Viking, and Wolfe, which are
popular with remodelers. Designer faucets, sinks,
and custom-made countertops in Corian or laminates are offered at discount prices. Its kitchen
remodeling center offers semicustom European-
style cabinets. Prices are just competitive on
Mitsubishi, Toshiba, and Samsung electronics; the
store specializes in larger-screen TVs. Scratched
and dented items and factory closeouts can lower
prices significantly off original retail, or spend even
less on a selection of used appliances. Delivery to
almost anywhere (evening delivery and installation);
extra charges for installations and hook-ups.

APPLIANCE SALES & SERVICE

*655 Mission Street, San Francisco. (415) 362-7195,
M–F 8:30–5:30, Sat 9–5. MC, VISA, AE, DIS.
Parking: street/pay lot.*
Bargain hunters will really appreciate the selection
of as-is blems and factory seconds on many brands
of small appliances here. These were once display
models, samples, discontinued styles, or closeouts;
all pieces are mechanically perfect and carry a
manufacturer's warranty. All accessories and parts

are carried for these lines, which include air purifiers, espresso makers, water filtration units, pressure cookers, and electric shavers. There are also hard-to-find appliances such as egg cookers, large juicers, and meat grinders. Brands include Braun, Cuisinart, Rowenta, Oster, Sunbeam, Krups, Bionaire, West Bend, and KitchenAid, all at competitive prices. The store will special order any new item and can provide or order any replacement part or accessory for small appliances. And it ships anywhere via UPS.

BOSE FACTORY STORE

Outlets at Gilroy, Gilroy. (408) 842-2541. Daily.
MC, VISA, AE, DIS. Parking: lot.
(Other outlet: Petaluma center.)
If your curiosity has been piqued by national radio commentator Paul Harvey's testimonials on Bose products, a trip to the Bose Factory Store will allow you to hear first-hand what all the fuss is about. For the uninitiated, Bose is an American electronics manufacturing corporation with worldwide distribution. It's also the largest speaker and amplifier manufacturer in the world—the Bose stereo system is factory-installed in Mercedes-Benz and many top domestic car models. Although some of the Bose audio products are sold through retail outlets, others, like the WAVE radio and Acoustic Wave Music System, are sold only on a mail-order basis or through one of the company's nineteen factory stores in outlet centers around the country. The factory stores also sell "factory renewed" Bose products at minimal to modest savings (10–30%). When a product is returned for any reason, it may eventually qualify as a "factory renewed" product (a special seal is displayed on the item). Before it can be resold, the item goes through a rigorous retesting and remanufacturing process at Bose. The performance of a renewed product is the same as a factory-new product; both are subjected to the same testing and quality standards and have identical warranties. At the outlet, the WAVE radio sells for $349 new, and $314 renewed; the Acoustic Wave Music System (with built-in CD or cassette player) is $997 new and $897 renewed. Take a seat in the separate Bose Music Theater inside the outlet for a thirty-minute audiovisual Bose product demonstration.

CALIFORNIA AUDIO & VIDEO

*9550 Main Street, Penngrove. (707) 795-9065,
(800) 866-1222. M–F 10–7, Sat 10–6, Sun 11–5.
MC, VISA, AE. Parking: lot.*

You'll feel right at home here with the wide range
of audio and video products. VCRs, TVs, stereo
components, car stereos, telephones, answering
machines, video cameras, and most other high-tech
gadgets can be ordered if they're not in stock.
Lines represented include Acurus, Aragon, M & K,
JVC, Panasonic, Zenith, Hitachi, Mitsubishi, Proton,
Quasar, Magnavox, Harmon/Kardon, Aiwa, Onkyo,
JBL, Polk, Denon, Carver, Nakamichi, NHT, Infinity,
Yamaha, Bogen, and Pioneer. California Discount's
prices are very good every day and it tries to beat
any advertised special sale price. The folks who
work here do their best to provide all the attention
and help you need, especially if you've driven a
distance to do business with them. You'll get a
sound perspective when buying a fine audio/video
system after spending time in the comfortable
environment of the home theater room. You can
get phone quotes over the free 800 number and
have articles shipped anywhere. *Directions: Take
101 to the Penngrove exit, go right on Old*
*Redwood Highway one and a half miles, then right
on Main.*

CAMBRIDGE SOUNDWORKS
CLEARANCE CENTER

*702 Dubuque Avenue, South San Francisco. (650)
225-9500. M–Sat 10–8, Sun Noon–6. MC, VISA,
AE, DIS. Parking: lot.*

Cambridge is not giving away the store here—
instead, it's mostly small change. Located in front
of Cambridge's distribution warehouse, this center
sells discontinued models, refurbished or returned
products, and out-of-box or open box speakers
and electronics for discounted prices. Most of the
time you're saving a teensy 10–20% off the regular
or sale prices of its other Bay Area store; more
rarely, you'll save 25–40% on a closeout model.
Anything that's carried by Cambridge may be
found here: Harmon Kardon CD players, Pioneer
receivers, VCRs from JVC, Sony cassette decks,
etc. Everything is fully warranted with a 30-day
return or exchange policy. Its location on a frontage
road north of the San Francisco airport makes the
Cambridge Soundworks Clearance Center convenient for a quick stop to prospect for bargains.

CHERIN'S

727 Valencia Street, San Francisco. (415) 864-2111. M–F 9:30–5:30, Sat 10–5. Cash/Check. Parking: private lot at 18th and Valencia.

They must be doing something right—they've been in business since 1892 (the decor hasn't changed much since then). This is a great source for home appliances: refrigerators, freezers, washers, dryers, ranges, and microwave ovens. Remodelers can find esoteric brands like Wolf, Viking Range, Caloric, Asko, Miele, Sub-Zero, U.S. Range, Gaggenau, and Traulsen. If you're updating or upgrading and covet European-style appliances, you'll have plenty of options here. Cherin's also sells mainstream brands like GE, Maytag, Amana, Thermador, Dacor, and KitchenAid. It specializes in built-in appliances. Contractor prices prevail for everyone. Its business is mostly referral since it rarely advertises, and its low prices reflect a minimal markup. No price quotes over the phone. Delivery is free within the Bay Area.

FAMOUS BRAND ELECTRONICS

Factory Stores of America, Vacaville. (707) 447-7085. Daily. MC, VISA, AE, DIS. Parking: lot.

Tandy Corporation, the largest electronics retailer, has a big umbrella covering stores like Radio Shack and Computer City. With its industry connections and many stores it generates a fair amount of overstocks and closeouts, makes special purchases from the many vendors it deals with, and refurbishes many returned high-end products that failed initially after purchase. This creates an interesting mix of everything electronic at its company-owned clearance stores. Browse around and you'll find CB radios, electronic organs, CD players, TVs, VCRs, boom boxes, compact stereo systems, telephones, and household electronics like bread makers, vacuums, indoor grills, juicers, battery-operated toys, and many more things to plug in. Brands include Sony, Norelco, Radio Shack, Seiko, Panasonic, Sanyo, JVC, Waring, Jensen, Uniden, and others. Prices are reduced 30–70% off every day, and most products come complete with full warranties.

FILCO

1433 Fulton Avenue, Filco Plaza, Sacramento.
(916) 483-4526. M–F 10–7, Sat 10–6, Sun 11–5.
MC, VISA, DIS. Parking: lot.
(Other stores: Chico, Citrus Heights, Folsom, Lodi.)
Filco offers an extensive selection in cameras, appliances, home entertainment, and electronics at minimal markup. Prices on cellular phones keep competitors steaming, but consumers have no complaints. Most major brands of 35mm cameras, accessories, and instant cameras are in stock at terrific prices. Kodak film is sold at cost. Filco's on-site processing is its loss leader. Jenn-Air, KitchenAid, Panasonic, Whirlpool, Amana, Sony, GE, Sub-Zero, Mitsubishi, Hitachi, Quasar, RCA, Onkyo, and Bose are a few of the major brands found in appliances and home entertainment.

FRIEDMAN'S MICROWAVE

2301 Broadway, Oakland. (510) 444-1119. M–F
10–5:30, Sat 10–5. VISA, AE, DIS. Parking: street.
(Other stores: Dublin, Hayward, Palo Alto, Pleasant
Hill, San Francisco, Santa Clara, San Rafael.)
I approach the purchase of a new appliance as if I were planning the invasion of Normandy. Enter Friedman's Microwave. It sells a full range of microwaves from the most basic and inexpensive models up to top-of-the-line types. The prices are competitive with superstores. Thanks to a price guarantee, weekly free classes in microwave cooking, trade-in allowance, and 20% discounts on accessories (including carts) bought with the microwave (10% thereafter), you come out the winner. Most of all, you'll appreciate the information provided by the staff in a sane, no-pressure atmosphere. The Oakland store is also an "as-is" center for GE microwaves.

FRY'S ELECTRONICS

1177 Kern Avenue, Sunnyvale. (408) 733-1770.
M–F 8–9, Sat 9–8, Sun 9–7. MC, VISA. Parking: lot.
(Other stores: Campbell, Fremont, Milpitas,
Palo Alto.)
Fry's is well established with tech types for computers and related products. Also, home and office electronics, high-tech toys and gadgets, TVs, boom boxes, cordless phones, speakers, CD players, cassette players, satellite dishes, and fax machines—enough to keep you wandering the aisles for hours. Very competitive prices!

HOUSE OF LOUIE

1045 Bryant Street (at Ninth Street), San Francisco. (415) 621-7100, (800) 99-LOUIE. M–Sat 9–6, Sun Noon–5. MC, VISA, DIS. Parking: small side lot; street.

House of Louie offers aggressive pricing on kitchen and laundry appliances, televisions, VCRs, and bedding. Its bilingual staff is appreciated by many consumers. It's also very sharp on prices! It can't always beat loss-leader "door buster" prices, but what you want usually isn't the "door buster" anyway. House of Louie offers an everyday and upscale selection of brands, including Wolfe ranges and cooktops, Bosch and Asko dishwashers, KitchenAid, Amana, GE, Whirlpool, Sub-Zero, Jenn-Air, Dacor, etc. You'll see Sony and Panasonic TVs from small "spare room" sets up to huge 53-inch Videoscope units; the more expensive the model, the greater the savings are likely to be. You can also resort to catalogs. Upstairs is a room full of mattress sets from Simmons, Beautyrest, BackCare, and Maxipedic at solid discounts. The furniture selection is rather ho-hum, definitely not for upscale buyers.

OEMI INC.

102 Grand Avenue (corner of Airport Boulevard), South San Francisco. (650) 872-6668. M–F 9–5, Sat 11–3. MC, VISA. Parking: lot.

If you're in the market for a typewriter of any configuration, basic to computerized, you'll find an in-depth selection at Oemi. Its prices are just about the lowest around because it often skips U.S. distributors to buy directly from manufacturers. Many repairs and some warranty work done on the premises. There are also some used manual machines. Oemi's prices on computers, printers, office copiers, fax machines, dictation equipment, overhead projectors, calculators, and cash registers are competitive with deep-discount chains. Many used, demo, discontinued, or closeout items available at extra discounts. Oemi also takes trade-ins and buys and trades equipment. All sales final!

ORION TELESCOPE CENTER

3609 Buchanan Street, San Francisco. (415) 931-9966; catalog requests (800) 447-1001. T–Sat 10–5:30. MC, VISA. Parking: lot.
(Other stores: Cupertino, Watsonville.)

Orion is the largest telescope firm in North America; its catalog is very helpful to consumers in the prepurchase stage. Get set to view celestial wonders by doing your homework, then contact the Orion Telescope Center. If you know what you want, you can order over the phone by credit card. Or you can stop by and pick the brains of the pros on the staff. You can gaze through models from Celestron, Pentax, Edmund Scientific, Orion, and Televue. Naturally, all the esoteric accessories you haven't even thought of buying, but will eventually, are available. Orion also sells binoculars, spotting scopes, photographic accessories, and telescope-making parts. And you're going to save 10–30% on anything you buy!

REED SUPPLY

1328 Fruitvale Avenue, Oakland. (510) 436-7171. M–Sat 9:30–5. Cash/Check. Parking: lot.

You'll be surprised at the selection of kitchen and laundry appliances that can be crammed into this relatively small space. Major brands, including status lines popular with architects and kitchen planners, are sold at very good prices. If you have special installation problems, you'll be referred to someone who can do the job. Reed also sells kitchen cabinets (Omega, Westwood, Mid Continent), bathroom vanities, custom counter-tops (including Corian, marble, and maple), green-house windows, water heaters, shower doors, wall heaters, Cadillac lines of faucets, and more. Something really esoteric on your list? You can special order from catalogs. Working on a low markup, Reed essentially sells to everyone at con-tractors' prices. Beware: At times the staff is stretched too thin for prompt service. Delivery charges relate to distance involved.

REMINGTON SALES & SERVICE

84 Second Street, San Francisco. (415) 495-7060. M–F 8:30–5, Sat 9–5.. MC, VISA, AE, DIS. Parking: lot.
(Other stores/outlets: Gilroy, Milpitas, Vacaville centers.)

At the Remington store you'll obviously find shavers and trimmers of all description for men and women (face, leg, nose, ear, mustache, etc.), as well as parts and accessories. But that's not all. There are knives for every use: Swiss Army knives, cutlery sets, and kitchen knives, Henckels, Buck knives, and other knives I'm not sure how to describe except that some looked fairly menacing (the Fury Scimitar, for example). A good selection of flashlights, Maglights, knife sharpeners, and whetstones, manicure sets, scissors (all uses), and travel aids complete the inventory. Discounts from minimal to fairly good. Service done on shavers at San Francisco store only.

SAN JOSE HONDA/SONY

1610 S. First Street, San Jose. (408) 294-6632, (800) 297-6692. M–F 10–7, T and Th 10–8, Sat 9–5:30, Sun Noon–5. MC, VISA, DIS. Parking: lot.

San Jose Honda/Sony is hard to beat with Sony devotees. An authorized dealer, its focus is on volume sales at discount prices, and it monitors the competition closely to make sure it beats everyone. TVs in all configurations and sizes including big screen. VCRs, 8mm camcorders, laser disc players, telephones, minirack stereo systems, and audio components at good prices, too. The showroom is filled with boxed units ready for your car trunk. The store can provide setup and delivery for a reasonable price.

SEARS FURNITURE & APPLIANCE OUTLET

1982 West Avenue at 140th, San Leandro. (510) 895-0546. M–F 10–7, Saturday 9–6, Sun 11–5. MC, VISA, AE, DIS, SEARS. Parking: lot.

If you're not adverse to a dent or scratch somewhere on the surface of a refrigerator, washer, range, freezer, or water heater, then the mammoth Sears Outlet in San Leandro may be just the place to go when you need an immediate replacement.

The appliances are out of carton and may be categorized as discontinued, previously used, and/or reconditioned. Outlet merchandise may be reduced 20–60% percent off original retail; however the average appliance markdown is 20–40% percent. These are worthwhile savings given the slim profit margins in this competitive category of the marketplace. The selection includes any of the major appliances that may have been sold at a regular Sears store, from top-of-the-line to the most basic level. Each item is tagged and noted with an explanation of its status—used, reconditioned, damaged, discontinued, etc. "Used" applies to anything that was delivered to a customer and then returned whether there was any "actual" use or not. The Sears Outlet also has many larger-size televisions (27-inch to over 60-inch screens) at good markdowns. A 52-inch RCA model (used, damaged, and reconditioned) was marked down to $1,339 from $1,999; a 50-inch Hitachi was $1,499 from $2,799 (also used, damaged, and reconditioned); and a 35-inch RCA Proscan was $1,299 from $1,999.

About half the 70,000-square-foot warehouse is filled with furniture from Sears' Northern California furniture departments and individual HomeLife stores. Upholstered pieces, formal and casual dining room sets, bedroom sets, occasional pieces, mattress sets, and lots of one-of-a-kinds and odd pieces fill the space. All products are fully warranted functionally. No warranty on cosmetic damages. All sales are covered by a 30-day return policy—return for any reason with sales receipt and accessories included. Not to worry, all the operating manuals are available, and essential operating parts are included. No delivery or installation is offered; instead, referrals are provided to local services/individuals. Typically, there are independent delivery trucks and personnel on-site ready to give immediate service. Merchandise can be held for three days while arrangements are made.
Directions: From Fwy. 880, take Marina exit heading west. Turn left at Merced, right at West Avenue to 140th Street.

SHARPER IMAGE OUTLET

Great Mall of the Bay Area, Milpitas. (408) 956-8373. Daily. MC, VISA, AE, DIS, DC. Parking: lot.
Merchandise in the Sharper Image catalog is high-tech and usually expensive. At its clearance center you'll save 20–50% on overstocks, one-of-a-kind products, samples, closeouts, returns, and slightly damaged items from its stores. Pick up executive toys and more eclectic and esoteric items like novelty phones, security gadgets, exercise equipment, jewelry, luggage, executive cases, golf and ski products, and just about anything else in its catalog. About 20–30% of the inventory is current at straight retail pricing.

TELECENTER

1830 S. Delaware Street, San Mateo. (415) 341-5804. M, W, F 9–6, T, Th 9–8, Sat 9–5, Sun Noon–5. MC, VISA, DIS. Parking: lot.
Telecenter's prices are very competitive with other stores and superstores. Telecenter carries brand names in kitchen and laundry appliances (popular new high-end appliances for remodeling projects), plus TVs, video equipment, stereos, and more. There's no aggressive sales bafflegab here. If you're working with a contractor, you'll get a contractor's discount if you can provide their name and license number. Modest delivery charges.

VIDEO ONLY

24040 Hesperian Boulevard, Hayward. (510) 785-1470. M–F 10–9, Sat 10–7, Sun 11–4. MC, VISA. Parking: lot.
(Other stores: Dublin, San Mateo, San Francisco.)
They keep it simple and specialize in selling TVs, VCRs, camcorders, and home theater audio. All the leading brands, too: Quasar, Panasonic, Toshiba, Hitachi, Sony, JVC, RCA, Magnavox, General Electric, Zenith, Yamaha, Technics, and more. Prices are very competitive with the big guys around town, and the service and pace of business is more consumer friendly. Keep track of local ads and you can hold them to their "double your money" low-price guarantee—though I doubt very many buyers have ever needed to.

WHOLE EARTH ACCESS

*2990 Seventh Street (at Ashby), Berkeley. (510)
845-3000. M–F 10–7, Sat–Sun 10–6. MC, VISA.
Parking: lot.*
(Other stores: San Francisco; San Rafael.)
Not only are the values and selection appealing,
Whole Earth Access is a neat place to shop. There's
a special emphasis on major home appliances,
power and hand tools, cameras, binoculars, and
sunglasses, plus an extensive consumer electronics
department with stereo systems, radios, VCRs,
camcorders, TVs, and a complete computer and
software department. Competitive pricing is a top
priority. You'll find leading brands in kitchen,
housewares, and home accessories departments,
plus mattress sets, lighting, home storage, and
appealing lifestyle furniture including popular pine
bedroom furniture for adults and children. Also,
look to Whole Earth for modestly discounted natural-fiber sportswear and shoes.

Also See

Under Cameras:
SAN JOSE CAMERA & VIDEO

Under Catalog Furniture Discounters:
**DAVID MORRIS CO.; DEOVLET & SONS;
GIORGI FURNITURE; MILLBRAE FURNITURE
COMPANY**

Under General Merchandise—Membership
Warehouse Clubs:
PRICE/COSTCO; SAM'S CLUB

Cameras and Photography

If you're looking for a camera that requires no fancy accessories or particular savvy, you're probably in the market for something under $100—a basic point-and-shoot, no-hassle model. Your best bet is to rely on local superstores, which frequently offer promotional pricing on these cameras. Check ads for KMart, Target, WalMart, and Circuit City, or visit Price/Costco or Sam's Club. On the other hand, if you're serious about your photography and investing in esoteric camera equipment, look in on the local resources listed below or consider the many mail-order companies that advertise extensively in publications like *Popular Photography*. Ordering by mail, especially when dealing with brand-name products, can be a time- and money-saving option if you've done your homework and follow sensible consumer guidelines. The trade-off for mail-order savings? You forgo the personal service and technical support that local camera shops offer. I've listed two mail-order companies that my shutter-bug friends consistently recommend for price and reliability. One other essential is required before tackling the advertisements, which can cover many pages: a magnifying glass!

ALPHA PHOTO PRODUCTS
380 Lang Road, Burlingame. (650) 696-9444, (800) 734-8745. M–F 9–6, Sat 10–5. MC, VISA, DIS, AE. Parking: lot.
Alpha Photo offers a lot to professionals: photographic supplies, graphic arts and presentation equipment, materials, and more. I suspect many consumers will focus on the albums, particularly wedding albums, not often found in retail stores (these are the fancy leather, premium-priced wedding albums sold in wedding-photo packages by most photographers). If you're willing to do the work of assembling an album, you can order all the components from a professional photographer's line carried at this distribution center. Several styles

and configurations are available. You choose the cover set, the leaves (pages), mats, etc. There are minimum orders for the leaves and mats (packages of six or twelve), but the prices are so reasonable you won't mind ending up with a few extras. Some components may have to be special ordered (like leather cover sets). Stop by and pick up a catalog. Located in a commercial business district east and south of the Broadway exit off 101.

B & H PHOTO-VIDEO (MAIL ORDER)

119 W. 17th Street, New York, NY, 10011. Orders: (800) 947-6628 (photo), (800) 947-1175 (video and imaging). Fax (800) 947-7008. Information: (212) 444-6670. MC, VISA, DIS.
Camcorders, VCRs, video monitors, videotape, printers, microphones, editing equipment, and other essentials for professionals fill this company's ad pages. Ordinary folks will zero in on binoculars, cameras, lenses, film, and accessories.

CAMBRIDGE CAMERA EXCHANGE, INC. (MAIL ORDER)

Seventh Avenue and 13th Street, New York, NY, 10011. Orders: (800) 221-2253. 24-hour fax order line: (212) 463-0093. Information: (212) 675-8600. Customer relations: (212) 255-3744. MC, VISA, DIS, C.O.D.
A good resource for amateurs and professionals— you could set up your own studio and darkroom by ordering from Cambridge. Some video cameras, camcorders, telephones, radios; accessories for all categories, too. Used department to sell and trade. Write for free Cambridge Camera catalog.

L.Z. PREMIUMS

241 E. Campbell Avenue, Campbell. (408) 374-3838. T–Sat 10–6. MC, VISA, and financing. Parking: lot.
L.Z. has a loyal shutterbug following for its prices on cameras, accessories, and developing equipment. Kodak film is sold at dealer's cost; Kodak processing is 30% off. Major appliances, electronics (VCRs, faxes, beepers, home and car stereos), cameras (new and used), camera gear, and cellular phones are also sold. The floor selection is very

limited, but their large catalog library extends your options. Prices reflect a modest markup, and delivery charges are reasonable. Forget hype and hustle; the staff is knowledgeable and low-pressure. No phone quotes.

PHOTOGRAPHERS LIGHTING

436 Bryant Street, San Francisco. (415) 882-9380, (800) 833-0060. M–F 8–6:30, Sat 9–5. MC, VISA, DIS. Parking: garage at 435 Bryant.
Professionals spend hours browsing through the inventory here. There are two angles to this operation: This company rents lighting equipment, grips, and medium-format cameras, and sells flashes, strobes, adapters, grip equipment, background paper, and other professional stuff. It claims to have the lowest prices on seamless paper in the country. Local pros wait for the first Saturday each December, when rental equipment with a lot of usefulness left is sold off.

PHOTOGRAPHERS STUDIO SUPPLY

432 Bryant Street, San Francisco. (415) 495-5145, (800) 447-5888. M–F 9–5:30, Sat 10–5. MC, VISA, DIS. Parking: garage at 435 Bryant.
This company serves the professional photographers and graphic arts firms that are concentrated in the SOMA area. The emphasis is on supplying products for mounting, storage, and presentation—allowing for direct purchase of many items that must often be bought through mail-order companies. Except for some very esoteric items, everything is discounted. Photography students, hobbyists, and other consumers seek out this resource to purchase albums, mount board, foam core, and archival papers for mats. All too often when one needs mat board for mounting, it can only be purchased in large sheets. Sizes here start at 8 by 10 inches. Many appreciate the use of the dry mount press and mat cutter here for a small fee. Check the bargain tables for "whatever." Don't hassle with street parking; pull into the garage across the street for Photographers Lighting.

PHOTOGRAPHERS SUPPLY

576 Folsom Street, San Francisco. (415) 495-8640.
M–F 9–5:30, Sat 9:30–5, Sun 11–4. MC, VISA.
Parking: spaces provided.
If you're a novice, bring a knowledgeable friend.
This is for serious photographers who buy film,
paper, and chemicals in quantity and relinquish
seminars at the cash register in favor of a discount
up to 25% on Kodak film. Everything for the darkroom too. Feel secure with its roster of brands:
Kodak, Fuji, Agfa, and Ilford films and papers for
starters.

SAN JOSE CAMERA & VIDEO

1600 Winchester Boulevard, Campbell. (408)
374-1880. M–Sat 10–6, Th 10–8, Sun Noon–5.
MC, VISA, DIS. Parking: lot.
Photo buffs looking for sophisticated and usually
expensive cameras and accessories will feel right
at home here. Most major brands are on hand:
Canon, Nikon, Olympus, Vivitar, Minolta, Pentax,
Hasselblad, Mamiya, Leica, Gitzo, Yashica, Ricoh,
Fuji, Bogen, Kodak, Metz and Beseler enlargers,
Kodak carousel projectors, and Gossen exposure
meters. Keeping up with the market, a full line of
advanced photo system cameras are carried, as
well as digital cameras. This shop aggressively discounts video cameras from Canon, Nikon, Quasar,
and Minolta, ruffling the feathers of other dealers
by not playing ball and offering products at higher
prices, as they do. This place is a hero to consumers.
For a close-up look at the world, check out the
binocular department. You'll probably get the lowest price in the Bay Area by shopping here. Save
gas if you're out of the area; order by phone and
have it shipped UPS.

Also See

Under Appliances, Electronics, and Home
Entertainment:
FILCO; WHOLE EARTH ACCESS

Under General Merchandise:
MEMBERSHIP WAREHOUSE CLUBS

Computers

The Bay Area abounds with computer stores. Trying to pick just a few and applying the label "bargain" is extremely difficult. Prices, products, locations, and the marketing direction of various stores tend to change so often I'm wary about making recommendations. There are so many variables to this market—whether you're buying a branded product or a clone, which system you're buying, whether you're trying to build one yourself, etc.—that it can hardly be covered with a few recommendations. Choosing a store on the basis of price alone may lead to nothing but frustration if the service and support you need is not part of the price. When canvassing other computer users I find that their advice is most often based on a special relationship they have developed with a particular store or dealer, though some choose stores based on price rather than support. Some hard cases think the best way to spend a day off is perusing the esoterica of the computer market at someplace like Fry's Electronics or Comp USA, while novices will undoubtedly end up on sensory overload and feel like their brains have been scrambled. Price buyers tend to be folks who can whip off the top of their system unit, pull a screwdriver out of their pocket, and add new chips, cards, drives, or other hardware without any apprehension at all.

I suggest networking with high-tech friends or user groups to lead you to businesses with a reputation for good prices and support. Your local user group is hands-down your best resource for all kinds of information, shopping recommendations, and free public domain software. Finding a dealer in the Bay Area is not difficult. After you've passed the novice stage, you'll find bargain-priced resources for software and add-on hardware (memory, modems, boards, et al.) located all over the Bay Area, particularly in Silicon Valley.

Two valuable Bay Area publications for information on microcomputers are *Computer Currents* and *MicroTimes*. They provide practical computer information for businesses, professionals, serious home users, and absolute novices. They have question-and-answer columns, let you know what's available in the Bay Area, and list services and products, events and classes to attend, and organizations and user groups to join. *Computer Currents* and *MicroTimes* are distributed from hundreds of locations in seven counties around the Bay. You're most likely to find them in local libraries, colleges, adult education facilities, record stores, video and electronic stores, and anyplace where high-tech people are likely to hang out. If you can't find one, call their offices 9–5. Another useful publication for the beginner is *Smart Computing*, written in "plain" English and directed to the novice and intermediate user. See below for information about where to find copies.

COMPUTER CURRENTS

(510) 527-0333 to find local distribution points or for subscription information.

MICROTIMES

(510) 934-3700 to find local distribution points or for subscription information.

SMART COMPUTING

(800) 848-1478 for information.
Available at most magazine counters.

Art, Craft, and Hobby Supplies

AMSTERDAM ART

1013 University Avenue, Berkeley. (510) 649-4800. M–Sat 9:30–6, Th 9:30–8, Sun 11–6. MC, VISA, DIS, AE. Parking: lot.
(Other stores: San Francisco, Walnut Creek.)
Here's an excellent resource with virtually everything for drafting, graphics, and fine arts. The store's second floor is chock full of graphic, architectural, and engineering resources. Discounts are from 20% to 40% on all major brands of art supplies and fine arts tools. You'll delight in the complete selection of fixings that makes it a cinch to prepare a flyer or notice for printing, even for an absolute novice. Amsterdam's fine paper department offers more than 700 types of papers. Fine writing instruments from Montblanc, Parker, Waterman, Sheaffer, Aurora, Tombow, and Lamy are all sold at 10–20% discounts. Amsterdam has a good selection of prefab frames at solid discount prices; precut mats, discounts on glass and framing sections for the do-it-yourselfer; and in-house custom frame orders competitively priced with other frame shops. Pay attention to special promotions and closeouts for super savings.

ANGRAY FANTASTICO

559 Sixth Street, San Francisco. (415) 982-0680. M–F 7–5:30, Sat 8:30–4. Cash/Check. Parking: street/lot.
Fantastico's warehouse has just about everything for craft-oriented people. It stocks an extensive selection of dried and silk flowers (exotic specimens you see beautifully arranged in fancy stores), plus all the makings to put them together: tapes, wires, ribbons, foam, etc. My favorite is florist ribbon in rolls for gift wrapping at one-third the cost of the Hallmark kind. Its aisle of ribbons is unsurpassed. Come here for holiday decorations and ideas. It also has baskets, plastic flowers and fruits, dollhouses, ceramics, garden statuary, and many

accessory items. Prices to the general public are usually 10–30% lower than stores closer to home, except for paper party supplies, which are competitive with all the other party discount stores. Nice wedding department, and 10% off on wedding and party invitations from several books.

ART EXCHANGE

77 Geary Boulevard, Second Floor, San Francisco.
(415) 956-5750. T–Sat 11:30–5:30. MC, VISA.
Parking: street.

The Art Exchange is a wonderful resource for those who have art that no longer fits their lifestyles. Perhaps they've moved, gone through a divorce, inherited art that doesn't suit their decor or taste, or redecorated. The gallery resells artwork, including paintings, sculpture, prints, and other objets d'art. The only requirement is that it be original: no reproductions like posters or photographs. The emphasis is on contemporary art. There are watercolors, monoprints, woodcuts, sculptures, carvings, etchings, oils, and more, at prices ranging from $300 to $3,000 (some works to $25,000) and including the works of famous artists like Henrietta Berk, Gary Bukovnik, Richard Diebenkorn, David

Hockney, Roy Lichtenstein, Joan Miró, and Robert Motherwell alongside those of lesser-known talents. Before you bring your art in, call the owner to discuss what you'd like to place on consignment, and its price. When the work is sold, the gallery gets one-third of the selling price. Documentation about the artist or the work is especially desirable.

ARTS & CRAFT SUPPLIES OUTLET

41 14th Street, San Francisco. (415) 431-7122.
M–F 9–4. MC, VISA. Parking: street.
(Other store: Annex, 50 13th Street, San Francisco.
Sat only 10–5.)

Arts & Craft Supplies is an outlet for an importer and distributor of many of the categories of merchandise you find in major arts and crafts supply stores: painting supplies, acrylic paints, pens, glues, lace, transfer type, paper goods, beads (lots and lots!), macramé, inks, brushes, basketry, doll parts and accessories, craft patterns and magazines, jewelry findings, jute, oil paints, floral supplies, wedding and shower favors, and more. Organization may not be the outlet's strong suit, but keeping such a convoluted inventory in order would defy all but the pathologically organized. Most folks like the mess—it seems more in keeping with one's expectation of an outlet. Pick up a shopping basket—I guarantee you'll find goodies you didn't know you wanted as you stroll along the long wall, with its merchandise dangling off Peg-Boards and stashed on shelves. Discontinued or surplus merchandise is usually at least 50% off original retail. (Expect some surprises—the company picks up some very interesting inventory, buying up entire booths at trade shows.) Small craft manufacturers or anyone else interested in volume purchases may have access to additional discounts. Inquire! Shop on Saturdays at the company's annex, located a block away.

BEESWAX CANDLE ART OUTLET

5743-D Landregan, Emeryville. (510) 547-8469. W only Noon–5:30 (or by appt.). MC, VISA, DIS. Parking: street.

Make sure it's Wednesday (or call for an appointment) before setting out to replenish your candle stock. This outlet sells two lines of candles: one specifically for Jewish holidays, the other perfect for anytime lovely candles are appropriate. They're made from honeycomb beeswax, which gives

them a distinctive finish. Most candles are sold in boxes or in pairs and priced 30–50% below retail as seconds or overruns. A 12-inch pair of dinner candles at retail runs about $10; for overruns you'll pay about $6. Pillars, fluted tapers, chime, and birthday candles in gorgeous colors add beauty to entertaining and special holiday occasions. The Shabbat, Chanukah, and Havdalah candles are dripless, virtually smokeless, and emit a fresh honey scent. Make your own candles after buying sheets of honeycomb beeswax and the candlemaking kits that are sold here. Beeswax candles in all shapes and sizes work especially well with rustic accessories and decorations that are popular now—the new "natural" look sweeping the home accessories industry. An unusual selection of candleholders are priced at $2 to $50. Add your name to the mailing list for invitations to special sales prior to Chanukah and Christmas. Call for new Berkeley or Emeryville address and extended hours in fall of 1997.

THE CANDLE FACTORY

*21 Duffy Place (at Irwin Street), San Rafael. (415)
457-3610. M–F 9–5, Sat 10–5. MC, VISA.
Parking: lot.*

Candles not only add atmosphere, but actually
tend to slow life down to a more relaxed pace. We
need to use them more often, instead of reserving
them just for special occasions. Increase your stash
by stopping by the Candle Factory, where you'll
find your senses overpowered by the combined
fragrances of the thirty-one scents used in candlemaking here. Because the candles are made on
the premises, you can buy at factory prices. These
dripless and smokeless candles are made of
organic domestic ingredients, and it's claimed
they outburn imported ones. Occasionally you'll
find specials when a wheel runs off color or a tint
proves unpopular. Seeking wellness? Then you'll
appreciate the line of holistic healing candles.

CANDLE OUTLET

*1010 North Idaho (between Howard and
Bayswater, off Amphlett), San Mateo. (650) 343-
0804. T–Sat 10–6. Cash/Check. Parking: street.*

At this fragrant and cozy little outlet, discontinued
candles, seconds, and occasional surplus candles
are reduced in price at least 50% off original
retails. The manufacturer keeps some very high
profile company: it supplies tapers and gift candles to trendsetting lifestyle stores, major department stores, and upscale gift stores and provides
candles under private labels for famous collections.
Except for the tapers, all the candles are scented
with fragrances made exclusively in France (vanilla,
cedar, bergamot, ylang-ylang, exotic woods, mel-
on/cucumber, etc.). There also are some aro-
matherapy candles with 100% essential oils in the
collection.

The candles are distinctive—rounds in several sizes
have inset designs around the sides of the candles,
including flowers, herbs, leaves, starfish, cinnamon
sticks, hot red peppers, even dressmaker buttons
(in silver or gold), or stars. The patterns are illumi-
nated as the candles burn down through the center

(no drips over the sides). Plain candle rounds come in a crayon-box range of colors. Assume anything wrapped in cellophane is first quality; other "bare" candles are usually seconds.

The candle beauties are pricey at retail—a 3- by-3-inch round $12 to $14 at retail is only $6 as a discontinued first ($5 as a second). A first-quality 4-by-6-inch round is $28 to $34 at retail, $12 at the outlet. 6- by-6-inch three-wick candles are $20 at the outlet; plain (but fragrant) 3-by-9-inch columns are $8, and square-shaped aromatherapy candles are $5. Dripless, smokeless, unscented tapers range in length to 24 inches. Lots of little candle accessories are left over from this outlet's production—terra-cotta pots, flat bases (tiles, recycled glass) to protect furniture, and other goodies. Locals stop in frequently to scout for bimonthly special promotions. Expanded hours between Thanksgiving and Christmas.

CHEAP PETE'S FRAME FACTORY OUTLET

4720 Geary Boulevard, San Francisco. (415) 221-4720. M–Sat 10–6, W–Th until 8, Sun Noon–5. MC, VISA, DIS. Parking: street.
(Other stores: 11 East Fourth Avenue, San Mateo; Montecito Plaza, San Rafael; 1666 Locust Street, Walnut Creek.)

If you have travel posters, prints, and family photos languishing in your closets and drawers because the cost of framing far exceeds the price of the picture, Cheap Pete's comes to the rescue with more than 10,000 ready-made frames in sizes ranging from 3- by-5 inch to 30- by-40 inch, including hard-to-find 4- by-6 and 5-by-5. The frames, available in metal, Plexiglas, and wood (styles for all decors), are wonderfully discounted. Also table-top, collage, and frames for gift giving. You'll achieve maximum savings (20–60% off) if you select a ready-made frame; on custom framing expect savings of 20–40% off pricey frame shops. Labor costs and overhead are kept down by doing custom work on a production-line basis. Also, volume purchasing of frames and using leftover materials result in the discount prices.

COLLECTOR'S CORNER ART GALLERY

2441 San Ramon Valley Boulevard #4, Diablo Plaza, San Ramon. (510) 829-3428. M–Sat 10–6, Sun Noon–5. MC, VISA. Parking: lot.

Collector's Corner sells original art—numbered and limited editions—at nicely discounted prices. Its inventory is quite eclectic, ranging from very modest prints to more expensive (investment) pieces priced in the hundreds and even thousands. By far the largest part of the selection is in the middle range of framed pieces selling for $195 to $350. Markdowns on designated pieces can reach 30–40% off comparable prices at other galleries. Those able to spend big bucks (thousands) might be able to order a piece of art that they have seen in another fine art gallery and save 20–40% on the framed piece. The selection will appeal to the sophisticated connoisseur as well as those who simply want an affordable lithograph. Written certification on everything guarantees authenticity. Artists in the collection include Pradzynski, Behrens, Rockwell, Eidenberger, Hatfield, Buckles, Thomas Kinkade, Mark King, Susan Rios, Barbara Wood, Jack Terry, G. Gordon Harvey, and many others. Framing prices are about 20–30% below typical frame shops.

DHARMA TRADING CO.

1604 Fourth Street (corner of F Street), San Rafael. (415) 456-1211. M–Sat 10–6. MC, VISA, DIS. Parking: lot.

If the textile artist in you needs an avenue for expression, Dharma Trading can provide the essentials for you to "paint your wardrobe." It carries dyes and coloring agents for fabric painting, silk-screening, batiking, etc. The company provides excellent information and how-to advice. It also offers a wide range of cotton and silk fabrics ready for dyeing. Even better, each piece in its extensive inventory of ready-made clothing for babies, children, and adults in "naked white" cotton and silk needs only a dip in the dye or a brush stroke before it's transformed into an original creation. Apparel includes baby sets, basic T-shirts, bodywear, dresses, jumpers, scarf blanks, rompers, and other styles. The store's yarn brings in many women, who carefully check for special markdowns on this out-of-the ordinary selection. Dharma satisfies the needs of "cottage industry" apparel manufacturers as well as just plain folks. To get the full picture, write or call for a catalog: P.O. Box 150916, San Rafael, CA 94915, or (800) 542-5227.

ELITE PICTURE FRAMES (MAIL ORDER)

1547 Jayken Way #B, Chula Vista, CA, 91911. (800) 854-6606. M–Sat 7–3:30. MC, VISA.

This mail-order company specializes in preassembled frames and wood sectionals for assembling your own frames at home. Many preassembled frames come complete with linen liners (some with gold or wood lips) in many different finishes: antique white, Renaissance gold, walnut, driftwood, cherry, oak, pewter, etc. Prices are good: a 12-by-16-inch frame ranges from $12.50 to $29.50. Custom wood sectionals are sold by the pair. The framing finishes available offer lots of design choices—traditional, ornate, contemporary, or natural, in widths ranging from ¾ to 2½ inches. Order two pairs for a frame and you'll receive four miter clips for easy joining. No special tools are needed, although wood glue is recommended for more secure joining. (Glue and hangers are not included.) To finish the project you may have to go to a local resource for mats and glass. Nielsen metal sectionals, linen liners, Fredrix stretched canvas, and oval stretched canvas are also available. The catalog features color pictures of its frames, but if you're still not certain about a particular framing finish, you can order samples for a small charge (to cover shipping). Call for a catalog and join all the corporations, schools, and galleries that have discovered this money-saving option for framing.

FRAMERS WORKSHOP

156 Russ Street, San Francisco. (415) 621-4226. M–F 9–5:30, Sat 9–2. MC, VISA. Parking: limited street (two spaces marked Tenant Only).

This is a do-it-yourself frame shop only if you buy all the materials and assemble them at home, an option for artists who find that the $6.39–$13.50 assembly charge adds up when they're framing many pictures for exhibit or sale. Aluminum framing and custom wood frames are available. You can select budget-priced materials to frame an inexpensive picture or print, or go first class with museum-quality materials for conservation mounting of fine artworks. Prices on aluminum frames are often lower than at do-it-yourself frame shops, even when all the work is done for you. Prices on basic conservation matting are also lower, but on the more elaborate fabric and French detail mats, Framers is competitive.

GENERAL BEAD

*637 Minna Street, San Francisco. (415) 621-8187.
T–Sat 10–4, Sun 1–4. VISA, MC. Parking: street.*
The General Bead store in San Francisco is a serious
bead wholesaler and the largest bead retailer in
Northern California. Anyone willing to meet wholesale minimums (which vary from item to item) can
buy at wholesale. However, those without resale
numbers will have to pay appropriate taxes. Those
interested in buying in smaller quantities will be
charged retail prices. The store's strength is its
high-fashion beads for the style-conscious client.
Its main focus is on glass beads and on Austrian
crystal pieces. The beads, in all varieties (ethnic,
glass, bone, shell, pearl, antique, sterling, crystal,
ceramic, brass, etc.) from around the world, are
not readily available anyplace else. With two floors
and 25,000 items in inventory, General Bead offers
artists fabric dyes and paints, metal studs, sequins,
and rhinestones, plus such "tools and fixins" as
jewelry findings and much more. Be warned: The
staff is geared toward working with professionals,
and there's no time for counter seminars for
novices about the esoterics of making jewelry.

GRAFTIK DIMENSIONS LTD. (MAIL ORDER)

*2103 Brentwood Street, High Point, NC 27263.
Catalog requests and orders (800) 221-0262. Daily
24 hours. MC, VISA, DIS.*
Graftik Dimensions Ltd. is a mail-order company that
publishes a catalog for consumers and volume frame
users, including smaller frame shops. Its prices are the
result of volume buying of framing materials. Most
small frame shops pay a premium price to keep a wide
variety of wood molding and aluminum framing on
hand. Graftik offers preassembled frames in 5-by-7 to
14-by-18 inches (some to 24-by-30 inches), with prices
ranging from $9.95 to $43.95. Several styles have
linen liners. Sectional metal/aluminum or lacquer-
finished frames are easy to assemble, with the
hardware, hangers, and spring clips provided.
Custom-made frames are just that—assembled at
the factory and shipped to you. Frames larger than
50 inches are shipped in sections with an easy
assembly kit. Turn page after page in the catalog
and you'll see that almost every style of frame
molding is available, whether you want an ornate
gold-finished carved frame, a faux stone finish,
burled wood, hand-lacquered, contemporary
wood, touches of silver or gold, or a frame with a

linen liner or antique brass corners. You don't have to buy blind. You can order a free sample of the metal or custom-made wood moldings. Precut acid-free mats, glass, and nonglare plastic in standard sizes are also available. Service is another point of pride for the company. Most orders are shipped within forty-eight hours. Shipping costs in many cases are offset by the fact that no sales tax is charged.

LEESEN INC.

700 Seventh Street, #122 (Baker Hamilton Building), San Francisco. (415) 703-0086. M–F 10–5, Sat 11–5, Sun Noon–4. MC, VISA. Parking: lot.

It would be easy to overlook Leesen Inc. while cruising through the labyrinthine corridors of the mammoth Baker Hamilton building. That's a mistake if you're looking for a dramatic gold-finished frame for a picture or mirror. Leesen frames are made out of a hardwood from China called "cham," which is used in construction, being especially good for lintels and other load-bearing applications. Most Leesen frames have handcrafted corner ornaments that are made from a chip-resistant resin compound. (This compound is different from the easily chipped plaster that some framers use.) Unlike most machine-made soft wood moulding frames with exposed seams, Leesen's corner ornaments are made to discreetly cover the seams of the joints. The detailed designs give the frames an elegant (sometimes ornate) look without being overpowering or overdone, making them suitable accents for many rooms. The frames are handfinished with gold leaf that will not dull or tarnish over time. Leesen is not a custom frame shop; the frames are fully assembled in popular sizes from 8" by 10" to 30" by 40". Those who have shopped around will find that the frame prices are substantially lower than the prices on comparable frames—even on many look-alike frames made from softer woods like pine (often imported from Mexico). Taking the savings even lower, the company's prices on plain or beveled mirrors are lower, and there's no charge for mirror assembly. Any way you look at it, these frames and framed mirrors offer a good value/quality/price ratio.

MITCHELL'S BEESWAX CANDLES

Factory Stores of America, Vacaville. (707) 446-6448. Daily. MC, VISA. Parking: lot.
Beeswax candles are virtually drip-free, burn smoke-free, and last longer than petroleum-based candles. Mitchell's Beeswax Candles are expensive—some would say extravagant—and are sold in gift stores around the globe. A pair of 10-inch silhouette tapers may be priced $20–$25 at these stores; but at the factory store you'll pay about $16. The store offers a complete range of pillars and tapers in a setting that's hard to resist.

SAN FRANCISCO MUSEUM OF MODERN ART RENTAL GALLERY

Building A, Fort Mason Center (at Buchanan and Marina), San Francisco. (415) 441-4777. T–Sat 11:30–5:30; closed August. MC, VISA. Parking: lot.
This gallery's goal is to give new artists exposure; you get an excellent chance to take part in the beginning of an artist's career at a very low cost. You can rent a painting, sculpture, or photograph for a two-month period, with the option of renting for another two months. If you decide to buy, half the rental fee applies toward the purchase price.

Rental fees vary: an artwork with a purchase price of $300–$399 rents for $44 for two months, while an $800–$900 work would rent for $72. Many corporate offices, restaurants, and film companies come here for fine art to display. A suggestion: When selling your home, rent a dramatic piece of art to increase the buyer appeal.

SAN FRANCISCO WOMEN ARTISTS GALLERY

370 Hayes Street, San Francisco. (415) 552-7392. T–Sat 11–6, Th till 8. MC, VISA. Parking: street.
This group has been around since women wore long skirts and wide brimmed hats as they did their Plein-Air sketching in the fields near San Francisco—in other words, more than 100 years. The gallery is staffed by its members and volunteers (many past members have acquired fame and fortune). Members' exhibits change every month and the expressions are diverse—abstractionists, realists, expressionists, landscaptists; painters, etchers, sculptors, etc. There is a rental gallery allowing art lovers to acquire an original piece on a payment plan, to take it home for a trial period before making a permanent buying decision, or just to borrow one for a limited period to brighten up a room for

a particular occasion. In the gallery stands, many smaller works of art are available at reasonable prices, a good starting place for beginning collectors.

STAMP FRANCISCO FACTORY OUTLET STORE

466 Eighth Street (bet. Harrison and Bryant), San Francisco. (415) 252-5975. T–F 10–5, Sat 11–3. Special die sales each month, second Sat only. MC, VISA. Parking: street.

At Stamp Francisco every second Saturday is a special sale day. Become a stamp maker by buying the essentials. First, buy the rubber dies for 25¢ each. Next, pick up a sheet of self-adhesive backing (cushion) for $4, and finally the blocks for 10¢–25¢ each. Some folks make their own wooden blocks. Discontinued and/or used stamps 25% off. Parents can create endless hours of fun and quiet activity for their children by collecting stamps and colored pads. Hone your do-it-yourself skills by taking one of the gallery's classes, held every third Saturday.

STAMPER'S WAREHOUSE

12147 Alcosta Boulevard., San Ramon. (510) 833-8764. M–F 11–5:30, Th till 7, Sat 9:30–5:30, Sun Noon–5. MC, VISA. Parking: lot.

If you think a little savings is better than none at all, you'll be satisfied with the 20% discounts reflected on the marked prices on stamps from 150 companies. This modest operation shows just how popular stamping has become. Customers are stamping papers (invitations, giftwrap, stationery, etc.), fabrics, lamp shades, and sundry other items. The costs on the paraphernalia can add up for the enthusiastic stamp crafter—stamps, stamp pads, inks, glitter, papers, and more. The warehouse offers more than 1,000 stamp images displayed along two walls of the outlet. Check the center tables for extra-special closeouts. *Directions: From Fwy. 680, take the Bollinger Canyon exit east. Turn right on Alcosta. Located in the Country Faire Shopping Center.*

STONE CANDLE OUTLET

650 University Avenue, Berkeley. (510) 849-3191. M–Sat 10–6, Sun Noon–5. MC, VISA. Parking: street.
Stone Candle is innovative. It conceived the "original glowing candle," and more recently the hidden-color concept (as the candle burns, beautiful colors magically appear). At the factory outlet, you can buy seconds with small imperfections; small balls cost $6.50, large balls, $9.50—even the beautiful ball that duplicates Grace Cathedral's stained glass window in the city. Occasionally, Stone's hand-sculpted wildlife candles show up; they're lifelike, with beautiful detailing, rich lustrous colors, and prices usually associated with collectibles.

STRAW INTO GOLD

3006 San Pablo Avenue (corner of Ashby), Berkeley. (510) 548-5247. T–F Noon–5:30, Sat 10–5:30. MC, VISA, DIS. Parking: street.
If your pleasure comes from knitting or crocheting a fine-quality "treasure," you'll want to use a natural fiber commensurate with the time you're going to spend making it. Straw Into Gold's customers approach this store as if making a pilgrimage to a religious shrine. Its attraction? One of the most impressive selections of fibers on the West Coast. This company serves a clientele of weavers, machine knitters, stores, and the public. The bargains are in the center aisle's baskets of closeout yarns and in the "cone" selection. It's much cheaper to buy off the cone, priced by the pound. You can save about 30% if you buy a whole cone (unused portions can be returned within six months for a refund). You'll also find notions, supplies, wonderful buttons, and more. Inquire about receiving a catalog and price list for mail orders.

UP AGAINST THE WALL

3400-D De La Cruz Boulevard, Santa Clara. (408) 727-1995. M–F 9–4:30, Sat by appt. only. MC, VISA. Parking: lot.
Catering to artists, galleries, and interior designers, Up Against the Wall primarily uses aluminum frames, as well as lovely wood framing materials, at prices about 15% below standard frame shops (higher discounts on quantity orders). If you have works to frame, you have two options: You can have the work done here from start to finish, or you can do it yourself at home, after purchasing the materials. This is a time-saver of special value

to artists who may be framing a number of pieces at once for a show or fair. Call for directions.

VALLEY ART GALLERY

1661 Botelho Drive, Suite 110, Walnut Creek.
(510) 935-4311. T–Sat 11–5. MC, VISA.
Parking: lot.
Valley Art exhibits, sells, and rents the work of established and emerging artists. Artists submit work to a jury of professionals for inclusion in its sales and rental program. There's a nice selection of original canvases priced $150–$3,000. More than 200 artists are represented. The gallery also sells fine crafts, jewelry, and sculpture by talented local artisans. Rental periods extend for three months starting at $10/month.

Also See

Under Food and Drink:
SAN FRANCISCO HERB CO.

Fabrics

General Fabrics

ALLEY KAT FABRIC OUTLET

1658 El Camino Real, San Carlos. (650) 596-8331. M–F 10–6, Sat 10–5, Sun 11–5. Cash/Check. Parking: street.

Do you sew? Then you must subscribe to the theory that "she who dies with the most fabric wins." If so, you must need more fabric to add to your pile. Alley Kat Fabric Outlet is worth checking out just to ogle the leftover fabrics the owner buys from apparel manufacturers and small local design houses. These are fabrics that you don't find at local fabric stores. That's good. You'll love the widths—most 60–64 inches. The selection: lots of cotton knits at $2.50–$3/yard, many in wonderful original prints that are perfect for children's sportswear; taffetas at $2.50/yard; a few bolts of heavy tapestry at $5/yard; a great selection of fleece; some woven dress fabrics; cotton/Lycra in solids and stripes; corduroy; rayon challis; flannel; velvets; Italian wools and linen; Gore-Tex; and more. Loved the table filled with button boxes selling at eight for $1 and cards of lace at $1/yard. Most fabrics are $5/yard (wools often $10/yard).

BOLTS END

2743 Castro Valley Boulevard (behind Burger King), Castro Valley. (510) 537-1684. T–Sat 10–5, Th 10–8. MC, VISA. Parking: lot.

Bolts End is overloaded with fabrics, lace, and trims, plus buttons, linings, and other paraphernalia, leftovers from apparel manufacturers. Prices are very good. The selection is always interesting, although somewhat eclectic. Check the bridal department for laces, headpieces, and some fabrics. Gussy up your home with home-decorating fabrics—cottons, brocades, tapestries, laces, and trims (fringe, gimp, piping, etc.). Discounts are 20–70% off retail. Good resource for buttons.

BRITEX FABRICS

146 Geary Street; 147 Maiden Lane, San Francisco. (415) 392-2910. M–Sat 9:30–6, Th 9:30–8. MC, VISA, AE. Parking: lot.

Britex is an institution, its four floors stocked to the ceilings with a most distinctive selection of fabrics. It's the place of last resort, where you go when you can't find a particular fabric anyplace else. Now there is a bargain angle: on the third floor, you'll see remnants and end cuts at drastic reductions. Additionally, each floor has a sale table. I won't claim that the trims, tassels, wonderful selection of buttons (about 30,000), bridal, and jewelry findings are bargain priced, but just learning what is available makes most people happy. The store's expanded home-decorating department offers many distinctive and well-priced fabrics that are more typical of those associated with restricted designer showrooms.

DISCOUNT FABRICS

501 Third Street (at Bryant), San Francisco. (415) 495-4201. M–F 10:30–5:30, Sat 10:30–3:30. MC, VISA. Parking: street.

The goal at Discount Fabrics' warehouse is to sell fabric by the bolt, but you can buy in any quantity you want. This outfit buys from a variety of sources, resulting in many terrific buys and some fabrics that are hard to picture in any application. Yet there are times when one wants inexpensive fabric of any kind for utility without regard to quality, color, or pattern—to protect plants from frost, cover furniture, provide insulation, use as drop cloths, whatever. There's a little of everything: merino wool knits and an extensive selection of velvet, felt, drapery yardage, sheers, raw silk, flannel, printed rayon, muslin, Lycra, vinyl, woven prints, knits (jersey and interlock), home-decorating fabrics (upholstery, drapery, linings), and more. Small craft makers don't have to worry about minimums and can utilize the full library of fabric catalogs from Eastern and New York suppliers to find what they need. Check for notions: excellent prices on bulk buttons, zippers, Velcro, etc. Special-order bridal fabrics at discount prices, too! Prices seemed very good across the board.

FABRIC FACTORY OUTLET

101 Clement Street (at Second Avenue), San Francisco. (415) 221-4111. M–Sat 10–6. Parking: street.

It's like buried treasure. A small, low-profile store jammed with fabric that will certainly pique the interest of anyone who's on the prowl for good buys. It's roulette shopping, with an unpredictable array of fabrics that are not your standard fare. Many appear to come from apparel manufacturers, and that's good. Some very interesting prints (good for children's apparel); usually some fancy stuff for after-five apparel (velvets, rayon faille, novelties); lots of cotton knits; occasional wools and linens; rayons in many guises; and even a smattering of home-decorating fabrics. Before leaving home, take an inventory of your notions so you'll know what to stockpile. Lots of buttons (packaged and loose), elastic, laces, trims, shoulder pads, etc. Prices are gratifyingly low: $1.09 to $3.99 on most yardage (home-decorating fabrics are higher).

M.I. DISCOUNT

2026 Shattuck Avenue (at Addison), Berkeley. (510) 704-8834. M–F 11–7, Sat 10–5, Sun Noon–5. MC, VISA. Parking: street/pay lots.

Fabric fanatics always on the prowl for bargains won't mind the hodgepodge selection of many old, outdated fabrics in all categories, along with some beauties and quality fabrics. M.I. Discount, a fabric liquidator, buys from many sources. Discounts average 60% off original retail. Some prices by the yard: 54-inch cottons or cotton blends and brocades for $8, quilter's cottons in 45- to 60-inch for $2.99 to $3.99, bolt ends of home-decorating fabric at $2–$6; check the $1 and $2 bargain tables for whatever is getting the price-cutting axe for the week. I particularly liked the extensive selection of special buttons (about 500,000 on hand), current and discontinued patterns, and Kirsch drapery hardware, all at 60% off. Polyester products like pillow forms and sheeting for quilts or upholstery show up from time to time.

STONEMOUNTAIN & DAUGHTER

2518 Shattuck Avenue, Berkeley. (510) 845-6106. M–F 9:30–6:30, Sat 10–6, Sun 11–5:30. MC, VISA, AE. Parking: street.

The owners of this shop have long-established connections with the apparel industries in Los Angeles and New York. They combine quality with modest to maximum discounts in purchasing and pass on savings of 10–60% to their customers. They bring in leftover designer wools and silks from Calvin Klein, Donna Karan, Ellen Tracy, Liz Claiborne, and others. Along with some ordinary fabrics, there's a superior selection of quality, (relatively) bargain-priced wool, silk, cotton, and rayon blends that are really quite special—the fabrics are much more elegant than the store. Love the bridal fabrics and accessories, French reembroidered lace with coordinating trims, the hand-selected bulk buttons to match with fashion fabrics, expanded selection of cotton for quilters, and patterns in stock always discounted 20%. Discriminating customers seeking fabric for sophisticated apparel rarely leave disappointed and look forward to discount coupons sent throughout the year to mailing-list customers.

THAI SILKS

252 State Street, Los Altos. (415) 948-8611. M–Sat 9–5:30. MC, VISA, AE. Parking: street.

Thai Silks is the retail division of Exotic Silks, an importer whose materials are used by artists, decorators, designers, yardage shops, quilters, and home sewers. Thai Silks has an extensive inventory of white and natural silks, hand-hemmed scarf blanks, and other items for artists to paint and dye, including ties, Christmas ornaments, and fashion accessories. There are exclusive prints, a dazzling array of fashion and bridal silks, velvets, and cut velvets. The prices are 20–40% off regular retail. La Soie lingerie is also available in a wide range of styles, fabrics, and prints. The first-quality silk gowns, chemises, kimono robes, teddies, camisole and tap pants sets, nightshirts, and pajamas are the most popular styles sold. Silk boxers for men in sizes 32–44. Women's sizes: P–XL. Prices are well below regular retail of specialty shops.

Home-Decorating Fabrics

ALAMEDA UPHOLSTERY SHOP

859 W. San Carlos, San Jose. (408) 295-7885. M–F 9–5:30. MC, VISA, DIS. Parking: street/back lot.
This shop caters to do-it-yourselfers, with its huge selection of upholstery fabrics, plus fabrics that can be ordered from most major manufacturers, including Waverly, Schumacher, Pacific Hide & Leather, Barrow Industries, and many others at a 25% discount. Draperies, vertical blinds, pleated shades, and miniblinds are sold for a 25–50% discount when customers measure and hang their own. Foam rubber is cut to order.

BY THE YARD

170-D Alamo Plaza, Alamo. (510) 837-8579. M–F 10–6, Th till 8, Sat 10–5. MC, VISA. Parking: lot.
If you'd like to buy a charming 100% cotton print fabric that usually retails at $25 for $7.99–$11.99, you'll love By the Yard. That's a fairly typical price range and discount on its lovely selection of factory overruns and first-quality goods tastefully displayed on horizontal rolls around the store. Most can be coordinated with current patterns from well-known wallpaper manufacturers. Hundreds of fabric sample books are also available for those who must see it "all" before making final choices. Fabric discounts are 25–70% off retail; order wallpaper at a 25–30% discount. Nice selection of trims. The staff's know-how and referrals to workrooms are helpful to the novice.

CALICO CORNERS

2700 El Camino Real, Redwood City. (415) 364-1610. M–Sat 10–6, Sun Noon–5. MC, VISA. Parking: lot.
(Other stores: Greenbrae, Pacheco, Sacramento, San Jose.)
The real bargains are not actually calico, but beautiful imported and domestic fabrics for upholstery, draperies, and slipcovers at 20–50% off regular retail. The emphasis is on first-quality fabrics, but you will find occasional seconds. Sample books further extend the selection with discount pricing. Capture the look of hot new trends with specialty rods, finials, home-decorating books, and publications. Calico Corners now has its own workrooms, if you can't do it yourself. With low prices, beautiful displays, and helpful clerks, these stores are an absolute pleasure to shop in.

D & S DISCOUNT FABRICS

1000 15th Street (at Bryant), Second floor, San Francisco. (415) 522-1098. M–F 9–5. MC, VISA. Parking: street.

D & S Discount Fabrics, near Showplace Square, is a warehouse-styled showroom that's well organized and stocked with surplus yardage from local fabric suppliers and fabric distributors. Regular specials set aside in sale bins might be where you'll find bolts of polyester, 118-inch, sheer-drapery fabric priced at $2/yard or antique satins at $3/yard. Those wanting recent or current fabrics for pillow making can consider hundreds of 24-inch pillow halves with finished edges at $3 each, or 24-inch and larger fabric pieces at $1.50 each. These are sample cuts from major fabric houses typically used in trade showrooms or by fabric reps. Larger, 1- to 4-yard pieces (often wing-display samples from trade showrooms) are priced well below wholesale. Other fabrics are available from large bolts. The outlet is strong on multipurpose fabrics that can be used for window coverings, bedding treatments, upholstery, etc. Vintage trims and fabrics (velvets from the 1920s, needlepoints, brocades and tapestries from the 1930s and 1940s) occupy a few tables and satisfy purists renovating upholstered pieces or making decorative pillows. Many trims, while new, replicate vintage trims. Individually priced vintage bed linens and tablecloths (from old estate homes in Europe) and old linen toweling priced $4.50 to $6.50/yard are acquired occasionally and add to this unusual selection. Discount priced Dacron or goose down pillow fillers are for sale. Utilize the D & S workroom for maximum convenience. Save 25% on current fabrics sold from sample books of local fabric distributors.

FABRICS & MORE

460 Montgomery Street, The Marketplace, San Ramon. (510) 277-1783. M–Sat 10–6, Th till 8, Sun Noon–5. MC, VISA. Parking: lot.

Fabrics & More is stocked with the latest home-decorating fabrics: lovely tapestries, chintz, jacquards, velvet, neutral cotton upholstery, sheers, and more. Overstocks offer the lowest pricing: $5/yard in the clearance corner, while prices on roll displays start at $12. Discounts are 20–60% off retail. Special orders at discount pricing are offered (buy more, save more). You'll find fabric from Schumacher, Braemore, Cyrus Clark, Waverly, Robert Allen, Harris, P. Kaufman, Bloomcraft, Covington, and many others. Need rods? There's the standard selection in stock, with more choices available from catalogs, at modest discounts. You can order elegant trims and tiebacks or pick up a tapestry pillow square. The staff is very knowledgeable, and advice is freely given. There is a $50 one-time charge for home visits. Once you have the fabric, the staff will arrange for labor. *Directions: From Fwy. 680, take Bolinger Canyon Road east to Alcosta. Turn right one block to Montgomery/The Marketplace.*

FURBELOWS
6050 Johnson Drive, Suite A, Pleasanton. (510) 463-0242. M–F 10–6, Sat 10–5. MC, VISA. Parking: lot.
Fur•be•low (noun) 1. A ruffle or flounce on a garment; 2. a piece of showy ornamentation. This store is aptly named, with its selection of trims, fabrics, and wallpapers. It offers an upscale selection at downscale prices. On wallpaper books from most well known companies you'll save 30% on papers, 20% on companion fabrics. Other fabrics, about

250, are sold for 50–70% discounts off bolts nicely arrayed around the store. These are home-decorating fabrics geared primarily to contemporary and traditional decors. You can always spend time looking through sample fabric books and special order what you need for a 20% discount; on large quantities, you may save even more. I was very interested in the sample selection of expensive, elegant decorator trims at a 20% discount by special order. Best bargain of all is the free decorating assistance by the talented and enthusiastic owners. They can arrange to have your project made for you. *Directions: Take the Hopyard exit from Fwy. 580. Located in the Pleasanton Square Shopping Center.*

KAY CHESTERFIELD MFG. CO.
6365 Coliseum Way, Oakland. (510) 533-5565. M–F 8:30–5, Sat 9–1. MC, VISA. Parking: lot.
The Kay Chesterfield Mfg. Co. specializes in reupholstering furniture for residential and commercial clients around the Bay Area; to serve its clientele, it maintains an extensive in-stock inventory of fabrics. Bargains come into play when the bolts are sold down to a relatively small amount of yardage. Additionally, the owners buy roll bal-

ances and discontinued fabrics from mills and often find deals that are too good to pass up. The deepest discounts are on small pieces, 1 to 8 yards. In any case, the minimum you'll save is about 50% off retail. Since fabrics can cost up to $50–$100/yard wholesale, some prices may be unnerving. The greater part of the selection falls in the $10–$30 price range. Many people who come in are making handbags, place mats, teddy bears, art, or craft projects. Very little in the way of drapery or bedspread materials. *Directions: Take 66th Avenue exit from Fwy. 880 to first light, and turn left (near Coliseum parking lot).*

MYUNG JIN STUDIO OUTLET

10 Liberty Ship Way #370 (Schoonmaker Building), Sausalito. (415) 331-8011. F only 10–4 (or by appt.). MC, VISA. Parking: lot.
Myung Jin Studio Outlet is top-notch for beautiful home-decorating fabrics. The owners design them in-house and have them made in India or the United States. These exclusive and expensive fabrics are sold to the design trade, and discontinued fabrics and mill ends await you at the studio. There are two primary fabric collections. First, the 54-inch

heavy cottons in both subtle and crisp colorations (stripes, checks), ikat prints, and solids to be used on leaning-toward-contemporary/informal furnishings. They'd also make great slipcovers. These are outlet priced at $8–$12/yard. Next, the exquisite rayon chenilles in unique weaves for more elegant and traditional applications are priced $35–$45/yard. Some fabrics are available in small quantities; others (mostly cottons) can easily accommodate any yardage requirements. Creative sewers with upscale inclinations will see many possibilities in the luxurious chenilles for making apparel. There's a small selection of beautiful silks. Finally, cones of chenille yarn (discontinued dye lots) are sold by the pound (about $15/pound)—of interest to weavers or knitters. Chenille throws and scarves, pillows, and chef aprons are ready to go for those without time to sew.

NORMAN S. BERNIE CO.

1135 N. Amphlett Boulevard, San Mateo. (650) 342-8586. M, W, F 8–4:30 T, Th 9–5:30, first Sat every month 10–2. Cash/Check. Parking: street.
The founder of this company is a fabric man from way back, selling mill ends to fabric retailers and

dyeing and printing "naked" fabrics for manufacturers. Bernie buys leftover current patterns of upholstery fabrics and other home-decorating and special-use fabrics. Often there are only 6 to 9 yards left on a bolt, not enough to cover a sofa, but maybe enough to cover dining room chairs, a small chair, or pillows. The fabrics are well priced, too! You'll also find full bolts of 60-inch denim (many types of stripes, plus solids in various weights); muslin (all weights and widths); cotton duck; sheeting; canvas; marine fabrics; drapery fabrics; scrims (gauzelike); occasionally luxury and liner furs by the pound or yard; chintz; raw silk; and lots more. A few fabrics got my yuck response, but for the most part I loved the selection. In the upstairs gallery you'll find full bolts of better-quality home-decorating and craft fabrics. Decorators and wanna-bes waste no time in snatching up yards of laundered jacquard for "shabby chic" treatments at $12.50/yard. Elegant damasks don't gather any dust either, with most priced at $22.50/yard. *Located between Peninsula Avenue and Broadway exits off Fwy. 101. Outlet faces freeway.*

POPPY FABRICS

5151 Broadway (near 51st Street), Oakland. (510) 655-5151. M–F 9:30–8, Sat 9:30–5:30, Sun 11–5:30. MC, VISA. Parking: lot.
Poppy Fabrics excels in its selection of upscale and distinctive fabrics for sophisticated shoppers. Many fabrics are just not found in the typical store's selection of home-decorating fabrics. P. Kaufman, Covington, Collins and Aikman are a few of its lines from major U.S. mills (some fabrics are exclusive imports). Create a *House Beautiful* result working with one of Poppy's unique French provincial fabrics, or choose an Italian tapestry—then embellish with a distinctive ribbon or braid from the trim department. A beautiful store, Poppy offers a nice level of customer support with knowledgeable staff, how-to books, and all the paraphernalia one needs to see a project from start to finish. Prices are discounted a little to a lot (20–60% off retail). Utilize Poppy's custom workroom services if you're too timid to go the do-it-yourself route. Design services and home consultations by experienced interior designers are another of Poppy's special benefits.

RODOLPH FABRIC FACTORY OUTLET

989 West Spain Street, Sonoma. (707) 935-0316. W & Th 11–2, or by appt. Hours subject to change during holidays. MC, VISA. Parking: lot.
This outlet focuses on unusual dye lots and remnants of fabrics traditionally sold only through interior designers. Fabrics normally priced from $80 to $120/yard at retail are offered via the outlet at $15 to $30/yard. There are beautiful colors and textures in a selection of silks, wools, and cottons found in contemporary and classical motifs. A great resource for those trying to capture that *Architectural Digest* image in their decorating projects, as well as a unique source for quilters and crafters. Also available, for $5 to $10/yard, is a selection of Jim Thompson Thai apparel silks. Call or sign up so you won't miss Rodolph's 3-day factory sale events every spring and fall.

S. BERESSI FABRIC SALES

1504 Bryant Street, Second Floor, San Francisco. (415) 861-5004. M, W, F Noon–2 Sat 11–3. Sales in fall and spring: M–Sat 10–5, Sun Noon–5. MC, VISA. Parking: lot.
S. Beressi, a local fabric wholesaler, gives the public a chance to buy a huge variety of first-quality leftover and discontinued fabric, thread, polyester fiberfill, and bedspreads from his upstairs warehouse. Prices are below wholesale to encourage fast sales and speedy removal. These materials are used not only for bedspreads, but for draperies, upholstery, slipcovers, costumes, apparel, and crafts. Fabrics purchased from mills on buying trips around the world include exquisite velvets, 120-inch drapery sheers, and silk damasks from Europe. Regulars at the outlet will recognize the almost prehistoric fabrics that get cheaper and cheaper every year. Call the office for weekday access anytime during the year, when prices are 40% off marked prices, or for sale dates (50% off wholesale) that usually start in mid-April and mid-October. Rely on Mr. Beressi for workroom referrals to suit your pocketbook—budget to best and priced accordingly. He's been around long enough to know everyone in the business.

Also See

Under Art, Craft, and Hobby Supplies:
DHARMA TRADING CO.

Under Famous Labels/Factory Stores:
LAURA ASHLEY

Under Other Bay Area Factory Outlets/Factory
Stores:
EMERYVILLE OUTLET

Under Children's Clothing:
**CHICKEN NOODLE; DONNA CAPOZZI; PETALS;
STORYBOOK HEIRLOOMS; SWEET POTATOES**

Under Draperies and Window Coverings—
Ready-Made:
ALL LISTINGS

Under Furniture and Home Accessories—
Catalog Discounters:
ALL LISTINGS

Under Linens:
MERCADO

Office Supplies

Three mammoth stores with locations all over the Bay Area dominate the office supply market. OfficeMax, Office Depot, and Staples are self-service operations selling a complete selection of basic office supplies and necessities. Prices at these chains are very competitive—each claims discounts of 30–70% off retail—and they're usually much lower than at other office supply or stationery stores. Both companies offer special services, including delivery, copying, printing, engraving, rubber stamps, and phone orders. Great resources for home, office, or back-to-school supplies. I shop each about equally, according to which has a store closest to wherever I'm shopping on any particular day.

ARVEY PAPER CO.
2275 Alameda Street (at Potrero), San Francisco.
(415) 863-3664. M–F 8–5:30, Sat 10–4. MC, VISA.
Parking: street/lot.
(Other stores: Oakland, Redwood City,
Sacramento, San Jose.)
Arvey offers the best selection of printers' supplies and papers of every description, plus graphic supplies, light printing equipment, etc. It caters to small to midsize businesses; the average consumer gets a fair shake, too! Arvey sells business machines, pens, janitorial needs, and lots more; its office supply section has expanded to keep up with the super office stores. If you're a big user of stationery supplies, get on its mailing list.

J. C. PAPER

1221 Diamond Way, Concord. (510) 798-5301. M–F 7–6, Sat 9–2. MC, VISA. Parking: lot. (Other stores: Hayward, Mountain View, Oakland, San Carlos, San Francisco, San Rafael, San Jose, Santa Rosa, Stockton.)

This company is handy if you've started producing your own letterhead, flyers, reports, or whatever, using the newer, more affordable laser or ink jet printers. Getting professional results is reflected in the paper you use. J. C. Paper's mission in life has been to supply the various print shops and offices with all their needs, but do-it-yourselfers can also stop in to shop and lay in a supply of papers. As paper specialists, J. C. Paper offers a better range of quality, finishes, weights, and color. Naturally, there are myriad envelopes to go along with the papers.

KELLY PAPER

1375 Howard Street, San Francisco. (415) 522-0420. M–F 7:30–5, Sat 9–1. MC, VISA, AE, DIS. Parking: lot. (Other stores: Concord, Oakland, Palo Alto, Sacramento, San Carlos.)

If you're a mailing-list customer you'll get the word on specials that should prompt you to stop in, stock up, and save money in the process. Like J. C. Paper, this company can keep the home office well supplied with paper for printing whatever.

Stationery and Party Supplies

Party supply stores have proliferated all around the Bay Area. Select the store that is closest to you, but note that particular stores may have something extra to offer. Here's the general profile that applies to the stores in this section: They all have a good selection of paper party products; paper plates, napkins, plastic utensils, table covers, and paper place mats are typically about 25% less than at well-known specialty stores. You'll frequently find lots of extras: bibs, crystal (plastic) hostess or caterers' trays and punch bowls, regular and helium balloons, party hats, favors, carnival-type toys for children, and more. Most stores have good buys on giftwrap; some also carry craft supplies, silk flowers, and baskets.

BOSWELL'S DISCOUNT PARTY SUPPLIES
1901 Camino Ramon, Danville. (510) 866-1644.
M–Sat 9–6:30, Sun 10–5. MC, VISA, DIS.
Parking: lot.
(Other stores: 5759 Pacheco Boulevard, Pacheco; 3483 Mt. Diablo Boulevard, Lafayette; Rosewood Pavilion Center, Pleasanton.)
Boswell's has wonderful gifts, gags, etc. Great selection of paper products in fabulous colors discounted 30%. Everything for weddings and parties for all ages and occasions. Trophy ribbons, stocking stuffers, jokes, toys, gag gifts, wedding and shower accessories, bandannas, inexpensive hats, and scads more. Depending on the size of your order, you can save up to 25% on wedding invitations. Craft and educational supplies, too! Individual store hours may vary.

THE CARD AND PARTY DISCOUNT OUTLETS

33 S. Capitol Avenue, San Jose. (408) 254-7060.
M–F 9:30–7, Sat–Sun 10–5. MC, VISA. Parking: lot.
(Other stores: 562 E. El Camino Real, Paulina
Plaza, Sunnyvale; 545 Meridian Avenue, Suite F,
San Jose.)
For help planning for a big event, you've come to
the right place. Not only will you find all paper
goods at 20–50% off, you'll also scoop up wrap-
pings and ribbons at minimum 20% discount and
catering supplies at 30–50% off. Greeting cards
are always 50% off retail, while the intriguing collection of closeout giftware (including stuffed
animals, ceramics, rubber stamps, stamping accessories, and frames) is also discounted 30–50%.
Lots of little goodies for tots, hats for grown-ups,
piñatas, and balloons complete the picture. Also,
wedding invitations at modest discounts. Those
with resale numbers can shop at its Cash & Carry
warehouse at 143 E. Virginia Street in San Jose,
(408) 287-3177.

CURRENT FACTORY STORE

Great Mall of the Bay Area, Milpitas. (408) 263-
5560. Daily. MC, VISA. Parking: lot.
(Other store: 190 Golf Club Road, Pleasant Hill.)
Over the years I'd speculate that anyone involved
with fund-raising efforts has come across the
Current company. It has two Bay Area outlets,
where overstock and discontinued merchandise are
sold at modest to very gratifying markdowns. Stock
up on stationery, greeting cards, gift wrap, paper
party supplies, stickers, gift items, ribbons, bows,
and more. Current keeps everyone in mind, so all
occasions, ages, and styles are well represented.

DIDDAMS DISCOUNT PARTY HEADQUARTERS

215 Hamilton Avenue, Palo Alto. (650) 327-6204.
M–W 10–7, Th–F 10–8, Sat–Sun 9:30–5. MC, VISA.
Parking: street.
(Other store: 10171 South De Anza Boulevard,
Cupertino.)
A great place for children's parties, but also reli-
able for all adult occasions! Balloon prices are really
sharp. Theme parties a specialty; lots of hats, host-
ess servers, and party accessories. You may save
considerably (up to 40%) on wedding invitations,

depending on the size of your order and the processing time involved; appointments and a minimum $50 processing charge are required for this service.

GREETINGS 'N' MORE

Tracy Outlet Center, Tracy. (209) 835-8378. MC, VISA. Parking: lot.
(Other outlets: Anderson, Pacific Grove centers.)
Stationery, bows, giftwrap, gift bags, paper party supplies, and an extensive selection of greeting cards for all occasions (at 50% off every day), Christmas paper all year round.

HALF PRICE CARDS

1212-J El Camino Real, San Bruno Towne Center, San Bruno. (650) 875-7113. M–F 10–6, Sat 10–6, Sun 11–6. VISA, MC. Parking: lot.
The greeting-card field has become fiercely competitive, which accounts for the increasing number of stores that sell half-price cards. Now a store devoted entirely to this concept has opened, selling mostly current line products that are heavily discounted by the manufacturers to gain market share. Half Price Cards offers a full range of greeting cards, more than 3,000 designs, at half the price charged by other stores. In addition to greeting cards, a large range of wrapping paper, gift bags, ribbons, bows, stickers, and gift items are priced at 20–75% below prices found at typical Hallmark stores. Gift items include frames, magnets, wind chimes, mugs, coloring books, crayons, children's books, and balloons. Note: No paper party goods.

THE PAPER OUTLET

Factory Stores at Vacaville, Vacaville. (707) 449-3442. Daily. MC, VISA, DIS. Parking: lot.
(Other outlets: Folsom, Gilroy, Lathrop, Milpitas centers.)
Stop by for giftwrap, gift boxes, ribbons, party goods and decorations, greeting cards, invitations, thank-yous, books, games and puzzles, plus paper products for the home and office at proper savings. These are selected closeouts and seconds. The wonderful stock of giftwrap (appears to be roll ends from giftwrap departments) is hard to resist.

PAPER PLUS OUTLETS

1643 and 1659 San Pablo Avenue (north of University Avenue at Virginia), Berkeley. (510) 525-1799. M–Sat 10–6, Sun Noon–5. MC, VISA. Parking: side lot.
(Other stores: 2924 College Avenue, Berkeley; 1309 Castro, San Francisco; 800 Texas Street, Fairfield; and Vacaville center.)

The store in Berkeley may be a bit of a mess, but the other outlets are neat and tidy. You'll discover satisfying bargains on discontinued and surplus inventory from the well-known Papyrus stores. There's a tantalizing selection of quality cards, giftwrap, and stationery at 50–80% off. The unique gift wrap is sold in single sheets; greeting cards are always at least 50% off; half off on gift wrap, children's books, small children's toys, and stuffed animals. Also photo albums, stationery in boxes or lovely portfolio packs, diaries, and more. A complete party-goods inventory at very competitive prices. You'll even find boxes for your truffles! The store at 1659 San Pablo is devoted to seasonal specials and is merchandised accordingly (some very special Christmas and Chanukah merchandise). Great source whenever you're planning theme parties around holidays.

PARTY AMERICA

1257 Marina Boulevard, Marina Square, San Leandro. (510) 297-5110. Daily. MC, VISA. Parking: lot.
(Other stores: Campbell, Cupertino, Dublin, Larkspur, Millbrae, Palo Alto, Pleasant Hill, Redwood City, San Carlos, San Jose, Santa Clara, Union City.)

Party America stores sell paper products for parties, plus balloons, Wilton cake-decorating supplies, hostess servers, etc. Giftwrap and cards are discounted 50% every day; wedding and party invitations from several catalogs at 20% discount. Good overall party resource.

PARTY CITY

1909 Mt. Diablo Boulevard, Walnut Creek. (510) 945-8200. M–Sat 9–8, Sun 10–5. MC, VISA, AE, DIS. Parking: street. (Other store: Sacramento)

150 stores around the country and growing. This is the first in the Bay Area, and the profile is similar to all the other party stores mentioned in this chapter. Good end-of-season half-price sales, frequent special promotions, and special discounts to local schools, caterers, restaurants, churches, synagogues, clubs, corporations, etc.

THE PARTY WAREHOUSE

221 Oak Street (at Third Street), Oakland. (510) 893-1951. M–F 10–6, Sat–Sun 10–5. MC, VISA. Parking: street.

(Other stores: Daly City, El Cerrito, San Bruno, San Francisco, San Leandro, San Mateo.)

The Party Warehouse discounts 20–50% on party necessities: theme party paper products, as well as wedding, juvenile birthday, and baby shower departments, which are quite impressive. Bargain prices apply on giftwrap, ribbon, classroom decorations, and Christmas and other seasonal decorations. Additional discounts are available for caterers, churches, and schools.

PAULA SKENE DESIGNS

1250 45th Street, Suite 240, Emeryville. (510) 654-3510. First Sat of every month, 9–3. Checks/VISA. Parking: street.

Paula Skene is a wonderful resource for premium-quality and elegant stationery, sold in galleries, museums, and fine stationery stores in the United States and Europe. These are cards that people do not throw away. Paula uses heavy, fine-quality paper and creates designs of deeply embossed and ele-gantly foil-stamped images that may require as many as seven passes through the presses. These cards are works of art, most worthy of framing. At the warehouse sales, the stationery is sold for 50% off retail. Occasional cards are about $1.75 each; boxed cards about $14 for 8; boxed stationery (20–30 sheets) for $12; and enclosures about 60¢ each. Not inexpensive (when compared to the discount card and party stores), but a solid value. You'll want to stock up and keep these beauties on hand for classy correspondence. To keep up with sale dates, make sure to have your name added to the mailing list. *Note: Corporate designs are a specialty. Look for the City Rock on Doyle Street and you won't get lost.*

Wedding Invitations

Many of the stores listed above sell wedding invitations from budget to midpriced books for modest discounts, typically 20–25% off published price lists. There are also many mail-order companies for invitations that advertise prominently in bridal magazines. Most have 800 numbers, special consultation lines, and unconditional guarantees. If you requested information from each company, you could fill a shopping basket with packets that include sample invitations, catalogs, and complete instructions for ordering. Mail-order prices are considerably less than the prices listed in most midpriced books carried locally, but there is a definite difference in the quality of the paper. In other words, for half the price, you'll get half the quality. Depending on how one wants to allocate the money in a wedding budget, and how important the quality or image conveyed by choice of an invitation is, the mail-order option may be an acceptable alternative to local stores. It's a very personal decision. I can guarantee that when it comes to the wording and many esoteric details of invitations, you'll wish you were sitting face-to-face with an experienced stationer.

Also See

Under Art, Craft, and Hobby Supplies:
AMSTERDAM ART

Under Food and Drink:
CASH AND CARRY WAREHOUSE; CENTRAL CASH 'N CARRY

Under General Merchandise—Discount Stores, Liquidators:
ALL LISTINGS

Under General Merchandise—Membership Warehouse Clubs:
PRICE/COSTCO

Food and Drink

6

I don't want to be accused of overlooking any common sense strategies, so forgive me if you think I'm stating the obvious. What was true thirty years ago is still true today: Savvy consumers can easily trim grocery bills by monitoring weekly ads for specials at local supermarkets. When prices are low, buy in quantity. If you have a freezer, stock up. Clip and use coupons, but only on products that suit your family's needs. Often coupons don't bring prices below store brands, or below featured specials on competing brands. Too often, they apply to products that have little nutritional value and offer "savings" on products you wouldn't buy otherwise. If it's convenient, shop warehouse supermarkets like Food 4 Less and Pak N Save. Price/Costco and Sam's Club are obvious money-saving sources if you can handle the multiple or oversize packaging on most products.

Farmers' markets: Check local papers for announcements of seasonal farmers' markets in your area. Produce fresh from the farm is usually—not always—offered at lower than supermarket prices. (Many folks are more concerned about flavor and freshness than price.) Local farmers' markets are open year-round in many communities. Booths selling gourmet edibles (mustards, vinegars, baked goods, sausages, etc.), esoteric greens, specialty vegetables, fresh cut flowers, and plants are delighting and expanding the bounty for shoppers. For a listing of Bay Area certified farmers' markets call (800) 897-FARM or (800) 949-FARM.

Bakery thrift shops: It's truly worth your while to check the Yellow Pages for the bakery outlets close to you and to include a stop at one on your way around town. Parisian, Oroweat, Langendorf, Kilpatrick, and many other bakeries maintain thrift stores to sell their day-old bread and freshly baked surplus. Savings range anywhere from 20% to 75% off retail, depending on the category. Buy a lot at one time; you can freeze whatever you don't use right away. My favorite? Oroweat/Entenmann's Boboli pizza breads sold half-price every day. Stock up for great freezer emergency rations.

BEVERAGES & MORE
2900 N. Main Street, Walnut Creek. (510) 472-0130. MC, VISA. M–Fri 10–9, Sat 9–9, Sun 10–7. Parking: lot.
(Other stores: Albany, Mountain View, Oakland, San Francisco, San Jose, San Rafael, Santa Clara, Santa Rosa, Sacramento.)
Along with its competitive pricing, Beverages & More offers a connoisseur's selection of wines, organized by country and varietal, that is accommodating to just about any budget—from box wines to fine vintages. If your dessert or drink recipe calls for an exotic liquor or liqueur, no problem. It would take you almost two years to work through the beer selection alone if you sampled a new beer every day. Conscientious hosts who want to provide nonalcoholic drinks, healthy punches, or fancy waters for their guests have hundreds of choices, too. In the "More" category are packaged specialty foods including mustards, seasoning mixes, candies, snacks, coffees, and teas. New deli counters are satisfying the palates of gourmets with cheeses, olives, meats, and sundry other offerings. Cigar aficionados can count on a good selection. The company's not timid about posting the prices of local competitors for comparison. Join ClubBev for special membership savings.

THE CANDY JAR FACTORY OUTLET
2065 Oakdale Avenue, San Francisco. (415) 550-8846. M–W 8–4. Before major holidays: M–F 8–4. MC, VISA. Parking: street.
The Candy Jar produces truffles for specialty candy stores and upscale shops. If you're willing to go off the beaten path to its plant, you can save a little or a lot depending on what you buy. Basic and deluxe truffles in more than a dozen flavors sell for $1 each ($1.25 to $1.50 elsewhere). In addition to truffles, it also sells oversize turtles (nuts and caramel) and other heavenly chocolate candies. The best everyday buys are on seconds (small surface imperfections), closeouts, and overruns. After holidays you may find deep discounts on packaged chocolates. You can stock up. Truffles stay fresh for five to six weeks, or even longer if refrigerated. Budget

watchers can buy truffles in any amount for a big event or wedding and handle all the packaging and wrapping themselves, or the Candy Jar Factory will do the packaging for you.

CASH & CARRY WAREHOUSE

452 Dubois Street, San Rafael. (415) 457-1040. M–F 8:30–5, Sat 8:30–3. Cash/Check. Parking: lot.
If you're cooking for a crowd or planning a big party, the Cash & Carry Warehouse may make your preparations easier—they offer institutional products used by restaurants, catering services, and schools. The paper and party products selection is as complete as most party supply stores listed in the Stationery and Party Supplies section, plus there is a good selection of janitorial products.

CENTRAL CASH 'N CARRY

190 Keyes Street (at Fifth), San Jose. (408) 975-2485. M–F 7:30–6, Sat 9–5, Sun 10–4. MC, VISA. Parking: lot.
(Other stores: 1315 16th Street, San Francisco; 1131 Elko Drive, Sunnyvale.)
Central Cash 'n Carry is another option for the party planner, especially if you're looking for paper and food products. You'll find restaurant-sized cans and jars of condiments, salsas, cheese sauces, and other sauces as well as ice cream toppings, punches, and syrups. Also many hostess and catering trays, bowls, and pans. Good paper party products, piñatas, and favors, too. This is a no-frills warehouse store with many institutional supplies. Delivery service available.

CHOCOLATE FACTORY OUTLET

1225 Eighth Street (off Gilman), Berkeley. (510) 558-8100. Daily 10:30–6. Cash/Check. Parking: lot.
In the warehouse kitchens behind the outlet, candymakers of the San Francisco Chocolate Company toil each day making thousands of varieties of truffles, chocolate-covered Oreo cookies, and novelty candies (you won't find Sees-type nuts and chews here). Fresh surplus inventory is sent to the immaculate factory store and sold for about 30% less than the prices charged by retail stores that sell the candies loose or in boxed products. Most truffles, in a palate of yummy flavors (all made without preservatives), are factory-outlet priced at $1; those with blems (small cracks in the shells) are about 50¢; chocolate-covered Oreos are 85¢ (retail $1.35

to $1.50). The company's products are featured by several catalog companies in seasonal gift packs—the same tin of Oreos that sold for $35 in one of the catalogs went for $19.95 at the outlet. This is a premium chocolate maker, and other small, fine-quality, cottage-style Bay Area candy-makers are invited to sell their products in a separate display at the outlet. All the goodies here will appeal to chocolate aficionados. Aspiring candy-makers will appreciate the opportunity to buy some of the "ingredients" usually available only to manufacturers who can meet thousand-pound purchasing minimums. Here, imported European chocolates are packaged in small quantities for home cooks. Those needing favors for weddings or special events (a big part of the company's business) should inquire about pricing. Additional benefits and savings can be derived from dealing directly with this manufacturer.

CHOCOLATE FACTORY OUTLET
1291 Fremont Boulevard (next to Fish Wife restaurant), Seaside. (408) 899-7963. M–Sat 10–9, Sun 11–5. MC, VISA. Parking: lot.
It's right out of *I Love Lucy*—chocolate tunnels and fast-moving conveyor belts. A tasty detour for visiting tourists. The decor here is a Willy Wonka fantasy come true. Pick up a plastic glove and any size box you want and ramble down the 40-foot chocolate bar. Choose your favorite or a variety of chocolates: truffles, turtles, peanut butter cups, caramels, English toffee, nuts, chews, and more. When you're done and the box has been weighed, you'll pay $8.95/pound (close to wholesale). If you're going to hide in the closet to eat these treats, then maybe you'll settle for a 1/4 pound bag of "bloopers" for $2. They may be ugly, misshapen, or stuck together, but they taste just the same as the firsts. The diet-conscious may opt for sugar-free chocolates at $10.95/pound—if you shopped at the factory's popular candy store in Carmel, you'd pay more like $12–$14/pound. Lovely gift boxes available. Locals and visitors alike can tour the factory anytime, or arrange for special chocolate-making classes.

COUNTRY CHEESE
2101 San Pablo Avenue, Berkeley. (510) 841-0752. M–Sat 9–6, Sun 10–5. Cash/Check. Parking: street.
Domestic and imported cheeses, meat products, dried fruits, nuts and seeds, grains, spices by the ounce, and health food items at wonderful prices

keep Berkeley residents happy. You'll love the old-fashioned country store atmosphere, with bins for scooping out grains and rice. I've found some pricey ingredients, like dried porcini mushrooms, at decent discounts. Inquire about discounts for co-ops and volume orders.

DELICIEUX FINE DESSERTS

48 Paul Drive, San Rafael. (415) 479-1020. M, W, Th 10–3 (call first). Cash/Check. Parking: lot.

This company sells its just-like-home-baked pies and cobblers for about half off. Its excess inventory is usually available after delivery and sales to farmers' markets, caterers, gourmet grocers, and restaurants around the area. The baked pies can be frozen indefinitely; otherwise they'll keep for about four to seven days. A cobbler serving 24 people (11 by 17 inches) runs about $22 at retail, about $12 as surplus production at the outlet. Pies can run from $2 to $6—more than pies from supermarket frozen food shelves, but there's no comparison. Hand-rolled and -shaped crusts create that homemade appearance, allowing you to pass off a pie as one of your own (if you're so inclined). The pie selection may change according to the season, but you can usually count on some favorite fruit flavors (love the strawberry rhubarb), nut pies, etc. Cobblers may be purchased by the piece or sheet.

EUREKA COFFEE

2747 19th Street (bet. Bryant and York), San Francisco. (415) 550-0625. M–F 8–4. Cash/Check. Parking: street.

This outfit sells one item: coffee beans. No cups, no high-tech coffeemakers, not even a fresh cup of coffee. If you consume quantities of coffee and prefer fresh-roasted beans to anything sold in cans at the supermarket, then buy a pound or two to sample the blends and you'll probably become a regular. Eureka roasts fresh coffee beans on the premises and supplies many restaurants and other food-service establishments. Six dollars a pound for French, Italian, Vienna, Colombian, Mocha/Java or the house roast ($6.50 for decaf), a solid 25-50% less than other high-profile coffee purveyors charge. I've sampled several of the blends and found the rich flavors so satisfying that I routinely replenish when I find myself in the area.

FARM RIPE COUNTRY STORE

2070 S. Seventh Street, San Jose. (408) 280-2349, (800) 628-3493. M-F 10-3 Jan-Oct, 9-4 Nov-Dec (Sat hours, Christmas season only). MC, VISA. Parking: lot.

At Mayfair Packing's warehouse store, you'll find Sugaripe housebrand prunes; dried apricots, peaches, pears, and apples; shelled or unshelled walnuts; also raisins, dates, almonds, cashews, filberts, and Brazil nuts, all selling at below supermarket prices. At holiday times inquire about gift packs, premade to your specifications. You can order by phone; they ship anywhere. *Note: The company may move to another location in the South Bay. Keep in touch through its catalog or 800 number. Write to Farm Ripe, PO Box 3487, Saratoga, CA, 95070.*

GROCERY OUTLETS

2001 Fourth Street, Berkeley. (510) 845-1771. M-Sat 8-9, Sun 9-7. Cash/Check/Food stamps. Parking: lot. (Other stores: Antioch, Fremont, Hayward, Oakland, Newark, Petaluma, Rancho Cordova, Redwood City, Sacramento, Salinas, San Jose, San Pablo, Stockton, Vacaville, Woodland.)

Specializing in closeouts, packaging changes, and surplus goods, Grocery Outlets (formerly Canned Foods) offers a constantly changing inventory at up to 40% savings every day. Be prepared to buy whatever the company has captured from the marketplace. Dry groceries, frozen and refrigerated foods, health and beauty aids, wines and beers, housewares, and general merchandise are backed with a 100% money-back guarantee. You may find well-known and unfamiliar brand names, as well as I've-never-seen-that-before products. Some excellent buys on gourmet and diet frozen dinners, gourmet ice creams, seasonal items, juices, and snacks!

HARRY AND DAVID

Factory Stores of America, Vacaville. (707) 451-6435. Daily. MC, VISA, AE, DIS. Parking: lot. (Other outlets: Gilroy, Napa, Petaluma, Tracy centers.)

Harry and David is a catalog company specializing in gourmet treats. Each catalog's tempting selection of gift baskets may include cheeses, candies, fruit (fresh or dried), jams, and more. You'll find products from the catalogs at the outlets, or you can order spiral-sliced hams, smoked turkey, gourmet steaks, snack foods, boxes of candy, baked sweets, very elegant tortes, and luscious cheesecakes, a company specialty. All are sold at the stores for 20-50% off catalog retail. They are every bit as good, wholesome, and fresh as what you'd get by ordering from the catalog; you derive the savings of buying direct. Other catalog items include gifts, home decor, kitchen-oriented products, and garden items from the Jackson & Perkins catalog.

HERMAN GOELITZ CANDY STORE

2400 N. Watney Way, Fairfield. (707) 428-2838. M-F 9-5. MC, VISA. Parking: lot.
Other outlet: (The Jelly Belly Store, Factory Stores at Vacaville).
Stop by for a sweet deal on candy. The Herman Goelitz candy factory in Fairfield is the company Ronald Reagan made famous. The factory store mainly sells first-quality, full-priced candies. However, there's always a selection of Belly Flops, Jelly Bellies that may be stuck together or oddly shaped, priced at $4 for a two-pound bag. (Normal Jelly Belly beans are typically $5.50/pound.) The

seconds are always fresh, tasty, and, just like first-quality candy, fattening! Finally, factory tours (M-F 9-3) are very popular for groups of all ages.
Directions: Going east on Interstate 80, take Chadbourne Road right to Courage, turn left to Watney. From 80 West, take the Abernathy exit, turn left on Chadbourne, left on Courage, and left on Watney.

JOSEPH SCHMIDT CONFECTIONS

3489 16th Street (at Sanchez, one block south of Market), San Francisco. (415) 861-8682. M-Sat 10-6:30. MC, VISA. Parking: street.
Joseph Schmidt makes premium chocolates—truffles are its best-known confection—sold at quality department stores. They're very expensive! A single truffle may sell for $1.50 to $2, or $25/pound and more at upscale stores. It's a lot more than mass-produced See's candy, but less than Godiva and Teuscher premium candies. This small store serves as an outlet and a test market, and is always stocked with a tempting selection of truffles and other candies, like chocolate-covered nuts and the exceptional candy sculptures (many holiday-themed) that are Joseph Schmidt hallmarks. Depending on

whose prices you use for comparison, you may be saving 25-50% off retail. Truffles in a tempting variety of flavors are just $1 each. The store is stocked with many appealing and unique gift-oriented candy assortments, perfect for hostess gifts or special acknowledgments.

LETTIERI & CO.

108 Associated Road, South San Francisco. (415) 873-1916. M-F 8-5. Cash/Check. Parking: lot. This company imports gourmet brands for delis, supermarkets, and gourmet food outlets. Specialties: olive oils, balsamic vinegars, pastas, fancy treats, desserts, jams, and syrups. Stock up on assorted bags of pastas for as low as 50¢/pound, 16-ounce jars of jam for 99¢, and balsamic vinegar of all ages with prices ranging from $1.99 to $13.95 a bottle. You'll pay more than wholesale, but quite a bit below retail. This small outlet is located in front of the office.

PLUMPJACK WINES

3201 Fillmore Street, San Francisco. (415) 346-9870. M-F 11-8, Sat-Sun 10-7. MC, VISA, AE. Parking: street. PlumpJack sells a surprising 150 wines under $10 and is committed to offering good values on all its wines, indicated by its printed "Compare Our Prices" list and price guarantee. The company specializes in Californian and Italian wines. You'll find familiar labels and vintners, as well as those more easily recognizable to connoisseurs. Stymied for a gift, or need a second wedding gift? Call or stop by and you'll get help putting together a case of wine that should delight wine aficionados. A 10% case discount helps, too! Delivery free anywhere in San Francisco; UPS otherwise.

PRICE RITE CHEESE

1385 N. Main Street, Walnut Creek. (510) 933-2983. M-Sat 9:30-7. Cash/Check. Parking: lot. Buy two pounds of cheese, save plenty; buy ten pounds, save even more. You'll find low-priced, high-quality jack, cheddar, and mozzarella and a vast assortment of fancy cheeses, Dutch and Indonesian spices, pâtés, and specialty meats at discount prices.

SAN FRANCISCO HERB CO.

250 14th Street (bet. Mission and South Van Ness), San Francisco. (800) 227-4530, (415) 861-7174. M-F 10-4, Sat 10-2. MC, VISA, DIS. Parking: street.

Go to the San Francisco Herb Co. for ingredients! Open to the public, it's a wholesale distributor of gourmet spices, spice blends, culinary herbs, nuts and seeds, medicinal herbs, organic herbs, traditional potpourri ingredients and fragrance oils. It does most of its business by mail and requires a $30 minimum to place an order—but three's no such requirement for outlet shoppers. You pay only one price: wholesale. Most products are available in 4-ounce, l-pound, and 5-pound sizes. Call and request a free catalog with potpourri recipes.

SMART & FINAL

24601 Mission Boulevard, Hayward. (510) 733-6934. Daily 7-8. MC, VISA, DIS. Parking: lot. (Other stores: 20 Bay Area locations—see Geographical Index.)

Smart & Final stores offer a spic-and-span shopping environment along with a fairly complete grocery selection; institutional foods; paper, party, and janitorial supplies; business and office supplies; and extensive frozen food and deli departments. Prices are sometimes higher than warehouse clubs, but there's no membership requirement. Labels in English and Spanish on most products. Its convenient and accessible locations are a boon to many underserved neighborhoods and communities.

TRADER JOE'S

337 Third Street, Montecito Plaza, San Rafael. (415) 454-9530. Daily 9-9. MC, VISA. Parking: lot. (Other stores: 17 Bay Area locations—see Geographical Index.)

You can be forgiven for not knowing about Trader Joe's if you're new to the area. Just about everyone else stops by to load up on gourmet foods and condiments, bakery products, cheeses, ready-to-serve wholesome gourmet specialties, wine, beer, health products, etc. There's a wonderfully casual and friendly ambiance to these stores, and prices are usually excellent on the often exotic offerings highlighted in every "Fearless Flyer" specials announcement. Some of the foods will please health-conscious consumers who want products without eggs, salt, sugar, MSG, dairy, or preservatives. The wine selection is so-so to superb; prices are excellent. Caveat: I wouldn't buy a case without first trying a bottle.

WINE CLUB

953 Harrison Street, San Francisco. (415) 512-9086. M-Sat 9-7, Sun 11-6. MC, VISA. Parking: lot. (Other outlet: 1200 Coleman Street, Santa Clara.) The wine connoisseurs I know have voted with their dollars! They've put Wine Club on their list of sources thanks to its pricing and selection. Anyone can shop and take advantage of its low markups, about 6-12% above wholesale. Budget shoppers can find a Chardonnay or Cabernet priced under $5 or $10, while serious connoisseurs can trim costs even when buying a world-class Burgundy at $78. Wines come from California, France, Italy, Germany, Spain, Portugal, Australia, New Zealand, Chile, Madeira, and elsewhere. If you're on the mailing list, you'll get "For Wine Lovers," the monthly buyer's guide, which lists most wines in stock followed by a designation of its value and availability. You can follow up with a phone order; UPS delivery or local courier service for a $15 flat fee for up to five cases.

Also See

Under General Merchandise—Discount Stores, Liquidators:
ALL LISTINGS

Carpets, Area Rugs, and Flooring

7

The evolution (some would say it's a revolution) of the carpet industry continues. On the manufacturing level, companies have merged and consolidated until the greater part of the market is controlled by just two companies. On the dealer level, buying groups have been formed (like True Value and Ace Hardware) to gain more leverage in buying. Through these alliances, they've combined advertising and marketing efforts. The major buying groups are recognized through their advertising as Trustmark and Carpet One and Carpet Max. Many local dealers have joined these alliances. While this is beneficial to the dealers, it does not allow consumers the wide latitude to comparison shop that they have enjoyed in the past. The Trustmark members are able to private-label their carpets, while Carpet One dealers sell carpets exclusively to their members. Price guaranties offered by members ensure that dealers are likely to keep pricing in line. Territories are protected to further control competition. Shaw Industries, the country's largest carpet manufacturer, upset the industry with its decision to enter the "retail" end of the business with Shaw Carpet Showplace stores (fourteen in the Bay Area). It's made comparison shopping more confusing by breaking with industry standards and pricing its carpet by the square foot rather than the square yard. (I think it's a clever ploy to make the carpet appear less expensive at first glance.) And major "big box" warehouse stores have added to the competitive marketplace pressure.

As a consumer, it is now more difficult to rely on brand identification and style names when making comparisons. To determine value, shoppers have to pay more attention to comparable qualities between carpets: the depth and density of pile, warranties and guaranties, stain-protection finishes, etc. When making comparisons, remember to multiply the square foot price by nine to get the equivalent square yard price when necessary, and be sure to note the type of padding and all aspects of installation, including removal and disposal of old carpeting. Make sure the bid is complete and that it includes all extras. Carpeting is often the single biggest investment you'll make in furnishing your home, so buy wisely!

Independent carpet stores and sources still abound, however, and these continue to offer exceptional values and selection. Certain stores specialize in buying overstocks and closeout patterns and colors. Some buy room-sized remnants or pieces from off-color dye lots. Others go in for bankrupt inventories. For these reasons, you can still save on your carpeting dollar.

When it comes to area rugs, there is a rug priced for you, whether you're a bargain hunter or rich and famous. New fiber developments and new looms driven by computer technology (the same concept as player pianos) have opened the market to everyone. Companies have also developed new rug sources in countries around the world, resulting in a broader range of rug prices. In addition, new

channels of distribution have been opened within the U.S. so that rugs can be purchased at stores that run the gamut from mammoth home improvement stores, warehouse clubs, and catalog companies to traditional specialty rug merchants and every retailer in between. In many cases, companies have developed special rug programs to sell to a particular type of retailer—thereby eliminating direct competition between various types of retailers. That makes it hard to comparison shop, since a rug shown at a major full-service retailer like Macy's is unlikely to be found at a discount store.

What counts most for many consumers shopping for an area rug is finding stores with a good selection from which to make a choice and a price orientation that suits a particular budget. A 9-by-12-foot area rug can be found for as little as $69 today. One thing that hasn't changed, today as yesterday: you get what you pay for. A higher price usually results in deeper pile, tighter weaves (or more knots or lines in handmade rugs), more complexity of pattern, better color development, and better fibers and finishes.

In this chapter I've included stores with selections oriented toward contemporary designs, casual decorative rugs, "new" rugs in reproductions of classic patterns, and transitional styles in both synthetic and wool fabrications in budget to better qualities. Before you buy an area rug, I recommend that you survey the marketplace with a visit to many stores. Once you've seen what the market has to offer, you'll be able to make a buying decision that reflects not only the aesthetics of your choice but the best price/quality/value equation for your budget.

Remember that it's a changing market. Always take your time, comparison shop, and consider all the factors. Be sure to check the listings in this book under Furniture and Home Accessories—Catalog Furniture Discounters, General Furnishings, and Furniture Clearance Centers. Many companies in these categories come through with exceptional prices on carpeting and area rugs.

General Carpeting, Area Rugs, and Flooring

A & M CARPETS

98 12th Street (corner at South Van Ness and Mission), San Francisco. M–Sat 9–5:30. (415) 863-1410. MC, VISA, DIS. Parking: street.
This is a family-owned business that keeps prices down with its low-rent location and no advertising. The owners also take advantage of special opportunities to buy discontinued area rugs from many manufacturers. Prices start at $59.99 for a 6-by-9-foot polypropylene and top out at about $899 for a wool. (Excellent selection priced under $300). The inventory is heavily oriented toward reproductions of Oriental-style area rugs, but there are some contemporary patterns. The selection also includes "art silk" (rayon blends) and berbers with fringe, but no sisals. Sizes from 2-by-4 to 9-by-12 feet. Good selection of inexpensive runners, even runners cut to size off a roll. Delivery anywhere in San Francisco for $25. If you're looking for "wall to wall" carpeting, check the rolls in the back for some good pricing.

CARPET SYSTEMS

1515 Bayshore Highway, Burlingame. (650) 692-6300. M–F 8:30–5, Sun by appt. Cash/Check. Parking: street/rear lot.

This offbeat location south of the airport can be attributed to the fact that most of the company's business is done with commercial and property-management companies. However, consumers can cross the freeway for Carpet Systems' excellent pricing. The showroom is neatly organized and well stocked with sample books from major carpet mills. You can go budget or top-of-the-line, or choose a contract carpet for your home office. Prices quoted include pull-up and disposal of existing carpets, labor, padding, and sales tax. A 30% deposit is requested with your order, the balance paid at installation. Nice, low-key setting and accommodating staff. *Directions: From SF/101 south, take Millbrae exit east to Old Bayshore and turn right. Going north on 101, take Broadway/Burlingame exit right to first light and turn left. Carpet Systems is across from Charley Brown's.*

CARPETS OF NEW ZEALAND

1940 Olivera Road, Suite C, Concord. (510) 689-9665. M–F 10–6. MC, VISA, DIS, AE, financing. Parking: lot.

Most wool carpeting is imported, entailing heavy freight, customs, and distribution costs. Cavalier Carpets, the second-biggest carpet manufacturer in New Zealand, bypasses traditional distribution and sells directly to customers. Thus, prices on wool carpets here are competitive with quality nylon carpeting, e.g., Ultron or Antron. You'll pay about half the price of competitors' wool carpeting. To extend your choices, the company sells wool carpeting from other manufacturers, also well priced. Your choices in pads are extensive. All carpets are moth-proofed and naturally resist soiling. Of course, you can borrow samples. You can have area rugs made from simple berbers or from carpets with more elaborate designs. Also, if you're some distance from the store, you can have the carpeting shipped to a local installer.

CONTRACTORS FLOORCOVERING OUTLET

818 Main Street #3, Pleasanton. (510) 417-0272.
M–F 1–5 or by appointment. Cash/check.
Parking: lot.

This doesn't look like your typical carpet store, and it's not. For one thing, without advertising and tucked away on the side of a building across from the historic Pleasanton Hotel, few would ever find their way to the door without a referral from a satisfied customer. Much of the owner's business is done with local developers (including upscale custom home developments cropping up in the hinterlands of southern Alameda County), with realtors preparing properties for sale, and with property managers. Anyone can stop in and go through the extensive selection of samples from major carpet, vinyl, laminate, and hardwood flooring companies. Prices for carpet, padding, and installation will appeal to the skinflint in all of us—with low overhead, markups are minimal. The owner's years as a sales representative for major carpet companies are invaluable when it comes to discussing the merits of each carpet and its appropriateness for your installation. You can borrow samples and order dye lot samples from the manufacturer.

Shoppers are bound to appreciate the owner's low-key informality, which strikes just the right note for comfortable shopping.

HALS CARPET & VINYL

7804 E. 14th Street (at 78th Avenue), Oakland.
(510) 632-1228. M–F 9:30–4:30, Sat 10–2. MC,
VISA. Parking: street.

Hal's location keeps overhead down; he also owns the building, employs no commissioned sales staff, and deals directly with each customer. His main clientele is apartment-building owners. Closeouts, mill drops, some seconds, and short rolls are sold at reduced prices for as much as 50% off original wholesale. You'll find moderate- to better-quality carpets among the mill rejects and special buys. Additionally, he stocks samples from major mills so that you can special-order carpeting in just the right color, style, and price range. Custom orders are sold for a minimal markup, and prices may vary with the type of installation and your skill at negotiating the lowest price after you've done some comparison shopping. Prefinished wood flooring from Bruce, Anderson, and Hartco, plus vinyl flooring from Armstrong, Tarkett, Congoleum, and

Mannington, are well priced. For a one-man operation, Hal's volume is impressive!

LAWRENCE CONTRACT FURNISHERS

470-B Vandell Way, Campbell. (408) 374-7590. T, W, F 9–5:30, Th 9–8, Sat 9–3. MC, VISA. Parking: lot.

Lawrence Contract Furnishers is one of the best resources for carpeting, vinyl floor coverings, hardwood flooring, and hardwood flooring kits from more than eighty companies. You'll probably have to arrive first thing in the morning to pat all the samples, and if you work fast, maybe you'll be done by closing time. After you've chosen your carpet, you can start again if you're shopping for wallpaper, draperies, or furniture from well-known manufacturers. Lawrence's discount system earns you average savings of 25–35%. Check the catalog library for additional resources. Most wallpaper books are discounted 30%. You're pretty much on your own, since decorator services are not available at these prices. Three times a year Lawrence has clearance sales on showroom samples, with prices reduced an extra 20–30%. *Directions: To find this out-of-the-way showroom from the San Tomas Expressway, take the Winchester exit in Campbell, go south to Hacienda, turn left, then right on Dell. Lawrence's is on the corner of Vandell and Dell.*

PIONEER HOME SUPPLY

657 Mission Street (bet. New Montgomery and Third), Fifth Floor, San Francisco. (415) 543-1234, (415) 781-2374. T–F 10–5 Sat by appt. Cash/Check. Parking: street/pay lots.

Taking one of the smallest markups around, Pioneer occupies a special niche in the marketplace, with pricing that its competitors are hard-pressed to meet. Amazingly, Pioneer has never spent a penny on advertising, depending instead on the loyal following it's acquired through more than forty years in business. The emphasis at Pioneer is now on carpeting and mattresses. The selection of carpeting and floor coverings is extensive. There's no push to trade up for bigger bucks and more profit. Just let them know your budget, and they'll point out the appropriate book, whether you're redoing an office with sleek contemporary contract carpeting or playing it safe with a conventional plush. If you live in the hinterlands, carpeting can be ordered and shipped directly to an installer in your area. I know some busy customers who are so confident of Pioneer's pricing and integrity that when they need a new box spring and mattress set they just call and say, "Send a new set." If you're like most people, you'll want to bounce on the mattresses first. No problem; when you stop in you'll have a variety of major lines in several price ranges to choose from. Delivery and installation are provided. *Note: Pioneer is closed Monday, Saturday, and Sunday, and weekday hours may vary since this "mom" is still fine-tuning her schedule.*

RUG DEPOT OUTLET

4056 Hubbard Street at 40th (across from Bay Bridge Shopping Center), . (510) 652-3890. M–F 11–7, Sat–Sun 10–5, MC, VISA (no checks). Parking: lot.

This is legitimate—a new warehouse concept for a major importer of machine-made and handwoven area rugs. This company is selling its "leftovers"— discontinued patterns, rugs from canceled orders, and surplus inventory at 40% to 50% off the retail of full-service stores. (Smaller savings may occur when prices are compared to promotional pricing at some discount stores, and more than 50% may be offered on many discontinued rugs.) With 20,000 square feet of warehouse space to show-case its inventory, the outlet's selection is quite extensive. It's a self-service operation, so start off by checking the hanging racks of samples that show rug styles and patterns available, with tags denot-ing sizes available in each pattern, fiber content, price, and location on warehouse floor.

Since this company imports a full range of rugs for distribution to retail stores around the country, you can buy 6-by-9-foot rugs in heat-set polypropy-lene, Oriental designs for $59.99, or in Southwest designs for $64.99; a Kirman-style machine-loomed 100% Belgian wool rug for $139; or a hand-knotted 160-line classic Aubusson Chinese wool rug for anywhere from $999 to $2,499. Other styles include scatter rugs and more. Sixty percent to 70% of the inventory is machine-made and imported from Italy and Brazil. Others countries include Belgium, Germany, India, Turkey, and China. Prices for a 6-by-9-foot rug start at $59.99. Rug sizes run from 2-by-3 feet to 9-by-12 feet, plus runners.

STYLER'S FLOOR COVERINGS, INC.

2249 Grant Road, Los Altos. (415) 961-8910. M–Sat 10–5. Cash/Check. Parking: lot.
You can relax here. The service is low-key, and the focus is on better carpeting (although you can buy budget, too), with some of the best brands coming from smaller mills on the West Coast. Markups are minimal, which leads to very competitive pricing. Major brands of vinyl flooring take care of baths and kitchens, and those prices are equally competitive. Large carpet samples and books can be borrowed for making sure that the color that looks so great in the store will look equally great at home. The lighting, wall color, and window orientation in your home can produce striking color differences from store lighting. Styler's licensed installers will see that the job is done to the highest standards.

TRADEWAY STORES WAREHOUSE

350-A Carlson Boulevard, Richmond. (510) 233-0841. M–Sat 10–5:30, Sun Noon–5. MC, VISA. Parking: lot.
(Other store [furniture only]: 10860 San Pablo Avenue, El Cerrito.)
If you're looking for good deals on carpeting, this gloomy warehouse for Tradeway Stores offers carpeting that has been written off as an insurance loss. Name-brand mills also dispose of overruns, excess inventories, seconds, and off-color carpeting. Stacked in rolls twenty feet and higher, the carpets will make you feel like you're walking through a mini Grand Canyon. I'm always impressed at the good buys on commercial carpets, which is why so many savvy architects and contractors make their way here. Prices are usually lower than original wholesale, and on the dogs that have been around too long, substantially lower. This is strictly a case of "what you see is what you get." You'll be impressed by the many fine-quality rolls, yet bewildered by others that seem unlikely to ever find a permanent resting place. There are no special or custom orders. Padding is sometimes available below wholesale. Tradeway

does not install, but will provide you with contractor references. All carpeting is ready for immediate delivery.

Remnants

CARPET CONNECTION

390 Bayshore Boulevard, San Francisco. (415) 550-7125. M–Th 9–7, F 9–6, Sat 11–5. MC, VISA. Parking: street.
Carpet Connection has a particularly choice selection of remnants, including many that are very effective in contemporary decors. You'll find stain-resistant carpets plus 100% wool and woolex blends. In many instances the remnant prices are below manufacturers' listed wholesale prices. Along with remnants, rolls of discontinued carpets are priced with bargain hunters in mind. There is a minimum installation charge of $75, and binding is $1.25/linear foot.

DICK'S CARPET ONE & AREA RUG WAREHOUSE

444 Lesser Street, Oakland. (510) 534-2100. M–Sat 9–5:30, Sun Noon–5. MC, VISA, DIS. Parking: lot. (Other store: 1065 Ashby Avenue, Berkeley.)
The carpet spectrum is covered, but the best values are found in the impressive selection of remnant carpets, from absolutely tacky to superb, and of course prices vary accordingly. What's nice about Dick's is that the remnants are in workable sizes, with many that will easily fit most room dimensions; there are even some large enough to cover two or three rooms. If you're inclined to buy a 6-by-9-foot rug in a midpriced ($200 to $500) or better range ($500 to $2,000), or if you're interested in larger sizes, Dick's offers an extensive and pleasing selection of rugs to review. Modestly priced polypropylene rugs start at about $200 for a 6-by-9-foot. The selection of rugs, from companies noted for innovative designs, cutting-edge fashion, or beautifully rendered reproductions of classics in wool or better-quality synthetics, is worth a special stop. Delivery charges are reasonable, usually $15–$25, depending on distance. *Directions: From Hwy. 880 take the 66th Avenue exit west to Oakport, turn right, and drive one mile to Lesser.*

FLOORCRAFT

470 Bayshore Boulevard, San Francisco. (415) 824-4056. M–F 8–6, Sat 8:30–5, Sun 10–5. MC, VISA, AE, DIS. Parking: street.

You'll find about 1,000 remnants in easy-to-see racks. Your best prices are on the "weird" sizes, because it's harder to sell a 7-by-20-foot rug than a standard 10-by-12-foot. Ditto for vinyl remnants. The selection covers about every type of carpet, including wool berbers, commercial carpets, graphics, loops, textures, and plush. Installation, cutting, binding, and delivery are provided. Kitchen remodelers will want to compare prices on Floorcraft's midpriced kitchen cabinets from Diamond, Omega, and Dynasty. You may be surprised to find that you'll save at least 10% off all those other "deeply" discounted prices advertised everywhere else, and maybe more on custom orders. Expect at least 15% lower prices than the warehouse superstores on custom orders for tubs, faucets, and toilets from Kohler, Moen, and Delta.

REMNANT WORLD CARPETS

5158 Stevens Creek Boulevard (at Lawrence Expressway), San Jose. (408) 984-1965. M–F 9–9, Sat 10–6, Sun 11–5. MC, VISA, DIS, AE. Parking: lot. (Other store: White Road Plaza, 1054 S. White Road, San Jose.)

You'll find more than 2,000 remnants from leading mills at good prices and 400 rolls of carpet. Want a take-it-with-you rug? Have it bound to your specifications. If you lack the fortitude to lay it yourself, you can have it installed. You can also special-order carpets from samples at very nice discounts, or pick up a bound area rug or hall runner from this extensive selection. Finally, check the vinyl flooring in rolls and remnants.

WOOD BROS. FLOOR COVERING, INC.

221 N. 16th Street, Sacramento. (916) 443-2031. M–Sat 8:30–5:30. MC, VISA, DIS. Parking: lot.

Wood Bros. has a huge showroom with rolls of carpets and vinyl flooring from major manufacturers (Trust Mark, Mohawk Excellence, Salem, Lees, Cabin Craft, Philadelphia, Evans & Black, Armstrong, Tarkett, Congoleum, Mannington, and more). The prices are already good, yet the staff is always willing to dicker a little. The best bargains are in the annex, where remnants are neatly organized by size up to 12 by 30 feet. Each piece is priced. (It drives me nuts when stores don't tag carpets, requiring you to ask for a price over and over again.) You'll be referred to licensed contractors for installation.

Helpful Hints

BERT'S CARPET WORKROOM
1751 Tennessee Street, San Francisco. (415) 641-8255. M–Th 9–4:30, Fri 9–3. Cash/Check. Parking: street.
Stretch your decorating dollar by making the best use of remnants or old carpeting. Maybe you're cutting down wall-to-wall carpeting to use in a bedroom, or you have some good remnants left over from a new carpet installation and you want to make runners or small area rugs. Worst-case scenario—your dog has chewed the edges of your expensive Oriental carpet. Call Bert's, one of the few companies around that specializes in binding. Binding is $3.50/yard; serging is $5.50/yard; fringing is $5/yard. Ask about costs on carpet repairs or a full line of Oriental fringe. Also, serging and binding of sisal carpets.

Also See

Under Furniture and Home Accessories—Catalog Furniture Discounters:
ALL LISTINGS

Under Furniture and Home Accessories—Furniture Clearance Centers:
MOST LISTINGS

Dinnerware and Kitchenware

AVERY'S

3666 Stevens Creek Boulevard, San Jose. (408) 984-1111, (800) 828-3797. M–Sat 10–6, Sun Noon–5. MC, VISA. Parking: lot.

Bargains go hand-in-hand with extra-special benefits at Avery's—courtesy strollers for the tots and starched linen hand towels in the lovely rest room. Avery's may have changed its pricing on some categories to appeal to bargain hunters, but it retains its lovely ambiance, fine selection of giftware, tasteful merchandising, and gracious service. The realities of the marketplace prompted its new discount policy: 30% off retail on most patterns of fine china (Noritake, Villeroy & Boch, Wedgwood, Spode, Lenox, Fitz & Floyd, etc.); 25–30% off retail on stainless and silver-plate flatware; 30–50% off on sterling flatware; and discounted stemware (excluding Waterford and Baccarat). A 50% discount applies to any leftovers, closeouts, whatever, found in its clearance room. Brides will want to register! Throw in its courtesy giftwrap, shipping, 800 number, and in-stock availability of most patterns and you end up with a full-price service and real values. Avery's is located behind Kiddie World at the back of the parking lot.

BIA CORDON BLEU OUTLET

1135 Industrial Road, San Carlos. (650) 637-8405. M–Sat 9–5. MC, VISA. Parking: lot.

This store serves as an outlet for plain and patterned Cordon Bleu porcelain dinnerware and bakeware. New inventory (overruns, discontinued patterns, slightly imperfect pieces) is added weekly, so you may want to visit more than once. Since the line is frequently featured in major store sales and promotions, the discounts vary accordingly, but you can count on 50% off "regular" retail—maybe more, in the case of missing lids and other such incomplete items. This outlet also caters to restaurant chefs and gourmet cooks; professional equipment and kitchenware are discounted about 20% off retail (even Calphalon, Le Creuset, All Clad, and Cuisinart). Along with the more popular items, you'll discover hard-to-find baker's equipment, like oversized pie plates (up to 12-inch), along with cake-decorating supplies, gadgets, utensils, pot racks, knives, springform pans, butcher-block carts, and other kitchenware. By mid-1998 the outlet will be moving into a new warehouse one block south on American (off Industrial).

CHICAGO CUTLERY, ETC.

Outlets at Gilroy, Gilroy. (408) 842-3810. Daily. MC, VISA. Parking: lot.

Whether you're cutting up tomatoes or a side of beef, you'll find a suitable knife at Chicago Cutlery at below department-store sale prices. You'll also find Wagner cast-iron skillets, Magnalite professional cookware, Colonial candles, and lots of other goodies. Your best buys are the discontinued items and seconds (not functional flaws; usually discolored wood handles on the knives or minute scratches on the Magnalite pans).

COOKIN'

339 Divisadero (bet. Oak and Page), San Francisco. (415) 861-1854. T–Sat Noon–6:30, Sun 1–5. MC, VISA. Parking: street.

This fascinating store is piled, stacked, jammed, and crowded with "recycled gourmet appurtenances," or, in plain English, used cookware. If what you want isn't made anymore or you can't locate it anywhere, it may be here. I'm not sure Cookin' qualifies as a bargain store, since the "old" things sometimes cost more now than they did originally, and many secondhand items are superior to the new stuff. The brands that made up Mom's or Grandma's kitchen are still available, but they're often made overseas and don't reflect the same quality. If you want anything copper, there's plenty. Cast iron, stockpots, bakeware, old measuring cups and utensils, exotic pastry items, molds, grinders, and more are sure to tempt. Count on dinnerware, soufflés, casseroles, custards, coffeemakers, waffle irons, glassware, and china. Not everything is old; occasionally there are closeouts at 25–45% discounts. Love the expensive professional-grade French pastry molds, bags, tips, and stuff for those Cordon Bleu recipes. If you're cleaning out your kitchen or disposing of an estate, call the owner, who's always on the lookout for good stuff.

COPPER KITCHEN AT VENICE GOURMET

625 Bridgeway, Sausalito. (415) 332-3544. Daily 9–6. MC, VISA, AE. Parking: street/pay lots.
Designers and restaurateurs are beating a path to the Copper Kitchen to buy the old Greek and Turkish molds, pails, bowls, buckets, and assorted pieces to use as fireplace pots, planters, or decorative accents. Old Turkish turban molds that sell here for $15 are often sold for $40–$50 in San Francisco's specialty boutiques. True to its name, you can find just about anything made from copper: heavy, new French cooking pots, new molds, graters, teapots, crepe pans, fry pans, stockpots, strainers, cookie cutters, wine coolers, pot racks and hooks, plus lots of charming, slightly tarnished old copper cookware. (Old pieces that have worn out their tin lining are not suitable for cooking, but they add wonderful charm to any decor.) Everything is discounted a little to a lot (some new pieces just a modest 10–20%); however, there's always a sale posted on a particular group of copper something. The best prices are always on the old pieces—the

Greek owner utilizes his direct connections to the old country to acquire these goods. You can shine up those old pieces, but I like them the way they are. Delicious gourmet deli with the best copper selection in the Bay Area, and a good reason to visit Sausalito.

CORNING REVERE FACTORY STORE

Great Mall of the Bay Area, Milpitas. (408) 934-9070. Daily. MC, VISA, DIS. Parking: lot.
(Other outlets: Folsom, Gilroy, Petaluma, Tracy, Vacaville centers.)
Corning and Revere products are the emphasis at this store: Visions cookware; Corelle dishes (open stock and boxed sets); Pyrex everything; Corningware bakeware and separate replacement lids; Revere bakeware and copper- and aluminum-disk-bottom pots and pans. The big discounts apply to Corning's and Revere's own lines, typically 20–60% off retail. The best buys are on 24- or 32-piece sets, such as Corelle and Corningware, in plain boxes. Overall, you'll find the best markdowns at the separate clearance store in Vacaville, where only discontinued products from Corning and Revere are sold at minimum 50% discounts.

CYCLAMEN STUDIO OUTLET

1825 Eastshore Highway, Berkeley. (510) 843-4691. M–F 11:30–5:30, most Sat 11–5. Cash/Check. Parking: lot.

Julie Sanders' whimsical ceramics appear in stores like Henri Bendel, Marshall Field, and their Bay Area equivalents. Stop in here to buy seconds, prototypes, and sample pieces. These ceramics are divided into dinnerware, platters, bowls, mugs, pitchers, and vases. Each piece is hand-painted and unique. Inspirations for the designs come from the great artists of the nineteenth and twentieth centuries, French Renaissance architecture, Mission furniture, and African textiles; combining sculptural shapes only adds to their originality. Five-piece place settings of dinnerware range at retail from $90 (solid colors) to $200. At the outlet, you're unlikely to find complete place settings all in one color, but you can expect a fun forage for accessories. Platters and other serving pieces in brightly colored glazes with dramatic designs, some with touches of gold, make wonderful gifts. The platters may range from $36 to $90 and lend themselves to serving many ethnic foods that are so popular in today's menus. Prices wholesale or below. All sales final. Shipping available, including boxes. Outlet faces the freeway.

DANSK FACTORY OUTLET

1760 Fourth Street, Berkeley. (510) 528-9226. Daily 10–6. MC, VISA. Parking: lot. (Other outlets: Carmel; Napa Factory Stores, Napa; Tahoe Truckee Factory Stores, Truckee.)

Dansk factory stores showcase all the products made by this fine company. Its lines are particularly appealing for their clean contemporary designs and functionality. Prices are typically discounted 30–60% on discontinued groups and factory over-runs. The stores are fun to visit, beautifully merchandised, and brimming with colorful, well-priced bargains. My favorite Dansk purchase: the 18-piece wineglass set packaged in a handy box with drawers that functions neatly as a storage unit.

DAVID M. BRIAN

1126 Broadway Plaza (at S. Main), Walnut Creek.
(510) 947-1991, (800) 833-2182. M–F 10–9, Sat
10–6, Sun 11–5. MC, VISA, AE. Parking: lot.
(Other store: Bon Air Center, Greenbrae. (415)
464-0344.)

I think of David M. Brian as the Gump's of Contra
Costa County and Marin. It's a pleasure to peruse
its elegant home accessories, decorative fine art,
giftware, dinnerware, kitchenware, and linens. It's
not a bargain store, but one bargain angle may be
of interest to you—30% discount on all sterling silver and silver-plate flatware by Towle, Reed and
Barton, Wallace, International, Oneida, Gorham,
Lunt, and Kirk Stieff, with interest-free, easy payment plans. Another plus is that almost every pattern is in stock. You'll also find 20–30% savings
offered every day on most informal and formal china
patterns. If you're buying a present, you'll love the
free giftwrap and free shipping within the Bay
Area—just another aspect of this first-class store!
Phone orders accepted.

FAMOUS BRANDS HOUSEWARES

Factory Stores of America, Vacaville. (707) 451-
2463. Daily. MC, VISA, AE, DIS. Parking: lot.
(Other outlets: Gilroy, Tracy centers.)

Here you'll find everything Rubbermaid, closet
accessories and organizers, picture frames, bakeware, cookware, gadgets galore, potpourri, kitchen
linens, pots, pans, serving dishes and platters,
glassware, microwave cookware, laundry-room
necessities, giftware, and more. The store offers
promotional items, discontinued styles, closeouts,
and regular merchandise at 20–70% discounts. It's
a subsidiary of the Lechters stores.

FARBERWARE OUTLET

Factory Stores of America, Vacaville. (707) 452-
0533. Daily. MC, VISA. Parking: lot.
(Other outlet: Folsom, Gilroy center.)

You'll be blinded by the gleam of Farberware's
stainless steel pots and cookware as you wander
through this outlet. Discounts are 25–40% off on
most items, but can go as high as 60% off retail.
Farberware also makes small electric appliances,
like toasters, coffeemakers, hand mixers, and
teakettles, as well as mixing bowls, measuring

cups, etc., all offered at minimal to large discounts. Millennium and Gourmetrix cookware is occasionally offered at modest discounts.

FRANMARA
560 Work Street, Salinas. (800) 423-5855. M–F 9:30–4:30. MC, VISA, DIS, AE. Parking: lot.
Franmara, a wholesale distributor to hotels and restaurants, has discontinued importing and distributing Pillivuyt French porcelain dinnerware. The Pillivuyt ("pilly-vwheat") dinnerware and serveware line offers a European look with traditional and contemporary designs. Its multifunctional qualities have made it a favorite with great cooks around the world. Each piece can go directly from the freezer to the oven or microwave. All the remaining inventory in Franmara's large warehouse is being liquidated—a process that may take a year or more. Everything is being sold below cost. Dinnerware and serveware patterns come in plain white or may be very special and decorative. It may be worth a stop to scout for some of the accessory pieces common to restaurants but not normally available in other dinnerware services. Corkscrews, barware, and pepper mills (items the company continues to

distribute) are also available at discount prices. *Directions: Take the John Street off ramp from Hwy. 101. Franmara is diagonal from Good Night Inn.*

HEATH CERAMICS, INC. (FACTORY OUTLET)
400 Gate 5 Road, Sausalito. (415) 332-3732. Daily 10–5. MC, VISA. Parking: lot.
The Heath Factory Store could well be the focal point of a trip to Sausalito. Overruns and seconds of tile for flooring, counters, and walls are available in extraordinary colors and textures at very worthwhile savings. The dishes and heat-tempered cookware that do not pass Heath's high standards are sold for 40% below retail prices. You'll find new glazes reflecting the latest looks in home-decorating trends, plus whiteware (dinnerware) in all shapes and special one-of-a-kind decorated plates. These savings are apt to keep you coming back to round out your dinner settings, to buy gifts, to purchase tile for a remodeling project, or to introduce a friend to the experience.

HERITAGE HOUSE

2190 Palou Avenue, San Francisco. (415) 285-1331. M–F 10–6, after 6 by appointment, Sat 10–5. MC, VISA, DIS. Parking: street.

Heritage House offers some special benefits that make it a solid alternative to the popular mail-order discount companies. First, the selection is distinguished by the many premium lines of imported European (some hand-painted) lines of china, stemware, and flatware and other lines that bear prestigious American designer names. Heritage House may be able to offer only minimal (10–20%) discounts on these lines, but that's better than none at all (and many are not available through mail order). On the more mainstream lines sold in department stores everywhere, prices are sometimes a tad higher than many mail-order companies, but still very competitive. If you're adding to your patterns, the staff is helpful about advising you when the manufacturers have scheduled sales and special promotions, so you can time your purchases for maximum savings. Brides get very special treatment, with a complete registry program and a telephone registry program for out-of-area brides. Appointments are preferred for bridal consultations;

with hundreds of patterns to choose from and combine, you'll appreciate the staff's expertise in helping you through the process of choosing the patterns you'll live with for many years. There are only two or three very upscale retail stores around the Bay Area that have a selection that rivals what you'll find here. Stop in too if you're shopping for tasteful gifts. The company has a most unlikely location: It's in an industrial park in the Bayshore area. Its modest exterior is in complete contrast to the beautiful showroom you'll encounter once you go through the doors. *Directions: From downtown, take the Army Street/Bayshore exit off Hwy. 101 to Bayshore. Turn left on Oakdale, right on Barnveld, and left on Palou.*

JANUS

261 Main Street, Los Altos. (800) 697-3500. M–F 10–6, Sat 9:30–5:30, Sun Noon–5. MC, VISA. Parking: street/rear lot.

Use the Janus 800 number to take the legwork out of gift buying. Or stop in and find a beautiful store featuring fine china, crystal, flatware (stainless, sterling, and silver plate), and giftware, with a discount policy that rivals many of the best mail-order companies. A few patterns in a few lines are not discounted, but 20% discounts are offered on Jean Couzon stainless (no one else does that). Minimum discounts start at 20% off retail; some are around 40%, and occasionally even more when manufacturers' promotions are added. Brands include Wedgwood, Christian Dior, Spode, Fitz & Floyd, Lenox, Noritake, Dansk, Villeroy & Bach, Royal Doulton, Reed & Barton, and other famous lines. Janus will ship anywhere!

THE KITCHEN COLLECTION

Factory Stores of America, Vacaville. (707) 446-7823. Daily. MC, VISA, DIS. Parking: lot.
(Other outlets: Anderson/Shasta center.)
The Kitchen Collection is a factory store for Wear-Ever and Proctor-Silex. Everything in kitchen essentials is covered, including other brands, like Meyer, Lincoln, Wilton, Anchor Hocking, Kitchen-Aid, and Hamilton Beach, all at a good price. There's a complete array of Wear-Ever pots and pans, pressure cookers, roasters, cake pans, and indispensable small electric appliances like toaster ovens, coffeemakers, juicers, popcorn makers, portable mixers, griddles, electric frying pans, woks, and Crock-Pots, as well as less essential but still useful devices. Sign up for the mail-order discount catalog.

LE CREUSET FACTORY OUTLET

Factory Stores of America, Vacaville. (707) 453-0620. Daily. MC, VISA, DIS, AE. Parking: lot.
(Other outlet: Gilroy center.)
Le Creuset cookware is exactly what you need for cooking comfort foods: stews and brews that need long, slow simmering or baking. If price has kept you away, check out the bargains on everything familiar (and unfamiliar) this company makes. First-quality pieces are discounted about 40%, seconds about 50%, and discontinued pieces and liquidations as much as 70% off retail. Don't pass up the other culinary accessories, like the never-fail screw-pull corkscrews, woks, and storage containers. Ships UPS anywhere!

LE GOURMET CHEF

Petaluma Village Factory Outlets, Petaluma. (707) 766-8893. Daily. MC, VISA. Parking: lot.
(Other outlets: Folsom, Napa.)
An irresistible store for browsing, buying and, to a lesser extent, bargains. The latest in gourmet cookware, gadgets, and accessories are almost as tempting as the gourmet edibles in jars, packages, bottles, and boxes (sauces, mixes, jams, marinades, vinegars, etc.). Value priced famous names: Cuisinart,

Krups, Henkel, Chantal, Meyer, Circulon, Fagor, Rowenta and Lodge cast iron cookware. Give your kitchen a culinary update by selecting some new fine cutlery, gourmet cookware, microwave bakeware, glassware, small electronics, kitchen gadgets, or accessories (salt and pepper shakers, mugs, cleaning aids, etc.). Except for kitchen gadgets and edibles, everything is priced at or below department-store sale prices.

LENOX FACTORY OUTLET
Outlets at Gilroy, Gilroy. (408) 847-1181. Daily. MC, VISA, AE, DIS. Parking: lot.
A large, elegant, and well-stocked store with Lenox china, stemware, crystal, flatware, and giftware (vases, picture frames, candles, coordinating paper products, etc.). Since Lenox now owns Gorham, you'll also find stemware, flatware (stainless, silver plate, and sterling), and Gorham giftware. Prices are discounted 30–50% off retail. Everything is almost invisibly marked as a second, yet the merchandise may in fact be first-quality surplus or closeouts. Some of the most popular patterns made by Lenox are sold on an open-stock basis. Phone quotes and orders are accepted on

the store's inventory; however, no special discounts are offered on merchandise that may not be carried in the outlet. The outlet is now carrying Lenox lamps and the Baldwin brass line (candlesticks, light plates, etc.) at about a 20–25% discount. UPS shipping anywhere!

MARJORIE LUMM'S WINE GLASSES
112 Pine Street, San Anselmo. (415) 454-0660. M–F 10–4, weekends by appt. MC, VISA, AE. Parking: municipal lot.
The serious wine buff doesn't want cutwork or ornamentation on glasses, obscuring the color and clarity of wine. If you're as serious about your wineglasses as you are about your wines, you'll want to pay a visit to Marjorie Lumm's warehouse/store. She has been at the helm of her own mail-order glass company for thirty years. Most of her glasses retail between $5 and $20 apiece; the most expensive is the Riedel Sommelier Burgundy, at $42. Bargain hunters will want to scrutinize the seconds, reduced 50% off retail. You may also find discontinued first-quality glasses sold at a considerable discount. Glasses can be engraved for a modest charge, and chipped or broken glasses can be

repaired. Call first about availability and store hours. Write for Lumm's catalog: P.O. Box 1544, San Anselmo, CA 94979.

MIKASA FACTORY STORE

1239 Marina Boulevard, Marina Square, San Leandro. (510) 352-1211. M–F 10–9, Sat 10–6, Sun 11–6. MC, VISA, AE, DIS. Parking: lot.
(Other outlets: 280 Metro Center, Colma; Anderson/Redding, Gilroy, Milpitas, Napa, Petaluma, South Lake Tahoe, Tracy, Vacaville centers.)
You have a chance to buy everything Mikasa here. Since it makes more than 300 patterns of dinnerware alone, you know there's a lot you haven't seen before. You'll also be energized by the prices, a tempting 20–50% off retail. At the outlet you'll find dinnerware, casual to fine china; casual and formal stainless flatware; cookware, bakeware, and casseroles; canisters; crystal stemware and giftware; linens; teakettles; pots and pans; vases; housewares; and more. Using Mikasa's special-order desk is the best way to order additional settings or pieces. UPS shipping available. Sorry, no giftwrap; all sales final.

NORITAKE FACTORY STORES

Outlets at Gilroy, Gilroy. (408) 842-9559. Daily. MC, VISA, AE, DIS. Parking: lot.
More than 200 Noritake patterns of china, crystal, stemware, glassware, and giftware, plus dozens of boxed sets, may challenge your decision-making abilities and keep you browsing. Everyday savings on first-quality wares range from 30–65% off. Savings are less, of course, when prices are compared to sale events at Bay Area stores and to mail-order companies. Some patterns may not be familiar—it would be impossible to find a store that carries everything that Noritake makes. On special patterns or closeouts, make sure you buy everything you need. Beautiful store. Phone orders and UPS shipping.

ONEIDA FACTORY STORE

Factory Stores at Vacaville, Vacaville. (707) 448-5803. Daily. MC, VISA. Parking: lots.
(Other outlets: Gilroy, South Lake Tahoe centers.)
You can't miss these stores, with their dazzling displays of silver-plated goods. You'll find overruns, vendor returns, excess inventory, and some seconds in traditional silver-plated hollowware, stainless and gold-electroplate flatware, gift items, leaded

crystal stemware and accessories, and melamine children's giftware. Expect 50–70% discounts off original retail. Tea sets, serving trays, casserole holders, picture frames, candleholders, most patterns of Oneida flatware, and food warmers are plentiful. Almost every item s available in prepacked gift boxes.

PFALTZGRAFF FACTORY STORE
Factory Stores at Vacaville. (707) 446-4984. Daily. MC, VISA. Parking: lot.
(Other outlets: Gilroy, South Lake Tahoe centers.)
Factory-owned and -operated, Pfaltzgraff Factory Stores offer the largest selection of Pfaltzgraff dinnerware and exclusive stoneware items made just for factory stores and catalog sales. Save 15% and higher on more than forty patterns with coordinating glassware, flatware, linens, and much more. Bridal and gift registry. Shipping available.

REED & BARTON
Outlets at Gilroy, Gilroy. (408) 847-5454. Daily. MC, VISA. Parking: lot.
Just what you'd expect from Reed & Barton: stainless and sterling silver flatware, silver plate, serving pieces, hollowware, storage chests, and more. The inventory is first quality, overruns, discontinued, and slightly irregular (usually on the silver chests). Discounts range from so-so to impressive. Also, Sheffield silver-plate serving pieces and Belleck china giftware from Ireland. A lovely store with an accommodating staff. Phone orders accepted.

ROBIN'S NEST
116 E. Napa (just off the Plaza), Sonoma. (707) 996-4169. Daily 10–6. MC, VISA. Parking: street.
Going to the wine country? Then stop off here for kitchenware, giftware, and gourmet cooking accessories and foods for 15–50% off retail (selected markdowns to 60% off). The best buys are on closeouts and special purchases. Uncommon wares from local artisans are especially appealing.

ROYAL DOULTON
Factory Stores of Vacaville, Vacaville. (707) 448-2793. Daily. MC, VISA, AE, DIS. Parking: lot.
(Other outlet: Pacific Grove, Gilroy centers.)
Slightly imperfect patterns of Royal Doulton, Royal Albert, and Minton china are sold at 40–70% discounts. Patterns not in stock can be special

ordered and shipped to your home; recently discontinued patterns are sold at clearance prices. Beatrix Potter, Brambley Hedge, Bunnykins, Toby Jugs, Character Jugs, and Crinoline Ladies giftware are sold at 20% discounts. You'll also find Royal Albert giftware and some crystal. Keep your eyes peeled for "extra specials" and markdowns around the holidays. You can special order anything in Royal Doulton, Royal Crown, or Derby. Don't worry about getting your china and giftware home: They ship via UPS anywhere, and most items are sold in gift boxes.

SILVER & MORE

Great Mall of the Bay Area, Milpitas (408) 934-9302. Daily. MC, VISA. Parking: lot.
(Other outlet: Gilroy center.)
At Silver & More you'll find displays of current silver, silver plate, and stainless flatware patterns from Towle, Wallace, and International Silver at 50% discounts, plus Gorham, Reed & Barton, Lunt, and Kirk Stieff competitively priced with the best mail-order companies. Waterford and Baccarat stemware and giftware are sold by special order at 20% off. These companies make several qualities of silver-plated giftware and hollowware: a lot of budget-priced trays, bowls, and candlesticks that offer the gleam but may not have the weight or quality engraving found on the better groups in stock. Check for special promotions of one kind or another, offered every week.

TOSCANA CERAMICS

601 Townsend Street (at Seventh Street), San Francisco. (415) 552-2118. W–Sat 11–5, Sun Noon–4, expanded holiday hours. MC, VISA. Parking: lot for Baker Hamilton Building tenants.
The Majolica tableware sold here, imported from Umbria and Tuscany, may reflect the art form of the Renaissance, but it meets current standards for food use. Many shoppers consider Majolica wares somewhat expensive when confronted with the current pricing at specialty gourmet and gift stores or from catalog companies. Toscana's prices are 20% to 50% less than competitors' prices on most items. For instance, an Umbrian Apothecary jar with portrait, 14 inches high, 7 inches in diameter, is $185 ($275 in catalogs); a dinner plate in the popular Rooster design, Galletto Verde, is $34 ($48 in catalogs); a Raffaellesco 12-inch serving bowl is

$80 ($120 elsewhere); a 17-inch serving dish is $78 ($155 elsewhere); a Geometrico 4-piece canister set is $375 ($500 elsewhere); and wine chalices at $35 are a bargain when compared to $55 at other stores. Antiquated designs that more closely represent the art form as it existed during the 14th and 15th centuries are available. They include reproductions of *Piatti da Pompa* (display portrait plates) that were produced in Umbria in the first quarter of the 16th century and large jugs and portage vessels painted in the *Stile Arcaico*, or archaic style, dating back to the 14th century. A bridal registry program is available on in-stock and eleven special-order patterns. Delivery takes about three months.

UNION STREET GLASS OUTLET
833 South Nineteenth Street, Richmond (888) 451-7752. M–F 10–3, Sat and Sun before Christmas. MC, VISA. Parking: street.
Union Street's Manhattan stemware design won the prestigious Niche design award in 1995. It's no wonder this line has become so popular with discriminating consumers. Its goblets, barware, bowls, and vases are elegant—and expensive: goblets retail for about $50 each. Each piece is hand blown,

signed, and dated. It's hard to figure what makes a second, since subtle variations on each piece enhance and emphasize the handmade look. Most collections here are embellished with 23-karat gold that will not scratch or wear off. You can choose goblets that have jewel tones drawn through the stem and gold leaf permanently fused into the design. For maximum versatility, the clear glass and gold-leaf treatments are the ultimate in elegance. From my perspective, the seconds at $10–$20 per stem, $5–$10 for a piece of barware, paperweights for $10, and bowls and vases at $35–$150 are genuine bargains. If you stop by and the door is locked, push the buzzer.

VILLEROY & BOCH OUTLET
Petaluma Village Factory Outlets, Petaluma. (707) 769-9029. Daily. MC, VISA. Parking: lot. (Other outlets: Ocean Avenue, Carmel; Tahoe/Truckee center.)
If you're cruising up Hwy. 101, take time out to visit the Villeroy & Boch Outlet, where shoppers delight in 20–70% discounts off retail (most dinnerware discounted at least 50% off retail). You'll find seconds and current pattern overruns, but it's

unlikely you'll find the company's newest patterns. Villeroy & Boch company makes about sixty patterns; at the outlet you'll find about twenty-five, including many of its best-known patterns, like Basket, Petite Fleur, Amapola, Siena, Mariposa, Botanica, Molina, Switch, Virginia, and its two popular Christmas patterns, Naif and Holly. You can buy a piece or a place setting from open stock. You're limited to the patterns in stock; no special orders for other patterns. However, you can call and order anything in stock and have it shipped UPS to your home. Villeroy & Boch also makes 24% lead crystal stemware. Prices on seconds and overruns range from $6 to $18. The Carmel store adds another angle—first-quality current and new lines, some reduced 20% off retail. Exchanges with receipt are allowed within one month.

Mail Order

Many mail-order companies offer the best of both worlds: good service and good prices on fine and everyday china, flatware (silver and silver plate), hollowware, crystal stemware, fine giftware, better jewelry, and collectibles. Check the back pages of almost any home magazine for starters. If a local retailer is having a special 40% off sale, then you may save just a few dollars. To avoid problems, keep careful records and copies of your order, ask for an estimated shipping date, and make sure you understand the company's return policy. There are trade-offs. For those starting or completing their own sets of china, crystal, or silver, there's no club plan to spread the payments without interest. On the plus side, you may avoid the California state sales tax (pending legislation); you can use toll-free 800 numbers to place your order; most companies have a national bridal registry; and shipping and insurance charges are very reasonable. Based on my experience, I can say that the companies listed here have good track records. Each may have slightly different pricing, availability, and shipping charges, so it's a good idea to get on the mailing list of each.

LANAC SALES
(800) 522-0047; fax (212) 925-8175.
Bridal registry, high-end patterns (Bernardaud, Haviland, Raynaud/Ceralene, Baccarat, etc.), gourmet cookware and electrics, giftware, and home accessories.

BARRONS

(800) 538-6340; fax (800) 523-4456.
Bridal registry, fine china, crystal, flatware, collectibles, and giftware.

MICHAEL J. FINA

(800) BUY-FINA; fax (718) 937-7193.
Bridal registry, good prices, some hard-to-find (at discount) patterns in china and stemware, better housewares, and jewelry.

ROSS-SIMONS

(800) 556-7376; fax (800) 896-9191.
Always my first choice for mail order. Most major brands, in-stock inventory, and bridal registry. Also fine jewelry, watches, nice giftware.

SMYTH

(800) 638-3333; fax (410) 252-2355.
Bridal registry; major brands of china, flatware, and crystal; jewelry; and watches.

THURBER'S

(800) 848-7237; fax (804) 278-9480.
Cover all your bases with this company's catalog.

Bridal registry and most mainstream china, flatware, and stemware patterns offered at discount.

Also See

Under Giftware and Home Decor:
ALL LISTINGS

Under Linens:
BED & BATH SUPERSTORE; HOME EXPRESS; LINENS 'N' THINGS

Under Jewelry and Watches:
ALL LISTINGS

Under Appliances, Electronics, and Home Entertainment:
WHOLE EARTH ACCESS

Under General Merchandise:
ALL LISTINGS

Under Late Listings:
WATERFORD WEDGWOOD OUTLET

Draperies and Window Coverings

AMERICAN DRAPERIES & BLINDS FACTORY SALE

1168 San Luis Obispo Avenue, Hayward. (510) 487-3500. Usually first Sat of May and Nov. 8:30–4:30. MC, VISA. Parking: lot.

American makes draperies and blinds; twice a year it opens its factory to the public to clear out miscellaneous stock, draperies in discontinued fabrics, production overruns, and odd sizes. Most draperies are priced between $20 and $60, a savings of 50–75%. Bring your required rod sizes and lengths. Expect traditional, three-pronged, French-pleated, lined/unlined draperies (double fullness), fan-folded and ready to hang with hooks inserted. You'll find a variety of colors, weaves, textures, and weights. Extrastrong miniblinds and verticals in alabaster and white are sold with a lifetime warranty in the twenty most requested sizes (custom sizes available, too). The sales usually occur on the first weekends in May and November. All sales final. Call anytime during the year and ask to be put on the mailing list.

CROW'S NEST INTERIORS

155 Railroad Avenue #C, Danville. (510) 837-9130. M–F 10–4, Sat by appt. MC, VISA. Parking: rear lot.

Since the fabric is the largest part of the total expense in drapery or other window treatments, Crow's Nest's 25–30% discount on fabrics helps considerably. Additionally, its workrooms provide excellent quality at fair prices. Designers work on a consulting basis for $45/hour, which is refunded when the drapery order is placed. In addition to draperies, Crow's Nest discounts Ohline, Woodfold, and vinyl shutters. You'll like the 25% discount on wallpaper and 20–25% on coordinating wallpaper fabrics, and you'll find the prices on bedspreads, comforters, window-seat covers, pillows, and upholstery equally pleasing. A two-thirds deposit is required with your order. Designers also offer complete design services, including furniture, carpeting, accessories, etc. at affordable prices.

THE DRAPERY OUTLET
590 Taylor Way, Belmont. (800) 371-6100. M–F 8–5, Sat 10–2. MC, VISA, AE. Parking: street.
For years this company has filled drapery orders for major stores. The outlet has a drapery workroom, a fabric warehouse, and the experience to handle almost any type of drapery treatment. You'll save on several aspects of the job. First on fabric, where markups are very modest. In addition to the in-house selection, you can plow through hundreds of sample books from major suppliers. You can go budget, better, or best; bring in your own fabric to have draperies made; or special order a fabric. You'll avoid the add-on markups taken by most major stores on every aspect of the job. If you need help, consultants will come to your home with samples, make recommendations for design treatments, and take measurements. The company gets you started and inspired with its display of treatments. Choose custom trims from sample books and hang the draperies from discounted Kirsch rods. A 50% deposit is required

before making the draperies. After buying new draperies you can rely on this company for other projects, such as slipcovers, duvets, comforters, and reupholstery.

WELLS INTERIORS CLEARANCE CENTER
41477 Albrae Street, Fremont. (510) 490-6924. M–F 10–6, Sat 10–5, Sun 11–5. MC, VISA. Parking: lot.
(Other stores: fourteen stores in Northern California; check Geographical Index.)
If you don't mind spending a little time scrounging to unearth your bargains, Wells Interiors offers hard-to-beat prices. This is where all the returns, double orders, customer mistakes, factory mistakes, etc. are sent from nineteen stores. Sizes and styles are limited, but even Wells' everyday discount prices are drastically reduced. For example, vertical blinds for patio doors that would normally sell for $80–$200 go for $50–$75. Wood blinds priced normally at $50–$200 per window are $25–$50 each. Keep your window measurements in your wallet so you can shop if you find yourself in the area. Repair service is available here for most blinds and shades. The company manufac-

tures its vertical blinds at this location—prices are very good! If you never get to the clearance center, stop by one of its fourteen Northern California stores. I have no trouble at all choosing Wells Interiors as a reliable source for value. I love the audacious signs posted in its stores comparing its prices to other local companies. *Directions: From Hwy. 880, take the Stephenson exit west. Turn left at Albrae, and follow around curve. Outlet faces freeway.*

THE YARDSTICK
2110 S. Bascom Avenue, Campbell. (408) 377-1401. M–F 9:30–8:30, Sat 9:30–6, Sun 10:30–5. MC, VISA, DIS. Parking: lot.
If you need draperies right away or you want luxury window treatments at budget prices, check the Yardstick. It usually has about 3,000 ready-mades (guaranteed 2½ fullness) from its own workrooms available for you to take home and hang. There's also a complete custom window-covering department using popular fabrics from Waverly, Robert Allan, Richloom, Covington, and others. Home-decorating services include furniture upholstering. Free in-home decorating service anywhere from San Francisco to Monterey. Kirsch and Graber drapery rods are always 30% off the manufacturers' list prices.

Also See

Under Carpets and Flooring:
LAWRENCE CONTRACT FURNISHERS

Under Furniture and Home Accessories—Catalog Discounters:
ALL LISTINGS

Under Fabrics—Home-Decorating Fabrics:
ALL LISTINGS

Flower and Garden

AW POTTERY

*601 50th Avenue, Oakland. (510) 533-3900. M–Sat
9–5. MC, VISA, AE, DIS. Parking: street.
(Other outlet: 2908 Adeline Street, Berkeley. (510)
549-3901.)*

Those who must limit their gardening to container
plantings will find pots for every situation at AW
Pottery. It's been a fixture in Berkeley for years,
but most shoppers have yet to discover its warehouse retail and outlet store in Oakland, north of
the Coliseum complex. The company imports
everything from tiny pots to gigantic vases and
urns, from rustic earthenware to porcelain (most
from its family-owned pottery studios in Malaysia
and China). It supplies nurseries locally and around
the country, national catalog companies, and
florists, and also handles direct imports for mega-
store chains and warehouses.

At both locations, AW Pottery sells imports to
consumers for about a 20% discount off prevailing
retail. (Marked prices do not reflect the discount,
which is given at the register.) For more impressive
savings take a look at all the seconds and damaged
pieces. If you can live with a chip or crack (from
minor to major) then you can pick up pots for
70–80% off retail (prices on seconds generally
range from 50¢ to $8. AW offers organized chaos;
with so much inventory and so many types of
imports—including teapots, small gift items, bonsai dishes and pots, and every variety of pot and
urn imaginable (glazed, unglazed, porcelain, etc.)—
keeping it all neat and tidy would keep the staff
working twenty-four hours a day.

CALAVERAS NURSERIES

1000 Calaveras Road, Sunol. (510) 862-2286. M–Sat, 8–4:30, Sun 8–3. MC, VISA. Parking: lot.
This firm grows many of the plants that it sells wholesale and directly to the public. Bring your list and landscaping plans and buy everything you need in one fell swoop at down-to-earth prices. Prices in 1997 were as follows: 1-gallon shrubs $3.40–$4.40; 1-gallon trees and vines $4.40–$5.40; 5-gallon shrubs $12.40–$16.40; 5-gallon trees and vines $16.40–$18.40; and flats of ground cover $11.95–$16.95. Prices on volume orders are reduced 15–20%; mix or match any plants that are the same price code and size. Call first to make sure that what you want is in stock. Delivery can also be arranged. For fall planting, time your buys for the Big Fall Clearance Sale!

COAST WHOLESALE DRY FLOWERS & BASKETS

149 Morris Street, San Francisco. (415) 781-3034. M–F 6–3, Sat 7–Noon. MC, VISA. Parking: private lot.
One glance at the warehouse and you'll get the feeling that they've scoured the forests and fields for unusual dry flowers such as hydrangeas, along with wreaths, oak leaves, pine cones, and more. Garlic braids, unique baskets, gourds, pods, and potpourri create a fragrant shopping environment. Lots of decorative accessories for ornamenting wreaths and arrangements, floral supplies, and beautiful fancy ribbons are also available. Prices are in line with other flower market vendors.

CONCORD SILK FLORAL

2061 Commerce Avenue, Concord. (510) 682-8088. M–Sat 10–5. MC, VISA. Parking: lot.
Allergies? Then your salvation is artificial flowers and greenery, but at bargain prices of course! If you have a resale number and are in the flower business, you'll get extra special prices on all the flowers, floral supplies, plants, baskets, and faux trees here.

COTTAGE GARDEN GROWERS

4049 Petaluma Boulevard North (up Pine Tree Lane), Petaluma. (707) 778-8025. Feb–Oct, daily 9–5; Nov–Jan, daily 10–4. MC, VISA. Parking: lot.
This nursery specializes in perennials, grasses, clematis, herbs, and many varieties of new and old antique roses. All plants are grown on the premises,

ensuring consistent care and quality, as well as acclimation to the region. You'll find more than 400 varieties (most offered in 1-gallon cans). Prices are very reasonable—$4.95 each, or choose any six for $28. The more common varieties are also at the big discounters (KMart, Home Depot, etc.) at slightly lower prices, but Cottage Garden's plants are fuller and healthier and get my money every time. If you have your heart set on a particular plant, call for availability and a list of all the plants carried.

COTTAGE GARDEN PLANTS

2680 Franklin Canyon Road, Martinez. (510) 946-9136. Sat 9–4. Cash/Check. Parking: lot.
This is a very different shopping experience. You'll drive down a quiet back road that leads to a lane that ends at Cottage Garden's 3-acre growing and selling area. There's also no phone on site, no comfort facilities, and only a cardboard table for transacting business. If you shop with kids, they'll love the chickens hopping freely around the plants. The owner, a landscape contractor, starts his plants from cuttings and seeds and specializes in both common and uncommon perennials, native grasses, woody ornamentals, and some trees. Rows and rows of plants (most in 1-gallon containers) are in various stages of growth. Unless you're really a plant pro, you'll need to wait for a "walk through" to identify the various plants, which are often not labeled. It's sometimes wet and muddy, so wear your oldest shoes. Type-A people might want to bring the morning paper to make the wait for service easier when too many customers show up at the same time.

The prices: Most perennials are $2.50 (1 gallon); woody ornamental shrubs, $3.50 (1 gallon); 15-gallon trees, $35–$40; trees in 24-inch boxes, about $120. Plants include: six to seven varieties of daylilies, penstemon, yarrow, cone flower, rudbeckia, salvia, agapanthus, amaryllis, Cransbill (true geraniums), verbenas, potato vine, clematis, hibiscus, sedum, lirope, camellias, scented barberry, dianthus, cotoneaster, butterfly bush, Mexican evening primrose, Japanese maples, crepe myrtle, bushes and trees, and more. The plants are "acclimated" (grown in the open) and are less likely to incur transplant shock. Finally, many customers have extended existing plantings (unusual varieties) by bringing in cuttings from their gardens for propagation. *Directions: From Hwy. 4 take the Alhambra Avenue exit south, turn right/west (about 300 feet) onto Franklin Canyon Road. Drive 1.7 miles, turn right on Wolcott Lane, look for signs.*

FLOWER TERMINAL

Sixth and Brannan Streets, San Francisco. Hours vary, generally M–F 2 a.m.–2 p.m., Sat hours for a few vendors 8–Noon. Cash/Check. Parking: street/lot.

Several wholesale nurseries are located in this block, selling cut flowers, houseplants, greenery, and floral supplies to the trade and the public. Don't expect information or advice. Vendors have neither the time nor the personnel for retail services. You are required to pay sales tax, unless you have a resale number. Highlights: Ira Doud and Floral Supply Syndicate are headquarters for ribbons, decorations, wrapping paper, wreaths, and other fixins for holiday decorating, floral displays, or table decorations. Silver Terrace is the largest of several vendors selling cut flowers, foliage, and plants. While prices aren't "wholesale" to the public, many items are simply not sold elsewhere at retail. From October through Christmas, anxious shoppers crowd these dealers to get a head start on their holiday decorations. Note: Only people with resale numbers are allowed to park in the lot in the early morning hours, and street parking can be a real problem!

FLOWERS FAIRE

360 Bayshore Boulevard, San Francisco. (415) 641-7054. M–Sat 8:30–6:30, Sun 9–5. MC, VISA. Parking: street.

People who live and work in this area stop by here to pick up roses, tulips, or tasteful mixed bouquets. For decades, this quick-service, budget-priced operation has specialized in carry-away bouquets. You'll get more blooms for the buck here than at your local supermarket. Flowers Faire offers several reasonably priced packages for weddings based on the use of seasonal flowers—and additional savings if it doesn't have to deliver. You can have it your way, but some flowers will cost more. If you become a frequent customer, you'll want to pick up a discount card.

LISA ARNOLD NURSERY SALES

9950 Calaveras Road, Sunol. (510) 862-9009. M–F 7–4; winter, Sat 8–4; spring/summer, Sat and Sun 8–4. Cash/Check. Parking: lot.

For a big landscaping job, go where the pros—landscape contractors and nurserypeople—go. Bring your "want list" and fill your trunk with trees, shrubs, ground covers, color, and specialty items like Japanese maples, bonsai, and palms. Some prices: flats $8.50–$11.50; 1-gallon $2.50–$7.50; 5-gallon $7.50–$16.50; and 15-gallon $30–$60.

MAINLY SECONDS

15715 Hesperian Boulevard, San Lorenzo. (510) 481-1902. M–F 10–5, Sun 11–5. MC, VISA. Parking: street/lot.

When warm weather rolls around and you're in a potting mood, you'll find good buys on an ample selection of planters and pots. True to its name, you'll find pottery seconds aplenty (usually stoneware or ceramic pots). The store also carries first-quality bargains in odd lots, closeouts, and direct purchases at discount prices—a consequence of its wholesale business. A 6-inch standard clay pot sells for about 69¢. You'll find standard terra-cotta pots, Mexican pottery, bonsai planters, ceramics from India, Chinese stoneware, and more. Everyday discounts on standard pots are 30% off marked prices, while seconds in every category are reduced 50% and more. Sometimes the pottery yard is overflowing, sometimes it's practically bare.

NOR CAL POTTERY PRODUCTS

2091 Williams Street, San Leandro. (510) 895-5966. M–F 10–4. Cash/Check. Parking: lot.

Nor Cal is an importer and distributor of pots and planters. It also imports many unique pots and planters used by landscape architects and interior designers. Since most of its pots are terra-cotta imported from Italy, a fair amount of seconds are accumulated—damaged in shipping, with cracks or chips. These seconds are usually 50% off retail. Occasionally, special pots get damaged, and then prices may be dropped to 75% off retail. There are bargains aplenty. You'll want to poke around each stack and pallet of pots, but ignore the excess first-quality inventory, also stacked outside, at full retail. At times, I've spotted fairly large terra-cotta pots (seconds) priced at $5 (well below wholesale).

If you approach Nor Cal with an "I'll take pot luck" mind-set, you'll probably be more than satisfied. *Directions: From Hwy. 880, take the Marina exit west. Turn right at Merced, left on Williams.*

ORTIZ POTTERY OUTLET

425 South Market Street, San Jose. (408) 286-3661. M–Sat 9–6, Sun 9–2. MC, VISA, AE. Parking: lot.

Behind San Jose's convention center, this outlet offers pallets, tables, and stacks of pottery containers, such as Italian terra-cotta, Gainey ceramics in more than fifty colors, and Mexican and Chinese pottery. These are closeouts and seconds at nicely discounted prices. Inventories from other manufacturers produce an ever-changing selection. Look for statuary items, such as fountains and birdbaths. Catalogs are on hand for special orders on some pretty upscale Italian pots, patio statuary, and garden accessories. You'll appreciate the umbrellas over the pottery yard on rainy days.

POTTERY & FLORAL WORLD

685 Brannan Street (at Sixth Street), San Francisco. (415) 543-5455. M–Sat 8:30–5, Sun 10–4. MC, VISA, AE. Parking: rear lot.

Customers become regulars, as every visit produces new treasures. The company's buyers are on the prowl for surplus and slightly imperfect inventory from manufacturers and importers to keep its three West Coast stores well stocked. They're successful, too! The pottery yard is stocked with standard Mexican terra-cotta pots, as well as unusual large urns (many with distinctive finishes), statuary, fountains, and outdoor benches and tables. Artificial flowers, mostly silk, are always in good supply at competitive prices. You'll also find giftware (love the surplus dinnerware from L.A. Pottery), baskets, Chinese pots, cookie jars, wax fruit, bath accessories, and holiday ornaments and decorations. Regulars hurry in each fall for decorations and fixins, then line up early for post-Christmas sales and return again in late spring for last-chance markdowns. Be advised: Some of the most interesting ribbons and Christmas decorations are imported by the company for wholesale distribution. To avoid conflicts with its retailers, these are not discounted to any great degree. Love those parking spaces at the back of the store!

REMEMBER WITH FLOWERS
24901 #B Santa Clara Street (off Jackson and Hwy. 92), Hayward. (510) 784-8990. M–F 9–7, Sun 9–6. MC, VISA. Parking: lot.
(Other store: 1553 A Street, Hayward.)
Remember with Flowers is a clearinghouse for fresh-cut flowers, selling surplus inventory from the Flower Market and local growers every day. Flowers are graded for shipping (1–5); Remember with Flowers buys flowers that have passed their tolerance for cross-country shipping (a 3 grade), but they're not bloomed-out or tired. All flowers are sold in bunches of ten or two dozen stems, the wholesale norm. Shop prepared to select the best of what's available. You may find freesias, chrysanthemums, hybrid lilies, alstromeria, roses, and baby's breath at about half the price of the supermarket. If you need just a one-day display of flowers, you may find everything you need in the markdown buckets near the front door; on which prices are reduced another 50% or so.

A SEPARATE ARRANGEMENT
5758 Shellmound Street, Emeryville. (510) 653-7227. M–Sat 9–6, Fri till 6:30, Sun 10–5. MC, VISA. Parking: lot.
East Bay shoppers don't have to cross the bridge to find super buys on fresh-cut flowers. Just take the Powell Street exit east off Hwy. 80 to the first light, turn right, and head for the orange building behind Lyon's restaurant. This good-sized shed-type building is filled with buckets of flowers and some house plants. The company supplies many flower kiosks in supermarkets and other retail operations with ready-to-go bouquets and bunches of individual blooms. The leftovers are sold to the public at deeply discounted prices. Usually in stock: roses, Casablanca lilies, tulips, alstromeria, carnations, mums, baby's breath, foliage, greenery, and more. Inquire about flowers for weddings or other special events (bouquets or centerpieces) and monthly floral design workshops. Accommodating staff.

A. SILVESTRI CO. FACTORY SECONDS

2635 Bayshore Boulevard, San Francisco. (415) 239-5990. M–Sat 8:30–5, spring and summer Sun 10–4. MC, VISA. Parking: lot.

Anyone navigating the roads to reach the Cow Palace or 3Com Park has probably noticed the displays of concrete statuary at the A. Silvestri showroom—a large complex that's been a fixture in the area for years. Indoor and outdoor architectural fountains, planters, benches, statues, religious figures, columns, bird baths, fish ponds, mantels, balustrades, and garden ornaments in many guises attract buyers from all over. Bargain hunters will want to check out the seconds selection, where anything from Silvestri's vast inventory may end up, particularly if it's cracked, chipped, oversprayed, or just real old. Prices are reduced by about half on these rejects. Some cracks can be easily camouflaged using a product like Bondo, a body filler for cars. Some buyers will feel that the cracks just add an antique authenticity to the piece. In any case, it's up to each buyer to decide if they can fix or live with the imperfections. Fountains will not include pump elements, but these can be purchased. Some exceptionally large seconds may be located in other parts of the showroom or yard. No delivery is provided on seconds, a consideration when buying a very large or heavy piece.

SMITH & HAWKEN OUTLET

1330 Tenth Street, Berkeley. (510) 525-2944. F–Sat 10–6, Sun 11–6. MC, VISA, AE. Parking: lot.

Smith & Hawken's outlet is partitioned from its very attractive full-service retail store and nursery. It has a separate entrance and offers merchandise in garden furniture, distinctive gift and dinnerware items, garden tools, plant food and fertilizers, fireplace tools, garden books, some apparel, and much more in the way of esoteric gardening and decorative items. Some merchandise may be slightly damaged or irregular, but most is discontinued catalog inventory reduced 25–75% off retail. *Note: I've found that hours change from time to time, so call first.*

SSILKSS

635 Brannan Street, San Francisco. (415) 777-1353. Daily 8–5. MC, VISA. Parking: lot.

Ssilkss, an importer, wholesaler, and manufacturer of artificial trees, stocks an impressive inventory of silk flowers, plants, and trees and offers the same discounts to everyone. Ssilkss makes a variety of artificial trees up to twenty-five feet tall: ficus, palms, flowering trees, and bonsai. Complete your presentation with baskets and dried material to coordinate with the silk flowers and greenery. Christmas starts in August here, with an extensive display of Christmas trees 4 to 15 feet tall and grapevine reindeer up to 6 feet tall.

SUNFLOWER WHOLESALE FLORAL SUPPLY

1243 Boulevard Way, Walnut Creek. (510) 947-0543. M–Sat 9:30–5:30. MC, VISA. Parking: lot. East Bay floral designers and wanna-bes flock to this upscale operation to get the very best in floral supplies. Since opening its operation to the public, word has spread that this is the place to go for inspiration and unique and high-end flowers and fixings. Amid the abundant floral displays are sample arrangements created by Sunflower's talented in-house designers that reflect the latest trends and sophistication in flowers, colors, and foliage. If you're clever at duplicating but shortchanged in creativity, you'll welcome the ideas that are provided. If you're lazy or in a rush, you can buy the

ready-to-go arrangements, which are very reasonably priced, considering the level of originality. I found prices competitive and sometimes a bit higher than some vendors at the San Francisco Flower Mart, but you get so many extras at Sunflower: excellent customer service and free advice, unique blooms (dried, paper, and silk), beautiful ribbons (silks, French wired, and other high-end exotics, which can be quite pricey), distinctive containers and objects for showcasing your arrangements (baskets, bowls, bird cages, papier-mâché boxes, twig chairs), wreaths made from out-of-the-ordinary materials, and some elegant home accessories (window boxes, stands, statuary, topiaries, pots, vases, etc.). I saw many things that I haven't seen at other floral supply outlets, which is what makes this company so special. There is a two-tiered pricing structure. Wholesale buyers must have a valid California resale license, and the general public pays the listed retail price (with additional discounts for quantity purchases). Hands-on classes with an emphasis on basic floral design techniques are offered throughout the year for a modest fee. In addition, free floral demonstrations by in-house and guest designers are frequently offered, particularly

during the fall and holiday open houses. Martha
Stewart would love this place!

Also See

Under Home Improvement:
HOME DEPOT

Under Art, Craft, and Hobby Supplies:
FANTASTICO

Under General Merchandise—Discount Stores:
PRICE/COSTCO

Furniture and Home Accessories

In this chapter, I've separated the listings into logical groups. All the stores mentioned offer substantial savings. Some have large showrooms with backup warehouse stock, allowing you to buy furniture directly off the floor, while others may have minimal or no stock on display and do most business through catalog orders. A few are clearance centers for full-service retail stores. When stores have focused on a particular category of home furnishings, e.g., office or baby furniture, I've created a separate section for them.

It's important to understand the system when buying furniture. When you place a custom order (as opposed to buying in-stock inventory), you usually have to wait anywhere from a few weeks to several months for delivery. The store you're buying from often has no control over turnaround time. For instance, the fabric you've chosen for a new sofa may be out of stock at the factory, or delivery may be delayed until the manufacturer schedules another production run. Often the store won't be aware of these problems until the piece is ordered from the manufacturer. Once the furniture arrives, there may even be additional delays if freight damage has occurred and the piece must be "finished" or "deluxed." It's hard to fathom how a china cabinet can be sent without shelves or hardware, but it does happen. When something goes wrong, it may seem to take forever to sort everything out. In most cases, the only way the store can alleviate the aggravation is to keep you informed. Patience is required when placing a custom order, whether you're trying to save a few hundred dollars or several thousand dollars on your furnishings.

Catalog Discounters

The businesses in this section sell furnishings primarily from manufacturers' catalogs rather than from in-house stock. They offer some of the best alternatives to high retail prices. The operations I have listed are all similar, in that they take a small markup. Many eliminate costly services and forgo advertising. Some of these places have no furnishings at all to show; others have quite a few. Buying furniture this way will usually enable you to save 20–40%. The discounts offered by these stores differ by degrees. Some offer little more than a very low price, while others combine a high level of service and design support with slightly higher prices. I'm confident that you'll be able to find the store that most fits your needs among the ones I've listed. Most have no credit plans other than MC or VISA. These stores may also focus heavily on two or three categories of furnishings. Therefore, I've cross-referenced them under the carpets, appliances, and draperies sections, or in instances where I felt it was more appropriate, I've placed the stores' listings in those categories. Note the cross-references to consider all your options.

ALIOTO & ASSOCIATES

644 Third Street West, Sonoma. (707) 996-4546. M–Th 9–5; F, Sat, eves by appt. Cash/Check. Parking: lot.

Alioto & Associates maintains a low profile compatible with Sonoma's pastoral image. Although the exterior resembles a new apartment house, the showroom is quite lovely. You'll find several room groupings complete with tasteful accessories providing a tempting assortment of furnishings from the manufacturers the store represents. Showroom prices reflect the manufacturers' suggested retail listing; you'll have to ask for the discount price. Of course, you can buy off the floor, but chances are you'll end up purchasing from the store's catalog resources. Alioto has an extensive selection of wallpaper books (average 25% discount); carpet and flooring (vinyl) samples from leading manufacturers; window treatments (blinds, pleated shades, woven woods); and fabric samples for draperies and upholstery. Alioto works with new homeowners and remodelers at the blueprint stage to help them avoid expensive mistakes. It controls costs by operating with a minimal markup, doing business on a cash basis, and being family owned. Using its interior design service, you can completely decorate your office or home. In addition to most major brands of high-end furniture, it can also order some "restricted" brands, although the discounts may be less. Phone quotes are given if you can provide all the specifics.

CHETT GAIDA INTERIORS

80 Carolina, San Francisco. (415) 558-9823. M–T 9–3:30, F 9–Noon. Appt. preferred. Cash/Check. Parking: street.
Chett Gaida is a pro who combines personal design service with good values. He generally serves an upscale clientele prepared to pay for quality, evident in middle- to high-end furnishings like McGuire, Henredon, Leathercraft, Aireloom, La Barge, Lane, Hekman, and others. If you're timid about making buying decisions involving thousands of dollars on furnishings you'll have to live with for years to come, you'll appreciate the time Gaida is willing to spend with you. That includes visits to trade showrooms, design expertise, and even home consultations. If you're interested in investing in a fine handmade Oriental rug, he can arrange visits to reputable wholesale rug showrooms. Gaida offers a peace-of-mind alternative for those who simply can't do it on their own. Deposits of 50% are required with an order. Appointments preferred.

DAVID MORRIS CO.

1378 Sutter Street (bet. Franklin and Van Ness), San Francisco. (415) 346-8333. M–F 9:30–5:30, Sat by appt. MC, VISA, 30- to 90-day interest-free payment plans. Parking: street.
You'll see just a few sample pieces of furniture on the floor, but David Morris offers good savings on custom orders from major catalogs. The store does a tremendous carpeting business and works closely with insurance companies on replacement claims. If carpeting is your top priority, you'll want to settle down with sample books from just about every carpet company. Inquire about Karastan and its Persian and Chinese carpets. Selecting new draperies or window treatments is a piece of cake. If you must see before you buy, you can arrange a preview trip to the Furniture Mart. David Morris also sells well-known brands of kitchen and laundry appliances, TVs, VCRs, and stereos. You'll save 30% on almost all purchases, including freight and delivery.

DEOVLET & SONS

1660 Pine Street (bet. Van Ness and Franklin), San Francisco. (415) 775-8014. M–Sat 8–5:30. MC, VISA. Parking: street/pay lots.

This store has been around for more than fifty-five years, and for good reason. The grown-up children of its original customers now get the same good values, prices, and service that their parents received years ago. You may have to ask someone to turn on the lights on the second and third floors for a good look at the bed, dining, breakfast, and living room furnishings. You'll find displays of very moderately priced goods in upholstered lines and case goods for the bedroom and dining room, plus major lines of kitchen and laundry appliances (including Wolfe, Viking, Gaggenau, Dacor, General Electric, Kitchen-Aid, and Sub-Zero), and vacuum cleaners. The store leans toward traditional and includes Victorian-inspired reproductions in uphol-stered furniture and case goods, and many oak pieces. It can usually offer immediate delivery on appliances and bedding. You'll find excellent prices on its large selection of carpets from several major mills, and count on a 25–30% discount off retail.

DON ERMANN ASSOCIATES

699 Eighth Street, Suite 100A, San Francisco. (415) 621-7117. M–F 9–5. MC, VISA. Parking: lot.

Don Ermann's new setting in the San Francisco Fashion Center represents an attempt to simplify his life and business. Old-timers may miss his ele-gant showroom, but they'll still find the enticing pricing that kept them coming back time and time again over the years. Like most other outfitters that offer quality furnishings at discount prices, Don and Joan Ermann can help you make your way through an extensive collection of furniture catalogs. You can purchase better lines of home furnishings, plus carpets, floor coverings, draperies, fabrics, executive office furniture, and wallpaper. The lines it carries are impressive. Some high-end examples are Brown Jordan, Hammary, Hekman, Glass Arts, Hickory Chair, La Barge Tables and Mirrors, McGuire Rattan, Taylor Woodcraft, Jasper Cabinet, Fremarc Designs, BarcaLounger Recliners, Ekornes Stressless Chairs, Koch & Lowy lamps, and Dunhill. Serious customers are taken to the Galleria or Showplace Square to evaluate potential choices. The owners are most accommodating: never pushy and very knowledgeable. Pricing is straightforward.

The store subtracts 40% from the retail price (from factory-published lists, not inflated retail lists). Delivery charges additional. If your time is precious, make an appointment so someone will be available to give you their undivided attention.

EASTERN FURNITURE

1231 Comstock, Santa Clara. (408) 727-3772. M, T, Th 9:30–8; W, F, Sat 9:30–5:30; Sun Noon–5. MC, VISA. Parking: lot.
Eastern has 50,000 square feet, featuring galleries by Century, Hickory-White, Bernhardt, Natuzzi, and Harden. Other manufacturers the store represents include Vanguard, Sherrill, Hancock & Moore, Hickory Chair, Lane, Hekman, Customcraft, Rowe, Kincaid, Maitland-Smith, and many more. You'll find leather furniture, youth furniture from companies like Lexington and Stanley, mattresses from Serta, recliners from Braddington-Young, plus many informal dining sets and occasional tables. Filling in the spaces are upholstered sofas, chairs, sectionals, entertainment centers (RCA Home Theatre is a specialty), and accessories. The backup inventory in the nearby warehouse may save you a possible three-month minimum wait. You can special order merchandise from the approximately 200 manufacturers Eastern represents. Prices are considerably less than full-service retail stores on most furniture lines carried. Beautiful showroom with elegant displays. Interior designers available.

GALLERY WEST

1355 Market Street (at Tenth Street), San Francisco Furniture Mart, San Francisco. (415) 861-6812. T–F 9:30–4:30, Sat 10–4. MC, VISA, financing. Parking: validated basement garage weekdays, street on Sat.
At Gallery West you'll have access to the wholesale showrooms of the Western Merchandise Mart. Browse through manufacturers' catalogs of sofas, chairs, bedroom and dining room pieces, occasional tables, lamps, accessories, draperies, window coverings, carpeting, and vinyl or hardwood flooring. Serious customers get to view possible selections in Mart showrooms in the building or at Showplace Square. The staff can provide complete design services at no extra cost when combined with major purchases. The usual discount reflects 25–40% off the prices in conventional retail stores. As a factory representative for Highland House

and Designer Gallery Ltd. (upholstery), Hekman Furniture, Sumpter Cabinet and Howard Miller (clocks, curios), and James Moder crystal chandeliers, Gallery West offers special discounts on these lines. Delivery is extra. You'll have to stop at the desk in the main lobby to get the okay to visit the Gallery West showroom. This building is not open to the general public.

GIORGI BROS.

212 Baden Avenue, South San Francisco. (415) 588-4621. M–Sat 9–6, F until 9. MC, VISA, financing. Parking: street/lot.

Giorgi Bros. is not an elegant store. To earn that description, it would have to carpet, paint, and triple its space to provide room for lovely vignettes that would do justice to the furnishings it sells. As it is, the store is usually crammed with about one hundred sofas, approximately fifty bedroom and fifty dining room sets, entertainment cabinets, grandfather clocks, mattresses, appliances, floor coverings, chairs, occasional tables, and more. Its buyer does an impressive job selecting fabrics for the upholstered pieces on the showroom floor. Additional inventory is kept in a nearby warehouse, helpful if you're in a rush. If you want to select your own upholstery pattern or finish, you can custom order through the catalogs. Across the street in the annex are informal kitchen and dining sets, children's furniture, and other articles. Another new showroom has been added just a half block away to showcase even more furniture. You'll see moderate- to high-end lines like Century, Hickory-White, Vanguard, Flex Steel, Bernhardt, Wexford Collection, Pennsylvania House, Lexington, Hammary, American of Martinsville, Weiman, Pulaski, Classic Leather, Stanley, Lane, Hekman, Harden, La Barge, Burton James, Borkholder, Henkel-Harris, Hancock & Moore, Hickory Chair and dozens more. Tags list Giorgi's discount price (at least 33% off prevailing retail), plus manufacturer's name and model number. With all this emphasis on its classy furniture selection, it's easy to overlook the appliances, home electronics, and floor coverings (carpet, vinyl, hardwood) at very competitive prices. The new parking lot across the street from the main store allows for leisurely shopping.

HOUSE OF VALUES

2565 S. El Camino Real, San Mateo. (650) 349-3414. T–Sat 9:30–5:30, F eve 7–9. MC, VISA. Parking: street.

Just when I think I've seen everything at House of Values, I'm directed out the door and down the street to the next showroom. There's an outstanding selection of furnishings that reflect all the latest design trends (including new shabby-chic slipcovered upholstery and Shaker-style pine, maple, and cherry tables and cabinets). My comparison surveys earned it high marks on pricing and values. Although it sells no carpeting or draperies, its in-store selection of fine-quality bedroom and dining room furniture, entertainment cabinets, occasional tables, lamps, upholstered goods, brass and iron beds, and mattress sets is quite extensive. Some famous names: Century, Hickory, White, Harden, Bernhardt, Burton James, Hekman, Garcia Imports, La Barge, Highland House, Lexington, Stanley, Lane, and more. House of Values takes one of the smallest markups around—a reason so many people drive miles to shop there. If you find the perfect piece on the floor, it's yours as soon as delivery can be arranged. You can custom order "designer lines" of furniture from its catalogs or showrooms at Showplace Square and designer fabrics by the yard for your own home-decorating projects. Need help? Then you'll appreciate the interior design service available at no extra charge. Worth a visit from anywhere in the Bay Area.

THE INTERIOR WAREHOUSE

7077 Village Parkway, Dublin. (510) 829-7280, (800) 547-8614. T–Sat 11–4 or by appt. MC, VISA. Parking: lot.

This charming catalog-furniture buying service has several choice pieces of upholstered furniture on its floor; hundreds of furniture catalogs; fabric, flooring, and carpet samples; window treatment displays; and wallpaper books. Even better, it's comfortable. The sales staff is friendly, knowledgeable, helpful, and very low key. Members of its entourage include Henry Link, Bernhardt, Pulaski, Lane, Hickory Tavern, Hekman, Fremarc, Dino-Mark Anthony, Brown Jordan, Cal Mode, Chapman, Weiman, La Barge, Habersham Plantation, McGuire, Stanley, and many more. The discounts on these lines are 20–40% off most retail pricing. On wallpaper and fabrics in sample books, discounts are

15–30%, or occasionally more, when the manufacturer is having a special promotion. The store's drapery and upholstery swatch selection is one of the finest in the East Bay. Carpeting is sold for 10% over cost. Custom wood shutters are 30% off! Resident designers can provide in-home consultations at approximately $60/hour. *Directions: From Hwy. 680 (north of 580 interchange) take the Alcosta exit east of Village Parkway, and turn right.*

JOHN R. WIRTH CO.

1049 Terra Bella, Mountain View. (415) 967-1212, (408) 736-5828. M–Sat 9–6. MC, VISA. Parking: lot.
If you're asked for a referral at the desk, just mention Bargain Hunting in the Bay Area. Then you can join South Bay and Peninsula residents who want to stretch their home-furnishing dollars on living room, dining room, bedroom, and outdoor patio furniture; mattresses; and accessories. You can spend hours eyeballing the wallpaper books, fabric swatches for draperies or upholstery, carpet samples (including area and Oriental), vinyl or hardwood flooring samples, even custom kitchen cabinets. Wirth can handle any window covering or treatment, including shutters. For additional choices on home furnishings not in the showroom, you can go to catalogs. The salespeople are experienced, helpful, and not pushy. The prices on furnishings (including freight and delivery) are discounted on the average about 35%. Note: No phone quotes, sales usually final, full payment expected before delivery. *Directions: Heading south on 101, take the Shoreline exit west. Terra Bella is the first street on the left; go one and a half blocks.*

LEON BLOOMBERG CO. & HOUSE OF KARLSON

80 Carolina Street, San Francisco. (415) 863-3640. By appt. only, M–F 9–5. Cash/Check/VISA. Parking: street.
Leon Bloomberg won't stay retired. He closed his furniture store a few years ago. Now he's back, leasing space from the San Francisco Furniture Gallery. His catalogs cover everything from patio furniture to bedroom sets (some hard to find at discount). There are also books of carpets and flooring samples. Leon and his staff work by appointment. A qualified interior designer is available to help with selections of furnishings and treatments: custom rugs, reupholstering, finishing,

window treatments, and bedcovers. Call first to discuss your needs and budget so that when you visit they can be prepared with suggestions or tell you whether they have access to the lines you have already selected. Phone quotes provided if you've got all the specifications. Naturally, savings are your incentive for checking in, and you can probably expect a solid 35% off retail. A 40% deposit is required to place an order; balance due on delivery.

MILLBRAE FURNITURE COMPANY

1781 El Camino Real, Millbrae. (650) 761-2444. T–F 10–6, W till 9, Sat 9–5. MC, VISA. Parking: street/city lot (side of building).

To be in a position to provide good value, it helps when you own your own building and warehouse. That way, you have the space to take advantage of special discounts on volume purchases when manufacturers make their offers. Millbrae Furniture fits the bill on both counts. Millbrae manages to cram in a good selection of furniture, appliances, bedding, carpets, draperies, and Sony and Hitachi TVs, making it a one-stop resource for consumers. On the first floor you'll find upholstered goods and

the appliance department, which showcases its upscale Sub-Zero, Dacor, and Wolfe lines, plus other consumer favorites. Go up to the second floor to bounce on the beds and check the dining and bedroom groupings. Finally, explore the basement for recliners and leather furniture. You can buy moderately priced furniture right off the floor, or mosey over to the back room, where there are cabinets full of manufacturers' catalogs that provide additional resources. On most items the savings run about 30% off prevailing retail prices; however, appliances are 10% over cost. Like most discounters, this store rarely advertises but does a steady business based on referrals.

NORIEGA FURNITURE

1455 Taraval Street (at 25th Avenue), San Francisco. (415) 564-4110, (800) 664-4110. T, W, F 10–5:30; Th 1–9 Sat 10–5. MC, VISA, DIS. Parking: street.

Noriega Furniture is appealing for its beautiful showroom, personal service, and decorator consultants. Its specialty is expensive high-quality furniture, and its manufacturers' catalogs offer furniture, carpets, draperies, wallpaper, beautiful artwork, and accessories at savings of at least 20% and as much as 33%. Noriega is one of the few resources in the Bay Area discounting Lladro and Hummel, as well as Waterford and Lenox lamps. Noriega also features Stickley Mission Oak furniture, Arts and Crafts lamps, and pottery. You can purchase European, American, and Oriental reproductions and accent pieces; distinctive accessories like etchings from Eidenberger and Kasimir; museum replicas; and original antique prints and drawings. Overall, you'll be dazzled by traditional furnishings from companies like Henredon, Karastan, Karges, Kindel, Marge Carson, La Barge, Widdicomb, and others. If you need help, Noriega's decorators will go to most Bay Area communities with samples. Located in the Sunset/Parkside district, one mile north of Stonestown shopping center.

R & R FRENCH BROS.

333 Alabama (at 16th Street), San Francisco. (415) 621-6627. M–F 9:30–6, most Sats 10–3. VISA/MC. Parking: street/lot.

French Bros. is an excellent resource for home furnishings, floor coverings, mattresses, and window coverings at very special discounts. Furniture selections can be made from its library of catalogs or by personally escorted visits to the Western Merchandise Mart and showrooms at the Showplace Square Design Center. Visits are arranged by appointment. Here's a partial list of the manufacturers represented: Stanley, Bernhardt, Pulaski, Lane, American Drew, BarcaLounger, Henredon, Coleman of CA, Baker, Bassett, and Lexington. The extensive carpet and vinyl flooring selection includes a wide range of residential and contract carpeting. As it is displayed gallery fashion, you won't have to exhaust yourself hauling heavy sample books around. Finally, prices are right on target for bargain hunters.

WESTERN CONTRACT INTERIORS

1702 Park Avenue, San Jose. (408) 275-9600. M–F 8:30–5:30, Sat 11–5:30. Cash/Check. Parking: lot.

If you're past the start-up phase of furnishing your home and are in search of quality furnishings at significant savings, you'll be in good hands here. When you want to sit down and get serious with your queries, I suggest making an appointment with a staff designer. Western's lovely showroom has sample pieces of furniture for starters and tasteful accessories, but it's hardly representative of the total resources available. You can order window coverings, mattress sets, bedspreads, carpeting, and furniture for any room in the house, or patio furniture for outside. Western has a contract division that you can also use as a resource for business and home-office furnishings. Many Silicon Valley executives have ordered ergonomic seating and office products for their offices, then go one step further and have their homes furnished by the residential side of the business. Space planning and more in-depth design service is provided. Expect to save 25–40% off full-service retail store prices on most lines.

Also See

Under Carpets and Flooring:
LAWRENCE CONTRACT FURNISHERS

General Furnishings

If you're into dollar-wise decorating, there are familiar stores all around the Bay Area that offer stylish furnishings and accessories at "getting started" prices. Stores like Cost Plus and Pier 1 offer low-cost furnishings—kitchen sets, informal chairs, tables, and sofas, plus the accessories and accent pieces to fill the empty spaces in your rooms. The Bombay Company is an excellent resource for accent pieces and accessories for those in the traditional mode.

BENICIA FOUNDRY & IRON WORKS, INC.
2995 Bayshore Road, Benicia. (800) 346-4645.
M–F 9–6, Sat 9–5, Sun 11–5. MC, VISA.
Parking: lot.
This company is a major manufacturer of metal beds sold to famous stores around the country. Everything is made by hand using traditional craft techniques. Traditional to contemporary styling is offered in a variety of finishes. The company is careful to avoid conflict with the retailers that sell its beds: No special or custom orders can be placed, nor does it sell anything from its current

wholesale catalog inventory. However, when orders are cancelled, a bed is returned by a retailer, or there is some imperfection in a finished bed, it is sold for a substantial savings: 35–50% off original retails. The selection is limited in terms of style, finish, and size, but it is worth a visit to see this unpredictable mix of "leftovers." You may find complete beds, a headboard only, canopy styles, daybeds, etc., in twin, full, queen, or king sizes. Recently, the company has expanded its manufacturing to include a very nice line of garden furniture and accessories made from cast aluminum and finished with a durable baked-on polyurethane powder coating. These are Victorian and classic designs of patio tables and chairs, lampposts, urns, planters, mailboxes, settees, benches, and more. Prices are very reasonable. You're on your own when it comes to delivery; however, a bed frame can be boxed and shipped for about $60. Assembly instructions included.

BOB'S DISCOUNT WOOD FURNITURE

2078 San Pablo Avenue (bet. University and Addison), Berkeley. (510) 848-6662. M–Sat 10–6, Sun 11–5. MC, VISA, DIS. Parking: street.

Need cabinets to store your collection of compact discs, books, or videotapes? This store has carved out a niche in the unfinished-furniture business as a specialist in bookcases. You can get custom sizing on most cases and cabinets here and protect your budget by buying woods in basic and budget pine, better in veneers of alder or oak, and best in solid oak or alder. You can buy off the floor from an extensive inventory of cases in many standard sizes: widths from 18 inches, heights to 96 inches, and standard depths at 9 and 12 inches. You may want a custom depth for compact discs. Buy unfinished cases or spend about 10% more for several options in stains or clear sealers. Glass or wood doors on some styles, also fixed or adjustable shelving. Prices are very good across the board. I particularly liked the extra quality features like mounting rails to anchor tall cases to walls. Finally, there are many options utilizing cabinet bases with bookcase tops—lots of versatility! Call for phone quotes, but take measurements first.

BUSVAN FOR BARGAINS

900 Battery Street, San Francisco. (415) 981-1405. M–Sat 9:30–6, Sun Noon–6. MC, VISA, revolving charge. Parking: street and pay lots.
(Other store: 244 Clement Street, San Francisco.)
Although not your typical furniture store, Busvan carries almost anything from its somewhat tired, but too busy to remodel store: furniture, rugs, pianos, antiques, paintings, books, bric-a-brac, and office furniture. The main floor is filled with new, discount-priced upholstery and mattress sets at excellent prices. Its newest focus is on deep-seated upholstery from some of the state's better-known manufacturers, who are using Busvan to expand their sales. The top floor is crowded with bedroom, dining room, and accent furniture in the budget to moderate price ranges, and occasionally some exceptional one-of-a-kind accent pieces (trade samples). Nestle your preteen or adolescent in style from its expanded selection of bedroom groups. Busvan offers a sea of RTA (ready-to-assemble) or lifestyle furniture, especially desks, bedroom pieces, computer furniture, bookcases, and entertainment centers. Its solid-pine unfinished furniture is priced to make other stores blush. Opportunistic buys lead to an eclectic selection of floor samples and factory closeouts. The basement features used furniture at rock-bottom prices. Although the staff is friendly and helpful, the size of the store makes it primarily self-service. All sales final. Reasonable delivery charges, or bring your own van; Busvan will pad your furniture and stash it in or on your vehicle free.

COMMINS DESIGN GROUP

990 Grant, Benicia. (707) 745-3636. M–Sat 10–5, Sun Noon–6. MC, VISA, AE. Parking: lot.
Commins' warehouse showroom in Benicia is an extension of its furniture manufacturing and design company. The company sells direct to consumers out of its impressive selling space at its factory. For contemporary furnishings that embrace classical design elements, a trip is mandated. Everything speaks of nature and the organic, with elegant faux finishes on all the pieces. I loved the dramatic chests, étagères, entertainment cabinets, wall units, consoles, bedroom systems, and glass-top tables with architectural pedestal bases. The many accessories on hand are from local artisans and importers, selling for appreciably lower prices than

elsewhere. Altogether, this upscale collection of distinctive furniture and accessories is in no way ordinary or predictable. You can acquire prototype samples, buy pieces off the floor, or opt for a custom design that allows you to choose the color of the finish and possibly some design modifications at no extra charge (or a very modest one). In this way you'll save about half of what you would have paid a designer or showroom. Also, glass tops for anything at really good prices.

COTTAGE TABLES CO.

550 18th Street (off Third), San Francisco. (415) 957-1760. W–Sat 1–5. MC, VISA. Parking: lot.
Tony Cowan builds superior-quality tables in the old tradition—from solid wood using dowel-and-glue construction. Each table is custom-made. A table that you buy from him will become a family heirloom. There's no inventory on hand, other than several sample tables to show the quality of his work, some style variations, and the woods and finishes used. A reasonably formal, solid cherry plank table 36-by-72 inches was priced at $1,800; a country pine table 33-by-60 inches was $1,200. You can have tables made in maple, walnut, pine,

cherry, or oak; in styles conveying a contemporary, country, traditional, or transitional feeling; with any of a variety of leg styles; and you can add a silverware drawer for about $150. Tony does not make chairs, but keeps several on hand that he can order for you from manufacturers' catalogs. He sells the chairs at cost, which amounts to almost a 50% discount to you—a nice accommodation for his customers. A 50% deposit is required with your order.

ENGLISH GARDEN FURNITURE & LIGHTING

128 Mitchell Boulevard, San Rafael. (415) 492-1051. M–Sat 10–4, Sun 11–4 (call to verify). Cash/Check. Parking: lot.
English Garden Furniture captures the look of Victorian garden furniture. It duplicates elegant designs from the 1700s to today in cast aluminum, and the pieces will last for years. The tables, chairs, and benches in these historical patterns reflect charm and grace and beautifully enhance traditional decors and gardens. The company has built furniture for the Embassy Suites Hotels and many historical mansions, gardens, and other public places. It also serves discriminating consumers who want good value and good design that's out

of the ordinary. Once you understand the quality of this furniture, the prices appear reasonable. When it comes to top-of-the-line garden furniture, you can find similar styles in each of the three major manufacturers' lines. A chair from English Garden Furniture at $195 is comparable to one that may be priced closer to $700. Charming dining sets (table and four chairs) in various patterns are available for $795 to $1,300. Tables are sold in small dimensions or large, and some are available with glass tops. The chairs and chaise longues are popular with city residents who want balcony furniture that is heavy enough to withstand wind and attractive enough to blend visually with interior room decors. Authentic reproductions of old baker's racks come with optional chopping blocks and wine racks, with or without brass trim. The company also excels in its selection of garden benches, light fixtures, chandeliers, lampposts, urns, authentic French doors, and anything custom you might desire. If you've passed the plastic-and-webbing stage and you're willing to invest in a lifetime set of garden or patio furniture, then you may want to consider this source before making any final selections.

FURNITURE EXPRESS OUTLET

667 Folsom Street (bet. Third and Fourth streets), San Francisco. (415) 495-2848. M–F 11–7, Sat 10–6, Sun Noon–5. MC, VISA, AE. Parking: street. Folks on the prowl for inexpensive furnishings will find most of what they need right here. There are easily assembled computer workstations, desks, TV carts, dressers, bookcases and shelving units, microwave/utility carts on casters, solid maple tables, affordable dressers and pine bedroom furniture (finished and unfinished) for teen or children's rooms, and home entertainment centers (as low as $39). This is not forever furniture, but the overall quality/price/value equation is solid and the prices are very appealing for budget decorating. Prices on many pieces were about 30% below those in a local department store "sale" ad posted on the wall. Everything is sold in boxes. Delivery can be arranged.

IGUANA AMERAMEX

301 Jefferson Street (at Third Street), Oakland.
(510) 834-5848. W–Sun 10–6. MC, VISA.
Parking: street.

In its 45,000-square-foot store, Iguana Ameramex sells furniture and home accessories imported from Mexico. The outstanding prices offered on almost all its inventory can be attributed to strategies that lead to savings in shipping (a significant overhead cost) and buying directly from manufacturers, craftspeople, and artisans, thereby eliminating middleman or distributor costs. The furniture, sold directly to the public, is similar to many recent collections of furniture showcased in several local furniture specialty stores and similar in design to furnishings being shown in well-known catalogs like Pottery Barn and Robert Redford's Sundance catalog.

The furniture has broad cultural appeal. It's most often made from pine and reflects the design roots of Mexico's colonial past. It's appealing to those who are trying to achieve a more relaxed and informal environment for their homes. The rustic nature of the wood and finish allows these pieces to blend nicely with furniture defined as Southwest, country, or traditional. Others might see a rustic pine armoire or console as an appropriate accent piece for a more contemporary room. Prices here are often 15% to 50% less than comparable styles in other stores or catalogs. Armoires in various configurations and sizes are priced from $350. The overall presentation of the store is best defined as eclectic clutter, with an array of furniture for many uses—armoires, occasional and dining tables, chairs, consoles, headboards, dressers, buffets, china cabinets, library units, chests, benches, etc.—crowding the huge space. Many pieces are one-of-a-kind, handpicked from a particular craftsperson's inventory during the buyer's monthly buying trip to small villages and manufacturing areas throughout the central and coastal regions of Mexico. Other basic pieces (armoires, chests, etc.) are replenished with each container shipment.

Adding interest to the overall inventory are the many special hand-carved pieces, and tabletops fabricated from barn doors or table bases that may have been made from oxen or donkey yokes.

You'll find some hand-painted pieces, some pieces made from mesquite wood, and some made from older or recycled wood. Tables with iron bases and glass tops are perfect for placement over area rugs. There's an intriguing selection of folk art, tabletop accessories, distinctive glassware (margarita glasses, etc.), hand-cast pewter tableware, Contera (carved stone) table bases and pedestals, and some Talavera ceramics in myriad designs from the Guanajuato, Michoacán, and Dolores Hidalgo regions. If a large pot for patio or garden use is on your most-wanted list, you're likely to find one here. Rustic, bisque-fired architectural pots in a variety of sizes and finishes are scattered throughout the store. Pottery prices are about half off the prices of other retailers.

LAMPS PLUS FACTORY OUTLET

15928 Hesperian Boulevard, San Leandro. (510) 278-5307. M–F 10–9, Sat 10–6, Sun 11–6. MC, VISA, AE. Parking: street.
(Other stores: Pleasant Hill, Sacramento, San Jose, San Francisco, San Mateo, San Rafael.)
Lamps Plus benefits from volume purchasing power (a thirty-eight-store lighting superstore chain along the West Coast and the largest specialty lighting chain in the country). It offers a lot, and while it can't be all things to all people, it comes close. I spotted the ordinary, ho-hum, and familiar styles seen in most home-furnishings stores, and some extra-special lamps and fixtures. Its subsidiary, Pacific Coast Lighting, is one of the largest lamp manufacturers, with a customer list that includes most department stores, specialty stores, and the hotel/hospitality industry. In a competitive market Lamps Plus offers consistently low everyday pricing, and at its clearance center in San Leandro, some exceptionally good buys.

30% to 50% of the display space is devoted to clearance inventory at the San Leandro store. Take notice of the tags and you'll be able to sort the regular merchandise from clearance merchandise. Black-and-white tags denote regular-priced merchandise with everyday pricing; yellow-and-white tags indicate that the item is "reconditioned"—it may have small cosmetic flaws on the finish, or it may have required reconditioning at the factory to repair any functional problem. These are all sold with the company's 100% satisfaction guaranteed policy, which applies to all its merchandise. Red-and-white tags represent closeouts or discontinued products from its own line of lamps from other Lamps Plus stores, or from factories anywhere in the world (these last products may or may not have been sold in a Lamps Plus store previously). The company uses its connections in the industry to make good closeout buys for its clearance centers and passes the savings along to customers.

The clearance inventory changes from month to month, reflecting whatever "buys" the company has garnered from its suppliers. There may be some delightful surprises from time to time, when exceptional values are captured. When the item is unique to the clearance center, savings may be from 10% to 60% off Lamps Plus original prices or estimated retail value. Can't complain about these manufacturers: Koch & Lowy, Halogen, Westwood, Fine Arts, Geo. Kovacs, Stiffel, and ceiling fans from Casablanca and Hunter. Lamps Plus can also special order fixtures from catalogs. Finally, it has about the biggest array of replacement lamp shades I've spotted in the Bay Area.

MANCINI'S SLEEP WORLD

968 El Camino Real, Sunnyvale. (408) 245-6251.
M–F 10–9, Sat and Sun 10–6. MC, VISA, DIS.
Parking: lot.
(Other stores: Los Altos, San Jose, Santa Clara.)
South Bay mattress shoppers can get a fair price from Mancini's. They'll also find one of the best selections from Serta, Sealy, Simmons, and Spring Air. The staff can give you the lowdown on the differences between brands and qualities so that you can make an informed decision, whether you're buying budget or top of the line. Check the bulletin board, where ads are posted from its competitors (one way to show that its pricing is solid). Prices include delivery and removal and disposal of old mattress sets. Mancini's also sells adjustable beds, futons, bed frames, headboard sets and a nice selection of children's furniture (lots of bunk beds).

NATIONAL MATTRESS CLEARANCE CENTER

15430 Hesperian Boulevard, San Leandro. (510) 481-1623. M–Sat 9–6, Sun Noon–5. MC, VISA, DIS. Parking: lot.

National, in business for sixty-six years, has such a large collection of mattresses and box springs that it could host a slumber party for hundreds. Its huge mattress department has two sections. First, you'll find new Simmons, Sealy, Serta, and Spring Air mattress sets at about 20% below the advertised department store "50% off" sales. Every manufacturer offers price groups ranging from budget to ultrapremium. So wherever you fit, you'll be sure to find a terrific value. You can do even better if you're willing to consider mattresses from the "as-is" area. That is where you'll find legitimate factory seconds and mismatched sets. Defects or flaws are carefully pointed out and explained when you're making a choice. Some flaws are obvious, but many are not. Factory seconds also carry a warranty, but for a shorter time. I spotted a top-of-the-line, king-sized set priced at half National's discount, first-quality price. Mattresses can be purchased without box spring units.

OAK 'N PINE FURNITURE

446 West Francisco Boulevard, San Rafael. (415) 453-6078. M–F 10:30–6, Sat 10–5. MC, VISA, DIS. Parking: lot.

You'll find an updated collection of rustic pine, country-style pine, and oak furniture. Working with a smaller markup, everything is well priced in the modest- to midprice range of furniture lines. Some collections are imported directly from Mexico, others originate from smaller West Coast companies. Customers can find beds and bedroom furnishings; tables, cabinets, and occasional pieces for the dining room; living room pieces; furniture for the home office; and entertainment systems, wall systems, stereo cabinets, TV stands, and bookcases priced about 25% below competitors. Many lines are transitional and reflect the informality that many are seeking for "real" family living. All furniture is assembled and can be purchased right off the floor for immediate delivery. You can special order other options from manufacturers' catalogs. This is a good place for younger couples getting started and anybody who wants good value.

RONEY'S FURNITURE

14000 Washington Avenue, San Leandro. (510) 352-4074. M–Sat 9:30–7, Sun 11:30–6. MC, VISA, DIS. Parking: lot.

Roney's warehouse (a former National Guard armory) is stuffed. The emphasis is on traditional or transitional furniture from major manufacturers. If you need it yesterday, you can buy sofas, chairs, and tables; living room, bedroom, and dining room furniture; and entertainment cabinets, recliners, lamps, and accessories right off the floor: Some of the most popular lines in furniture are ready to go—lots of weekend country collections and better reproductions of the classic Arts and Crafts styles. Prices are nicely discounted, whether you buy a piece off the floor or opt for a custom catalog order. Whether you're buying your first piece of furniture with a minimal budget or upgrading, Roney's offers many options for most budgets. Expect a small delivery charge. If you're in the mood for a good browse with the hope of finding a great bargain, give Roney's a whirl; you're sure to become a regular.

SLEEP SHOP LTD./KIDZ & TEENZ LTD.

1530 Contra Costa Boulevard, Pleasant Hill. (510) 671-9400. M–F 9:30–7:30, Sat 9:30–6, Sun 11–5. MC, VISA, DIS. Parking: lot.
(Other stores: Antioch, Dublin, Lakeport.)

This very complete store makes a profit through volume sales rather than high markups. A diverse selection of brass and iron beds (at least thirty-six models) and daybeds (about twenty-four models) are available from Elliotts, Wesley Allen, Fashion Bed Group, and Elm Creek. Sleep tight on mattress sets from Simmons, Serta, Sealy, and Spring Air that are always available at less than department store sale prices. Sleep Shop aggressively discounts special buys and mattress sets with discontinued covers. Delivery charges are minimal. If your tots are ready to leave their cribs, check out the extensive selection of juvenile and teen furniture in the Kids & Teenz Ltd. department. With eighteen vignettes and more than sixteen bunk beds on display, you can find just the right look to suit your child's personality. Parents appreciate that many companies are offering suites of furniture with classic and clean lines that can leave home with the kids when they set up their own households. Stanley, Camelot, Nordwins, Boyd, Silver Eagle, Vaughn, and Tempo are companies making the grade at Kids & Teenz Ltd. Special orders may take a few extra weeks or months, but the prices discounted at least 30% make the wait worthwhile.

STANFORD FINE FURNITURE & DESIGNS
6925 Central Avenue, Newark. (510) 745-9962. M–F 8:30–4:30. Cash/Check. Parking: lot.
If you want to achieve a designer look in upholstered furniture without designer prices, go where designers go: Stanford Designs. This company makes its own lines of sofas and does a lot of custom work. (Loved the new shabby-chic style, a slightly loose slipcover over a muslin-covered sofa.) There are several ways to get a deal at Stanford. First, sample pieces can be purchased off the factory salesroom floor. Next, you can go back to the warehouse and check the inventory of discontinued fabrics. Pick your sofa, sectional, sleeper, or chair style, your fabric, and your quality— you'll get such a deal! Pay extra and you can have coil-spring construction, down pillows, and so on. Otherwise, Stanford uses kiln-dried hardwood

frames, double bracing, HR 30 foam cushions with a ten-year guarantee (even the best companies often use only 1.85-density foam), and lined skirts. Shopping this way takes a little initiative. If you're trying to achieve a certain look, bring in a picture, find the fabric, and prepare yourself for extra customization charges. Services also include reupholstery and slipcovers. You'll still come out way ahead. A 50% deposit is required with the order, balance before delivery.

TRADEWAY STORES
10860 San Pablo Avenue, El Cerrito. (510) 529-2360. M–F 9–6, Sat 9–5:30. MC, VISA. Parking: street.
At Tradeway you'll find discounts on high-end pieces and some fairly ho-hum furnishings. It has contracts with several manufacturers like Thomasville, Dixie, Hammary, Broyhill, Universal, American Drew, Lexington, Bassett, American of Martinsville, Drexel-Heritage, Kincaid, Miles Talbott, Berkline and others. When furniture isn't delivered to a retailer for whatever reason, the manufacturer avoids shipping it back across the country by redirecting it to Tradeway. Everything is

"detailed" (repaired) if necessary and then priced at about 40–50% off original retail. Anything marked "as-is" has been part of a redirected inventory. Savvy shoppers case the store frequently to latch on to the unusual high-end designer pieces that show up from time to time. Other furniture lines are also stocked as needed to balance out this unpredictable incoming inventory. For the most part they're budget- to moderate-priced lines of upholstered furniture; dining and bedroom furnishings are also discounted. The furnishings are jammed haphazardly into several rooms on two levels. If you're looking for farmhouse-style kitchen tables, inexpensive dinettes, recliners, bunk beds, student desks, or family room sofas, Tradeway has lots of potential. Also a good selection of bedroom and dining room furniture. Delivery on purchases of more than $750 is free from San Leandro to Vallejo; otherwise delivery is priced according to distance.

WAY TO GO

2107 Broadway, Redwood City. (650) 306-1144. M–Th 10–8, T, W, F 10–6, Sun 10–6 (closed Sat). MC, VISA, DIS. Parking: rear lot.

Way to Go is a boon to the just-getting-started crowd and for those who want attractive, functional furnishings at no-nonsense prices. Everything in this store is sold in a box, whether it's a large 8-foot home entertainment three-piece cabinet system or a small kitchen utility cart. More than 500 assembled pieces are displayed for a buyer's consideration. Six of the best American manufacturers of ready-to-assemble furniture supply the goods, including Sauder Woodworking, O'Sullivan, and Bush Industries. You'll be surprised at how sophisticated and attractive RTA furniture has become. Many pieces are assembled with clips and fastenings, while some need a little glue to finish the process. (The owner suggests that all you need is a lot of patience and a margarita to see you through the job.) Many popular wood finishes and furniture styles are represented so that it's a simple proposition to find something that fits right into your decor. Oak, cherry, honey maple (Shaker-style pieces), black or white matte, white-washed finishes, etc.

are available on most types of furniture. You carry out boxes and assemble computer workstations, bookcases, microwave, VCR, or TV carts, entertainment centers, beds, dressers, cabinets, hutches (dining room or kitchen), and assorted, versatile storage pieces. You can pay as little as $75 for an oak entertainment center, or $359 for a Shaker-style honey pine-finished unit. You can also buy daybeds, futons, or mattresses. Prices are backed up with a price guarantee, and (if you're all thumbs) assembly can be arranged for an extra fee. Unopened boxes can be returned within ten days for a store credit. Delivery service available for a fee.

THE WOODEN DUCK

2919 7th Street, Berkeley (one block north of Ashby, across from Whole Earth Access). (510) 848-3575. M–Sat 10–6, Sun Noon–5. MC, VISA. Parking: Lot.

The Wooden Duck offers consumers good value and new options in buying furniture. The store is a showcase for an intriguing array of new reproduction pine furniture (some made from old wood), old pieces from Indonesia (many 95 to 100 years old), new teak garden furniture, new and old boxes and trunks, and other surprises that come with each new shipment. This company is reflective of a recent trend where many antique dealers and stores noted for selling reproductions are buying up furniture in former colonies in lieu of buying from Europe due to price and supply considerations. New sourcing is occurring in Vietnam (French), India (English), Eastern Europe as well as Indonesia. The Wooden Duck is both a retailer and wholesaler of furniture, and its warehouse-styled store is set apart by its extensive selection of imports and lower pricing. Some new reproduction pieces (chairs, armoires, tables, etc.) are made from pine, finished with coat of wax to achieve a light honey color. They closely resemble furniture associated with the English country pine-look. The pine bed side tables, bedroom dressers with curved fronts, and small consoles, were priced about 20–25% lower than other stores in the area. Another customer pleasing category is its teak garden furniture, similar to styles shown in many high profile gardening catalogs. These garden benches, tables, and chairs were 30–50% lower in price than similar catalog versions. The new teak furniture is made from plantation teak grown specifically for furniture making. Those looking for a table for a kitchen or dining room, and want a piece with a bit of history, should take a look at some of The Wooden Duck's old teak tables. Bear in mind that these teak tables bear no resemblance to the teak furniture sold as Danish Modern (so popular in the 1950s and 1960s). Furniture manufactured in Indonesia in the 19th and early 20th century was made to suit the tastes of European settlers or government officials (primarily Dutch or British colonials). The old teak pieces, usually tables and assorted cabinets and armoires, resemble the old oak and mahogany furniture that's usually associated with antiques from England and Western Europe. When the original finishes have been obscured with use, The Wooden Duck has had the tables refurbished with a shellac-based French polish which results in a lovely patina. These old pieces have been purchased from buying expeditions to small villages throughout Indonesia. The tables are priced according to quality of finish, size, thickness and cuts of wood, condition and generally range from $450 to $900. Most tables are made without nails and joined with mortise and tenon joints. It should be noted that some pieces do reflect an "ethnic" and Asian influence, but most are decidedly European in design with classic styles familiar to consumers. Wooden Duck is expanding its inventory and developing new sources so it is a store that bears watching. Its corner location is easy to spot—there's always a display of furniture set outside the entrance to catch the eyes of passing motorists.

Also See

Under General Carpeting, Area Rugs, and Flooring:
PIONEER HOME SUPPLY

Under Linens:
DREAMS

Under Appliances, Electronics, and Home Entertainment:
WHOLE EARTH ACCESS

Mattress Buyers Beware

Beware the mattress "discounters" that have pro-liferated around the Bay Area. Ads promising hard-to-believe prices are most often a lure to an aggressive bait-and-switch sales pitch. It seems that some sales personnel have the attitude, "If you can't sell them, insult them." Mattress sets from major manufacturers sold at these outfits are often made expressly for the discounters. From my comparisons, you can buy better quality and receive greater value when purchasing a mattress set from the sources listed here. Hints for savvy shopping: When you canvass the market for mat-tress sets, you're likely to end up very confused by the many names from the same manufacturer you find at different retail stores. Large stores and chains with volume accounts usually pick their own names for the manufacturers' groups they buy; they may also decide upon special fabric patterns and colors for the ticking. Most independents will sell mattress sets with the manufacturers' original names. By carefully studying the components dis-played in a manufacturers' cut-out samples—the number of coils; turns and gauge of the coils; weight, thickness, composition, and layers of the cushion elements; type of suspension system; and relative price range—you'll soon figure out that a specific manufacturer's Pontiac Supreme at Store A is equivalent to Buick Ultra at Store B and on a par with Oldsmobile Maximum at Store C. Many manufacturers have enlarged the selection at the high end of the market, offering mattresses with more design and comfort features, and accordingly higher prices.

Baby and Juvenile Furniture/ Equipment—New and Used

You might as well decide where to shop for baby furniture and equipment on the basis of conve-nience and selection, unless you want to go end-lessly in circles, comparing prices to save a few bucks. It's a very competitive market—kept that way by manufacturers who closely control distribu-tion of various style groups to selected retailers. The opening of baby "superstores" has increased the pressure on independents. They've responded with more service, expert advice, and pricing that keeps them in the game. The stores in this section are all very competitive and noteworthy for keeping prices as low as possible. I've included stores that also sell quality used furnishings, along with the new. Other Bay Area resources for budget- to moderately priced baby furniture and equipment: Toys 'R' Us, Wal-Mart, KMart, and Price/Costco.

BABY SUPER—ROCKERWORLD & FURNITURE FOR KIDS

1523 Parkmoor Avenue, San Jose. (408) 293-0358. M–W, Sat 10–6; Th–F 10–8:30; Sun Noon–5. MC, VISA; layaway. Parking: lot.
(Other store: Baby & Kids Bargain Outlet, 1881 W. San Carlos, San Jose.)
Almost supermarket-sized, this store is great for one-stop shopping. It offers an extensive selection, both in quality and quantity, of baby and toddler equipment and furniture for tots and the juvenile market. Buy everything you need for the first eighteen months: infant clothing, diapers, blankets, cribs, high chairs, Portacribs, adult rockers, playpens, car seats, and more. There's a complete furniture selection for infants through teens. Crib suites (cribs, dressers, changing tables, etc.) and youth furniture add up to one of the best selections of furnishings found anywhere in the Bay Area. John Boyd, Kemp, Stanley, Dixie, Henry Link and Childcraft, Play Space, Morigeau, Berg, and Vermont Tubbs are some of the lines. Furniture prices are nicely discounted. The selection of rockers and gliders is appealing. They're great all the time, for anyone. Be sure to check the Baby & Kids Bargain Warehouse, where discontinued merchandise, floor samples, and more budget-priced lines of goods are sold.

BABY WORLD

5854 College Avenue, Oakland. (510) 655-2950. M–F 10–6, Sat 10–5, Sun Noon–5. MC, VISA. Parking: lot.
Baby World provides new and used children's equipment, furniture, and toys. There's a wide array of riding toys (try to leave without one if you're shopping with your toddler). The playthings range from popular classics up to the latest in high-demand amusements. This is an excellent source for grandparents who need to set up a baby room. The selection of cribs, playpens, bassinets, high chairs, and car seats is quite extensive. The prices are great!

CHILDREN'S FURNITURE WAREHOUSE
525 66th Avenue, Oakland. (510) 562-9876. M–Sat 10–5, Sun Noon–5. MC, VISA, layaway.
Parking: lot.

The selection itself makes Children's worth a visit. For best buys check the clearance corner for extra markdowns. Thanks to its large warehouse for backup, most items are in stock for immediate use. Prices on cribs are competitive, but often a little higher than some of the other stores in this section. You'll find displays of toddler-sized play tables, chairs, and other furniture to coordinate with the various styles of cribs, adult rockers, and all the baby equipment on your list.

KIDS AGAIN
6891 Village Parkway, Dublin. (510) 828-7334. M–Sat 10–5, Th until 7, Sun Noon–4. MC, VISA.
Parking: back lot.

Kids Again, a store with multiple personalities, sells new brand-name lines of baby and youth furniture at discounts up to 30% off retail. After browsing through its floor inventory of infant, child, and teen furniture, extend your options even more by turning the pages in manufacturers' cata-logs. Special orders involve a few months for delivery, but you'll end up delighted with your savings. Several popular lines of crib and juvenile bedding (sheets, bumper pads, dust ruffles, quilts, shams, etc.) can be ordered from catalogs at 10–25% off suggested retail. Kids Again is also a consignment store—a big one. Buy or sell your children's clothing (sizes 0–10), toys, furniture equipment, or your still-wearable maternity clothing. The Fashion Court is set aside for consignment clothing for women, with an emphasis on better-quality, classic, casual, career, and special-occasion clothing. All that grown-up furniture from Furnish Again (see Used/Consignment Furniture) is from Kids Again's recent expansion into consignment furnishings for adults.

LIL' THINGS
McCarthy Ranch Marketplace, Milpitas. (408) 942-8060. M–Sat 9–9, Sun 11–7. MC, VISA, AE, DIS.
Parking: lot.
(Other store: Westgate Mall, San Jose.)

Superstores have come to the baby industry! After visiting this store, you'll wonder how the independent specialty stores can survive the awesome competition in price and selection that Lil' Things represents. The stores are impressive: new parents will be overwhelmed with the selection of "everything" that baby needs (and probably doesn't need), while grandparents will wonder how they ever managed without the paraphernalia that is de rigueur for today's parents. The selection is all encompassing, with choices that range from budget to best, whether you're buying cribs, strollers, car seats, gliders, or potty chairs. The baby furniture department showcases many vignettes (cribs, dressers, changing tables, etc.). Breast pumps and feeding essentials (1,000 bottles in stock) should ensure that infants get their nourishment in the most effective way. The clothing and shoe department has labels that parents are very familiar with and like; prices are often the same as in the labels' outlet stores. This company overlooks nothing: There's a baby gift registry, in-store photo studio, haircut salon, classes for parents. Just try to leave empty-handed!

LULLABY LANE & KIDS FURNITURE CLEARANCE CENTER

570 San Mateo Avenue, San Bruno. (650) 588-4878. M–F, W until 9, Sat 10–5:30, Sun 11–5. MC, VISA, AE, DIS. Parking: street/rear lot.
(Other store: Kids Furniture [juvenile only], 532 San Mateo Avenue, San Bruno.)
Opened in 1947, Lullaby Lane is now three separate operations. The first stop for bargain hunters is its clearance center, where closeouts, floor samples, and discontinued and slightly damaged items are sent over from its two other stores and sold for up to 50% off regular store prices. Grandparents can shop the clearance center to pick up a used crib for when baby comes visiting. Next, the main store, a few doors away, at 556 San Mateo Avenue, has an extensive selection of baby "everything." Think you can save more elsewhere? Take Lullaby Lane up on its offer to meet any price. Kids Furniture, just a few doors from the main location, is filled with nicely discounted juvenile furniture.

TOTALLY 4 KIDS/BABY DEPOT
Great Mall of the Bay Area, Milpitas. (408) 934-0454. Daily. MC, VISA, AE, DIS, layaway. Parking: lot. (Other stores: located within Burlington Coat Factory Stores at Westgate Mall, San Jose; across from Southland Mall, Hayward.)
A subsidiary of Burlington Coat Factory, some stores are freestanding as Totally for Kids, others occupy a large space within Burlington stores. Either way, the end result leads to an impressive selection of merchandise geared toward the needs of newborns to kids age 14. Whether you're setting up a nursery as a first-time parent, buying back-to-school clothes for a second grader, picking up toys for a birthday party, or finding the best breast pump, car seat, or stroller, you'll find selection and good prices. Everything is backed by a "lowest price" guarantee.

Also See

Under Furniture—Catalog Discounters:
ALL LISTINGS

Under Recycled Apparel:
GENERAL INFORMATION

Furniture Clearance Centers

CANE AND REED IMPORTS, INC. CLEARANCE OUTLET
222 Littlefield Avenue, South San Francisco. (650) 589-8822. M–F 10–4 (closed Noon–1). MC, VISA. Parking: lot.
Cane & Reed is an importer of wicker furniture, baskets, and accessories; it sells its line to better department, furniture, and specialty stores and handles special import programs for catalogs and major stores. It satisfies the needs of distinct market niches with a budget-to-better range of products. Discontinued and excess inventory, canceled orders, some pieces with small imperfections, but mostly first-quality pieces are sold for 40–60% off retail. If you're in need of wicker furniture (chairs, love seats, occasional tables, armoires, bedroom furniture, stools, dining groups); home accessories, including baskets, trays, tabletop accessories, decorative birdcages, and decorative wicker accessories; or picnic baskets and more, then stop buy to see what's new in the clearance room. Baskets generally priced from $2 to $20; accessories and furniture from $10 to $200. Some good gift buys

(imported ceramics and pottery, dinnerware, tea-for-one sets, and more) can be found in the miscellaneous tabletop-accessories section.

There's usually some white wicker furniture and also some styles in tricolor (blue and rose accents on a washed finish), tables with wrought-iron bases, and natural brown wicker pieces. Most furniture items are bulky—customers with larger vehicles and trucks will find it easier to haul away their good buys. No delivery or shipping available. Parking-lot sales, held twice a year, yield some sensational buys; be sure you're on the mailing list for an invite. Directions: From north or south on Fwy. 101, take South Airport Boulevard exit east. From north turn right, from south turn left on Utah, right on Harbor Way (turns into Littlefield).

CORT FURNITURE RENTAL CLEARANCE CENTER
2925 Mead Avenue (off Bowers), Santa Clara.
(408) 727-1470. M–F 10–7, Sat 10–6, Sun 11–5.
MC, VISA, AE. Parking: lot.
(Other store: 600 Dubuque, South San Francisco;
1830 Hillsdale, San Jose.)
Sometimes you need budget-priced furniture ASAP! Cort's "retired furniture" goes on sale when a line has been discontinued from its rental inventory or the pieces are too tired to pass muster with rental customers. In any case, you'll save 30–70%. The rental business has gone upscale, so the better the quality and condition of the item, the higher the price. Sofas, lamps, mattresses, pictures, and just about anything Cort rents might be found, but no appliances. Most furnishings come from mid-price manufacturers. You'll also find office furnishings. Delivery is extra.

FRELLEN'S CLEARANCE CENTER
6800 Goodyear Road, Benicia. (800) 707-7888.
M–Sat 10–6, Sun 11–5. MC, VISA. Parking: lot.
When spring rolls around, or at anytime during the year, shop here for excess and clearance inventory or canceled orders from Frellen's full-service retail

stores in San Ramon and San Rafael. Additional inventory shows up when the owners can swing a great special purchase from their vendors (better patio-furniture manufacturers) on factory-discontinued groups (colors, styles, etc.). Everyone wins—the manufacturers clear their warehouses, Frellen's keeps its showrooms uncluttered, and consumers get the savings. Although there may be some occasional "as is" floor samples, everything is first quality.

At the clearance center you'll find furniture from manufacturers like Tropitone, Mallin, Brown Jordan, Woodard, Samsonite, and Homecrest, which produce patio furniture in aluminum, wrought iron, tubular steel, and rattan. These companies also make many accessory items, like chaise longues, side tables, gliders, and carts, that allow you to add to your sets year after year—something that's hard to do when you've purchased inexpensive sets from discount stores and warehouse clubs. At the clearance center, savings range 20–40% off the original retail-store prices. At regular retail and when the goal is to purchase a set that will last for many years, expect to pay $400 to $800 for a table

and four chairs or $600 to $1,000 for a table and six chairs. Prices increase with swivel or tilt chairs, upgrades in fabrics, etc. Take your purchases out of the clearance center in a box and you'll maximize savings. Delivery and assembly charges are extra, and all sales are final. Another angle: Shop just before Christmas and you're likely to save 30% on artificial Christmas trees (including the Barcana line); after Christmas you'll save even more, but by then the selection may be pretty picked over. *Directions: Take the Lake Herman Road exit off Hwy. 680; the clearance center is in the Benicia Industrial Park.*

FUTON SHOP FACTORY OUTLET
2150 Cesar Chavez Street (formerly Army Street, between Fwy. 101 and Third Street), San Francisco. (415) 920-6801. M–Sat 10–5, Sun 11–5. MC, VISA, AE, DIS. Parking: street.
Futons have gone mainstream. The frame styling is more sophisticated, and fabrics used for covers reflect au courant design trends and may also be the same as fabrics on popular upholstered furniture lines. The Futon Shop has grown with consumers' acceptance of futons, with twenty-two

specialty stores and this one clearance center. At any one time you'll find two to three dozen discontinued futon frames, slightly damaged floor samples (usually finish flaws or scratches), and out-of-box frames. Savings are 20–50% off original retail. The best deal here is on the closeouts on futon covers, usually marked down to 40–50% off original retails. Futon mattresses, usually floor samples, are sometimes reduced about 30%. Tables and other accent pieces and closeouts from the Futon Shop stores fill the spaces around the warehouse floor and add to your bargain options. Delivery is available for an extra charge.

LEPÉ & DWYER DESIGNER OUTLET

385 Bel Marin Keys, Suite G, Novato. (415) 883-8200. M–F 10–4. MC, VISA. Parking: lot.
With this concept there's no guarantee, but if you're willing to gamble, a visit may lead to a home furnishings jackpot. This outlet is an outgrowth of the business Lepé & Dwyer (a custom-sewing workshop) conducts with Bay Area designers and their clients. The outlet, next to the workshop, handles designer leftovers and offers an unpredictable mix of bargains—from little accessories under $20 up to $1,000 or more for original custom-designed furniture. Inventory may include elegant bedding ensembles, draperies, pillows, and table coverings that were made by Lepé & Dwyer for showcase houses, or pieces they've made just for the outlet.

Local designers place furniture, accessories, and antiques from the showcase houses in the outlet after the event has concluded. Stashed around the outlet you'll find pictures, lamps, mirrors, sconces, baskets, etc. Designers and stores are placing the occasional canceled order and mistakes from their regular design business there as well. If you're open to good buys in whatever form they're presented, a visit can be fun. If nothing else, you may find some bargain-priced leftover yardage from Lepé & Dwyer's workroom, and you can engage their services in creating a treatment. *Directions: From Hwy. 101, take the Bel Marin Keys exit.*

LIMN EXTRA & CLEARANCE CENTER

290 Townsend Street, San Francisco. (415) 543-5466. M–F 9:30–5:30, Sat–Sun 11–5:30. MC, VISA, AE. Parking: lot.

Limn is a specialty-furniture retailer whose furnishings reflect best-quality European manufacturers, including more than 500 Italian and other European firms often found in Metropolitan Home. Its style is classic contemporary, design oriented, and appeals particularly to architects and a younger, affluent clientele. The Townsend Street retail showroom is filled with distinctive and unusual furnishings. Many of the contemporary pieces provide the eclectic note needed to spark a ho-hum room. All this superior design comes at a big price, which is why it's worth checking Limn Extra—a separate, 5,000-square-foot area that takes all the main showroom's discontinued samples, color changes, and slightly damaged merchandise. Additionally, the company makes selective buys of manufacturers' closeouts or surplus inventory whenever it can to satisfy the budgets of price-conscious customers who may not be able to afford the regular showroom inventory. Limn Extra offers savings on upholstered furniture from the main showroom, plus lighting products and accent pieces (distinctive chairs, tables, tabletop accessories). Savings range from 15% to 50%. Delivery service available.

NOW & THEN ANTIQUES

730 Scott Court, Novato. (415) 892-4436. M–Sat 11–6, Sun 11–4. MC, VISA. Parking: street.

This is an unlikely pairing—an outlet for a major Bay Area–based importer of rustic pine furniture sharing space with a collective of antique dealers. The furniture is sent to the outlet when it is freight-damaged, discontinued, or otherwise flawed in some way, or when a custom order is canceled. It is then repaired and priced at 20–50% off retail. The look is familiar—similar styles are showcased in the pages of the Sundance and Pottery Barn catalogs as well as in several stores around the Bay Area. The furniture is manufactured in a small community in Southern Mexico, where workers build each Segusino piece of furniture by hand based on the rustic styles of Spanish-colonial designs. The furniture is made from distressed wormwood carefully recycled from disassembled 50- to 250-year-old buildings. This old wood is used for decorative components, such as panels or doors, and gives each piece a one-of-a-kind appeal. Kiln-dried pine is used for the framing and structural components. After construction, each piece is hand waxed with a medium honey finish and accented with hand-forged wrought-iron hardware. The furniture has a chameleonlike quality that blends well with a variety of decors and products. Some 1997 bargains: a refurbished two-door bookshelf unit was priced at $449 (retail $700 or more); a $120 five-drawer nightstand would be about $170 at retail; a console table at $299 would be $425 at retail; a Santa Fe dining room chair was $126 ($156 at retail).

The selection changes frequently. At any time you may find coffee tables, end tables, dining tables, chairs, cupboards, armoires, chests, nightstands, headboards, buffets, benches, and accessories. If additional pieces or companion pieces (like extra dining room chairs, additional chests, etc.) in the line are needed, special catalog orders can be arranged at prices pleasing to bargain hunters. Delivery is free in Novato for small pieces; otherwise delivery arrangements can be made for a fee. *Directions: Now & Then is in the old gray Feed*

and Grain building on Scott Court, nestled next to Hwy. 101 at the De Long Avenue exit.

Office Furniture

BERKELEY OUTLET
711 Heinz Avenue, Berkeley. (510) 549-2896. T–Sat Noon–6. Cash/Check. Parking: street, limited on-site.

This outfit gives new meaning to being "tucked away." It's piled and jammed with office furnishings that range from old and ugly to nearly new and up-to-date. Bay Area corporations rid themselves of used office furniture by selling to companies like this one. Because it buys in huge lots and provides no services, prices are very low for better-quality pieces like heavy-duty file cabinets from insurance companies (they take a lot of use). You'll spot brands like Steelcase, General Fireproofing, Knoll, Allsteel, Art Metal, Herman Miller, Hayworth, and Hamilton. Most of the items are geared for offices or businesses where real work is done, rather than providing front-office glamour or image. Customers are referred for delivery services.

BIG MOUTH

1129 Airport Boulevard, South San Francisco.
(650) 588-2444. M–F 9–5:30, Sat 10–4. MC, VISA.
Parking: lot.

With a name like Big Mouth you might expect lots of fast talk and hustle; instead you'll find seasoned experts who buy used office furniture at a bottom price and pass on the savings to you. If you need top-notch, fire-safe, lockable files with full suspension, there's always a good selection on hand. You might be surprised that used file cabinets are sometimes as expensive as new, until you realize that there's a wide range in quality and durability. It's easy to find a new four-drawer cabinet for around $100, but chances are it does not compare to a used commercial-quality one. Check in for desks, chairs, tables, and lots of odds and ends. Good deals are frequently offered on slightly damaged new desks. If you must have new furnishings, a visit can be arranged to a wholesale distributor to make your selection; Big Mouth will place the order and give you a very substantial discount. Extra discounts for large lot orders.

THE DESK DEPOT

89 Pioneer Way, Mountain View. (415) 969-3100.
M–F 9–6, Sat 10–5. MC, VISA, AE, DIS.
Parking: lot.

This place specializes in used office furniture. You can also buy computer furniture, partitions, chairs, coat trees, tab card files, chalkboards, school desks, and wastebaskets. Some new pieces are stocked at 20–40% off list price.

JUST CHAIRS CLEARANCE OUTLET

525 Fourth Street (near Bryant), San Francisco.
(415) 543-5575. M–Th 9–5:30, Fri 9–5, Sat 10–5.
MC, VISA. Parking: street.

If you spend long days at the computer and your back is sending pain messages, it may be time for a new chair. Chairs are a specialty here—chairs to address the ergonomic needs of the users and chairs designed to eliminate work-related back, neck, and wrist disorders. Major corporations have utilized this store's expertise in selecting proper seating for their workforces. Increasingly, Just Chairs is serving the home-office market. Anyone working from the home has the same requirement for appropriate seating as corporate employees (maybe more so, since there's no one to pay compensation for time off or down time due to back, neck, or wrist disorders). If you've underestimated the difference a chair can make in comfort and efficiency, you'll quickly see the light after sitting in a variety of ergonomically designed chairs. As with all specialized products, the more features and technology involved, the more expensive the item. Custom-configured chairs (for height, weight, use, etc.) from the retail showroom can cost from $500 to $1,500. In a separate room behind its second-floor showroom, Just Chairs' clearance outlet offers consumers the chance to buy better-quality office and work chairs at discounted prices. Expect 30 to 40 different chair styles priced from $98 to $395 (retail values from $130 to $550). Some of these chairs are not seen in the retail marketplace, because they are primarily sold through contract design companies. In addition to clearance inventory from its showrooms, some chairs represent special purchases from manufacturers that regularly do business with Just Chairs. The fabrics may have been discontinued; an order may have been canceled, leaving the manufacturer in a bind; or the manufacturer may simply wish to clear out excess inventory. The selection usually includes basic computer chairs, multi-use computer chairs, executive multi-use chairs, comfortable conference chairs, stacking chairs, reception or guest chairs, and occasionally some stools. Features may include tilt and swivel, pneumatic seat-height adjustment, and adjustable armrests. If you take your chair away in a box, you'll save on the modest assembly charge.

RUCKER FULLER SOUTH

750 Brannan Street, San Francisco. (800) 736-3735. M–F 8–5. MC, VISA. Parking: lot.
If you're starting business in a day or two, don't worry; whiz by, do your shopping, and arrange for immediate delivery. There's also a large selection of used stock. The savings on the samples and closeouts range from 40% off retail to below cost. The used furniture is priced according to condition and original price; save 40–60% off original cost. There's an expanded selection of home-office furniture, computer furniture, and lots of desks, credenzas, files, tables, and chairs for any use. Need to rent? You can—everything from panel systems to complete wood offices. Delivery will cost. You'll

rejoice when you find the parking lot behind the store.

SAM CLAR OFFICE FURNITURE
1221 Diamond Way, Concord. (800) 726-2527. M–F 9–6, Sat 10–4. MC, VISA. Parking: lot. (Other stores: 6801 Dublin Boulevard, Dublin; 341 13th Street (bet. Webster and Harrison), Oakland.) Some of the office furnishings in Sam Clar's "used department" may be a little dated, but they're functional and cheap. Others are nearly new, with today's business looks, but of course they're more expensive. Everything is priced and, for the most part, firm. Many customers head right for the new "factory closeouts" (desks, files, and more) unloaded by major manufacturers and priced for beginning entrepreneurs. You can often save by combining new merchandise from the main floor with used furniture pieces. Nice selection of ensembles that work well in a home-office environment, especially when sharing space with guest or other family-use rooms.

Also See

Under Furniture and Home Accessories—Catalog Discounters, Clearance Centers:
ALL LISTINGS

Under Office Supplies; Stationery and Party Supplies:
ARVEY PAPER CO.; OFFICE DEPOT; OFFICEMAX; STAPLES

Under General Merchandise—Membership Warehouse Clubs:
PRICE/COSTCO

Used/Consignment Furniture

Used furniture stores have been around forever, but there's a new way to buy used furniture—from consignment stores that specialize in selling furniture and home accessories. These stores have struck a responsive chord with shoppers. They are a boon for consumers who lack the time and inclination to canvass garage sales and thrift stores, attend auctions, or search through classified ads—for many, the potential for greater savings does not make up for the time involved. On the other side, those redecorating or downsizing their households with furnishings too good to give away may consider consignment shops a viable alternative to garage sales or classified ads.

Generally, consignment furniture stores are very discriminating. They're willing to take furniture in good condition that still has consumer appeal. Antiques, heirlooms, old pieces with personality, and fine-quality furniture from recognized manufacturers top their most-wanted lists. Some stores do accept pieces that may be somewhat dated, reflecting furnishing trends throughout the last 30 years, because those pieces are often good candidates for painted or faux finishes. A run-of-the-mill dining room set of fairly recent vintage (1970s pecan finish or 1980s bleached oak) can be transformed with a little paint, ingenuity, and new seat covers.

Store owners will want to discuss your piece in detail before accepting it on consignment. A picture of the item is very helpful. Most shops will also accept fine collectibles, art, chandeliers, and home-accessory items (lamps, area rugs, etc.). Upholstered pieces must be really special and in top condition to attract the interest of consignment store owners. Any documentation that can be provided on the history of a piece is a benefit. Some of the smaller shops maintain a photo gallery or album to show pieces that are available for sale but not on their showroom floor. (This often applies to large pieces that are awkward to move from the seller's home.) In that case, the shop acts much like a broker, bringing buyer and seller together.

The furniture owner (consignor) and consignment shop typically split the selling price. The division depends on each store's policy, which is spelled out in advance. Some may pass on a greater share to the consignor, but levy a floor charge for showing the piece in their store. Generally, store owners work closely with clients to set prices. Setting a realistic price is the best means to arrive at a timely sale. It's important to understand the store's policy regarding price reductions or whether it will accept or present offers for less than the original asking price. Consignment periods may range from 30 to 90 days before the furniture must be removed from the floor. Owners unwilling to reclaim the furniture are usually offered several options—drastically reducing prices, donating the pieces to charity, or in some cases, allowing the store to auction the merchandise. There are treasures to be found in all these stores.

Since consignment stores share so many similarities, I'm providing a just a brief profile of the stores listed below to avoid being redundant. Keep locations of these stores in mind and allow a few minutes for a quick stop whenever you're driving through the area.

CONSIGNED FURNISHINGS CO.

150 Longbrook Way, Suite D, Pleasant Hill. (510) 798-8556. T–Th 11:30–8:30, Fri–Sat 11:30–9, Sun Noon–5. MC, VISA. Parking: lot.
Tasteful interior that's neat and clean. Appears to show more old pieces and antiques, along with mainstream furnishings. While the older pieces have the most personality, there's also a selection of more recent used furniture. Also, a consignment fine-jewelry department.

CONSIGNMENT PLUS HOME FURNISHINGS, INC.

1299 Parkside, Walnut Creek. (510) 927-6600. M–Sat 10–6, Sun Noon–5. MC, VISA. Parking: lot. (Other store: 4250 Rosewood Drive, Pleasanton.)
This store stands out in the crowd, with a 15,000-square-foot showroom that has all the amenities of its former tenant, an upscale furniture store. The large space, lighting, and carpeted floors are very effective in displaying the furnishings and accessories that consumers all over Contra Costa County have placed on consignment here. The overall selection is quite diverse, with furniture from every design period—traditional, Arts and Crafts, Oriental, contemporary, etc.

The consignors receive 60% of the final selling price. Merchandise that has not sold will be marked down 30% every 30 days. Furniture will be picked up free within the local area; reasonable charges for greater distances. Call in advance if you are bringing items directly to the showroom. Buyers can arrange delivery for a charge. *Directions: one block north of Ygnacio, one block east of North Main.*

CORNUCOPIA

1444 South Main Street, Walnut Creek. (510) 256-4486. T–Sat 10–5, Sun Noon–4. MC, VISA. Parking: street.

You'll be helping out the Wellness Community (a support network for people fighting cancer) with your purchases, consigned furniture, or donations. Furniture shows to advantage in this charming cottage with real-life room settings. Consignors claim 60% of the selling price, the remaining 40% supports the charity. Progressive markdown policy.

COTTRELL'S

150 Valencia Street, San Francisco. (415) 431-1000. M–F 9–5:30, Sat 9–4:30. MC, VISA. Parking: street.

The interior is gloomy and the dust level is high, but there's a vast inventory, ranging from new to almost ancient furniture—some good, some downright ugly, and most well priced. With a little inventiveness, those willing to take paint brush to wood may end up with a real conversation piece. Delivery in the city is free on purchases of more than $100.

FURNISH AGAIN

6891 Village Parkway, Dublin. (510) 828-7334. M–Sat 10–5, Th till 7, Sun Noon–4. MC, VISA. Parking: lot.

A separate but integral part of the Kids Again family (listed under Baby and Juvenile Furniture/Equipment). Furniture for grown-ups (living room, dining room, bedroom, accessories, etc.) on consignment.

HARRINGTON BROS. INC. MOVING & STORAGE

599 Valencia Street (corner of 17th Street), San Francisco. (415) 861-7300. M–Sat 9–5. MC, VISA, AE. Parking: street.

Twenty-something apartment dwellers do well at Harrington Bros.—lots of possibilities if the goal is to create an eclectic, art deco, or contemporary environment. Harrington Bros. is chock-full of furniture and accessories from the 20s through the 50s. I saw furniture that's gone from very much the rage, to really tacky, and back again. Most furniture comes from estate sales.

HOME CONSIGNMENT CENTER

1901-F Camino Ramon, Danville. (510) 866-6164.
M–Sat 10–6, Sun Noon–5. MC, VISA, ATM.
Parking: lot.
(Other stores: 400 Main Street, Los Altos; 1888
South Norfolk Street, San Mateo.)
Home Consignment has the size and space to
handle lots of furniture. Trucks deliver new "old"
furniture twice a day. There's usually some new
furniture from model homes, and occasionally new
furnishings from trade showrooms. Initial consignment period is 45 days. The consignor receives
60% of the selling price. A fine-jewelry department
is staffed with an experienced jeweler, and cases
are full of beautiful jewelry. Delivery is extra; also
charges for consignment pickups. *Directions: From*
Hwy. 680, take Crow Canyon exit east to first light.
Turn left on Crow Canyon Place, go one or two
blocks, curve left on Camino Ramon. The store is
behind Marshalls.

JUDITH FROST AND COMPANY

81 Encina Avenue, Palo Alto. (650) 324-8791. T,
W, Sat 10–4, and by appt. Cash/Check.
Parking: street.
This is a somewhat elitist collection, with prices
that range from $5 (on accessories) to thousands,
showcased with real panache. When pieces are
too large to move into the store, pictures are posted on a bulletin board for prospective buyers to
consider. Count on a nice selection of old pieces,
antiques, occasional chairs, new and used sofas,
and Oriental accessories. Upon completion of a
sale, the original owner receives 60% of the price.

KABARI ESTATES

554 Ygnacio Valley Road, Walnut Creek. (510)
932-6600. M–F 10–6, Sat 10–5, Sun 11–5.
Cash/Check. Parking: rear lot.
It's much larger inside than the exterior would indicate. Two floors of furnishings, antiques, china, silver, etc. are nicely displayed. The owners prefer to
preview furnishings to make sure consignments
conform to their standards—very discriminating.
Consignors take home 60%.

MAGGIE'S DRAWERS

121 S. Murphy Avenue, Sunnyvale. (408) 730-9300. T–F 10–7, Sat 10–6. MC, VISA, AE. Parking: street/rear lot.

South Bay furniture buyers might want to cruise through Maggie's Drawers. Maggie, a designer, maintains a studio-style consignment furniture store and design office, where other designers send their goofs or sample pieces (including gifts and accessories) from mansions after "showcase" tours/exhibitions. Some upscale furnishings come from individuals. Prices are set about 60–70% off original prices.

NATIONAL FURNITURE LIQUIDATORS

845 Embarcadero, Oakland. (510) 251-2222. M–Sat 10–5, Sun 11–4. VISA, MC, AE, DIS. Parking: lot.
(Other store: 1110 Van Ness Avenue [at Geary], San Francisco.)

Major hotels renovate their guest rooms every few years, not because the furniture is worn out, but to give their guests fresh, up-to-date surroundings and to keep up with the competition. The furniture comes from major San Francisco tourist hotels, boutique hotels, and hotels noted as luxury out-of-town escapes—names well known to Bay Area residents. The furniture from the better hotels is generally high quality, has been well maintained, and usually has been put only to light use, since tourists and business travelers tend to be out and about, not sitting around in their rooms.

The furniture that is being replaced is resold by companies like National Furniture Liquidators. Scout here for furnishings for vacation homes or primary residences—extra chairs, tables, lamps, sofas, sofa beds, bedroom furniture, and desks. The selection of furnishings is ever-changing. Pricing is determined by condition and is also affected by supply and demand. Prices do change on individual pieces and are frequently reduced when the company is overstocked. Lamps are often priced at $5–$25, occasional chairs at $25–$65, bedroom furniture from $25 to $125. Check the walls for framed pictures, mirrors, and artwork. National has a split personality of sorts. In addition to its hotel furniture, it also sells new budget-quality furniture to those who may have little money to spend but still prefer to buy new furniture. (You won't have any trouble telling the difference between the two types of merchandise.) Shoppers should also expect to find some pieces that are a little tired (but priced accordingly), but there's more than enough tempting and attractive furniture and accessories to justify a visit.

ONE OF A KIND
390 State Street, Los Altos (415) 949-3393. M–Sat 10–5. Cash/Check. Parking: street.
(Other store: 14485 Big Basin Way, Saratoga.)
You'll take home 80% of the selling price, but you're charged $6 a square foot for floor-space rental. That's an incentive to price right, so furniture sells quickly. Some consignors just place small pieces that show the style and finish of a complete set (the remainder staying in their possession), to trim rental costs. Also, collectibles and art objects get lots of space, and the big boys' toy section (golf collectibles, etc.) is unique.

POPIK FURNITURE CO.
935 Main Street, Redwood City. (650) 368-2877.
M–F 9–5:30, Sat 9–5. MC, VISA, AE, DIS.
Parking: street.
The children and grandchildren of Popik's original customers have sustained this business for fifty-four years. The original family is still at the helm, supplying Peninsula shoppers with new and used furniture. Furniture is bought outright, and then most pieces are "spruced up" in the refinishing shop in the back of the store. At first glance it may not be obvious that much of the furniture is used. It's unlikely you'll find antiques, but many pieces are definitely "vintage." If you're set on finding a piece to slipcover, stencil, or personalize with a faux finish, this is a good place to start. After fifty-four years, the interior of the store is a little tired, and furniture is crammed throughout. New furnishings and bedding are geared for the budget crowd rather than an upscale market, but the prices are all nicely discounted. Free delivery. If you have furniture to sell, call to schedule a home evaluation (no tired sofas wanted).

Also See

Under Furniture and Home Accessories—
Clearance Centers:
ALL LISTINGS

Giftware and Home Decor

CLAY ART CERAMICS OUTLET

239 Utah Avenue, South San Francisco. (415) 244-4970. Th 1–4. Cash/Check. Parking: street.
Clay Art/About Face makes ceramic masks, banks, bathware, and housewares (teapots, cookie jars, salt-and-pepper sets, mugs, tissue dispensers, candlesticks, and toothpick holders), sold through gift shops around the country. The decorative ceramic masks are made in about seventy images, including the company's original limited editions. They can get very expensive with the addition of feathers, jewels, or other design elements. The tabletop and home accessories collections combine functional creativity with sophisticated whimsy. Lots of animal motifs. Everything in the seconds room is discounted about 50% off wholesale, and the flaws are no big deal (usually painting defects).

COHN-STONE STUDIOS

5755 Landregan Street, Emeryville. (510) 654-9690. M–F 10–5:30 (closed 1–2:30). MC, VISA. Parking: street.
The artists at Cohn-Stone studios have earned a reputation for quality and design. Their contemporary handblown glassware, distinctive bowls, vases, perfume vials, paperweights, and plates have been exhibited in some of the nation's top galleries and fine arts specialty stores. Save 50% on seconds that may have a bubble or a scratch; they may be too big or too small, experimental, or discontinued. There's a good range of gift-priced beauties from $10 to $200, although some very special pieces may be priced from $300 to $750 (lamps). Anything made by Cohn-Stone is destined to be a tasteful, timeless gift or a wonderful accent for your home. All sales final.

COLLECTIBLES OUTLET

1899 W. San Carlos Street, San Jose. (408) 288-6027. M–F 10–6, Th until 9, Sat 10–5, Sun Noon–5. MC, VISA. Parking: back lot/street.
For classy collectibles, you can't do better than the Collectibles Outlet. Here are just a few of the names: Hummel, Lladro, David Winter and Lilliput cottages, Precious Moments, Dept. 56, Royal Doulton, Waterford, Nao, Swarovski, Boyd Bears, and many other brands of status bears and dolls (Madam Alexander, too)—and more! Naturally, your first question should be, "Are these authentic?" The answer: Yes! The proof: the registered trademark on each piece. Even though most of the inventory is discounted starting at 20% off retail, prices may be as much as 40–70% off original retail on special purchases and closeouts set out in the clearance room. The Collectibles Outlet is simply marvelous!

COUROC FACTORY STORE

501 Ortiz Avenue, Sand City. (408) 899-5479. M–Sat 10–5. MC, VISA, AE. Parking: street.
When in Monterey, make a beeline for the Couroc Factory Store, about five minutes away, in Sand City. This classy giftware (mainly bowls, trays, and serving pieces) is unique for finished designs hand-inlaid into a secret-formula phenolic resin compound, then buffed to the singular luster of satin blackness characteristic of Couroc products. The line is popular with tourists who seek tasteful mementos of California visits; natives may find all the designs appealing. Prices on seconds are 50% off retail. Expect to spend $27.50 to $75 for trays, depending on size. Group tours of the factory can be arranged in advance. *Directions: From Hwy. 1, take Seaside/Del Rey Oaks exit, go to Del Monte Boulevard, turn left at stop sign, left again at Contra Costa.*

CRATE & BARREL OUTLET

1785 Fourth Street, Berkeley. (510) 528-5500. M–Sat 10–6, Sun 11–6. MC, VISA, AE, DIS. Parking: lot.
Picture what you find in Crate & Barrel's "lifestyle" stores: bright, contemporary, functional home accessories. Out-of-season, discontinued, and occasionally damaged goods are sent to the outlet from the full-service retail stores. Discounts are 20–70% off original retail, although many discounts are in the more modest 25–30% range.

Check every nook and cranny of this colorful and creatively merchandised outlet. Crate & Barrel's popular basic stemware and barware are carried at retail store prices. Returns and exchanges.

EVANS CERAMICS GALLERY

1421 Lincoln Avenue, Calistoga. (707) 942-0453. Daily 10–5. MC. Parking: street.

Evans Ceramics produces designer vases and art pieces in raku, a firing process in which exotic finishes are achieved by pulling pieces directly out of a yellow-hot kiln. Evans's gallery is filled with one-of-a-kind prototypes, seconds, and overruns at clearance prices. The 40–70% markdowns vary with the status of the pieces. Evans's art evolves with design trends. Newer pieces and color palettes are continually being developed. The latest? Beautiful slumped and blown glass.

LA CASA REAL WAREHOUSE SALES

817 Arnold Drive #7, Muir Business Park, Martinez (¼ mile west of Price/Costco). (510) 370-2707. M–F 10–5, Sat 10–2 (by appt.). Cash/Check. Parking: lot.

Although not obvious to consumers, many wonderful decorative home accessories (including La Casa Real's) give no hint of their Mexican origins. They're sold in high-profile lifestyle stores, by national catalog companies, and in gift departments of major stores. Mexican artisans and suppliers have a great deal more to offer than what you typically see in Tijuana or in local flea markets.

La Casa Real's warehouse is where bargain hunters can buy the showroom samples at prices reduced 30–50% off retail. You'll find an eclectic selection of goods—angels in many forms, pottery, ceramics, pewter, decorative hand-painted wood furniture, forged iron tables and chairs, wall art, frosted handblown balls, vases and glassware, planters, Tang Dynasty–inspired, hand-painted ceramic horses, and more. Fifty-two suppliers contribute to the collection. Contributing fine artists and craftspeople have works that have been shown in galleries and museums throughout the U.S. and Mexico. Most individual pieces are signed by the artists—like the large contemporary handblown glass plates (lovely when displayed on a stand), or the numerous handcrafted and -painted wood boxes, iron roosters, sculptures, and lovely pewter plates and serving pieces. Many samples are one-of-a-kind, and prices range from $2.50 to $5,000 (for a large hand-painted armoire). Call first to verify hours, which vary seasonally or during trade shows. *Directions: From Hwy. 680 take Hwy. 4 to the Morello exit. Turn left on Arnold Drive.*

LUNDBERG STUDIOS

131 Old Coast Road, Davenport. (408) 423-2532. Daily 10–4. MC, VISA, DIS, AE. Parking: street.
Lundberg Studios is the recognized leader in Tiffany art-glass reproductions. Pieces sell in fine galleries and world-renowned stores. A Lundberg paperweight retails for $200–$400, a Tiffany-style lamp also in the hundreds! At any time in the studio there are usually seventy-five to a hundred seconds that are discounted about 50%. Lamps, paperweights, vases, crystal, and glass perfume vials may have minor flaws, or they may be discontinued.

In exchange for the seconds' low prices you may have to forgo Lundberg's prestigious signature. If you are an art-glass collector, the trip to Davenport will be worthwhile.

•

MASLACH ART GLASS STUDIO & SECONDS STORE

44 Industrial Way, Greenbrae. (415) 924-2310. T–Sat Noon–4. MC, VISA. Parking: street.
The elegant displays in this outlet showcase the many original pieces produced by Maslach. The goblets are very popular, when they're being produced. What's not readily apparent is that most of these beauties are seconds reduced about 25–50%. Maslach's distinctive marbles, a great favorite with collectors, are priced from $10 to $90 at retail, and happily, much less as seconds. You may find paperweights, bowls, sculptures, and new designs. The designers are constantly innovating and creating new treasures. Just about anything will qualify as a beautiful gift. Great wedding presents!

NOUROT GLASS STUDIO

675 E. H Street, Benicia. (707) 745-1463. M–Sat 10–4, Sun Noon–5. MC, VISA. Parking: street.

Works by Nourot are in the collection of the Corning Museum of Glass. If you would like to own a museum-quality piece of art glass that is individually crafted in the ancient tradition, be sure to get on the Nourot mailing list for special promotions, when selection is best and bargains abound. Special sales events are scheduled on the weekend before Mother's Day, the second weekend in August, and the first weekend in December. Retail prices are steep, but the quality is impeccable. Sale prices reduced 50% make them more affordable.

R. STRONG GLASS STUDIO & GALLERY

1235 Fourth Street (at Gilman), Berkeley. (510) 525-3150. M–Sat 10–4:30. MC, VISA. Parking: street.

Randy Strong designs and creates distinctive handblown goblets, vases, sculpture, and paperweights, many of which have 22-karat gold leaf fused to the glass. His unique works are seen at fine exhibits and in arts and crafts magazines. Prices at the studio's gallery are 20–75% off regular retail prices. The outlet's prices range from $10 to $58 for goblets and paperweights (seconds); special sculptures and platters can cost more (first-quality pieces are also available at slightly higher prices). R. Strong's handblown solid-glass gold hearts and hollow iridescent hearts make wonderful romantic gifts for many special occasions. The studio also features some special works by other artists at reduced prices. The main entrance to the studio is on the side of the building.

RED ROSE COLLECTION CATALOG OUTLET STORE

826 Burlway, Burlingame. (415) 347-6300. Fri 3–8, Sat 10–5, Sun 10–2. MC, VISA, AE, DIS. Parking: lot.

This catalog outlet store is just a jog off the freeway (near the Hyatt Regency), making a quick detour mandatory for anyone scouting for clever, inspirational, and whimsical gifts for adults or children. As you stroll through the outlet, think about graduation, showers, weddings, and any other gift occasion on the horizon. The outlet is filled with catalog overstocks, reflecting the merchandise found in its "lifestyle collection" of quality products and unusual gifts for home and garden, plus books, handicrafts, posters and framed art, CDs, candles, Christmas items, romantic dresses, fashion jewelry, and other delights. These "leftovers" are sold for 30–75% off original catalog retails.

Many women are bound to favor the dresses, kimonos, caftans, and sets that are chosen to provide a casual elegance for everyday and social occasions. A global influence is evident in the jeweled and vivid colors, original prints, and soft, free-flowing natural-fiber fabrics. Sizes Small to Large, one-size and Plus sizes. The fashion jewelry keys into the more spiritual aspects of the catalog with amulets, runes, Celtic designs, and many ethnic-inspired, handcrafted designs. Sterling silver, brass, gems, and natural stones are among the materials in the eclectic jewelry selection. Red Rose regulars will want to keep up with the frequent transfusions of new "closeout" inventory. *Directions: North Broadway exit east off Fwy. 101. Burlway is the first street north of the Hyatt Regency Hotel off the Old Bayshore Highway.*

SAN FRANCISCO MUSIC BOX

Great Mall of the Bay Area, Milpitas. (408) 956-9427. Daily. MC, VISA, DIS, AE. Parking: lot. You'll love the melodic greeting from dozens of music boxes when you enter this outlet, which serves as a combination clearance center and retail store. Not everything is discounted—look for tags or display signs with red dots to zero in on the special discounts. Music boxes come in any number of surprising configurations: figurines, water globes, stuffed animals, masks, trinket boxes, picture frames, watches, ornaments, and more. Don't worry, closeout or discontinued merchandise will be in working condition.

SMYERS GLASS STUDIO

675 E. H Street, Benicia. (707) 745-2614. M–Sat 10–4 (daily Nov and Dec). MC, VISA. Parking: lot. Smyers Glass is known throughout the country for its fine handblown stemware. A favorite of young brides and those who love to entertain, Smyers glass is sold in fine stores such as Neiman Marcus, Gump's, and Nordstrom. In addition to his handblown stemware, Stephen Smyers creates beautiful paperweights, bowls, vases, and perfume bottles. Seconds in the studio sell for 50% or more off retail. Special sales the first weekends in May and December offer exceptional buying opportunities.

TAKAHASHI HOME DECOR OUTLET

235 15th Street (corner of Kansas), San Francisco.
(415) 552-5511. M–Sat 9:30–5. MC, VISA.
Parking: street.

For bargains on home accessories, check out the clearance corner at Takahashi, a fifty-year-old San Francisco company that imports high-quality decorative and practical items for the home from Japan. It wholesales its line to prestigious catalog houses—Horchow, Charles Keath, Ballard Designs, Smithsonian, Winterthur, and many others. Famous gift stores also carry the Takahashi line, and many of its products selling in its outlet remind one of a familiar piece seen before, elsewhere. A space has been set aside inside the beautiful retail/wholesale gallery for the clearance outlet, where first-quality samples and discontinued or surplus inventory is sold at 50% discounts off retail prices. New pieces are added to the outlet selection almost daily. Majolica fruit plates and pictures, English teatime sets, French-style planters, an enormous selection of bathroom sets, and an even larger choice of fine mugs are always in evidence. Depending on when you shop, you may also find small porcelain jewelry boxes, picture frames, magnets, mama-san aprons, place mats, vases, cookie jars, celadon dinnerware, etc. Many items are one-of-a-kind; others are available in unlimited supply. Design collections are versatile, with some reflecting the subtle quality of Japanese design, others replicating traditional European and English designs, plus some hard-to-find masculine styling and even children's storybook-inspired dishes. Good values may be found on the showroom inventory of Japanese painted screens, scrolls, wooden panels, architectural trim, urns, Tansu and other accent pieces, and textiles.

TUESDAY MORNING

239 Third Street, Montecito Plaza, San Rafael.
(415) 453-9816. All stores: M–Sat 9:30–6, Th until
8, Sun Noon–6. MC, VISA, DIS. Parking: lot.
(Other stores: Danville, Fremont, Pleasanton,
Sacramento, San Mateo, Saratoga, Sacramento,
Sunnyvale, Walnut Creek.)

Texas-based Tuesday Morning has built its success and reputation on the uniqueness and quality of its inventory. Prices are promised to be 50–80% off original retail on excess inventories from manufacturers around the world. If you currently shop at other discounters, like T.J. Maxx or Marshalls, the prices on some merchandise may be merely competitive, or they may be much better. Everything is relative! The company's opening "events," held four times a year, draw shoppers attracted by the prospect of buying both the expected and unexpected: Oriental rugs; crystal and silver-plated giftware; housewares; porcelain lamps; bed, bath, and table linens; paper products; Christmas and holiday paraphernalia; baskets; children's toys and apparel; men's furnishings; even some furniture. You'll see some very famous names attached to the inventory. Everything is first quality. Wow! Cash refunds and returns allowed. Selections vary from store to store. Special shopping opportunities are offered to selected mailing-list customers (big spenders). Opening events scheduled generally for mid-Feb or March, May or June, mid-Aug or Sep, and mid-Oct to Dec.

WE'RE ENTERTAINMENT

Outlets at Gilroy, Gilroy. (408) 848-4311. Daily. MC, VISA, AE. Parking: lot.
The company licensed to sell this whimsical giftware sends its closeouts and discontinued inventory to this store. Calvin and Hobbes, Curious George, *Star Trek, Star Wars,* Winnie the Pooh, the Pillsbury Dough Boy, Harley-Davidson, Elvis, Coca-Cola, and Mickey Mouse and other Disney friends are just a partial list of famous icons found on the novelties, music boxes, ties, magnets, key chains, T-shirts, caps, boxers, etc. Markdowns of 30–40% make it tempting to stock up on a bag full of little gifts for friends and family members of all ages.

WHIMSICAL WORLD OF JUDIE BOMBERGER SECONDS OUTLET

65-H Hamilton Drive, Novato. (415) 883-3072. M–F 9–5. MC, VISA. Parking: lot.
Judie Bomberger manufactures a line of whimsical contemporary crafts for the home that sell in galleries and gift stores around the country. Some of her most popular pieces are the rusted metal sculptures mounted on a rod for garden staking. The dancing ladies, cats, rabbits, and assorted

winged critters are classified as seconds when they have a touch too much rust. Most people don't quibble when that translates to prices discounted 50%, ranging from $7 to $90 (most at $12 to $45). The fanciful and carefree indoor metal sculptures (mounted on rods attached to stands) are painted with layers of bright acrylic coatings—each piece has a character all its own. Reproductions of original watercolors are mounted and ready to hang. The seconds may have small dents at the edge or an almost imperceptible surface scratch. These are priced as seconds, at $17 to $35. Occasionally you may also find Judie's candleholders or unique furniture pieces.

ZELLIQUE ART GLASS
701 E. H Street, Benicia. (707) 745-5710. M–Sat 10–4. MC, VISA. Parking: street.
Zellique offers handblown art glass designed by Joseph Morel. If you don't mind a slight imperfection that you probably can't even see, then you'll save about 50% off retail. The collection includes paperweights, perfume bottles, bookends, vases, individual sculptures, bowls, and lamps. For the best selection, schedule a visit when Zellique, Smyers, and Nourot join forces for special open-house events on the weekend before Mother's Day and the first weekend in December. Get on their mailing list for these special events.

Also See

Under Dinnerware and Kitchenware:
ALL LISTINGS

Under Linens:
BED & BATH SUPERSTORE; HOME EXPRESS; LINENS 'N' THINGS

Under General Clothing:
BURLINGTON COAT FACTORY; MARSHALLS; STEIN MART; T.J. MAXX

Under Jewelry and Watches:
CRESALIA JEWELERS

Under Furniture and Home Accessories:
IGUANA AMERAMEX

Under Furniture and Home Accessories—
Used/Consignment
ALL LISTINGS

Under General Merchandise:
ALL SECTIONS

Under General Merchandise—Membership
Warehouse Clubs:
PRICE/COSTCO

Under Special Sales and Events:
ALL LISTINGS

Home Improvement

When it comes to home-improvement projects, it's hard not to mention HomeBase and Home Depot. These two warehouse stores dominate the market with vast selection and deep discount pricing. Similar in operation, they offer an in-depth selection of everything you need to build and fixture a home from the blueprint stage to the final step of landscaping and fencing. Most consumers are satisfied with the overall quality offered in the selection of products. However, if you're looking for more luxurious and expensive products, you may have to use specialty sources and forgo any hope of a bargain. Considering the sheer number of people who besiege these stores every day, both companies do a fair job with service, but they'd have to triple the staffing to provide the one-on-one attention that most of us would like. To that end, each company offers many special events for do-it-yourselfers. Think of these stores when buying plumbing, fencing, paint, tools, lighting fixtures, lumber, paneling, windows, sprinkler systems, hardware, garden equipment and supplies, window blinds, flooring, kitchen and bath cabinets and fixtures, electrical supplies, patio furniture, barbecues, and more, more, and more.

BLACK & DECKER
Factory Stores of America, Vacaville. (707) 453-1256. Daily. MC, VISA. Parking: lot.
You'll discover that Black & Decker makes lots of helpful and innovative gadgets and Handy Andy aids, in addition to its well-known line of tools and garden equipment. Everything in the outlet is priced at least 25% off retail. (The company sets prices to undersell its competitors.) You'll see "service products" (reconditioned items that carry a full two-year warranty and often are sold at 50% off retail); blemished cartons; and discontinued models. It may be worth a visit to buy a new cordless drill, palm grip sander, router, Workmate, variable

speed drill, power miter saw, circular saw, Groom 'N' Edge garden trimmer, buffers, hedge trimmer, or One Touch lawn mower. Black & Decker gets into the kitchen in a big way; you'll also find a variety of small electrical appliances at the same discounts.

C. H. BULL

233 Utah, South San Francisco. (415) 468-4530. M–F 8–5. MC, VISA. Parking: lot.
C. H. Bull and its Western Hardware division are major suppliers of tools for line workers, electricians, auto mechanics, carpenters, iron and steel workers, and manufacturing and industrial plants in Northern California. These tools are industrial-rated and may cost more than home-rated tools, even at discount. However, prices here are substantially discounted from manufacturers' lists. On products that serve both the industrial and home markets—Stanley tapes, vise grip sets, block sanders, saws, hammers, and other hand tools—prices are competitive with the warehouse stores. Western has no sales gimmicks or loss leaders, just low dealer prices every day. Located off Airport Boulevard, about one block from Price/Costco.

CALDWELL BUILDING WRECKERS

195 Bayshore Boulevard, San Francisco. (415) 550-6777. M–F 8:30–5, Sat 9–4:30 (Nov–Feb M–F 8–4:30). MC, VISA. Parking: street.
Caldwell Building Wreckers recycles building materials and offers new distributors' closeouts, plus seconds and liquidated stock. It's a labyrinth of rooms stocked with both new and used building materials. I was impressed with the variety in the hundreds of new windows and doors (exterior and interior). You'll discover well-known brands in wood frame windows and patio doors, most dual glazed (French door units, too). Also check out the decorative molding. You can go basic and budget-quality, or trade up to something really special and upscale. Either way, you'll be saving considerably. You can trim your building costs by buying recycled lumber, plywood, beams, mirrors, used bricks, cobblestones, occasionally slabs of granite and marble. The lumber is fully dried, avoiding the twisting that occurs later if it's too green. Also, Caldwell can custom cut special beams or sizes for you. I can't get too excited about used toilets, sinks, or bathtubs (unless they're Victorian style), but they're in stock, too. Delivery can be arranged.

CERAMIC CIRCUS

438 Francisco Boulevard W., San Rafael. (415) 456-0282. M–Sat 9–4:30. MC, VISA. Parking: lot.
You'll find Ceramic Circus in back of Tilecraft, an upscale tile company. It's a familiar story—special purchases, seconds, returned, and discontinued items. Discounts are 50–70% off original retail. You'll find more floor tiles than anything else, but there are some countertop and wall tiles. I noted one flooring tile marked down from $4.50 to $1.90. The selection is limited, so while it's probably not worth driving a long way, stop by if you're in the area. *Note: The entrance is on Rice Street.*

DESIGNER'S BRASS

280 El Camino Real, San Bruno. (415) 588-8480. M–F 8:30–5:30, Sat 9–5. MC, VISA, ATM. Parking: lot.
Check out Designer's Brass if you're replacing nondescript bath, kitchen, or door fixtures. With luck you'll find something you like among the many discontinued bathroom and kitchen faucets, fancy front-door locks, and indoor knobs, all deeply discounted. If you buy regular inventory, discounts vary with the amount of sale ($100 and more) and according to what line you buy and how much you buy of it. This outfit carries status brands that ordinarily cost far more than the budget-to-moderate models at HomeBase, etc. Very nice selection of the latest in kitchen and bathroom fixtures and accessories (pulls and knobs for cabinet doors).

ITALICS WAREHOUSE SALES

1476 66th Street (west of Hollis, south of Ashby), Emeryville. Fri only 10–4. (510) 547-1872. Cash/Check. Parking: street.
Today's homeowners are taking tile from the entryway down the hall and into all rooms of the house. New sizes and grout colors that camouflage soiling add to tile's appeal. Its only drawback? The price—combined with the cost of installation—is out of range for many homeowners.

Italics, with a focus on high-end tile, opens its warehouse every Friday for bargain shoppers. Most of its selection is imported from Italy. The designs are reproductions of natural stone—marble, slate, limestone, granite, patio terra-cotta, etc.—all suggesting the look usually associated with Mediterranean villas, which has been one of the hottest trends in the past few years. Tiles for other applications include wall tiles in glossy or satin finishes, bright or neutral colors, and sizes from 6-by-8 inches to 8-by-13 inches. Japanese porcelains in a rainbow of pastels or solid colors are good choices for countertops. Take a peek at the company's classy retail showroom (a half-block away, on the corner of 66th Street and Hollis) to see how these products will appear in actual installations. Friday warehouse openings allow bargain hunters a chance to eyeball the inventory closeouts, overstocks, and odd lots, which may be reduced 30-50% off the showroom's retail prices. Don't expect fancy displays at the warehouse; most tiles are sitting in boxes, with a few sample tiles for viewing. The fixings—setting thinsets, mastics, and grouts—are available for do-it-yourselfers. Although Italics does not provide installation services, the store may be able to put you in touch with tile contractors.

KEN'S GLASS

2905 Senter Road (at Lewis), San Jose. (408) 578-5211. M–Sat 9–5, closed W. Cash/Check. Parking: lot.
Ken offers great prices because he cuts corners: no secretary, virtually no overhead, no delivery, no installation, no cutouts on glass or mirrors (although he will trim edges to size), and a cash-and-carry policy. Ken stocks first-quality glass and mirrors, as well as seconds with a substantial price differential, in all sizes and shapes. He has a good selection of precut sizes of glass and mirrors for shelving, picture frames, rounds for tabletops, and mirrored closet doors. Look for bronze and clear beveled mirrors. Check all his bargains before deciding; you'll find many price options (40–80% discounts), whether you're covering an entire wall with mirror or simply replacing a broken window.

THE KITCHEN TABLE

151 Third Street, San Rafael. (415) 453-2662. M–F 9–4, Sat 9–2. Cash/Check. Parking: street.
This small shop is hardly more than a shed. The floor is covered with sawdust (you may be too by the time you leave), and the smell of glue pervades.

You'll see work in progress: butcher-block tables and countertops being built. Each butcher-block item is made to the customer's specifications. Drawers, knife racks, wine or glass racks, shelves, microwave platforms, and more can be made to accessorize the tables. Since they're handmade, you won't find the smooth edges and perfectly finished surfaces typical of mass-produced butcher-block products; these are more like antiques. They're finished in your choice of oil or urethane. Custom services are usually costly, but not here. You may save 40–60%, depending on where you do your comparison pricing. A table 48 inches long, 24 inches wide, 4 inches thick, any height, runs $200; one 27 inches long, 18 inches wide, 4 inches thick is $90. Orders can usually be filled in a couple of weeks. Call for a phone quote.

MAJOR LINES "AS-IS" WAREHOUSE

235 Bayshore Boulevard, San Francisco. (415) 647-9066. M–F 8–5, Sat 9–4. MC, VISA. Parking: lot.
If you're clever you can do a lot with the options available at Major Lines, distributor for Merillat custom kitchen and bathroom cabinets. This mid-priced line offers standard features like roll-out trays, a furniture-quality finish, and wipe-clean interiors. There are several styles, finishes, and cabinet fronts available. You can buy veneers or solid wood-face frames or practical, easy-to-clean melamine laminates. The bargain angle starts when you enter the warehouse, where discontinued (some just with style modifications), slightly damaged, or otherwise marked down cabinets are shown. At times, you may find enough cabinets in one style to completely outfit a kitchen or bath. More often, you'll find just a cabinet or two for the utility room, small bath, etc. Prices are about half off contractor pricing. (I spotted many pieces at $49.) Some inexpensive cabinets are in stock for the do-it-yourselfer in two-door styles in natural oak at near contractor pricing. All sales final.

McINTYRE TILE CO.

55 W. Grant Street, Healdsburg. (707) 433-8866. M–F 9–4, Sat 10–4. MC, VISA. Parking: street.
McIntyre Tile is sold directly through architects and interior designers. Its handcrafted, high-fired stoneware and porcelain tile is available in many beautiful colors, at about $12/square foot. Call and request a selection of samples in your color

range. If you see one you like, inquire about its seconds, which are half price (about $3/square foot) and may be off-color or slightly warped, but otherwise structurally sound. Allow plenty of time to pick and poke through the seconds. *Note: The store closes for lunch, 12:30–1:30. Get on its mailing list.*

THE MOULDING COMPANY

2310-D Bates Avenue, Concord. (510) 798-7525. M–F 8–5, Sat 9–1. MC, VISA. Parking: lot.
East Bay consumers should stop by this warehouse (wear a sweater on cold days) to select moldings or decorative trims. Most moldings (crown, base, casings, cove, etc.) are available in finger-jointed pine (paint grade), stain grade, and primed. A few moldings are stocked in oak, while other woods are available by special order (including mantels and columns). Sorting out the choices is made easier by reviewing the company's six-page catalog, which illustrates the type, dimension, and style of its molding. (This will be mailed on request.) The company supplies many smaller establishments with molding for resale, sells to many contractors, and offers consumers pricing that's substantially lower than the local home-improvement superstores. My comparison surveys revealed savings of about 35–40% on average. You can send your contractor in to make purchases, or, if you're a determined sort, do it yourself. It's not that hard to do if you plan each cut carefully and practice first on an extra length of molding. If you're doing several rooms, an investment in a chop saw makes the whole enterprise easier. Delivery is free in Contra Costa County and to other areas on larger orders. *Location: Bates is off Port Chicago Highway.*

NORSTAD POTTERY

253 S. 25th Street, Richmond. (510) 620-0200. M–F 9–5, Sat 10–3. MC, VISA. Parking: lot.
Norstad Pottery produces distinctive, beautiful, and functional stoneware planters, tableware, and vases, plus bath, kitchen, vegetable, and bar sinks that are handcrafted from stoneware clay fired to approximately 2,400 degrees. Each piece is hand-thrown and -decorated; therefore, each is different. Norstad's dinnerware, platters, and baking and serving dishes appeal to those shopping for contemporary aesthetic designs. Its sinks and stoneware are typically sold through architects and

specialty tile and bath showrooms. Bargain hunters check the Richmond showroom for seconds that may have slight color imperfections or something as minor as a pinhole in the glaze. These are visual flaws that don't impair product integrity. Discounts on seconds are 25–40% off retail. Catch sales in April and early December, when everything is reduced 25% and seconds are reduced an additional 40%.

POST TOOL & SUPPLY

800 E. Eighth Street, Oakland. (510) 272-0331. M–Sat 8–5, Sun 10–3. MC, VISA, DIS. Parking: street.
(Other stores: Fremont, Modesto, Sacramento, San Carlos, San Francisco, San Jose, San Rafael, Santa Rosa, Stockton, Vallejo.)
Post is all set up for serious tool users, offering high-quality brands: Milwaukee, Skil, Hitachi, DeWalt, Ryobi, Porter-Cable, Makita, and others. You'll usually find drill presses, bench grinders, table saws, hand tools, jacks, vises, wrenches, socket sets, electric tools, air tools, electric saws, lathes, and tool boxes. Everything is fully guaranteed and comes in the original factory packaging.

Prices are sometimes a tad higher than at HomeBase or Price/Costco, but the trade-off is expanded selection, customer service, and support.

R.V. CLOUD

1217 Dell Avenue (Irrigation) and 3000 S. Winchester (Plumbing), Campbell. Irrigation, (408) 374-8370; Plumbing, (408) 378-7943. M–F 8–5. MC, VISA. Parking: lot.
When landscaping your yard and installing a sprinkler system, stop by R.V. Cloud, a major wholesaler of irrigation supplies for contractors and perfect for do-it-yourselfers. Do everyone a favor and do some homework first: The staff is busy! You can buy pipe, fittings, sprinkler heads, timers, regulators—in short, everything you need. You'll pay about 10% more than contractors, which will save you about 20–30% off the prices at building-supply stores. The plumbing department is through a separate entrance at the other end of the building. You can order plumbing supplies, water heaters, pumps, and bathroom, kitchen, and laundry fixtures (toilets, sinks, tubs, and faucets) from catalogs. Kohler, Price Pfister, Moen, Delta, Grohe,

and others are stocked. R.V. is a good source for high-end fixtures. Keep an open mind and you may find really special prices on discontinued fixtures that offer quality you probably can't afford if you buy current stock. Special plumbing fixtures for the handicapped can be ordered. The quality ranges from standard to superlative. The merchandise comes in sealed boxes, so be sure to research style and color selections before coming in. Local delivery can be arranged for a nominal fee. *Note: R.V. is not open on Saturdays.*

RAFFLES FANS

1244 Fourth Street (corner of Fourth and C), San Rafael. (415) 456-6660. M–Sat 10–5:30. MC, VISA. Parking: street, lots.
Raffles specializes in ceiling fans and offers everything savvy value-conscious shoppers need: expertise, good service, and competitive prices. Raffles sticks with the proven leaders in the field: Casablanca, Hunter, and Emerson. Prices range from $99 to $2,500. Most sales fall in the $199–$500 range. It's important to evaluate first what charges are involved in installation, particularly if a new ceiling outlet must be put in. When shopping around, be sure to compare apples to apples: Some stores may quote prices that do not include fan blades, a light fixture, or fitting. Raffles offers good discount prices up front and stands behind its prices with a guarantee "to meet or beat any advertised or written quote."

STONELIGHT TILE FACTORY

1651 Pomona Avenue, San Jose. (408) 292-7424. Sat 9–5. Cash/Check. Parking: lot.
Stonelight Tile is a glazed tile with an unusually dense body made chiefly of natural clays instead of talc (used in most commercial tile) for a natural look that contributes to its great popularity among architects and designers. Stonelight's "boneyard" has stacks of leftovers and seconds (surface irregularities, color imperfections, or chips). The savings are considerable: Normal retail for these tiles is in the neighborhood of $7.50–$25/square foot. Seconds sell for 50¢ to $2.50/square foot, and overruns are $3–$5/square foot. You may have to pay full price for trim pieces if they are not in the seconds or overrun selection. Boxes cost, so bring your own. Finally, do yourself and the busy staff a favor—take measurements and have quantity esti-

mates ready before visiting. If you want to eyeball the first-quality tile, stop by the showroom at 609 South First Street.

TOOLS & MORE!

Outlets at Gilroy, Gilroy. (408) 842-1992. Daily. MC, VISA, AE, DIS. Parking: lot.
Just the ticket, "Tool Time" folks. This is an outlet for the Tool Warehouse chain, out of Troy, Michigan, and generally unknown to West Coast shoppers. While shopping partners are cruising through the apparel outlets, spend some time looking at all the gadgets, tools, doodads, and other clever goodies that make up this store. Some interesting stuff: 8-foot garden windmills; hand tools; assorted power tools, including cordless drills (minimum to maximum powers); pocket torches; magnifiers; clamps; levels; talking alarm clocks; lighted screwdrivers; videos; polishes; grout coatings; and altogether lots of things you'd expect to see in a catalog geared for basic, innovative, and original handyman/woman helpers. Prices are discounted 30–70% off the Tool Warehouse retail prices.

Getting the Job Done— Helpful Hint

THE TRADES GUILD

Alameda County (510) 547-3337; Contra Costa County (510) 820-2766; Marin County (415) 454-5272; Peninsula (650) 573-7337; South Bay (408) 297-3337; and San Francisco County (415) 777-3337.
The Trades Guild is a free consumer referral service that specializes in the building trades, so if you're unsure of the type of worker you need, it can help. Everyone who calls speaks to a real person (no voice mail) who will talk to you about your job, then refer you to several members in your area who do the type of work you need. In addition to the contractor names and telephone numbers, the Trades Guild will also relay comments about the contractor from his/her previous customers. The guild continuously solicits feedback about its members through postage-paid "Opinion Cards" that are sent to consumers who use the service. Contractors referred by the Trades Guild must meet strict membership criteria before they can be referred to the public. Contractors must be

licensed by the state and bonded. The guild veri-
fies all insurance information, checks for complaints
on file with various consumer agencies, requires a
personal interview at the contractor's place of
business, and requires five written references from
previous customers. There is no charge to consumers—the service is supported by membership
dues. The next time you need a carpenter, tree
trimmer, painter, carpet installer, landscaper,
plumber, electrician, or someone for earthquake
retrofitting, give the guild a call. This service provides a peace-of-mind alternative to plucking
names willy-nilly out of the yellow pages.

Also See

Under General Carpeting, Area Rugs, and
Flooring:
FLOORCRAFT

Linens

General Linens

BED & BATH SUPERSTORE

*555 Ninth Street, San Francisco. (415) 252-0490.
M–F 9:30–9, Sat 9:30–7, Sun 10:30–7. MC, VISA.
Parking: lot.
(Other stores: 590 Second Street, Oakland; 5201
Stevens Creek Boulevard, Santa Clara; 2675 Santa
Rosa Avenue, Santa Rosa.)*
Of course it has bed linens from brand-name manufacturers, even some designer lines. Prices are
discounted 20–40% on current, first-quality merchandise every day. You can give the bathroom
the once-over, too. You'll find a wonderful collection of closet organizers and gadgets. Don't miss
the housewares and kitchen department.
Farberware, Fitz & Floyd, Mikasa, Rubbermaid,
and Copco are a few of the lines in dinnerware,
cookware, accessories, and giftware. All the stores
are beautifully merchandised and well stocked,
although sometimes it takes a ladder to reach the
nearly ceiling-high shelves.

BEDSPREAD IMAGE

*39201 Farwell Drive, East Mowry Shopping
Center, Fremont. (510) 795-0539. M–F 11–7, Sat
11–6, Sun 12:30–5. MC, VISA, AE, DIS.
Parking: lot.*
Bedspread Image should definitely be on your list of
places to shop for bedspreads, daybed cover sets,
sheet sets, and decorative pillows. Bedspreads
and comforters from major mills are discounted
15–35% off retail. Prices on bedspreads range
from $49 to $329 (for a top-of-the-line custom
spread). The selection caters to most decors, from
country cute to nouveau contemporary.

DECORATOR'S BEDSPREAD OUTLET

5757 Pacheco Boulevard, Pacheco. (510) 689-3435. M–Sat 10–6, M till 7:30, Sun Noon–5. MC, VISA, DIS. Parking: lot.
(Other Stores: Fair Oaks, Pleasanton.)
Here's a selection of bedspreads, goose down comforters, daybed ensembles, Dacron-filled comforters, decorator pillows, and dust ruffles, offering depth and variety to suit almost everyone's taste and needs (there are many high-quality bedspreads for upscale shoppers). If you're also covering windows, consider ready-made draperies at prices lower than major store sales. On regular, first-quality merchandise, you'll save approximately 25% off prevailing retail. On custom orders you can save 30–40%.

DISCOUNT DEPOT

2020 San Pablo Avenue, Berkeley. (510) 549-1478. M–F 10–7, Sat–Sun 10–6. MC, VISA, DIS, AE. Parking: street.
(Other Stores: 520 Haight Street and 1620 Polk Street, San Francisco; 5350 Clayton Road, Concord; Futon Depot, Westgate Shopping Center, San Jose.)
Discount Depot comes in handy for new Cal students building their nests. They can pick up affordable linens and simple furnishings, a discount-priced futon and frame (budget to better versions), or a carton containing one of the contemporary RTA furnishings that make up much of the inventory. Usually a screwdriver is the only tool needed to put together a computer desk, end or coffee table, cart, bookcase, small eating table, etc. Find starving-student discounts on pillows, tablecloths, sheet sets, towels, and throw rugs. Mattresses and box springs from Serta and Simmons are discount priced for those who prefer traditional sleeping modes. Delivery can be arranged for about $25 to areas within a reasonable distance of each store.

DREAMS

921 Howard Street (at Fifth Street), San Francisco. (415) 543-1800, (800) 419-1200. M–F 10–7, Sat 10–6, Sun Noon–5. MC, VISA, AE, ATM. Parking: free adjoining lot/street.

For starters, Dreams is a great place to shop for down comforters and other down products (feather beds, pillows). Since most comforters are made on-site, you can specify the weight of the fill, the design stitch, and the covering fabric, allowing you to buy budget to top quality. The price you pay for whatever you choose results in excellent value and solid bargains. There's also a ready-to-go selection. You can decide on the type of down fill by examining the various down products on display. More information is provided by the staff on fill power and loft, and on the thread count and fiber detail for the covering. You can also bring in your down comforter to be cleaned by Dreams' German down-cleaning plant, which gently refluffs old down as it cleans. The service department can replace or repair your comforter cover (pillows too) and add or delete fill for reasonable charges. There's a very nice discount fabric selection for making duvet or futon covers, or you can bring in your own fabric or sheets to have one made (seamstresses on-site work with amazing speed). If you need odd-size linens or bed coverings, bed skirts, shams (any kind of bedding accessory), or window treatment, your problems are over. Making custom slipcovers has become a specialty—use the store's fabric on your furnishings and you're likely to save a little more. Dreams also sells competitively priced mattress sets and brass and metal beds (including daybeds); brand-name bed linens and a tasteful selection of throws, afghans, and decorative pillows round out the selection—all nicely discounted.

FIELDCREST CANNON

Folsom Factory Outlets, Folsom. (916) 351-0849. Daily. MC, VISA. Parking: lot.

I found excellent buys here in every category, including scatter rugs, blankets, sheets, comforters, and towels. The selection of table linens was not very extensive, nor were the discounts great. Price tags specifying "compared to" denote first-quality products; those saying "if perfect" are irregulars. The best buys are on irregulars, with 40–60% discounts off retail. The flaws were not obvious; in fact, I couldn't identify any. Loved the discounts on the upscale line of Charisma sheets. Returns for full refund or charge-card credit with receipt. Beautiful store!

HOME EXPRESS

39125 Fremont Hub, Fremont. (510) 795-7111. M–Sat 9–9, Sun 10–7. MC, VISA, DIS, AE. Parking: lot.
(Other stores: Citrus Heights, Concord, Dublin, Fresno, Pinole, Rohnert Park, Sacramento and South Sacramento, San Jose, San Leandro, Santa Clara.)

Home Express can fill your linen needs for dining, kitchen, bath, and bedroom with better-quality, brand-name merchandise at discounted prices. You'll find linens, kitchenware, housewares, gadgets, gourmet foods, RTA furniture, small electronics, organizers for every room, patio furniture, barbecue gear, vacuums, and more. Shoppers appreciate the stores' pleasant ambiance, tasteful seasonal displays, and sizzling new trends in home decor. Everyday prices are equivalent to department store sale prices, with familiar brands at discounts of 10–60% off regular retail.

LINEN FACTORY OUTLET

475 Ninth Street, San Francisco. (415) 431-4543. T–Sat 10–4. MC, VISA, DIS. Parking: street.

Linen Factory Outlet is connected to Western Linen, which sells textiles for kitchen, bed, and bath to department stores, hotels, restaurants, caterers, and small specialty stores. Being small, it can fill orders for special sizes that are often hard to buy from manufacturers. You'll find irregulars, overruns, and discontinued items from its stock. Among them are the classic bistro-check tablecloth in many colors and European damask table-cloths/napkins in 100% cotton. Look for imported items, such as famous British woolen blankets, throws, and high-end flannel bed linens. Each Saturday there are several items on special.

LINENS 'N' THINGS

Great Mall of the Bay Area, Milpitas. (408) 934-9288. Daily. MC, VISA. Parking: lot.
(Other stores: Citrus Heights, Pleasanton, Roseville, Sacramento, San Jose.)

Bigger is better—especially as represented by Linens 'n' Things' superstore concepts. This powerhouse national chain (more than 140 stores) offers 20–50% discounts off department store prices every day and backs them up with a price guarantee. Its stores stock a wide selection of linens in every category for the home. That's just the beginning, since the stores go on to provide "things" like picture frames, framed art, everything for entertaining, kitchenware (pots, pans, dishes, cutlery, etc.), small electronics, organizers, and tasteful home accessories and accents. It relies on some of America's leading companies to keep customers happy: Braun, Cuisinart, Calphalon, Krups, Farberware, and linens from Laura Ashley, Croscill, Waverly, Martex, Bill Blass, Adrienne Vittadini, and others. It's not hard to duplicate a picture-perfect bedroom with the coordinated groups of upscale linens in very current patterns.

MERADA DESIGNS

150 Starlite Street, South San Francisco. (650) 875-7627. M–F 10–6, Sat 11–5. Cash/Check.
Parking: lot.
Merada manufactures bedding primarily for the hospitality industry and furniture stores (often for display beds). Surplus spreads, comforters, etc. are sold at considerable markdowns in its outlet, but

most people prefer to use Merada's workrooms to have standard treatments (comparable to ready-made quality) made at very modest labor charges. You can custom order fabric from the many sample books available in Merada's design room upstairs and save 25% off book prices, or bring in your own fabrics or bed sheets for fabrication.

Merada offers a compromise that may solve the problem of getting just the effect you want within your budget. Most custom workshops are geared to service the high-end design trade, and the workmanship and construction is superior to almost anything available in the ready-made form. However, the labor charges, which do not include the fabric (and possibly extra yardage requirements), put custom services out of reach for many consumers. Some 1997 labor prices on queen sized fabrications (fabric not included): $25 for an unlined dust ruffle with rolled hem and a 4-inch band around the deck, $110 for a quilted bedspread (requires minimum 12 yards of fabric and includes fill and backing). Choose in-stock 54-inch, 100% cotton print surplus fabrics from the company's regular production, and total fabric and labor costs are about $139 for a queen-sized quilted bedspread. Coverlets, including backing and filling, are $100; duvets with zipper are $30; and simple shams with envelope back are $20 (with flange edge and welting, $28). Window treatment fabrications are also offered at reasonable labor charges, so you can extend your treatments to include slipcovers, draperies, curtains, cornices, swags, etc. Be sure to check yardage requirements if you're bringing in your own fabrics. Most treatments can be completed within two weeks of fabric availability. Also, fabrics suitable for multiple uses are available from a bargain table. *Directions: take South Spruce Avenue from El Camino Real.*

PAPER WHITE LTD. WAREHOUSE SALES
769 Center Boulevard, Fairfax. (415) 457-7673.
Quarterly sales. MC, VISA. Parking: lot.
The linens from paper white ltd. convey a romantic and nostalgic theme. The company designs and imports a high-end line in pristine white linen, linen/cotton blends, and luxurious Italian cottons. Many groups are lovingly trimmed with handmade lace, embroidery appliqués, or cutwork. It's not hard to find linens that are similar to this line at much lower prices, but close inspection will reveal the difference—finer fabrics, superior embroidery, and designs that reflect owner Jan Dutton's discriminating design talent. If you're on paper white's mailing list, you'll get sale invitations that will lead to 40–60% markdowns on the "leftovers": discontinued items, slightly soiled or (insignificantly) flawed but always lovely linens. For the bedroom, you'll find duvet covers, window panels, dust ruffles, pillows, bedcovers, and shams; for the dining room, place mats, tablecloths, and napkins; plus home accessories, aprons, pillows, etc. Other treasures can be found in a special selection of christening gowns to last through several generations, and accessories for babies. Call or write for a sale notice (usually in March, May, September, and December).

SPRINGMAID WAMSUTTA FACTORY STORES
Outlets at Gilroy, Gilroy. (408) 847-3731. Daily.
MC, VISA, AE, DIS. Parking: lot.
(Other outlet: Vacaville center.)
Rather than going upscale (with accompanying higher prices) like so many linen discount stores, this clearance outlet maintains a bargain-basement image and about the lowest bed linen prices I've

seen. The inventory is limited to closeouts and selected irregulars (not much in table linens); if you're not too particular about pattern or color, you'll find rock-bottom prices on sheets, mattress pads, blankets, pillows, comforters and bedspreads, and Pacific silvercloth. Exchanges and refunds with receipt.

STROUDS

500 El Camino Real, Menlo Park. (415) 327-7680 or (800) STROUDS. M–F 10–9, Sat 10–7, Sun 10–6. VISA, MC, DIS, AE. Parking: lot.
(Other Stores: Corte Madera, Dublin, Newark, Pleasant Hill, San Francisco, San Jose, San Mateo, Sunnyvale, Walnut Creek. Outlets: Strouds Super Outlets in Tracy, Vacaville centers.)
Strouds is a specialty off-price linen operation that offers top-quality products at decent discounts on virtually everything for bed (including down comforters), bath, kitchen, and dining room. The selection includes current colors and styles (many top-of-the-line). Using its special order program, you can coordinate wallpaper, window coverings, and accessories with your linen selections. In-home service for custom window coverings. The Super Outlets in Vacaville and Tracy offer moderately priced linen lines, more special promotions, closeouts, and irregulars unique to those outlets. Also, clearance inventory from its full-line stores at great prices. Return policies are very liberal.

WARM THINGS FACTORY STORE

180 Paul Drive (Terra Linda Industrial Parkway), San Rafael. (415) 472-2154. M–Sat 10–5, Sun Noon–5. MC, VISA. Parking: lot.
(Other Stores: 3523 Haven, Unit F, Menlo Park, open Nov–Apr only; 6011 College Avenue, Oakland; 3063 Fillmore, San Francisco.)
Everything from budget to best means everyone has warm and cozy nights! Warm Things provides all you need to know about loft, fill power, fabric, and design variables, plus good value. Its selection includes its top-of-the-line, European-style baffle construction in channel or box designs; 100% cotton cambric covers (230- to 360-thread count); and for lean budgets, light- and medium-weight goose down comforters. Everything at the Warm Things factory stores sells for 40–50% off its catalog prices. Warm Things also sells down pillows, featherbeds, boots, goose down bathrobes, wool mattress pads, slippers, many styles of down jackets, and throws.

Duvet covers are available in many fabrics, including damask, sateen, flannel, denim, and vegetable-dyed cotton. *Note: The Menlo Park store is open only from November to April.*

Mail Order

Because of shelf and display space limitations, local stores are limited in providing all your options for accessorizing. The companies listed here offer discounted prices, ranging from modest to very impressive, on a wide selection of linens in all quality ranges for children's and adult rooms. You're much more likely to see everything available in a particular pattern. You'll also find many esoteric bedding accessories and hard-to-find products. Call and request a catalog.

TOUCH OF CLASS *(800) 457-7456*
THE LINEN SOURCE *(800) 431-2620*
DOMESTICATIONS *(800) 746-2555*
THE COMPANY STORE (DOWN SPECIALTY)
(800) 356-9367

Also See

Under Furniture and Home Accessories—Catalog Discounters, General Furnishings, Clearance Centers:
ALL LISTINGS

Under San Francisco's Factory Outlets and Off-Price Stores:
ESPRIT OUTLET

Under General Clothing:
BURLINGTON COAT FACTORY OUTLET; MARSHALLS; T.J. MAXX

Under Giftware and Home Decor:
CRATE & BARREL OUTLET; TUESDAY MORNING

Wallpaper

I'm all for saving money, but if you're going to use a local store's wallpaper books, do the right thing and give it your business. It's very expensive for independent dealers to maintain an inventory of hundreds of wallpaper books for customers. Your local store may indicate when sales are likely to occur, so saving money becomes a matter of timing if you can't use the resources listed below. Also check the listings under Furniture and Home Accessories—Catalog Discounters, General Furnishings; Fabrics; and other cross-references listed here for stores that maintain an extensive selection of wallpaper books and then sweeten the process with nice discounts.

THE WALLPAPER CONNECTION

Crow Canyon Commons, San Ramon. (510) 275-8055. M–W, Sat 10–6, Th–F 10–7, Sun Noon–5. MC, VISA. Parking: lot.

This charming, cozy, boutiquelike wallpaper and home-decorating store has bins full of wallpaper (many with matching borders) discounted 25–75% off retail ($10.99–$15.99). After you see those, spend some time leafing through the library of books from companies that read like a Who's Who of wallpaper; you'll save 20–35% on those offerings. Companion fabrics are discounted 15–20% off list. If Waverly and other fabric companies are your choice, you can also order comforter ensembles, draperies, and window treatments at 20% savings. If you need window coverings, bedding treatments, or a chair reupholstered, take a gander at the fabric swatch books. You'll save a little to a respectable amount, depending on what you're ordering. Miniblinds and shades are competitively priced with the "big boys."

WALLSTREET FACTORY OUTLET
2690 Harrison Street (near 23rd Street), San Francisco. (415) 285-0870. M–F 10–6, Sat 9–5. MC, VISA, AE. Parking: street.
This is the city's best resource for wallpaper at bargain prices. In the front, about 1,000 current wallpaper patterns are stocked in bins at 40–50% off retail book price. About 500 borders and 75–100 companion fabrics are stocked as well. Check the back room for overruns and discontinued patterns at even greater discounts. Wallstreet stocks 500 wallpaper books for special orders at 30–50% discount. Its lovely displays and mockups help customers picture the finished room (its emphasis is on coordinating papers, fabrics, and borders). For best results, come with an open mind and prepare to be versatile. You can borrow samples for evaluation. If you start your decorating project with the wallpaper choice first, it's a cinch to coordinate the other elements.

Also See

Under Draperies and Window Coverings:
CROW'S NEST INTERIORS

Under Fabrics:
BY THE YARD; FURBELOWS

Under Carpets and Flooring:
LAWRENCE CONTRACT FURNISHERS

Under Furniture and Home Accessories—Catalog Discounters:
INTERIOR RESOURCES; JOHN R. WIRTH CO.; NORIEGA FURNITURE

Flea Markets

Attending flea markets has become a national weekend pastime. Here are some of the better-known markets in the area, held regularly throughout the year. Other markets occur on some other basis, maybe monthly or annually, and can be fantastic sources of bargains because they aren't as well attended as the listed ones. Check your local paper for notices of these events. Best bets: The San Jose Flea Market is the largest and maintains a reputation for the most reliable selection of everything from A to Z. The Foothill College Flea Market is distinguished by the number of artists and artisans who regularly offer some very original wares.

BERKELEY FLEA MARKET

Ashby BART Station Parking Lot (Adeline and Ashby), Berkeley. (510) 644-0744. Sat–Sun 8–7. Parking: free. Admission: free.

CAPITOL FLEA MARKET

3630 Hillcap Avenue (Capitol Drive-In), San Jose. (408) 225-5800. Th 7–5:30, Sat–Sun 6–5:30. Admission: 50¢ Th, $1.25 Sat, $1.50 Sun (children under 11 years free).

CHABOT COLLEGE FLEA MARKET

2555 Hesperian Boulevard, Hayward. (510) 786-6918. Third Sat each month 8–4. Parking: free. Admission: free.

DE ANZA COLLEGE FLEA MARKET

21250 Stevens Creek Boulevard, Cupertino. (408) 864-8946. First Sat every month 8–4. Located in campus parking lots B and C; over 850 vendors. Parking: $2. Admission: free.

FOOTHILL COLLEGE FLEA MARKET

12345 El Monte Road (corner Freeway 280), Los Altos Hills. (415) 948-6417. Third Sat every month

8–3. Parking: $1. Admission: free.
Noted for its antiques and collectibles, art, fine
arts, plants, toys, books, jewelry, household items,
clothing, etc. Benefits Foothill Theatre Guild.

GENEVA SWAP MARKET

Geneva Drive-In, 607 Carter (behind Cow Palace),
Daly City. (415) 587-0515. Sat–Sun 7–4. Parking:
free. Admission: Sat 25¢, Sun 75¢ per person.

MIDGLEY'S COUNTRY FLEA MARKET

2200 Gravenstein Highway South (off 101, west to
Sebastopol 5 miles), Sebastopol. (707) 823-7874,
(800) 800-FLEA. Sat–Sun 6:30–4:30. Cash only.
Parking: free. Admission: free.

NAPA-VALLEJO FLEA MARKET AND AUCTION

303 Kelly Road (off Highway 29, halfway between
Napa and Vallejo), Napa. (707) 226-8862. Sun 6–5.
Parking: $2. Admission: free.

OHLONE COLLEGE SUPER FLEA MARKET

43600 Mission Boulevard, Fremont. (510) 659-
6285. Second Sat each month 8–4. Parking: $1.
Admission: free.

PIER 29 ANTIQUE & COLLECTIBLES MARKET

Pier 29, San Francisco. (415) 956-5316. Sun 9–5.
Parking: street, pay lot. Admission: $2.
Vendors are vetted to ensure quality of selection.
Emphasis on antiques, handcrafted goods, col-
lectibles, vintage clothing, etc., all sold comfort-
ably from this indoor flea market

SAN JOSE FLEA MARKET

1590 Berryessa Road, San Jose. (408) 453-1110.
W–Sun dawn to dusk. Cash only. Parking: pay lot.
Admission: free.
The largest flea market in the United States, with
the largest number of regular vendors, offering a
smattering of everything from clothes to furniture.
Plants, pottery, toys, flowers, T-shirts, and children's
apparel are very popular. Don't miss produce row!

SOLANO DRIVE-IN FLEA MARKET

Solano Way and Highway 4, Concord. (510) 687-
6445. Sat–Sun 7–4. Parking: free. Admission: Sat
25¢, Sun $1.

General Merchandise

Discount Stores

You don't always have to drive miles out of your way to go bargain hunting. Throughout the Bay Area, discount stores like Target, Wal-Mart, Payless, Kmart, and Pay 'N Save do a respectable job of pricing merchandise lower than full-service retail stores. Companies like Service Merchandise advertise frequently, have many locations in the area, and consistently offer excellent values. They're good for all types of merchandise, particularly housewares, giftware, consumer electronics, jewelry, toys, and sporting goods. They cover almost every area except major home furnishings, apparel, and larger appliances. They are very competitive with each other, so comparison shopping pays off if you take the time to check catalogs before you buy.

Liquidators

Small liquidators abound all around the Bay Area, selling novelties, food items, health products, paper and party supplies, household goods, baskets, toys, whatever. So it's hardly worth the time and expense of driving out of your way to shop at any particular one. These places often have names like "$1.99," "Everything's a Buck," or, my favorite, "98 Cents Clearance Center Stores." Some stay strictly within the bounds set by their names; others have prices much higher than the names would suggest. By all means, cruise through the aisles of these stores if it's convenient. You may find some real deals, but sometimes you'll leave thinking it's all a bunch of junk.

MACFRUGAL'S

200 Serra Way, Milpitas. (408) 946-9605. M–Th 9–9, F–Sat 9–10, Sun 10–7. MC, VISA. Parking: lot. (Other stores: 19 Bay Area locations call (800) 800-9992 or check Geographical Index.)

MacFrugal's is strictly bargain basement. It buys carloads of closeout merchandise and sells at deeply discounted prices (40–70%). Goods include such diverse items as candles, linens, toys, books, housewares, giftware, and clothing. A great selection of Christmas ornaments and goodies is stocked every year.

ROBERT'S WAREHOUSE

2665 Pleasant Hill Road, Pleasant Hill. (510) 274-9620. M–Sat 10–7, F 10–9, Sat 10–7, Sun 11–6. MC, VISA, DIS. Parking: lot.

Robert's Warehouse sales trade show samples, manufacturers' overstocks, liquidations, and bankrupt inventories of new merchandise. Although you can never predict exactly what you'll find, you can expect candy, gourmet foods, kitchen gadgets, silk flowers, used videos, stuffed animals, toys, books, costume jewelry, stationery, housewares, bathwares, music boxes, prints, crystal, and gifts for everyone. Pickins' are especially choice after Robert's has cleaned out entire booths from the Gift and Gourmet trade shows. You'll save 50–75% off retail.

Membership Warehouse Clubs

Almost everyone has a cluster of cards in their wallets, but probably none is more valued than a membership card to Price/Costco or Sam's Club. People in all economic and social levels consider themselves privileged to qualify for membership. By now thousands of Bay Area consumers have discovered the delights—and the hazards—of shopping at a warehouse club. Nearly everyone has a tale to tell along the lines of "I just went in to buy toilet paper and came out with a new TV" or, in other words, "Every time I shop, I end up spending an extra $100 to $200 on completely unplanned purchases." It's hard to resist the prices and the tempting selection of new items. "Grazing" down the aisles tasting vendors' new products guarantees that you'll leave with a full stomach and basket. Each club provides an extensive variety of consumer goods (electronics, computers, apparel, books, food, beauty items, tires, housewares, giftware, fine jewelry, watches, tools, etc.) and office and institutional products, but don't expect an in-depth selection of anything. Each company makes buys at prices that allow it to undersell the competition. The trade-off: Many items are sold in extra-large quantities or packaged as multiples—a disadvantage for some individuals or small families. Surprisingly, the clubs manage to capture a fair amount of "high-demand" merchandise. At times, I've spotted Reebok, Adidas, and Nike athletic shoes, Dooney & Bourke and Liz Claiborne handbags, Guess? jeans, Rolex watches, Cross or Montblanc pens, Waterford crystal, and other items from consumers' "most wanted" lists. Each club continues to innovate and expand its offerings. Call for membership requirements. See the Geographical Index for the Price/Costco or Sam's Club locations near you.

Special Sales and Events

A.S.I.D. DESIGNERS SALE

The Galleria, 101 Henry Adams, and The Showplace, 2 Henry Adams, San Francisco. (415) 626-2743. Sale dates in Jun and Nov advertised in major Bay Area newspapers. Sale hours: Sat 9–5, Sun 11–4. MC, VISA. Parking: free lots. Admission: $10.

Every year, A.S.I.D. (American Society of Interior Designers), sponsors two sales (in June and November) to benefit its local chapter programs. These sales are an opportunity to buy fine-quality, high-end furnishings at up to 40% off showroom list prices. Some pieces appear to come right off the pages of *Architectural Digest* and others are comfortably familiar. If you're shopping for elegant pine armoires, chinoiserie, tansu, antique reproductions, lamps, framed prints or original artworks, wicker furniture, Oriental rugs, chairs, sofas, dining furniture, tables and occasional pieces, leftover fabrics, or just about any other home furnishing, you can anticipate tempting items at these sales. Some are slightly damaged, but they're the exception. Many lines are not displayed through retail furniture stores, which makes the opportunity to see and buy the samples particularly appealing. A.S.I.D. members staff the sale and charge $10 admission to cover their costs. It's advisable to bring carpet, paint, and fabric samples for matching. Delivery arrangements can be made. Watch for announcements in local newspapers for these sales. The lines that start by 8 a.m. on Saturday are followed by a real crush during the first hours of the sale. Come Sunday for more elbow room and last-chance markdowns.

AMERICAN INDUSTRIAL CENTER SALE

2325 Third Street (bet. 20th and 22nd streets), San Francisco. Sale info: (415) 621-1920. First Sat in Dec 9–4. Cash/Check. Parking: street.

Every year this cavernous industrial building, the American Industrial Center, opens its doors to the public for a most unusual sale opportunity. It's the place to go if you want to scope out some unique bargains. Plan to spend a few hours walking the halls, keeping your eyes posted for balloons, sandwich boards, and signs to lead you to the sale participants. Each year the traffic increases as word spreads that this is the only opportunity one has to buy certain very upscale merchandise. Because of market sensitivity, I can't mention companies by name, but I can give a few clues to the types of merchandise that you can find. For starters: an expensive line of handknit sweaters for women and men; several fashion jewelry manufacturers (lines that sell under the glass at posh stores); home accessories, including many sold through national catalogs and at chic and trendy special boutiques locally; bath and body products (many in elegant packaging); fashion hats; and several charming lines of children's apparel. It's a different environment, yet rest assured that security guards are on hand to ensure your comfort and safety. The sale is usually held on the first or second Saturday in December. Sign up on someone's mailing list so that you'll get sale announcements for future sales. I'd start at the 2325 entry on Third

Street (corner of 20th). Look for sale flyers that identify the participants and spaces where the doors will be open for your shopping adventures.

CONCOURSE SAMPLE SALES

The Concourse, between Seventh and Eighth streets, Brannan and Townsend, San Francisco. Info: (415) 864-1500 ext. 462. Sat–Sun Thanksgiving weekend; one Sat in June. Cash preferred/Checks okay with many participants. Parking: pay lots. Admission: $3.

Tenants of the Gift Center and Fashion Center, and many importers, distributors, manufacturers, and designers rent booth space at the Concourse for these mammoth events. Some participants never show up anyplace else to sell their samples, overruns, or leftovers. Each sale is frenzied from the moment the doors open. The inducement for consumers? Wonderful prices, usually 50% off original retail. Categories of merchandise: apparel for the whole family; body, bath, and beauty products; baskets; giftware; silk plants; fashion jewelry; leather goods; household goods; stationery; holiday decorations; home accessories; and more. Watch the *Chronicle* and *Examiner* for sale announcements and clip the $1-off coupon for admission.

EMERYVILLE STROLL

Free stroll maps available at Doyle Street Cafe, 5515 Doyle Street (off Powell), Emeryville. Stroll starts Thanksgiving weekend and continues through first two weekends of Dec. Sat–Sun 10–5.
The Emeryville Stroll showcases the many designers, wholesalers, manufacturers, artisans, etc. who have facilities or studios in the area. The mix is unusual and eclectic. After picking up a map, you'll need your car to navigate the area. You may find sophisticated and contemporary men's ties; fine art glass (very fine vases, paperweights, bowls, etc.); wonderful hand puppets and stuffed animals; fun-themed string lights and night lights; contemporary glass oil-burning lamps; table linens; women's artwear and accessories; silk sachets, pillows, ribbons, and handcrafted personal accessories; fine-quality fashion jewelry, notecards, and handcrafted gifts; and assorted other gift-appropriate merchandise. Altogether, twenty-five to thirty-six individual companies open their doors for this popular event. *Directions: Take the Powell exit east from I-80 to start the stroll. Parking is readily available throughout the area.*

FIRELIGHT GLASS SECONDS SALE

1000 42nd Street, Emeryville. (510) 652-6731. Daily 11–5 (Fri before Thanksgiving until Dec 23). MC, VISA. Parking: lot on side of building.
Firelight Glass puts on a glow every year. The warehouse is always well stocked with tables of contemporary, clear-glass, oil-burning candles. It's a breathtaking display! I'd have to describe the quality-control inspectors at Firelight Glass as "picky, picky, picky" since I can't spot the flaws that make up the seconds sold at this annual factory sale. As seconds the candles are priced at 30–40% off (most at 40%), from $9 to $50. Many styles are offered in graduated sizes. Pick up just one, or a trio for a more dramatic display. I find these to be wonderful all-purpose gifts, and, generally speaking, they're appealing to almost everyone. Buy some just to tuck away for a "little gift" for some person or occasion later in the year. Go all the way and buy a small or large bottle of clean-burning Firelight lamp oil. The candles in cylinders, rounds, triangles, prisms, squares, cubes, obelisks, and other artful

shapes (like the new side-filling chimney lamps) come with a lifetime Fiberglass wick. Some candles are sold as sets with incentive pricing (usually three candles in graduated sizes), although these candles can be purchased individually. Whatever you buy, you'll appreciate the careful packing and boxing done at the counter. Add wrap and ribbon, and your gift is ready to go. Note: These boxes will not withstand the stress of shipping or mailing. Store is closed on Thanksgiving. *Directions: Traveling north or south on San Pablo Avenue, turn east on 43rd Street. Go to Adeline, turn right, then turn left on 42nd Street. This company is located south of Powell Street off Interstate 80.*

FURNITURE MART SAMPLE SALES

1355 Market Street (at Tenth Street), San Francisco. Info: (415) 552-2311. One-day Sat sale dates announced in May and Nov, 9–5. MC, VISA, AE. Parking: pay garage off Market. Admission: $6.
It's hard to get past the desk and into the showrooms at San Francisco's Furniture Mart, but the doors open wide to the public during Sample Sales twice a year. The Mart has over 300 showrooms in two buildings (one ten-story, one eleven-story).

The Mart reflects the entire spectrum of home furnishings and accessories—from tacky to terrific, from budget to best. Approximately eighty showrooms participate in each sale. Prices are close to wholesale, possibly less on some items. Expect to find a little of every category: area rugs, upholstered furniture, case goods (dining, bedroom, occasional tables), lamps, lighting, pictures, mirrors, and great home accessories! Delivery service is available at extra cost. Watch the *Chronicle* and *Examiner* for sale announcements, or call to have your name put on the mailing list for sale notification.

GIFTCENTER SAMPLE SALES

888 Brannan Street, San Francisco. (415) 864-SALE. Dates: Sat sales in early Nov; usually in May before Mother's Day. Admission: $3.
Tenants of the Giftcenter combine with other manufacturers' reps, importers, and distributors to present a tantalizing shopping excursion. Booths and tables are set up on four levels of the Giftcenter; you won't want to leave until you've canvassed each floor. Fashion jewelry, women's designer clothing, giftware, housewares, linens, bath and body products, kitchen items, novelties, picture

frames, and gifts for any occasion are on display. Check the Pink Section of the Sunday *Chronicle/Examiner* for sale announcements and $1-off coupon for admission.

NOMADIC TRADERS WAREHOUSE SALE
1385 Ninth Street, Berkeley. (510) 525-5854. Daily 10–6 (Fri after Thanksgiving till Dec 31, closed Christmas). MC, VISA. Parking: street.
The focus at this yearly sale event is on sweaters for the sporting crowd and their cold-weather activities. Sweaters are made and imported from Uruguay, Peru, China, Nepal, and other foreign locales. Original knits in natural fibers translate ethnic traditions into contemporary designs. Look for great colors (and neutrals); interesting designs and patterns; and light, medium, and heavyweight versions in many hand-knit and hand-loomed, primarily unisex styles. Pick a cardigan, pullover, or vest. The sweaters usually are sold through stores that cater to the outdoor industry; discounts at the sale are 25–60% off retail on current and past-season styles. The new "fashion" sweaters in chenille, patchwork, and embroidered designs for women are very nice. Pick up a pair of warm socks, a knit cap or hat, mittens, a scarf, or a blanket—other items imported by the company. In the past few years, the company has developed a tempting line of sportswear, related separates, dresses for women, and shirts for men. Made both locally and in Bali, the clothes have a familiar look—loose, unstructured, oversized, and contemporary. Wonderful fabrications in rayon, fleece, and knits in rich colors and prints are discounted 30–60%.

SAN FRANCISCO BAY AREA BOOK FESTIVAL
Concourse Exhibition Center, Eighth and Brannan Streets, San Francisco. (415) 908-2833. Generally first Sat–Sun in Nov (call to verify), 10–6. Admission: adults $2/day, children 12 and younger free. Parking: street/pay lots.
The small press revolution started in the Bay Area. That's evident when you peruse the booths at the book festival, where these small presses showcase the fruits of their labors. Book lovers appreciate the opportunity to see many titles that they may overlook when browsing through local bookstores. Mainstream publishers participate as well. Bargain hunters can fill their book bags with good deals, as most participants offer modest to maximum

discounts on many of the titles in their inventories. Books run the gamut of topics from A to Z (children's books included). Authors readings and appearances, combined with book-related events, contribute to the appeal of this event.

Sporting Goods

BENT SPOKE

6124 Telegraph Avenue, Oakland. (510) 652-3089.
T–F 11–6, Sat–Sun 11–5. MC, VISA, DIS.
Parking: street.
The owners travel the state buying used bikes
from various law-enforcement auctions. That must
account for the wide variety of "wheels"—with little pink girls' bikes, tricycles, three-wheel bikes,
and mountain, hybrid, and road bikes filling up all
the space in this store. Some bikes look like
they've spent time languishing outdoors at the
mercy of the elements, while others are spiffy and
like new. Prices start at $19 for kid's bikes, about
$30 for adults. Bikes are reconditioned, and better
bikes have a limited warranty. Budget-priced
mass-market bikes (those sold at Kmart, Toys 'R'
Us, and other big chain stores or warehouse clubs)
are not warranted. Look around for special deals
on new closeout models from manufacturers like
Redline BMX, Jamis, Bianchi, Norco, and Nishiki.

No bikes are bought directly from consumers.
Good resource for families!

DEMO SKI

1101 E. Francisco Boulevard, San Rafael. (415)
454-3500. M–Sat 10–6, Th–F until 8, Sun 10–5;
winter hours: M–F 10–8, Sat 10–6, Sun 10–5. MC,
VISA. Parking: lot.
Demo Ski rents and sells top-of-the-line skis, ski
equipment, and snowboards for discount prices.
Customers have the opportunity to try before they
buy. During the summer the store switches gears
to sell in-line skates, water skis, and tennis rackets.
Major brands include Burton, Rollerblade, Salomon,
Nordica, H.O., and Wilson. When you're ready to
buy, you'll save about 20–30% on water skis and
boards, vests, and accessories; 20–30% on tennis
rackets (plan on $20 extra for professional string-
ing); and 20–50% on snow skis and boots.
Snowboards, in-line skates, and accessories are

always 10–15% off. Demo Ski also offers 15–20% discounts on quality sunglasses from Vuarnet, Ray-Ban, Revo, Serengeti, Oakley, and Suncloud.

FRY'S WAREHOUSE SPORTS
164 Marco Way, South San Francisco. (650) 583-5034. M–F 9:30–6, Sat–Sun 10–5. MC, VISA, AE. Parking: street.
(Other stores: 1495 E. Francisco Boulevard, San Rafael.)
For golf or tennis, Fry's offers value, selection, and discounts on better pro-shop lines of shoes, clothing, and equipment. Slip into shoes from Nike, Adidas, Wilson, K-Swiss, Foot-Joy, Reebok, or Dexter. Also, equipment from Wilson, Lynx, Power Bilt, Ping, Dunlop, Spalding, Hogan, MacGregor, Mizuno, Titleist, Cobra, Ram, Callaway, Daiwa, Cleveland, Yonex, and Taylor Made. These are not seconds or closeouts. While a discount operation, it provides tennis racket stringing and free club fitting with its golf-swing computer.

GUS' DISCOUNT FISHING EQUIPMENT
3710 Balboa Street (bet. 38th and 39th Avenues), San Francisco. (415) 752-6197. M–Sat 8–5. MC, VISA. Parking: street.
If words like *crocodile*, *pencil popper*, or *super-duper* mean anything to you, read on. Gus' Discount Fishing Equipment is an experience! The prices entice regulars to stop in almost daily on their way to the water to see what's new. Serving as a West Coast wholesale distributor for Master, Rapala, Cossaks, Trophy, Dot Line Nets, and Abu Garcia, Gus' also buys factory overruns, salvage losses, and inventory from liquidations. Everything is discounted 25–60% off original retail. You'll find equipment for salmon, trout, freshwater, saltwater, and surf fishing. The terminal tackle selection deserves careful scrutiny. Check the lures from Luhr Jensen, Bass Buster, Hopkins, Diamond Gigs, and Panther Martin. All rods and reels are guaranteed.

KARIM CYCLE

2800 Telegraph Avenue, Berkeley. (510) 841-2181. M–Sat 11–6, selected Sun Noon–5. MC, VISA, ATM. Parking: street.

This company's location close to the Cal campus is a definite advantage. Students come in when the semester begins to buy a bike and often return at the end of the year to sell it back. The company is careful to protect the integrity of its business. The seller's personal identification is required for all transactions, and Karim clears all bike registrations with local police departments. The selection covers bikes of all descriptions: mountain, road, hybrid, three-speed, and a few children's and tandem bikes are usually in stock. Prices are set according to condition and usually offer 40–60% savings off original retail. Karim usually has a recent inventory printout with descriptions and prices of better bikes. Mountain bikes start at $199; otherwise expect to spend $99 to $1,000 (on top-quality bikes). Before putting the used bikes out for sale, each is reconditioned and further supported by a thirty-day free service policy for any adjustments. Karim also sells new bikes and always has several deeply discounted closeout models in stock from well-known manufacturers. If biking is not your thing, you can rent or buy in-line skates and new and used snowboards. Finally, you often can trade in your old bike on a new and better model. Located three blocks north of Ashby at Stuart.

LAS VEGAS DISCOUNT GOLF

3211-L Crow Canyon Place, San Ramon. (510) 275-1234. M–Fri 10–7, Sat 9:30–6, Sun 11–5. MC, VISA, AE. Parking: pay lots.

Consumers can do armchair comparison shopping by checking Fry's, Nevada Bob's, and Las Vegas ads to see which place is offering the best deals. Las Vegas sells major brand-name gear for golf and tennis. Golfers will find Ping, Powerbilt, Lynx, Titleist, Hogan, MacGregor, Daiwa, Spalding, Mizuno, Yamaha, Palmer, and Taylor Made among others. Everything is discounted at least 20% and can be far greater, depending on special buys.

NEVADA BOB'S DISCOUNT GOLF

1975 Diamond Boulevard, Concord. (510) 680-0111. M–F 10–9, Sat 9:30–6, Sun 10–5. MC, VISA, AE, DIS. Parking: lot.
(Other stores: Belmont, Fremont, Modesto, Rohnert Park, Sacramento, San Jose, San Leandro, Stockton, Suisun.)

With more than 300 franchise stores, Nevada Bob's has considerable volume purchasing power. It will also beat any "verifiable" price on current pro-line equipment. Each store's experienced, professional staff ensures that customers are fitted for their build and ability. Along with balls, bags, carts, accessories, and "extras," shoes at 30–50% discounts deserve your attention. Give the apparel racks the once-over and you're sure to end up looking like a golf pro at nicely discounted prices.

NORDICTRACK "FACTORY DIRECT"

Outlets at Gilroy, Gilroy. (408) 842-4721. Daily. MC, VISA, AE, DIS. Parking: lot.
(Other outlets: Vacaville center.)

The company sends its reconditioned equipment, overruns, closeouts, and past season models to its factory store, and showcases first-quality equipment there as well. Current season, first-quality equipment is full priced. The best buys are found on reconditioned equipment and discontinued models, where markdowns can exceed 40% off original retails. Shop for fitness and exercise equipment, cross-country skiers, treadmills, strength-training equipment, riders, and abdominal exercisers.

NORTH FACE FACTORY OUTLET

1238 Fifth Street, Berkeley. (510) 526-3530. M–Sat 10–6, Sun 11–5 (extended holiday hours). MC, VISA, AE, DIS. Parking: street.
(Other store: 1325 Howard, San Francisco.)

The North Face manufactures high-quality outdoor equipment and colorful, long-lasting sportswear. Prices start at 20% off retail and dive from there. These price reductions are applied to seconds, overruns, and discontinued items. Casual tops, pants, shirts, sweaters, etc. for men and women (some unisex) can be classic or colorful. You'll find Gore-Tex and other high-tech fabrics in the company's outdoor clothing, rainwear, and skiwear. North Face backpacks, sleeping bags, lumbar packs, tents, and duffels are always in good supply and reduced 20–40% off. You'll even find hiking boots, and boots discounted. Soft luggage, carry-ons, and business cases made from sturdy cordura nylon are appropriate for both a Manhattan boardroom and a Jumla yak caravan. Get on the mailing list for the outlet's biggest sales.

PLAY IT AGAIN SPORTS
1601 Contra Costa Boulevard, Concord. (510) 825-3396. M–F 10–7, Sat 10–6, Sun 11–5. MC, VISA. Parking: lot.
(Other stores: fifteen in the Bay Area; see Geographical Index.)
At Play It Again Sports, most of what is sold is used; each Bay Area store may have a different mix of merchandise. Prices on used goods are discounted about 50% off original retail. You can buy, sell, trade, or consign equipment for football and soccer (including shoes), golf, street hockey, baseball/softball, and racquet sports; roller skates and Rollerblades; exercise equipment and weights; and water, downhill, and cross-country skis. No weapons or bowling balls. The store is geared mainly to weekend athletes and beginners (children or adults) rather than the serious sportsperson. Brands would be midpriced if sold new. The stores carry some new merchandise and samples. I suggest that hardpressed parents give this outfit the once-over. And call before coming in, especially if you're bringing something to sell or consign. The staff keeps a list of special requests and will notify you when or if the merchandise comes in.

SPORTMART
1933 Davis Street (Westgate Center), San Leandro. (510) 632-6100. M–Sat 9:30 a.m.–9:30 p.m., Sun 10–7. MC, VISA, DIS. Parking: lot.
(Other stores: Concord, Daly City, Emeryville, Milpitas, Sacramento/Roseville, San Jose, Santa Rosa, Sunnyvale, Vacaville.)
These stores offer a great selection of bikes ($60–$400); equipment for skiing, bowling, tennis, golf, water sports (skis, Boogie boards), fishing, and camping; and sports and workout apparel, shoes for every sporting activity for the whole family, and exercise equipment. You'll find brand names, a wide range of prices representing budget to better in the lines carried, and an in-depth selection that far surpasses almost all competitors. Each category is well supported with an endless array of accessory items. My comparisons show

that Sportmart trims prices to beat the competition from a little to a lot every day. Competitors' loss leaders may undersell it on occasion, but its price guarantee takes care of that. Very accommodating return and refund policy.

WILDERNESS EXCHANGE

1407 San Pablo Avenue, Berkeley. (510) 525-1255. Sun–W 11–6, Th–F 11–8, Sat 10–6. MC, VISA, DIS. Parking: lot.

Wilderness Exchange serves backpackers, climbers, mountaineers, campers, and cross-country skiers. It sells closeouts, sales rep's samples, blems, and overstock from more than thirty outdoor companies at discounts of 15–40% off retail. Another angle: About 20% of the inventory is used (high-quality, cleaned, and reconditioned if needed), most often sold for at least 50% off original retail. Buy, sell, or trade your way to good deals. Call to inquire about availability of any specific item or brand of equipment you have in mind.

About Bikes—Strategies for Buying New Bikes

Once you understand how distribution works, you'll see why it's very difficult to select any particular bike retailer as a source of bargains. Bike manufacturers protect their markets by creating a carefully balanced network of dealers, ensuring that each store is able to serve a particular market area profitably. To that end, manufacturers "suggest" a minimum selling price for the dealers. In the Bay Area, it appears that most dealers sell bikes at the "minimum suggested price." Therefore, the market is very competitive, with no one dealer offering substantially lower everyday prices. Of course, each store holds a few sales during the year, but if a dealer holds too many, or attempts to lower prices too much, other dealers complain to the manufacturer and the offender is in jeopardy of losing the line. So everyone plays along. Since the Bay Area is considered a year-round market, you don't have the predictable end-of-season blowout sales prevalent in ski equipment. Also, since the bikes are expensive, dealers control their inventory so that they can offer a good selection without becoming overstocked. If you're buying a better bike for off-road or heavy street use, you'll want to spend at least $300 to get reliable components. Each step up—to $500, $700, or higher—buys you better braking, shifting, frame materials, etc. Choosing which brand to buy is a very subjective decision. If you're in a good shop, the staff will spend time determining your anticipated use, where you'll be using the bike, perhaps even what trails you plan to ride on, and then you'll need to try several bikes to see how they handle. To buy at a bargain, first spend time evaluating the various models, make your decision, and then watch for a sale. Another option: cycling or bike publications for mail-order companies. Many have discounted prices, but you'll have to forgo after-purchase service and support, something you may regret.

If you're not interested in the better bikes, you won't have any problem finding bikes in the $100–$300 range. Sportmart, Wal-Mart, Toys 'R' Us, Kmart, Price/Costco, Sears, Play It Again Sports (used), and others are likely resources. Don't overlook classified ads or sheriff's department or police auctions. Refer to listings in this section that profile the best sources for used bikes—a good alternative when money's tight and for many out-of-state students who need a bike just for the school year.

Also See

Under General Merchandise:
ALL SECTIONS

Toys

BASIC BROWN BEAR FACTORY

444 De Haro Street (off 17th Street), San Francisco. (415) 626-0781. M–Sat 10–5, Sun Noon–5. MC, VISA, AE, DIS. Parking: street.
Basic Brown Bear's line is known for the quality of its plush fabrics and the appealing personalities of its critters. Here you'll find B.B. Bear, Beary God-Mother, and FOBs (friends of bears) like Chocolate Moose and Mother Goose. Prices range from $5 to $250 (a gigantic, fully jointed grizzly bear with leather paws), but the median price is $25–$30. You may want to return with your children at another time for a captivating tour and bear-making demonstration. Call for tour information for individuals or groups. Lots of fun!

FOLKMANIS

1219 Park Avenue, Emeryville. (510) 658-7677. M–F 9:30–4:30. MC, VISA. Parking: street.
This factory-second store features some of the most creative puppets on the market—weird and won-derful animals, from cuddly to creepy. Poor puppets. Some are flawed, discontinued, or production samples, but these lovable creations offer hours of entertainment for the child in all of us because of their appealing, lifelike appearance. Just try to resist the new "robins in a nest" or "mice in a box" or the cockroaches, dinosaurs, dragons, otters, dogs, bears, and more. They're far superior to the typical puppet; in fact, they look more like stuffed animals. Witches and other extraordinary "folks" are also part of the family. Prices on seconds with minor flaws range from $5–$25, at about 50% off retail.

LAKESHORE'S LEARNING MATERIALS

1144 Montague Avenue, San Leandro. (510) 483-9750. M–F 9–6, Sat 9–5, Sun Noon–5. MC, VISA, DIS, AE. Parking: street.
Lakeshore Learning Materials supplies teachers and educators (preschool and elementary grades) and nursery school and day-care operators with educa-

tional toys, games, teaching materials, books, play equipment, and more. Parents are free to shop for their children and find bargains in Lakeshore's large clearance center in the back. Stop by for 25–75% savings on overstocked, discontinued, returned, and slightly damaged items. You'll find a constantly changing selection of toys, teacher aids, and equipment. I noted many books (some teachers' copies with answers), clear plastic boxes for treasures, little nylon backpacks, even classroom tables, large activity carpets, and miscellaneous small toys. Pick up a catalog when you enter the retail showroom, since many catalog items are not displayed.

SAFARI ZONE

1410 Park Street, Alameda. (510) 522-1723. M–Sat 10–6, Sun 11–5. Cash/Check. Parking: street.

A companion store to Toy Safari (a block away), this store has a high testosterone level. It's geared to boys eight and older and men still collecting childhood memories. It's a resale shop specializing in models, games, videos, transformers, space paraphernalia (great for Trekkies and Lucas fans), and collectible toys (including old tin toys). If your children are not sentimental about their toys, bring them in for trade or sale, rather than let them gather dust. Your credits can also be used at Toy Safari (see below).

SANRIO SAMPLER

Factory Stores of America, Vacaville. (707) 447-3721. Daily. MC, VISA. Parking: lot.

If you've got little girls, chances are you've had to buy from Sanrio's popular "Hello Kitty" line of novelties, school supplies, party goods, lunch boxes, stationery products, cosmetic and beauty sets, craft sets, and other goodies. Sanrio Sampler offers 50% savings on many discontinued items. About 40% of the store is discount—it annoys me to no end that the rest is at full price. If you stick to the marked-down merchandise you can stock up on birthday party presents that will save you expensive last-minute sorties to local stores.

TOY GO ROUND

1361 Solano Avenue, Albany. (510) 527-1363. M–Sat 10–5, Sun Noon–5. MC, VISA. Parking: street.

A consignment and resale store that's well stocked with toys, books, records, games, tapes, and even skates for budget-strapped parents. Nice preschool selection of developmental toys, and a wall of books priced to gladden the hearts of parents of budding bookworms.

TOY LIQUIDATORS
Factory Stores of America, Vacaville. (707) 448-7314. Daily. MC, VISA, DIS. Parking: street. (Other outlets: Anderson/Redding, Folsom, Gilroy centers.)
Toy Liquidators is one of the country's largest toy firms, selling large quantities of closeout inventory from a wide variety of toy makers, including Mattel, Fisher Price, Hasbro, Tonka, and Playskool. There are typically about 1,300 toys, dolls, and games in stock at any one time. Stop by for little treasures or big-ticket items. Prices are kept low because there is no advertising of individual brands or stores.

TOY SAFARI
1330 Park Street, Alameda. (510) 522-0825. M–Fri 10–6, Sat 10–6, Sun 11–5. Cash/Check. Parking: street.
Teach your children a little about business and commerce. Have them gather up their toys in good condition and bring them in to sell. The owner is obviously a parent of boys, since much of the inventory is geared toward boy stuff. Lots of action figures, Matchbook cars, Nintendo, models, developmental toys for tots, books, puzzles, some Barbies, and collectibles, including *Stars Wars* toys for children under the age of 10.

Also See

Under General Merchandise:
ALL SECTIONS

Under General Merchandise—Membership Warehouse Clubs:
PRICE/COSTCO

Under Recycled Apparel:
GENERAL INFORMATION

Under Baby and Juvenile Furniture/Equipment:
ALL LISTINGS

Outlet Center Shopping

Approach shopping at outlet centers with the right expectations and you'll come away satisfied. If you're unrealistic and expect wholesale pricing or 50% discounts everywhere you shop, then you'll wonder what all the fuss and hype is about. Many stores offer discounts that I can only call modest. If you find that prices are just as good at department store sales—well, maybe they are. Yet each manufacturer's store offers far more of its own lines than you'll ever see in any one store, so your choices are much greater. Combined with the overall aspect of value pricing, and the concentration of so many attractive factory and off-price stores in one location, it's hard to spend a few hours shopping without leaving with several bags of good buys. Finally, there are usually several exceptional tenants at each center whose discount prices will more than satisfy your thriftiest inclinations.

Unlike conventional malls, outlet malls are usually located away from urban areas to avoid placing manufacturers in competition with retail stores that sell their products. Many manufacturers benefit greatly from their outlet stores. They can make more money selling their merchandise directly to the public than selling it to an off-price retailer or discount store. As department stores have moved heavily into developing their own private-label lines and direct-import programs, many manufacturers have been propelled into the outlet business to maintain their profits and production. Outlet centers have popped up all over Northern California. These are typically destination centers—at a comfortable distance from the major retail stores and shopping malls in the Bay Area, but close enough for a day's outing of shopping thrills, savings, and fun!

A word about timing: Just like every kind of retailer, outlet tenants have special sales that pile savings on already discounted merchandise. Holiday week-ends or any national holiday where substantial numbers of people have a day off are prime time for a day of outlet center shopping. Individually, some outlets have their own timetable for special sale markdowns or events. Unless you've ensured that your name is on the store's mailing list, you may never get the word on these special sales. Fortunately (for those concerned about mailing lists and junk mail in general), most companies are very proprietary about their mailing lists.

For a complete profile of the outlet stores found in the centers closest to the Bay Area (and in most outlet centers around the country), refer to the individual listings under the appropriate category.

Greater Bay Area Outlet Centers

For a listing of stores in each center, see Geographical Index.

Shasta/Anderson

SHASTA FACTORY OUTLETS

1856 State Highway 273, Anderson. (916) 378-1000. M–Sat 9:30–8, Sun 11–6; winter M–Sat 9:30–6, Sun 11–6. Parking: lot.
A good stopover on your way north on I-5. Closest Polo/Ralph Lauren Factory Store. *Directions: 8 miles south of Redding. From I-5 North: Anderson-Deschutes Road exit; from I-5 South: Deschutes Road exit.*

Folsom

FOLSOM PREMIUM OUTLETS

13000 Folsom Boulevard, Folsom. (916) 985-0313. M–Sat 10–8, Sun 10–6. Parking: lot.
Charming and appealing villagelike complex and a convenient detour for Tahoe travelers. More than

50 stores. Famous labels: Nike, Jones New York, Off Fifth, Carter's Childrenswear, and more. *Directions from Bay Area: I-80 to Highway 50 to Folsom Boulevard exit, turn left.*

Gilroy

OUTLETS AT GILROY

681 Leavesley Road, Gilroy. (408) 842-3729. M–Sat 10–8, Sun 10–6. Parking: lot.
Located 30 miles south of San Jose. More than 150 factory stores. Famous labels: Ann Taylor Loft, J. Crew, Lenox, Laura Ashley, Anne Klein, Nike, Birkenstock, Etienne Aigner, Liz Claiborne, Kenneth Cole, and more. *Directions: From 101 South, take the Leavesley exit left.*

Milpitas

GREAT MALL OF THE BAY AREA

447 Great Mall Drive, Milpitas. (408) 956-2033; tours: (800) MALLBAY (625-5229). M–F 10–9, Sat 10–8, Sun 11–7. Parking: lot.

The 1.5 million-square-foot project (the former Ford Motor plant) includes 9 anchors and 185 specialty retailers (primarily off-price tenants and manufacturers' outlets). Famous labels: Off Fifth, St. Johns, Mondi, Moda, Hero, Donna Karan, Bebe, Florsheim, Carter's Childrenswear, and more. *Directions: Located off 680 and 880 at the intersection of Montague Expressway, Capitol Avenue, and Main Street.*

Napa

NAPA PREMIUM OUTLETS

629 Factory Stores Drive, Highway 29 and First Street, Napa. (707) 226-9876. M–Sat 10–8, Sun 11–7. Parking: lot.

An outdoor center in the heart of the wine country, with more than 40 factory-direct stores. Famous labels: Ellen Tracy, Cole-Haan, Tommy Hilfiger, Nautica, Timberland, TSE Cashmere, MCM, BCBG, Dockers, Kenneth Cole, Kasper ASL, and others!

Pacific Grove

THE AMERICAN TIN CANNERY PREMIUM OUTLETS

125 Ocean View Boulevard, Pacific Grove. (408) 372-1442. Sun–Th 10–6, F–Sat 10–8. Parking: lot.

A lovely, airy, enclosed shopping outlet mall with more than 50 tenants. Famous labels: Anne Klein, Carole Little, Joseph Abboud, Woolrich, and more. *Directions: Easy access from Highway 1, Pacific Grove exit. Follow signs to Cannery Row and Aquarium. American Tin Cannery is one block past the aquarium.*

Petaluma

PETALUMA VILLAGE PREMIUM OUTLETS

2200 Petaluma Boulevard N., Petaluma. (707) 778-9300. M–Sat 10–8, Sun 10–6. Parking: lot.

A village-themed outdoor center with more than 50 factory stores. Famous labels: Ann Taylor, The Nap Outlet, Petite Sophisticate, Evan Picone, Off Fifth, Villeroy & Boch, and more. *Directions: From 101, take E. Washington Street to Petaluma Boulevard, turn right.*

San Leandro
MARINA SQUARE
Marina Boulevard West at Fwy 880, San Leandro. M–F 10–9, Sat 10–7, Sun 11–6. Parking: lot.
Very convenient outlet/off-price center located in the middle of the Bay Area. Famous labels: Ann Taylor Loft, Talbots Outlet, Eddie Bauer, Nordstrom Rack, Mikasa, and more.

St. Helena
ST. HELENA PREMIUM OUTLETS
3111 N. St. Helena Highway, St. Helena. (707) 963-7282. Daily 10–6. Parking: lot.
A small center, distinguished by its status tenants—Donna Karan, Movado, Coach, Brooks Bros., and others. *On Highway 29, one mile north of Christian Brothers Winery.*

Vacaville
FACTORY STORES AT VACAVILLE
321-1 Nut Tree Road, Vacaville. (707) 447-5755. M–Sat 10–8, Sun 10–6. Parking: lot.
Halfway between San Francisco and Sacramento. More than 125 stores—a shopper's shuttle takes some of the legwork out of visiting the many shops in this center. Famous labels: Barbizon, Le Creuset, Royal Doulton, Johnston & Murphy, Naturalizer, Etienne Aigner, and more. *Directions: From 80 East: take 505/Orange Drive exit at Orange Drive, turn right to access center entrance. From 80 West: exit at Monte Vista Avenue, first right onto Monte Vista, left at Nut Tree Road.*

Lake Tahoe region
TAHOE-TRUCKEE FACTORY STORES
12047 Donner Pass Road, Truckee. M–Sat 9:30–6, Sun 10–6. Parking: lot.
A relatively small center with 11 tenants. The large Villeroy & Boch and Dansk factory stores are the main attraction. *Directions: Located one-eighth mile east of the Agricultural Inspection Station. Take the Donner Pass Road exit from I-80.*

Tracy
TRACY OUTLET CENTER
1005 Pescadero Avenue, Tracy. (209) 833-1895. M–Sat 10–8, Sun 10–6. Parking: lot.
About 40 tenants. Famous labels: Anne Klein, Liz Claiborne, Rockport, Jones New York, Sony, Oshkosh B'Gosh, and more. *From 205, exit at MacArthur Boulevard.*

Glossary of Bargain-Hunting Terms

Whenever an item is for sale to the public at 20–50% under retail, common sense tells you there must be a reason. I have tried in each entry to give you an explanation; the answer generally falls into one or more categories described by the following terminology used in retailing.

discontinued or manufacturer's closeout: Apparel or products that are no longer being manufactured. In most instances this does not affect the merchandise, but if parts may need to be replaced, it could cause a problem.

floor sample: A model displayed in the store.

freight damage: Even if only one or two items in a shipment are broken, burned, chipped, or marred, for insurance purposes the entire lot is designated "damaged." This merchandise may be noticeably damaged; often, however, it is actually in A-1 con-dition but was part of a large shipment that met with physical mishap.

gray market: Also known as "parallel importing." Refers to the overseas purchase of foreign goods by independent companies who are not autho-rized U.S. dealers for those goods. The goods are then sold in the United States by off-price and dis-count retailers who compete with the owners of the U.S. trademarks for those goods. Not having to pay for service, warranties, or advertising, the gray-market merchants can undercut the prices of the U.S. trademark owners.

in-season buying: Whereas most retailers buy pre-season, a discounter will often purchase in-season, relieving the manufacturer of merchandise that is old from manufacturer's standpoint but still new to the public.

irregular: Merchandise with minor imperfections, often barely discernible.

job lot: Goods, often of various sorts, brought together for sale as one quantity.

jobber: A person who buys goods in quantity from manufacturers or importers and sells those goods to dealers.

keystone: Traditional retail markup. Based on the wholesale price being doubled, i.e., a $50 wholesale price results in a retail price of $100.

knock-off: A copy of a highly acceptable design. These may be nearly authentic renditions or shabby imitations. Some manufacturers and designers make their own knock-offs in different- or lesser-quality materials for off-price stores and chains.

liquidated stock: When a company or business is in financial trouble, the stock it has on hand is sometimes sold to merchandisers, at prices much lower than retail in order to liquidate the assets of the company.

loss leader: An item purposely priced low (sometimes at a loss) to get you into the store.

odd-lots: A relatively small quantity of unsold merchandise that remains after an order has been filled.

off-price retailing: The sale of major brand merchandise at reduced prices.

open stock: Individual pieces of merchandise sold in sets, which are kept in stock as replacements.

overruns: An excess of products, similar to surplus and overstocks, but generally due to a manufacturer's error.

past-season: Goods manufactured for a previous season.

retail: The selling of merchandise directly to the consumer.

returns: Orders returned to the manufacturer by retail stores because they do not arrive on time.

Fashion discounters are able to buy this merchandise below cost from the manufacturer.

samples: An item shown by the manufacturer's representative to the prospective merchandiser/buyer for the purpose of selling the product.

seconds: Merchandise with more-than-minor flaws, which may affect the aesthetic appeal or performance of the product.

surplus overstock: An excess quantity, over and above what is needed by the retailer.

wholesale price: The cost of goods to the retailer, except in discount shopping, when consumers can buy at or near this price.

wholesale to the public: This term is often used inappropriately by discounters. From my perspective, "wholesale" is the price the seller pays for the merchandise. If that same price were passed on to the consumer, a discount retailer would make no profit. When a discounter is able to buy merchandise for less than the manufacturer's original published wholesale price (at liquidations, end-of-season closeouts, etc.), it is possible for the discount retailer to add a markup and sell the merchandise for the original wholesale price or for even less.

Late Additions

DESIGN VIA CARIOCA OUTLET
2123 Bryant Street, San Francisco. (415) 642-9321. T–Sat 11–5. MC, VISA. Parking: street.
Classic, contemporary, and eclectic are terms descriptive of the unusual mixture of home accessories and occasional furniture imported by this company. The designs reflect Brazil's unique blend of African, Asian, and European cultures. Yet everything is designed with a California sensibility. The company makes an extensive variety of bowls (most to be used decoratively), trays, decorative buckets, candleholders, and other accessories from heavy polished aluminum. The cast aluminum garden tables and chairs work as well inside as outside. All the designs are contemporary reinterpretations of classic styles. Discontinued designs, some pieces with slight finish imperfections, and samples are sold for 30% to 60% off retail. These are the decorative accessories you'd typically expect to find in design-oriented, upscale home furnishings boutiques. Parking is tough during the week, but a cinch on weekends.

HCL HANDBAG & LEATHERGOODS OUTLET
1111 East Francisco Boulevard, Suite B, San Rafael. (415) 458-8228. M–F 10–4. MC, VISA. Parking: lot.
You'll save 40–60% off original retails on discontinued styles, seconds, samples, and returned goods at HCL's new clearance outlet. This company's status, high-end, and expensive line of handbags (in plain and signature leathers) and small leather goods are usually sold "under the glass" at fine stores around the country.

LILLI ANN OUTLET
275 Brannan Street, San Francisco. (415) 908-2888. MC, VISA. Parking: street.
Lilli Ann is back in business under new ownership. This is good news for its loyal customers who've

relied on the company for dressier sportswear and classic women's suits with a touch of elegance. Many of these women have felt abandoned by other companies who've trained their sights on a younger, more fashion-forward customer. The new Lilli Ann has retained the styling so appealing to its mature customer base, yet is introducing new updated collections so that women of all ages can shop the outlet. Suit skirts are often available in 18", 24", and 36" lengths. Suits and sportswear are fabricated in quality polyesters, microfibers, wool blends, and ultra suedes. The past season and current overruns are sold for 50–70% off retail. Outlet prices on suits range from $50 to $120; on sportswear (jackets, pants, and tops) from $15 to $95. Sizes: 4–20. Keep an eye peeled for the company's men's collections. Better sportswear under the Practical label and R. Herd sweaters made from mohair, angora, and natural fiber blends are nicely discounted. All sales final.

THE MULBERRY NECKWEAR OUTLET
1002 Second Street (at A Street), San Rafael. (415) 457-1577. Hours M–Sat 10–5. MC, VISA. Parking: street.

A great outlet for men's silk ties and boxers, typically sold through major department stores. Prices on discounted ties from the company's five contemporary collections are below wholesale at $5–15. Boxers are usually $14.

WATERFORD WEDGWOOD OUTLET
Outlets at Gilroy, Gilroy. Phone: Pending. Daily. MC, VISA, AE. Parking: lot.

This is a "coming attractions" kind of listing. Since the outlet had not opened at press time, I was not able to obtain firsthand all the particulars of the outlet's inventory and pricing. However, based on my visit to a Waterford Wedgwood outlet in Liberty Village, New Jersey, I expect the outlet will be beautiful. Count on finding stemware, giftwares, lamps, and china, but not necessarily in your favorite pattern or at deeply discounted prices. Look for great buys on overstocks and discontinued gift items.

Store Index

Store Index

Geographical Index

Subject Index